DATE DUE

DEC 1 9 1986		
MAR - 6 1988		
APR 1 7 1988		
MAY 2 6 1988		
NOV 1 4 1989		
NOV 3 0 1989		
APR 2 8 1990		
JAN 1 1991		
APR 2 6 1993		
NOV 2 2 1995		
APR 1 3 1998		

DEMCO NO. 38-298

Chile at the Turning Point

LESSONS OF THE SOCIALIST YEARS, 1970–1973

edited by
Federico G. Gil, Ricardo Lagos E.,
and Henry A. Landsberger

translated by
John S. Gitlitz

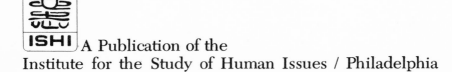ISHI A Publication of the
Institute for the Study of Human Issues / Philadelphia

Manufactured in the United States of America

Library of Congress Cataloging in Publication Data:

Main entry under title:

Chile at the turning point.

    Translation of Chile 1970–1973.
    Based on the conference held at the Institute of Latin American
Studies of the University of North Carolina at Chapel Hill, Apr. 27–May
7, 1975.
    Includes bibliographical references and index.
    1. Chile—Politics and government—1970-   —Congresses.
I. Gil, Federico Guillermo. II. Lagos Escobar, Ricardo.
III. Landsberger, Henry A.
F3100.C474513   320.9′83′064   79–10311
ISBN 0–915980–88–6

For information, write:

Director of Publications
ISHI
3401 Science Center
Philadelphia, Pennsylvania 19104
U.S.A.

Acknowledgments

We are indebted to the Ford Foundation and to the University of North Carolina at Chapel Hill for financing the Chapel Hill Conference, for which the essays and commentaries in this book were written. We are thankful to Hugo Castillo, Patricio Chaparro, Alberto Cisneros-Lavaller, Juan del Aguila, Douglas Kincaid, Daniel Levy, and Rose Spalding for their aid during the conference. Mrs. Elena M. Tomaro and Frederick W. Robison deserve special thanks for their assistance in the organization of the sessions. The Institute of Latin American Studies of the University of North Carolina provided logistical and administrative aid. Mrs. Anne Westbrook and Knut Walter helped in the translating and typing of the Spanish edition. We are also indebted to Professor Roberto Etchepar.eborda, who read portions of the Spanish manuscript and gave us useful suggestions.

We wish to express our special gratitude to John Gitlitz, who translated this volume, to Douglas Kincaid, Rowena Morrison, and Leah Florence, who assisted with the editing, and to Mrs. Anne Westbrook, Juan del Aguila, and the staff of the Institute for Research in Social Sciences at Chapel Hill, who typed the English version.

Finally, we want to thank Joel Jutkowitz and Betty Crapivinsky-Jutkowitz, Directors of the Institute for the Study of Human Issues, for their kind interest in the project and Janet Greenwood, also of ISHI, for her assistance in the production of the book.

FEDERICO G. GIL
RICARDO LAGOS E.
HENRY A. LANDSBERGER

Contents

Introduction

FEDERICO G. GIL
RICARDO LAGOS E.
HENRY A. LANDSBERGER

On September 11, 1973, Chilean democracy came to an end. Until then Chile had presented an unusual scene in the political panorama of Latin America. Almost from the moment of the country's independence, political life had remained firmly anchored in the constitution. With only two interruptions (both of short duration), its history from 1830 on was one of consistent democratic practice, characterized by constant expansion of the social and political base participating in the system. Though many may question the true nature of this "formal" or "bourgeois" democracy, the continuous process by which new social sectors were gradually incorporated into the decision-making structure cannot be denied. That fact has been amply demonstrated in any number of studies.

The collapse of Chilean democracy was preceded by an effort to build what many saw as a second road to socialism. In the words of Salvador Allende, "Chile faces the necessity of beginning to build a new road to a socialist society: . . . , a pluralist road, one foreseen by the classical theorists of Marxism but never before put into practice. . . . Chile is today the first nation on earth called to follow the second model of transition to a socialist society."[1] But the social system of Chile had shown signs of extraordinary strain even before Allende's rise to power. Insufficient economic growth and greater demands for popular participation in the benefits derived from such growth as there was had combined to produce severe tensions. As long as increases in the gross national product permitted Chilean society to satisfy the needs of new social groups, as long as the demands were small in relation to growth in GNP, the system could absorb new sectors that wanted to participate in the

1

benefits of a "modernized" society—or, at least, a society en route to modernization. But when economic growth decreased and the rate of incorporation of new sectors increased, a crisis in Chile's democratic order was clearly imminent.

The *coup d'état* signified, on the one hand, the violent end of that second road President Allende had sought to construct; on the other, it brought into being yet another military-authoritarian state in Latin America. These two faces of the *coup* have given rise to a variety of analyses and discussions. The bibliography, be it academic, political, or merely propagandistic, is already enormous.[2] And the events in Chile have raised numerous questions. Does the attempt to implant socialism within a liberal democratic system inevitably lead to the appearance of an authoritarian state which smothers that attempt? In other words, are the two linked in a causal relationship? Was the *coup d'état* an inevitable outcome of the "Chilean road to socialism"?

Will a democracy, as it was practiced in Chile in 1970, permit a transformation so profound as to facilitate the movement of a society toward socialism? Is the reply to this question so resoundingly negative as to render any such attempt futile from the start? If those who have won an electoral victory threaten to transform society, will those who hold the reins of power in a modern state consent to surrender them out of respect for the existing rules of the political game? Or will they respect those rules only when the system itself is not called into question? When it is, do the rules cease to function? Do they become, in effect, self-destructive? Without doubt this is an old theme, but, to some extent, it is one which the Chilean experience made real for the very first time.

In light of the Chilean experience, the reply to these and other questions would seem clear: the second road to socialism is not viable. On the contrary, the attempt to traverse it leads almost inevitably to the destruction of the democratic system within which the attempt is made. Violence (involving, of course, abandonment of the long-established rules of the game) is the necessary end of the second road. This reply, however, is far too simple to explain the complex reality of Chile between 1970 and 1973. To state it *a priori* is to ignore all sorts of factors that should enter into an analysis of the tragic outcome—particularly those relating to the management of the process. How were the innumerable day-to-day problems confronted? What mechanisms were used to articulate the new society? What economic variables were utilized? How can we account for their success (or failure) and the consequent impact on the viability of the model? And we should not neglect the errors (or successes) of the political leadership of the government and the opposition in using their respective strengths.

It is tempting to use this line of analysis to explain the present Chilean regime, but we should not ignore another very influential theme in the contemporary literature.[3] This is the argument that bureaucratic-authoritarian regimes in Latin America emerge basically as a result of the rigidity of social structures. This rigidity limits the rate at which new sectors, struggling to obtain a larger portion of the benefits of development, can be incorporated into the system. (It is assumed, of course, that development is occurring or has occurred.) A time comes when it is no longer possible to maintain the rhythm of incorporation, and at this point the system collapses. From that moment, if new sectors are to be incorporated, others must forego or at least decrease their share of the benefits—a share to which they have been accustomed for generations. Sectors which face losing ground then begin to ignore the formerly sacrosanct rules and resort to solutions based on force. Force becomes a means by which privileged groups seek to conserve what they fear losing, what they feel is legitimately theirs. Moreover, this phenomenon occurs precisely in those countries which seem the most advanced in the region—those in which economic growth (in many cases initiated by industrialization policies of import-substitution during the 1930s) has generated corresponding social growth in the sense of the emergence of stronger, more demanding social classes. An ever stronger industrial proletariat demands and obtains greater benefits. However, for these benefits to be distributed, there must be sufficient economic "elbow room," room for both more investment and more consumption. Thus, according to this theory, development in the long run generates the end of the democratic system. The authoritarian state arises, although certainly in a form far different from the traditional, nineteenth- and early twentieth-century dictatorships that still exist in some tropical countries (and more than one temperate one) in the region.

According to this interpretation, again, what happened in Chile was almost inevitable. The military *coup* did not take place just to block construction of a socialist state; it would have occurred regardless of the kind of civilian government ruling in Chile. Perhaps the *Unidad Popular* experience accelerated the *coup*'s arrival, but it would have taken place anyway, since Chile's defective social structure impeded the rapid economic growth necessary to satisfy an ever larger and more demanding working class. During the 1960s the peasants had registered to vote in massive numbers. For the first time they were able to exercise that right independent of the will of their *patrón*. Agricultural labor unions had become increasingly numerous and active. For many observers, this awakening of the peasantry was the straw that broke the back of the system's capability to integrate new sectors.

There are, then, two questions to be asked regarding the emergence of the dictatorship on September 11, 1973. First, was the Chilean road to socialism (or, as Allende preferred, the political road to socialism) viable? Second, did the military regime emerge in response to social tensions resulting from the inadequate development of Chilean society during the preceding forty years?

The editors of this book had these two queries in mind when they organized the conference, "Chile: 1970–1973, Lessons of an Experience," from which this work is drawn.

The conference was held at the Institute of Latin American Studies of the University of North Carolina at Chapel Hill from April 27 to May 7, 1975. The editors resolved to invite as participants a small group of "actors" in the Chilean experience, as well as a number of qualified "observers." Within the context of the above questions, our plan was to extend the analysis to other social processes with a certain similarity, even though these might be distant in time or geographic space from the Chilean phenomenon.

To structure the discussion, we tried to limit our attention to four main themes: a description of what happened in Chile during the period 1970–1973; the "causes" of the failure; the nature of the military regime imposed after the violent end of the experiment; and, last, the possible effects of these events on other political settings. After almost forty hours of formal presentations, commentaries, and debates, the participants as well as the organizers concluded that it might be useful to publish the material. To this end, while merging the last two themes, the editors have kept the original format. (Not all the essays appearing in this volume were presented at the conference, and those that were presented are published here in somewhat different form.) Thus the book is divided into three sections.[4]

The five essays and three commentaries in Part One all seek to describe the three years of the *Unidad Popular* government. The section begins with the work of Jorge Tapia Videla, who, in a remarkable *tour de force*, describes and analyzes different aspects of the period. He proposes that the experience can be classified chronologically in three phases. This scheme is particularly illuminating and useful for understanding the roles of social and economic interest groups during each phase, as well as the means by which these groups expressed themselves. The options open to each of the contending political forces and the various ways in which the struggle developed are analyzed in detail. Tapia describes clearly how, as the contenders became radicalized, the traditional arenas for resolving conflicts in a society based on a state of law (e.g., the National Congress) gave way to others, forming the basis of a society of conflict (factories, farms, universities, unions, etc.). Similarly, the various social and economic interests that in normal times delegated power through mechanisms of representation (e.g., political parties) now took power into their own hands, refusing to act through intermediaries. In other words, the confrontation of social classes in Chile began to occur directly, without intervening structures capable of mediating the intensity of the conflict. Tapia Videla suggests that recognition of this step, by which a political system of conciliation moved toward one of confrontation, is crucial to understanding what occurred.

The essay by Sergio Bitar is more than a mere description of the economic aspects of the *Unidad Popular* government. It is also an analysis of the interaction of economic and political factors. The author argues that two elements must be adequately understood by those wishing to move an economy toward socialism. First, it is necessary to study carefully the rhythm and velocity that modifications in the economic structure should assume. There will inevitably be a temporal lag between the implementation of economic changes and their impact on the correlation of forces in the political arena. A profound change in a given economic structure can produce the desired political effects only after the diverse participants in the productive process have adapted to the new situation. Moreover, the short-term effects produced by the changes may be diametrically opposed to those which are sought. This lag must be taken into account by those who wish to introduce profound changes in a society's economic structure.

The second element, closely linked to the first, concerns the compatibility of long-term structural changes with short-term economic policies designed to resolve immediate problems. The dilemma seems to involve difficult choices with obvious political consequences. Bitar uses these two elements to analyze the various economic disequilibria which were produced during the Allende administration. Finally, he offers a number of hypotheses about the conduct of specific social classes when confronted by various economic policies.

Clodomiro Almeyda describes Chilean foreign relations during the Allende period. His essay analyzes in detail the theoretical focus that gave meaning to the foreign policy of the *Unidad Popular*, tying it to internal policies in a harmonious and coherent whole. Almeyda explains why it was necessary to give priority to the principle of nonintervention (rather than to "socialist internationalism") and how, in order to contribute to the construction of a socialist society, foreign policy was subordinated to domestic factors. In addition to his observations specifically on foreign policy, Almeyda comments on the management of other sectors (in comparison with the foreign policy sector). For example, he explicitly devotes certain paragraphs to economic policymaking, in this way shedding light on his views of the "errors" that explain or help to explain the failure of the Chilean experiment. Unfortunately, prior commitments prevented Almeyda's participation in the conference itself, so his ideas were not subject to commentary, nor could he participate in the debates. (The same occurred in the cases of Pío García and David Baytelman.)

Baytelman's essay focuses on the "classical" problem of all socialist experiences: the legal nature of land ownership and the identity of that owner (the state, cooperatives, individual peasants, etc.). Baytelman begins by explaining that in Chile this problem was never resolved, in part because of the preconceived theoretical positions found within the "lefts." He then moves to a detailed description of the Chilean case, suggesting hypotheses to explain the poor results in agriculture and the fall in production. The latter, in the author's opinion, was greater than predicted, even considering the drastic changes which occurred in the structure of land tenure and exploitation. The reader of these pages is impressed by the inability of the Allende government to expose the familiar "Achilles' heel" of other socialist experiments. However, in Chile the problem was exacerbated by the lack of a uniform policy for the agrarian sector.

Pío García traces in detail the stormy history of the conception and development of the Social Property Sector, i.e., of the newly nationalized industries—a history as full of polemics within the *Unidad Popular* as of political skirmishes between the government and the opposition. He explains clearly how the *Unidad Popular*, by permitting the survival of important economic bases of bourgeois monopoly power, and therefore of its ability to manipulate the middle sectors and disrupt the economy, may have contributed to creating propitious conditions for the military *coup*. But he also suggests, in considerable detail, that advances in the creation of the Social Property Sector were at the same time an important impetus behind the "revolutionary process."

The commentaries which follow these five essays are observations, subsequently revised by their authors, on the papers presented at Chapel Hill. In the majority, only stylistic and editorial changes have been made. Hence, their tone is frequently colloquial. We sought purposely to maintain the spontaneity of the commentators' reactions.

In Part Two (Causes of the Outcome), there are two basic documents. In the first, Radomiro Tomić, after reviewing Chilean development prior to 1970, undertakes to weigh those factors that, at the beginning of the Allende administration, favored and hindered its chances for success. For Tomić, the basic reason for Allende's failure was the fact that the government never defined its final objective. Was the "second road to socialism" to lead to an entirely new socialist model? Or was it simply a different means of reaching one of the existing models, those which we know exist today in the various countries where socialism has been implanted? According to Tomić, both affirmations could be found within the *Unidad Popular*, and this ideological confusion was its fatal weakness.

A second fundamental cause of Allende's failure, notes Tomić, was the government's decision not to expand its social base. Specifically, it failed to reach a political agreement with the Christian Democratic party, particularly at the beginning of Allende's administration, when the most progressive sectors—in Tomić's opinion—controlled the party. Without entering into an analysis of who was responsible for the failure to reach an understanding, it is worth emphasizing that there was a generally shared belief in the seminar discussions that such an understanding would have greatly improved the experiment's chances for success. In these discussions, many events that affected relations between the Christian Democrats and the *Unidad Popular* were elucidated.

Luis Maira prefers not to speak of causes but of "different scenarios" in which the various social and economic forces confronted and clashed with one another. In his opinion, five such scenarios can be distinguished: political institutions, political leadership, the economy, the military, and the international arena. For Maira, these do not form isolated compartments, but are closely interwoven and overlapping. The *coup* cannot be explained by any one alone, but the interaction of the five does explain the events leading to September 11. In his essay, Maira focuses entirely on the first scenario, studying the manner in which the opposition slowly chipped away at the power of the presidency. In essence, his argument emphasizes two points: a) the left was incapable of understanding that successful implementation of its program depended on institutional continuity, even in a situation where "the rules of the game had meaning only under relatively normal conditions and could easily be frustrated the moment the established order was seriously questioned"; b) since the left did not possess an absolute majority within the Chilean political scene, the *Unidad Popular*'s program could be implemented only if the pattern of political conflict continued to be "tripolar." However, tripolarity existed only during the presidential campaign. Within a few months after Allende assumed power, the right was already maneuvering to create a bipolar vision of the conflict—"democracy or Marxism."

These two facts represent for Maira the "institutional rocks" that blocked the Chilean road to socialism. He continues with a detailed description of how the other branches of government began to attack the "strong presidency" character of the Chilean Constitution. On August 22, 1972, their actions culminated in the declaration by the Chamber of Deputies that certain actions of the executive were unlawful. (Note that the Congress did not declare the government itself illegal, but only some of its actions. This legal subtlety passed unnoticed in the rapid succession of events following the statement.) With this declaration the opposition completed construction of the institutional setting necessary to stage a military *coup d'état*.

In his chapter, Hugo Zemelman examines a number of political errors committed by the *Unidad Popular*. He begins by asking himself whether the Chilean road to socialism resulted from a conscious strategic decision or was imposed by existing reality. Zemelman notes the difficulties involved in moving from the trenches of opposition to government responsibilities—resulting more from a lack of knowledge of public administration than from the need for more precise programs dealing with the problems of transition. In the search for such programs, ideological problems not previously clarified appear and must be resolved. From yet another perspective, Zemelman reexamines the problems of relations with the Christian Democrats, of the "middle sectors," and of the organic unity (largely absent) of the *Unidad Popular*. Internal divisions reemerged constantly and finally led to a situation where popular support for the government "was fragmented into areas of influence that, besides structuring political control of the masses, prevented the organization of their support into an active force, beyond existing partisan structures. If the electoral majority were to become a significant force, it needed to be transformed into a unified political organization. More specifically, the requisite of a majority is fulfilled only when it is present in organized form." For many observers, this lack of unified, organic leadership was the principal cause of failure.

Silva Solar's and Tomić's commentaries help to clarify the tortuous road the government had to traverse if it wanted a dialogue with the Christian Democrats. Tapia Valdés' version of why the conversations failed in one specific case may be one-sided, but the delicacy of the subject matter reveals the difficulties of negotiating. It is far easier to search for conciliation within a given political or economic system than to reach agreements on its modification, albeit partial. From the perspective of those seeking less radical change, an error in evaluation by the *Unidad Popular* might constitute the point of no return. This anxiety was always present in the negotiations. What guarantee could be offered that an agreement would not mean the end of the very system that permitted the various interests to negotiate in the first place?

The discussion which followed these papers was at times heated and often exciting. Unfortunately, lack of space has prevented us from including it here. In general, it dealt with many of the same points. The question of who was responsible for the rupture between the government and the Christian Democrats occupied much of the debate. Yet other topics were also suggested for consideration: the degree of uniqueness of the Chilean case, the left's lack of technical preparation—in contrast to 1964—for its electoral victory, the absence of any real knowledge of military attitudes, etc.

Part Three contains analyses of more general topics relating to the Chilean experience. Schmitter and Stern both examine the repercussions of what happened in Chile on other areas, particularly in "Latin" Europe. Soares, in his essay, considers other models, such as Brazil, which now seem to serve as a guide to the Chilean *junta*. Bulé, in his essay, and Nun in his commentary, focus on the specific characteristics of the authoritarian states emerging on the continent. Finally, Landsberger and Linz compare the Chilean tragedy with that of the Spanish Republic. Their article offers a vision of the past, surprising in the similarity of both the problems faced and the form of their resolution.

In reviewing the results of our efforts, we editors find that we have overlooked many topics. The reader may note others. The distance between goals and achievements is all too often great, and we fear that this may be the case here.

The first and most obvious omission is that of any systematic analysis of the military, whether referring to Chile in particular or to Latin America in general. Although it is true that, with respect to the latter, the recent literature is relatively abundant[5] (particularly when compared with the situation prior to 1960), as far as Chile is concerned it is still very scarce. It seems that the long-established reputation of the Chilean armed forces as "professional and nonpolitical" made social scientists feel it would be uninteresting to study them in depth. Thus, virtually nothing has been written, except for the work by Joxe,[6] a doctoral dissertation,[7] and a study of the motives for the 1925 military intervention.[8] None of these sheds much light on the present phenomenon. Certainly more will be written in the future. Our desire was to have initiated this discussion—which will be long and emotionally charged—with some original work. Unfortunately, we were unable to find anyone with the time and/or the expertise to undertake such an exercise. We sought someone who could have replied to such elemental questions as why regimes of this type—all very similar in their basic characteristics—are emerging throughout Latin America. Why do the armed forces, who—to define them negatively—do not form part of the oligarchies or highest income sectors, nevertheless, once in power, adopt policies that serve these minorities? Or, to reverse the coin, how do oligarchies manage to "sell" the vision that they are the depositories and sole defenders of the "Western and Christian" world, when in fact this position is a transparent defense of their privileges? To reply that the "military are the iron fist of the bourgeoisie" seems hardly more than a slogan. The answer is much more complex, and when it is found, we will have advanced considerably in our understanding of the phenomenon. It will undoubtedly include as an important element, or at least one worthy of mention, the training of these armed forces in the United States. (It is curious, however, that many important North American values— e.g., those referring to human rights, basic liberties, the electoral systems, etc.—do not seem to be "transmitted" with the same efficacy as others—e.g., the benefits of the capitalist system and "free enterprise.") On the other hand, to say that one is dealing in many cases with "middle class military coups"[9] seems, given the policies now pursued, to dwell in the past. In the Chile of today this thesis would be very difficult to defend.

Our examination of the military would also have had to study the appropriateness of specific policies of the *Unidad Popular* concerning its relations with the armed forces. Luis Maira touches on this topic only in passing, despite the fact that he considers it one of the five scenarios that explain the outcome of September 11. Nevertheless, our knowledge is still very insufficient, and this is a major omission.

Although it appears fleetingly, another virtually absent protagonist is the Central Intelligence Agency. The definitive history of the CIA's role in the Chilean tragedy is still to be written. Two important reports—the result of investigations by the United States Senate—appeared some time after our seminar had concluded.[10] In April, 1975, we knew no more than what had been published in the press and what President Ford had admitted in his famous press conference of September 16, 1974—that the United States had intervened to "help and assist the preservation of opposition newspapers and electronic media and to preserve political opposition parties." All this had been done in the name of the "best interest of the people of Chile."[11] Without discussing the moral issues implicit in this declaration, it seems clear that the activities of the United States were no surprise to the leaders of the *Unidad Popular* government. As one of them present at our discussions stated, "It was something with which any analysis would have had to deal." Determining the degree of importance this intervention had in the final outcome (assuming that someday we know its true dimensions) will be a difficult task. Nevertheless, it is worth emphasizing that no one at the seminar sought to exaggerate that intervention: it contributed to the outcome, but it was not the determining cause. The *coup* was produced by a combination of factors, among which internal elements were most important. This, of course, does not lessen the seriousness of that intervention nor its future implications, whether within Chile, where so many "sacred" images have been destroyed, or, on a broader level, in relations between Chile and the United States.

Another closely related topic that is absent or referred to only in passing is that of imperialism or, more specifically, the "invisible blockade" by the United States. Although the impact of the "Allende Doctrine" in relations with the United States is mentioned, it is considered less in the context of those relations than as an element determined by the internal politics of the *Unidad Popular*. This is not an inadvertent oversight; to some extent, it results from the conviction, shared by the conference participants, that the blockade and similar actions did not have the decisive character that some would attribute to them. They did occur and can explain many problems (particularly the economic difficulties caused by the strangulation of foreign trade), but they were not of overwhelming importance. As with the CIA, this does not mean we should conclude that they need not be mentioned or, as some have maintained, did not exist. For our purposes, it seemed more important to focus discussion on those problems that could be affected by the action of Chileans and to analyze the barriers facing any society attempting to move toward socialism. The invisible (or, as in Cuba, visible) blockade would be one of these and hence deserves consideration. But to devote space and time to quantifying the importance of the blockade might have proved less rewarding than to examine any of the other topics with which we dealt. To the extent that the blockade was considered, it would have been more useful to focus discussion on how to confront such challenges.

Another theme that is not clearly treated concerns the "uniqueness" of the Chilean experience. The entire book assumes that the reader has considerable knowledge about Chile. Starting from this premise, we do not indicate what is unique to the complexities of the Chilean situation. Through 1970 Chile had a long history of solid and mature political institutions, an advanced level of social development compared to the rest of Latin America, powerful workers' organizations with clear ideological bases, and well-established, doctrinaire political parties (we refer to the major parties). These and other elements, too numerous to list, attest to Chile's uniqueness, and we assume that these peculiar traits are well known. Moreover, they explain many of the problems treated in the following pages. For example, when participants discuss at length the inability of the left to build a unified political structure, they affirm an almost self-evident fact. One has to know the history of each of the parties to understand how difficult it was for the *Unidad Popular* to move from theory to practice—a fact not discussed by any of our participants, despite the urgent need for just such a discussion.

Permeating all the events of the fateful years from 1970 to 1973, and the many questions they raise, is Salvador Allende himself, who adds an important element of uniqueness to the Chilean case. No one analyzed the role played in the Chilean process by the personality of its leader, so here, too, an important problem is overlooked. It is true that the *Unidad Popular* was characterized by the importance (perhaps too great) of the political parties within the government, which limited the influence of individuals charged with implementing policies. Nevertheless, it is very clear that Allende played a key role in the Chilean left. It was he who persevered in advancing the idea of the *Unidad Popular* (previously known as the Front for Popular Action, or FRAP)[12]—a coalition that would bring together the various sectors of the Chilean left and use the existing institutional mechanisms to gain control of the government. Allende maintained this position without vacillation, often in the face of opposition within his own party and from other political groups who felt that power could not be obtained through an institutional strategy. We do not intend to present here a history of political positions. Allende's favored line for his party was defeated in any number of Socialist congresses. Thus, although social processes cannot be explained entirely by the individuals who intervene in them, one can still say that to a large extent the *Unidad Popular* was the fruit of Allende's perseverance. Its creation as the political expression of Chilean workers reflected much more than the will of one man, but we cannot deny the importance of his role. For these reasons, it is difficult to understand why Allende, once he became President, had such difficulty transforming a political combination, so useful for obtaining electoral victory, into a government apparatus capable of unified policymaking. One reason is that his exaggerated respect for the desires of the individual coalition parties impeded every effort toward unity. One could go on proposing hypotheses about the role of Allende's presidency in the Chilean experience, but suffice it to say that this is another element we did not examine closely.

Although the organizers of the conference were aware that the Chilean case is somewhat unique, it was decided nevertheless to analyze its impact on other regions and environments. This was difficult, and we are only partially satisfied with the results we obtained. The essays here are directed more to studying how Europe interpreted the Chilean experience than to observing how this experience actually influenced the development of European political processes. (To what extent, for example, are the new positions of the Italian and French Communist parties, if not strongly influenced, at least colored by what happened in Chile?) It has often been noted that the Chilean failure was more a political than a military defeat, caused by the loss of support of the "middle sectors." Perhaps we can interpret the new European policies precisely as efforts to avoid such a situation by preserving certain values especially dear to these sectors. Is it true that each time the Portuguese Socialist party moves its position nearer to the center (thus moving to the right) it bears in mind the Chilean experience? Mario Soares refers to Chile constantly, particularly in emphasizing the need for greater discipline in economic productivity. Here an analysis such as that outlined above could have been useful.

Finally, in our enumeration of what this book is not, we must point out that it is not an evaluation of the Chilean experience. We never intended to review the accomplishments and failures of government policy during the *Unidad Popular*'s three years in Chile. This book does not contain statistics on the economic sector: production, growth in GNP, distribution of income, employment, balance of payments, etc., except where these are necessary to support a particular argument. Nor do we analyze what occurred in education, health, or basic services, etc. On the one hand, the *Unidad Popular* is too recent a phenomenon to make such an evaluation feasible or to permit comparison of the Allende administration with previous governments. On the other, the distorted use of statistics by the present rulers makes such a task very difficult. The various essays in this volume seek to elucidate something considered more essential—the viability of the experiment as a whole—than measuring each success or failure of the *Unidad Popular* by the traditional indicators. Such measuring is more appropriate for a government that rules within a given system; in Chile, where the challenge was to change the system, it is essential to "measure" whether the road chosen to accomplish that change was adequate and whether the experience can serve as a model for other societies. This is what we have sought to do.

It is perhaps important to add a few final comments. The visions presented here of what happened in Chile reflect a wide spectrum of Chilean society and diverse ideological and political positions. Nevertheless, any reader familiar with Chile will notice that some positions are not represented. The organizers were aware of this from the beginning, but the opportunities for a fruitful exchange of ideas were only possible within a limited segment of the ideological rainbow. We reluctantly came to the conclusion that if we attempted to include the entire spectrum, the possibilities for dialogue would be practically nil. Those actors who, during the three years of the *Unidad Popular* government, preached the defense of democracy, and who today make a mockery of it, showing that they do not believe in the rules of the game they established and claimed to defend, could not easily be invited to participate in a discussion of the Chilean experience. The dialogue with those sectors of Chilean society has been lost, perhaps forever. There is only hope that new generations will be able to renew it. On the other hand, we must also admit that, though the point of view of what is generally known as the "revolutionary left" is occasionally reflected in some of the essays, none of the participants truly represented that current of thought. In addition, it must be recognized that what happened in Chile stirs deep emotions. It is difficult to maintain the calm and academic objectivity necessary for analysis. We do not believe it overly optimistic to feel that we have achieved some degree of success.

As always happens in conferences of this kind, at the last moment some of the participants originally on the program were unable to appear. This was the case for Clodomiro Almeyda, Pío García, Gabriel Valdés, Joseph Grunwald, and also of a number of "actors" and social scientists who still live in Chile, for whom participation would have meant exposing themselves to reprisals by the military *junta*. Some of these Chilean scholars sent valuable contributions, which, except for the chapter by P. Bulé, could not be included in the limited space of this volume.

To conclude, the peaceful atmosphere of Chapel Hill and the privacy of the meetings permitted us to have a very rewarding week of exchanging ideas. Needless to say, the editors have not been fully capable of capturing herein every dimension of the discussions. We add only that during that week we relived the Chile we once knew, a Chile which today is dead.

We know that, when it is reborn tomorrow, the new Chile will differ from the old; we hope that the enduring values which made that small nation so civilized, so open, and such a lover of freedom will again prevail.

NOTES

1. Salvador Allende, *Primer Mensaje al Congreso Nacional* (May 21, 1971).

2. By way of example, there are already two attempts to compile bibliographies: Jirina Rybacek-Mlynkova, *Chile under Allende: A Bibliographical Survey* (mimeograph, n/d); and Eli Williams, *The Allende Years: A Union List of Chilean Imprints* (Boston: G. K. Hall and Co., 1976). For an attempt to order and classify (by the ideological orientation of their authors) the most important publications, see Arturo Valenzuela and J. Samuel Valenzuela, "Visions of Chile," *Latin American Research Review* 10, 3(Fall 1975), pp. 155–175.

3. On this point, see Guillermo O'Donnell, *Modernización y Autoritarismo* (Buenos Aires: Editorial Paidos, 1972), and in general all the writings of that author and of Fernando Henrique Cardoso on Brazil, Enzo Faletto on Chile, Jose Luis Reyna on Mexico, etc.

4. Since, inevitably, all four themes are discussed as a whole, it is hardly necessary to indicate that this division is made only to facilitate the orderly presentation of the essays. For example, in the papers describing what happened, many comments point directly to the "causes" of later failure.

5. See the summary of this literature presented by Abraham F. Lowenthal, "Armies and Politics in Latin America," *World Politics* 27, 1(October 1974), pp. 107–130.

6. Alain Joxe, *Las Fuerzas Armadas en el Sistema Político Chileno* (Santiago: Editorial Universitaria, 1970).

7. Bory A. Hansen, "Military Culture and Organizational Decline: A Study of the Chilean Army" (Ph.D. dissertation, UCLA, 1967).

8. Frederick M. Nunn, *Chilean Politics, 1920–1931: The Honorable Mission of the Armed Forces* (Albuquerque: Univ. of New Mexico Press, 1970); *The Military in Chilean History: Essay on Civil-Military Relations, 1810–1973* (Albuquerque: Univ. of New Mexico Press, 1976).

9. This thesis, advanced by Joxe, was first formulated by José Nun in a study of *coups* from 1920 to 1930 in Argentina, Brazil, Chile, etc. See José Nun, "The Middle Class Military Coup," in Claudio Véliz (ed.), *The Politics of Conformity in Latin America* (Oxford: Oxford University Press, 1967).

10. U.S. Senate, 94th Congress, 1st Session, Report No. 940465, *Alleged Assassination Plots Involving Foreign Leaders: An Interim Report of the Select Committee to Study Government Operations with Respect to Intelligence Activities* (Washington: U.S. Government Printing Office, 1975); and U.S. Senate, 94th Congress, 1st Session, *Covert Action in Chile 1963–1973: Staff Report to the Select Committee to Study Governmental Operations with Respect to Intelligence Activities* (Washington: U.S. Government Printing Office, 1975).

11. *New York Times,* September 17, 1974, p. 22.

12. In 1952 Allende was the presidential candidate of the People's Front, a combination including the Communist party and a faction of the Socialists. In 1958 and 1964 his candidacy was supported by the Front for Popular Action (FRAP), a coalition of the Communist and Socialist parties (the latter having been reunited in 1956) and other minor groups. The *Unidad Popular* added to these the Radical party and Christian groups (the MAPU) that had abandoned the Christian Democratic party in 1969.

PART ONE

The Three Allende Years:
An Overview

The Difficult Road to Socialism: The Chilean Case from a Historical Perspective

JORGE TAPIA VIDELA

This article is divided into three major sections. In the first I describe in general terms the major traits which define the Chilean political system during the period 1952–1970. In the second section I attempt to describe in chronological sequence the experience of the *Unidad Popular* government. In the third I try to present briefly the "causes" which, in this article and in other works, have been considered critical to understanding what occurred in Chile.[1]

Treating the government as the central political actor, I have distinguished three different periods in the experience of the government of the *Unidad Popular*. During the first period or phase of the government, the political system conserved in essence its traditional characteristics. The mechanisms for conciliatory resolution of political conflict continued to maintain a high degree of legitimacy, and the stability of the system was not threatened by serious problems. The government implemented policies in various areas and was capable of achieving important advances, while the opposition appeared disorganized and confused. In contrast, during the second phase the initiative held by the government was lost to an increasingly well-organized opposition. The efficacy of the government coalition was hampered by a series of problems—not a few of which led to serious internal disagreements about the policies and strategies that should be followed on the road to socialism. These internal and external factors began to undermine both the legitimacy of the system and its traditional mechanisms for resolving political conflicts. In this sense, it seems

19

clear that when the electoral mechanism lost its legitimacy, the system had reached a critical point of tension and polarization. For this reason I fix the beginning of the last phase of the *Unidad Popular* government in March, 1973—the date of the last congressional election. From that moment until the military *coup d'état,* Chile appeared to live in an atmosphere of "permanent and accelerated crisis."

THE EVOLUTION OF THE CHILEAN POLITICAL SYSTEM, 1952–1970

The Chilean economy during the period prior to 1952 was characterized by a considerable expansion of the industrial sector, while the traditional structures of exploitation and life in the agricultural sector remained unchanged; rapid population growth accompanied by high indices of urbanization; an increase in state intervention in social and economic life, reflected in the sustained growth of the bureaucracy; the progressive incorporation of traditionally marginal sectors into the modern economy, following industrialization and the expansion of the service sector; and, finally, progressively more acute problems deriving from Chile's dependent economy, which at once combined problems typical of subsistence single-product export and industrial economies.[2]

Chilean society was extremely differentiated, and the values and life-styles of the different social strata varied widely. Class relations reflected systematic discrimination against the lower levels and minimal vertical social mobility. The principal means for social advancement—education, wealth, and politics—were so closely linked as to inhibit the movement of lower-class sectors. In practice social mobility occurred more often within classes than between them, an assertion graphically supported by statistics on the distribution of national income.[3]

The political parties and dominant groups in Chile kept social tensions in check through the systematic use of cooptation. This permitted the political process to absorb new groups, who thus gained access to the exercise of power and its privileges. In this sense the experience of the *Frente Popular* of 1938 provides the most objective example of the political style which characterized Chilean democracy.

The alliance of the revolutionary parties (Socialists and Communists) with those parties supposedly defending the interests of the greater and lesser bourgeoisie was oriented in essence to preserve political control in the hands of the *parties of the middle class* and to reinforce Chilean *parliamentary* democracy. Implicitly the coalition affirmed that political competition in a pluralist society can take place, to the advantage of all participants, through the use of electoral mechanisms. This was the essence of liberal democracy. Thus the so-called revolutionary parties accepted the electoral road as the only route to political power, and the search for compromise among the various groups gradually became the general rule.[4]

Social and political pluralism, by recognizing implicitly the veto power of each and every politically articulated social group, led to social stalemate and political stagnation. In fact, these conditions were intimately linked to the very limited flexibility of Chilean social structures. Within each important social group there were subgroups desirous of maintaining the *status quo* in order to preserve their own positions of relative advantage *vis-à-vis* their social peers. Their advantage stemmed from a greater capacity to articulate political demands, which in turn gave them a "privileged" position within the system's "pressure politics." At the national level the immediate consequence of the social stalemate was the accentuation of the very rigidities which had produced the stalemate in the first place. Thus, in short, social stalemate led inevitably to political stagnation, in turn reinforcing the tendency (and necessity) for seeking compromise. Under the system just described, every social group capable of organizing itself politically in defense of its interests with some degree of "efficacy" gained *de facto* veto power *vis-à-vis* other social groups. This stalemate was the critical element in the "dynamic equilibrium" which characterized Chilean sociopolitical development during the period.[5]

In this fashion an imbalance among economic, social, and political factors developed, giving rise to frustrations in important sectors of the middle and working classes. In 1952 these precipitated an electoral realignment which reflected two clear trends. First there was a general rejection of political parties and, more specifically, of the traditional coalition structures which had served to maintain the *status quo*. These were embodied in the Radical party, which had formed the hub of every recent government. Second, new expectations emerged which, though still not clearly defined, favored creation of effective mechanisms for distributing the benefits of development. Both trends implied a challenge to the system, its institutions, and the traditional political style. In the long run they produced major destabilizing effects.

The populist orientation of the Ibáñez government, with its unstructured political support and its domination by immediate and contradictory interests, precluded any serious attempt to transform the system. The traditional political parties—the Conservatives, Liberals, and Radicals—proved incapable of capitalizing on discontent and integrating the new sectors that sought a political voice. On the contrary, the old parties continued to be preoccupied with their own intra-congressional game and with their permanent conflict with the executive. Every attempt to expand their electoral support failed because they did not try to present consistent political alternatives. The vacuum was filled by two new political actors: the *Frente de Acción Popular* (Front for Popular Action, FRAP) and the Christian Democratic party (PDC). Both organizations, utilizing the substantive electoral reforms approved at the close of the Ibáñez government, profited from discontent and mobilized the electorate. Unlike the older parties, they promised change, and during the following decade they produced profound modifications in the system.[6]

These alternatives were articulated in an integrated manner for the first time during the presidential campaign of 1958. Because the electoral battle was fought among four contenders, the candidate who represented the most conservative interests won by a tiny margin; but the most significant development of the election was the high percentage of voters who opted for candidates favoring structural reform.

The government of Jorge Alessandri (1958–1964) was distinguished by its conservative-technocratic character and its orientation toward the past. It reflected the traditional parties' separation from the new interests and the demands for new political alternatives and forms of organization. As a result, the reforms introduced during the Alessandri government, similar to those of the "Alliance for Progress," were more symbolic than effective and did not respond to the needs of the moment. The opposition skillfully mobilized the ensuing discontent; this was particularly true in the case of the Christian Democrats, who captured the support of wide sectors which historically had been loyal to the traditional parties. The result was an electoral battle in 1964 polarized around the figures of Salvador Allende and Eduardo Frei. Trying to prevent a victory by the candidate of the left, the traditional actors threw their support to Frei. Consequently, his triumph cannot be interpreted entirely as an expression of massive desire for change. It seems clear that the victory was due to the combined support of two sectors. The first consisted of the middle class, which had deserted the Radical party in 1952 and had supported Alessandri in 1958. Basically, as suggested above, the middle class seemed exclusively oriented toward an immediate economic goal, namely a greater share in the benefits of economic development. The other sector which supported Frei's candidacy was that which had traditionally supported the Liberal-Conservative coalition. Threatened in 1964 by a Marxist triumph, it opted for the lesser of two evils.[7] Six years later, in 1970, both groups would abandon the Christian Democrats to support Alessandri—for practically the same reasons.

Nevertheless, with the triumph of the Christian Democrats the first explicit attempt to transform the system began. The intent was to modify all structures which traditionally had blocked resolution of "Chile's global crisis."[8] The party's program—which would affect various socioeconomic sectors—emphasized those social factors linked to the organization and integral participation of all groups.[9]

Fundamentally, the goal of the Christian Democratic program was to reduce the various inequalities among Chilean social strata, largely through the use of existing legal and institutional mechanisms. In 1964 the replacement of the system by a clearly defined alternative was not yet suggested. From the government's point of view, the objectives were to be achieved by a political strategy that sought approval for specific policies through *ad hoc* support from those parties which might identify at least partially with the measures. Fulfillment of the program thus depended on the greater or lesser ability of the government and the Christian Democratic party to maintain control and leadership. The process would be, by definition, gradual and orderly. To follow such a strategy it was necessary to define priorities and choose between effective political participation and socioeconomic change. Frei's choice was to favor the latter.[10] Nevertheless, the need to maintain sufficient electoral support for the time necessary to achieve the party's objectives remained undiminished. This required the concentration and expansion of the government's power and base of support.

One of the most significant results of the Frei period was a profound transformation in the level and intensity of political participation. The magnitude of growth in the electorate is revealed by the following statistics: in 1952 the electorate numbered approximately 1.1 million voters, while in 1970 it had increased to about 4.4 million—practically 50 per cent of the total population. This abrupt quantitative expansion produced important effects on political parties and the political system as a whole. As each of the parties sought to establish a unique identity capable of drawing future support at the ballot box, interparty ideological divisions became greater and the electorate more polarized. In time, this process added to the already existing rigidity of Chilean institutions, further decreasing the possibility for achieving minimum consensus within the traditional channels of parliamentary democracy.

Although the politically mobilized mass was organized through structures at the base and/or at intermediate levels, the direction and control of these structures was highly centralized. To this end, both the Christian Democrats and the Marxist parties initiated similar and competitive activities. In actual practice, their main targets were those groups usually considered "marginal." Thus, popular and union organizations proliferated: Mothers' Centers (*Centros de Madres*), Neighborhood Clubs (*Juntas Vecinales*), Communal Centers (*Unidades Comunales*), Committees of Homeless Persons (*Comités sin Casa*), and similar base organizations. There was also significant organizational growth in the countryside; numerous independent syndicates were created which would eventually play important political roles.[11]

The increase in union organization during the Christian Democratic administration was dramatic. At the end of 1964 there were about 270,000 Chilean labor union members, of whom slightly more than 1,600 were peasants. Partisan political mobilization, stimulated by the deepening process of agrarian reform and changes in the labor legislation, increased these figures by the middle of 1970 to about 127,000 peasant union militants and total union membership to around 550,000. To these should be added about 250,000 employees and workers in the public sector, who were organized professionally into associations such as the State Employees Association (*Asociación de Empleados Semifiscales*, ANEF), the National Federation of Health Workers (*Federación Nacional de Trabajadores de Salud*, FENATS), and others. Although technically these associations were not labor unions, in practice they acted as if they were. Thus one could say that by the end of 1970, syndical organizations had a total membership of about 800,000. It is worth noting that efforts to control and lead these groups—whether long established or recently incorporated into the system—were ineffective. In general, they had a high degree of decision-making autonomy and negotiating power.[12]

Increasing political participation was not limited exclusively to the working class and the expansion of organizations. In the agricultural sector, the National Society of Agriculture (*Sociedad Nacional de Agricultura*, SNA) increased its membership by 60 per cent between 1966 and 1969. The SNA consisted principally of cooperative organizations and unions of employers and medium landowners.[13] Similarly, the SNA contributed to the formation of the Union of Agricultural Employers (COSEMACH), which initially included 20 provincial federations with 124 affiliated unions, some 10,000 activists, and 20,000 associated members. While the SNA maintained a conciliatory attitude toward the government, the COSEMACH developed a style of open and violent opposition, going as far as armed resistance to expropriations by the Agrarian Reform Corporation (CORA).

Identical expansion of political participation occurred among entrepreneurial, industrial, and commercial associations. Their activities were directed toward interest-group goals—in essence the defense of private property against redistributive policies. They mobilized existing private bodies (the Production and Commerce Federation, the Industrial Development Society, the Chamber of Commerce, and the like) and also revived semi-inoperative organizations (the retailers association, AMPICH). Toward the end of the Christian Democratic administration, the Production and Commerce Federation asserted that "entrepreneurial movements" represented some 600,000 persons—including large, medium, and small entrepreneurs.[14]

In addition, government policies contributed to rising expectations and popular discontent. Even though the government enjoyed a relatively favorable economic situation, it still could not ameliorate the problems which resulted from Chile's slow economic growth; these included inflation, monetary devaluation, unemployment, and underemployment. As a result, the frustrations of vast sectors of the lower and middle classes were intensified—not to mention the groups in high society which were totally alienated by specific policies of the government. These trends were reflected in the widespread use of direct pressure tactics—strikes, seizures, and collective protests. The tension even penetrated governmental institutions. In the army for instance, there was the October movement known as the *Tancazo*. The judicial branch went on strike for the first time in the history of the country. Thus the system revealed the first signs of instability.

The Christian Democratic experience showed once more that the stagnation of the Chilean political system could not be ended without widespread and effective popular mobilization, albeit with some degree of central political leadership and control. The Chris-

tian Democrats were caught between their relatively imprecise ideological goals and the need for pragmatic administration of policies.
The party's vacillations contributed to the fragmentation of specific, conflicting interests. At the same time, important internal divisions within the PDC limited its capacity for political leadership.

Even the government's most sincere efforts to promote rapid
changes achieved little. The case of political participation is illustrative and, in this sense, perhaps one of the most interesting of
the period. In spite of the formal commitment of the Christian
Democrats to popular participation in government decisions, these
remained in the hands of party leaders, technocratic groups within
the public administration apparatus, and influential and syndical
sectors. All these were actors who, because of their location within
the system, could effectively advocate their demands. As a result,
innovations in policy were always subject to the willingness of
these groups to absorb the costs of such changes.

Even so, the Christian Democrats initiated a process of major
significance. The inability of Chilean institutions to cope with the
demands of ever-more-numerous organized groups provoked not
only doubts as to the system's rationality and effectiveness but
also calls for its total replacement.

By 1967 recognition of the need for a new order could be perceived within the core of the PDC. In that year the so-called "non-
capitalist road to development" was proposed as a modification
necessary to achieve Frei's "revolution in liberty."[15] Although the
"noncapitalist road" failed to win the party's approval, it stimulated
internal discussion, leading to the first important division in the
PDC. The party's left wing departed to organize the Movement for
United Popular Action (*Movimiento de Acción Popular Unitaria*,
MAPU). Meanwhile, it was becoming obvious that the impressive
electoral support the Christian Democrats had received at the beginning of their administration was deteriorating.

By 1967 maneuvering for the next presidential campaign had
begun. In an atmosphere of violence and increasingly serious economic and social problems, a three-way electoral battle took
shape: Allende on the left, Alessandri on the right, and Tomić in
the center.

In the preceding municipal and congressional elections, the
National party and the so-called independent forces identified
with it had received increasing voter support. Its leaders realized
that behind a political figure like Alessandri they had an excellent
chance for victory. Therefore, it made no sense to them to again
support a Christian Democratic candidate, especially when the

Christian Democrats had named Radomiro Tomić, whose platform was "almost without differences" from that proposed by the left.

From the outset of his campaign, Tomić proposed a "revolutionary democratic and popular" program, whose success would depend on the "unity of the people."[16] Because motivations for support from conservative forces (alliance and/or fear) were absent, his only hope for expanding his electoral base lay in gaining the support of sectors which traditionally had voted for the left, and when his strategy for creating a widely based movement that included such groups failed, his chances of victory were minimal—particularly since within the Christian Democratic party itself there were groups on the right that were quite unenthusiastic about his candidacy.

Considered as a whole, the program of the *Unidad Popular* (UP) was the clearest call for qualitative change in the Chilean system. For this reason, it is interesting to explore briefly some of the circumstances of its origin and development. In my opinion these circumstances produced effects which, in the long run, limited the viability of the left's political program.

From a historical perspective, there are at least four considerations of immediate relevance. First, following the 1964 elections, the major parties and the FRAP alliance adopted substantially different strategies. The Communist party explained the electoral failure as resulting from the fact that the country was not yet ready to give majority support "to Socialists and Communists alone." Hence the Communists' strategy was directed toward creating a popular movement with a "wider social and economic base." The party then began efforts to achieve unity with progressive sectors of the national bourgeoisie. The Communists' contacts with the Radical party, which after its 1965 Congress had moved to a more left-wing position, acquired special importance.

In contrast, the Socialist party in 1967 stated that "revolutionary violence . . . is the only means for reaching political and economic power."[17] Not only did the Socialists reject the electoral road, but they also rejected—beyond the least doubt—the idea of forming any coalition based on a multiclass alliance. Nevertheless, the idea of returning to the electoral struggle slowly regained some degree of support—if no enthusiasm—within the party. Toward 1969, when the candidate of the coalition was to be chosen, the Socialists were still divided over goals, strategies, and preferred candidates.

These basic differences in orientation between the two principal actors of the coalition added to the historic battle for supremacy which had always divided them. As a result, the parties and smaller movements in the coalition showed clear differences from the beginning. Their consensus on basic questions of program and strategy rested on a weak base, perhaps no more than the implicit understanding that what was important was to preserve the coalition, even if this demanded "nondecisions" as its price.

Second, given the context in which the *Unidad Popular* candidate was chosen, it seems clear that Salvador Allende was not necessarily the most popular figure. This was particularly the case in his own party, where he achieved a narrow victory. It gradually became evident that Allende was receiving less support and had less authority and influence than in 1958 and 1964.

Third, it is worth emphasizing the nature of consensus on the program. Unlike what had happened in 1964 and on other occasions, there was no concerted effort to define the key points of the program in terms of intermediate goals and strategies to facilitate coherent government action. In some cases this seemed to reflect skepticism about the likelihood of victory, in others the conviction that the important thing was electoral triumph—afterwards there would be time for details. Lastly—and no less important—it reflected the conviction among some sectors that any attempt to spell out the key concepts of the program would lead inevitably to internecine clashes. In the long run these apprehensions proved critical. Apart from the program's real commitment to effect profound changes in Chilean society, there was no apparent agreement on goals or strategies—so basic to a program advocating revolutionary transformations.[18]

Finally, Allende's triumph clearly cannot be interpreted as a mandate for radical change by an immense national majority. As has been shown in a number of electoral studies, the hypothesis of a gradual shift to the left in the Chilean electorate has no empirical validity whatsoever. The election of Allende can be explained better by reference to the three-way electoral battle.[19]

From the beginning the ability of the *Unidad Popular* administration to act was constrained by its relatively limited electoral support, which limited its popular legitimacy.

THE UNIDAD POPULAR: A HISTORICAL VISION OF THE TRANSITION TO SOCIALISM

An analysis of the Allende government's activities and their effects on political, social, and economic affairs will permit us to evaluate the problem of qualitative change in the Chilean system. Perhaps the most crucial aspect is the shift from a political style based on conciliation to one of confrontation. This movement may serve as a framework for the crisis and breakdown of the *Unidad Popular*'s "historical project."

To this end our analysis distinguishes between three different phases of the Allende administration. Each was characterized by different actions and styles of government. Considered in sequence, they show how the government affected and was in turn limited by changes in the Chilean political system.

During the first phase the system preserved, although under stress, many of the traditional characteristics of parliamentary democracy. As the government stepped up implementation of its major policies, however, the level of polarization sharply increased. This led to the second phase, which was characterized by tension and the progressive erosion of legitimacy—the traditional source of the system's stability. Finally, in the third phase, the old style of conciliation was replaced by open confrontation. The latter came to be seen as the only way to resolve political conflicts based on demands no longer negotiable.

The First Phase

1. Achieving Power: The Program and Its Political Effects

From the beginning, the *Unidad Popular*'s rise to power severely strained the Chilean political system. Its program, after all, called for replacement of the existing system by one avowedly socialist. The Chilean road to socialism would lead to a new kind of state, economy, and society. Yet this transformation was to be within the framework of existing norms and institutions. Indeed, that was to be the essential characteristic of the Chilean socialist transformation. It sought to initiate a revolutionary process which would avoid the high social costs traditionally associated with major revolutions.

In concrete terms, the *Unidad Popular* program specified intermediate goals which when put into practice would ensure the achievement of socialism. Yet, because of the multiclass and multiparty nature of the coalition, various critical aspects of the program were left vague—for example, the definition of exactly what was meant by a "socialist society." In time this vagueness would impose serious constraints on government action.

The planks in the program that caused the gravest conflicts

were those defining the political and economic goals of the coalition. The social, cultural, and international political planks reflected minimal but uncontroversial agreement.

Politically, the government's program proposed the double task of protecting, enforcing, and expanding the democratic rights and privileges of the workers while at the same time altering the existing political institutions. The purpose was to transfer political power to the workers and the people as a whole, along with the prerogatives such power confers. The new power structure was to be built from the bottom up through a process of democratization at all levels, accompanied by popular, organized mobilization.

The main objective of the government's economic policy was to change economic structures in order to end the power of national and foreign monopolies and large landowners. To this end, the program proposed the creation of three property sectors: "social, mixed, and private." It also proposed to accelerate agrarian reform, reorganize the *minifundia,* and establish some form of cooperative ownership and land exploitation. It suggested development policies which would assign high priority to solving the immediate economic problems of the majority as well as the chronic woes of the Chilean economy. In addition, all economic policies were to be based on planning.[20]

Although the victorious coalition was committed to implementing these policies, its actions were severely limited by the nature of its electoral triumph. First, the impact of Allende's victory produced a crisis in the already weak national economy. The gravity of the situation forced the outgoing Frei government to take emergency measures in order to avoid economic collapse. Even with these, however, the economy did not recover the levels it had achieved prior to the presidential election.

Second, because none of the candidates had obtained an absolute majority, the Chilean Constitution required that the election be resolved by the National Congress, which would choose between the two candidates who had received the most votes—in this case Allende and Alessandri. Traditionally this situation led to negotiations in which the first-place candidate—always recognized as the virtual President-elect—was confirmed by Congress. In 1970, however, powerful groups sought to use the constitutional mechanism to block Allende by giving the election to Alessandri. Their efforts were frustrated by an agreement between Allende and the Christian Democratic party in which the Christian Democrats supported Allende in exchange for approval of an agreement expanding and refining certain constitutional guarantees. A Statute of Guarantees, designed "to preserve pluralist society in its political, social and cultural aspects," won rapid approval.[21]

The ratification of Allende's victory by the Chilean Congress and the Statute of Guarantees both emphasized what the foundation of the revolutionary process should be. Changes were to be made within the structure of existing institutions.[22]

Finally, the *Unidad Popular*'s victory signified no more than the partial conquest of political power. The coalition controlled only the executive branch; both chambers of Congress remained in the hands of the opposition. Even though the Chilean Constitution gave the President a high degree of administrative autonomy, policies designed to change the system were virtually untenable without the collaboration of Congress. Thus, a second limitation arose from the fact that the *Unidad Popular* sought revolutionary changes within the existing legal and institutional framework while controlling only a minority in Congress.

2. Government Organization and Policies

During the first phase, government activities focused basically on three closely linked policy objectives: a) economic recovery, b) initiation of the transition to socialism, and c) expansion of the government's political base of support. Implementation of these policies generated a dynamic process which greatly conditioned the orientation and strategy of the government thereafter.

In practice, for the coalition's program to be implemented efficiently, a high degree of internal cohesion around goals, strategies, and specific means was necessary. Similarly, to ensure approval of its most important policies, the program depended on at least a partial continuation of the traditional mechanisms for resolving political conflict. At first this seemed workable, for along with paralysis in Chile's most conservative sectors, the *Unidad Popular* could count on considerable sympathy within the Christian Democratic party. To this was added the support and/or neutrality of two important institutions: the Church and the armed forces. The latter acted in line with the so-called Schneider doctrine.

Nevertheless, certain organizational decisions within the government coalition had profoundly negative consequences in both the short and long run. Most important was the decision to establish a quota system for distributing political and administrative duties at all levels among the parties and movements of the coalition. This opened the door to internal battles—exacerbated by sectarianism—for control of leadership and political patronage.

Within the coalition there rapidly emerged the basis for internal political stalemate and the division of the state bureaucracy into feudal fiefdoms controlled by individual parties. From the beginning, unified, centralized political leadership was notable for its absence. The impact of this on government activities would be felt later on.

Still, the economic recovery and the initiation of the transition to socialism revealed considerable dynamism on the part of the government. It was aided by the availability of resources and by the paralysis of the opposition, both of which facilitated political initiative.[23]

To stimulate economic recovery, the government sought to rapidly redistribute income in favor of the poorest sectors of Chilean society. Measures were adopted to stimulate demand, thus forcing an increase in supply through renewed use of idle or underemployed productive capacity. Inflation was to be controlled initially by forcing business to absorb most of the cost of increased salaries in the form of reduced profits. The government could follow such a policy because of the simultaneous presence of three factors: the existence of large stocks, the existence of accumulated surpluses and/or profits in the private sector, and finally the existence of sufficient international reserves to combat bottlenecks in internal production with imports.

To initiate the transition to socialism, the government focused its actions on two fronts: creation of a Social Property Sector (SPS) and acceleration of agrarian reform.

Efforts to form the SPS were concentrated in three basic areas: a) the reappropriation of basic resources; b) nationalization of the banking system; and c) nationalization of monopolies and strategic industries in the industrial and distributive sectors.

A) THE REAPPROPRIATION OF BASIC RESOURCES[24]

The demand that the government take over control of basic industries—one of the traditional battle flags of the Chilean left—had come to be expressed by ever broader sectors of society. During the Frei administration, the "Chileanization" or "negotiated nationalization" of the copper industry had stimulated the formation of a broad consensus on the necessary components of a nationalistic policy. Now the nationalization of the large copper mines became the central issue in political debate over a government proposal for a constitutional amendment requiring state control of all basic mineral resources. The reform was approved unanimously by the National Congress, giving the government the necessary authority and instruments to make copper, nitrate, and iron mines state property. At the same time, the state negotiated ownership of the steel and coal industries. None of these measures encountered domestic political opposition. Nevertheless, the nationalization of the copper industry, which provided, under the terms of the Allende Doctrine, no compensation to the North American companies, provoked the first significant crisis in relations with the United States. This occurred, of course, within the atmosphere of latent hostility which had characterized relations since Allende took office.

B) NATIONALIZATION OF THE BANKING SYSTEM

The transfer of private banking to state control was one of the government's first measures, announced at the close of 1970. Until the appropriate bill could be sent to Congress, the government used the temporary means of stock purchases by the Development Corporation (CORFO), working through the *Banco del Estado* with credit from the Central Bank. Its strategy—as in the nationalization of the industrial sector—was based on the use of existing "legal opportunities" as a means for avoiding congressional action. In time, the expanded use of this method caused deterioration in relations between the government and the opposition.[25]

C) NATIONALIZATION OF THE INDUSTRIAL SECTOR

In order to incorporate productive, distributive, and commercial monopolies into the Social Property Sector, the government preferred to use existing legal mechanisms. These, according to its interpretation, allowed the state to intervene in and to take over economic activities where production was for some reason threatened—by lockouts, strikes, nonfulfillment of social laws, etc. The government proceeded to take such action in a significant number of firms. Often its hand was forced by labor groups, through strikes, occupations, claims of sabotage, and work stoppages. As a result, industries and businesses of a widely varying size, production, and economic significance—the majority of which were not among the government's targets—were nevertheless included within the Social Property Sector.

Finally, the government acquired still other businesses, particularly in the distributive and commercial sectors, through mechanisms similar to those used in the transfer of the banking system.

Efforts to purchase shipbuilding firms and the paper company, the *Compañía Manufacturera de Cartones,* encountered stiff resistance from stockholders, who were supported by the opposition parties and by business groups.[26]

In the agrarian sector, the government drastically upped the pace of expropriation yet was able to do so without modifying the existing legislation. During the first eighteen months the *latifundio* finally disappeared; at the same time the government abandoned the *asentamientos** used by the Frei administration, replacing them with groups of reformed properties called "Agrarian Reform Centers" (CERAs). The CERA program included a new salary system and a new system for reinvesting profits. Throughout the Allende years, the agrarian reform process was seriously disrupted by activities of groups on the extreme left. Through direct actions such as illegal seizures of agricultural properties, the Revolutionary Peasant Movement and others tried to force the reform to become more radical. These pressures created a situation of anarchy in the countryside, with both political and economic effects. The government responded with a policy of persuasion, but whether because it lacked the political will to control the process or because peasant expectations were fanned by the activities of groups that remained outside the coalition, such efforts met with little success.[27]

The *Unidad Popular's* short-term political goal was to expand and institutionalize its base of mobilized support. This was indispensable for any attempt at rapid and total transformation of Chilean society, including not only its dominant values and myths but also its political institutions, social structures, leadership, and government policies. Moreover, mobilized support was particularly vital to a movement which had achieved power through elections and which sought to channel its actions within the institutional framework of the society it wished to change.

The Chilean situation was further complicated by the highly developed political system, characterized by extensive political and social pluralism, electoral participation, and organization of working class, peasant, neighborhood, and economic pressure groups. The *Unidad Popular* was cognizant of this reality and postulated its immediate political task as the unification and expansion of its popular support. This support was to be mobilized around the broader, more long-term policy goals of the coalition.

---

*The *asentamiento* was defined as a transitional form of organization for the reformed sector in agriculture. Basically it was a productive and administrative unit formed around the borders and population of the expropriated *latifundios.*

During the campaign, the *Unidad Popular* had already established the *Comités de Unidad Popular* (CUP), mass organizations for political and electoral mobilization. Their long-term purpose was to prepare popular social and political groups for exercising power and for carrying out the changes (such as the Assembly of the People, electoral reform, and administrative decentralization) which would institutionalize participation at all levels and in all areas of public policy.[28]

In addition, the *Unidad Popular* had formulated a set of policies—known as the "first forty measures"—to be applied immediately upon assuming power. With these, the government hoped to placate the demand for policies whose execution would require considerable time. The "forty measures" had an immediate electoral purpose and were not designed to initiate profound changes; they were limited to responding to the immediate economic aspirations of the masses and to some general expressions on public morality to be applied by the coalition once in power.

Principally because of the government's minority institutional character, its need to reinforce its campaign support became more acute after it took office. During the first phase, the government's program for economic recovery worked to this end to the extent that it involved populist measures which did not demand important sacrifices from the middle class or from popular sectors. On the contrary, these groups were favored by the wage policies, price controls, and employment policies of the *Unidad Popular*. As a result, the government was able to increase its percentage of the vote from 36.2 per cent in the presidential election to 49.7 per cent in the municipal elections of April, 1971.

Nevertheless, there were early indications that the *Unidad Popular*'s capacity for transforming its electoral base into permanent mobilized support was limited. The importance of the CUP as a mechanism for participatory decision making was minimized, and decisions remained in the hands of party leadership. In practice this reflected two concrete problems. One was the political parties' fear that they might lose their capacity for recruitment and their desire to keep control of organizations which, because of their composition, enjoyed a certain autonomy. The other was the total absence of cohesion and strategic or tactical agreement within the coalition. Such agreement would have allowed abandoning the traditional pattern of interparty competition over individual and immediate interests. On the contrary, in the struggle for control of public administration, nationalized firms, and mass organizations, the divisions within the coalition were exacerbated. Moreover, while disagreements surfaced within the coalition, the government faced an ever larger and more united political opposition.

All this impeded efforts to mobilize strong and continuous political support, and as a result the government opted for seemingly halfhearted, day-to-day attempts to organize the population. There was no effective ideological or political penetration of the masses, for under the circumstances popular support was necessarily limited to organizations directly under the *Unidad Popular*'s control. This lack was apparent in the government's defeats by a united opposition in the parliamentary by-elections of Valparaíso (July, 1971), O'Higgins, Colchagua, and Linares (January, 1972). These defeats acquired more significance in that they reflected a drop in electoral support from April, 1971—despite the success of the government's short-term economic policies and, in the latter three provinces, the intensification of agrarian reform. The *Unidad Popular* also failed initially to create effective structures for worker participation at all levels in government decisions. At the national level, for example, neither the National Peasant Council,[29] created in 1970, nor the National Development Council, formed in February, 1971, were able to operate. Thus the planning of crucial economic and social policies continued to be carried out by traditional policy makers.

In the mining, industrial, and agricultural sectors of the SPS, direct participation of workers in decision making was also minimal. Policy decisions were normally left to the higher reaches of government, and their implementation was entrusted to the administrators of individual firms. The latter often identified more with the immediate interests of their parties than with the general policies of the government. This problem came to be known as the "crisis of middle-level leadership." Thus, from very early in Allende's administration, the government confronted a double dilemma: on the one hand, it was unable to establish mechanisms for effective popular participation in policymaking and administration, and on the other, it was unable to implement and coordinate policies for change in the different sectors.

Recognizing this crisis, the *Unidad Popular* met at Arrayán in January, 1972, to attempt its resolution. But the declaration of the party leaders summarized in the "Arrayán Agreement" produced no improvement. This was the outcome even though President Allende himself frequently declared that he would introduce whatever qualitative changes were necessary to implement the agreement.[30] Inefficacious political leadership served only to worsen internal conflicts, and the coalition continued to act as before.

The *Unidad Popular*'s political, economic, and social policies during the first phase undoubtedly produced profound changes in the Chilean political system, but their principal impact was that they substantively altered the conciliatory nature of the system, paving the way for a system of confrontation. Through the 1970 presidential election, three clearly defined groups of political actors participated in Chilean politics: the left, the center, and the right. Each represented economic and social groups whose interests conditioned the course of politics. Because of their position, the actors of the center—principally the Radical party and later the Christian Democrats—played the pivotal role around which the traditional politics of compromise revolved. Consequently, leadership of the political process lay in their hands.

The *Unidad Popular*'s rise to power began a gradual process of polarization which became more serious with the government's rejection of any compromise implying a reformist strategy. From the coalition's point of view, if the process of transformation were to be taken seriously, no compromise was possible on policies critical to the construction of socialism.[31]

To some extent, the *Unidad Popular* realized that, as the process of change began to affect dominant interests, these would increasingly seek to block government policy initiatives in Congress and wherever else possible. The failure of the coalition to mobilize its political support, and the limitations generated by its policies, gradually led the opposition to assume the initiative. Soon it was pressuring the government to return to the traditional style of political conciliation and to abandon its program. The situation grew more critical for the government after the emergence of ultra-leftist mass movements, in many cases inspired by the Revolutionary Left Movement (MIR). Thus the entire system shifted toward confrontation, and political instability became more pronounced.

There is general consensus that the policies of the *Unidad Popular*, with respect both to the economy and to the formation of SPS, were successful in the short run. But as time passed, new conditions seriously limited the government's margin for political maneuvering.

Any process of change will generate major disequilibria. For the *Unidad Popular*, which sought to eliminate a dependent capitalist system, this was emphatically so. Yet that system was intended to continue functioning normally even as it was gradually being replaced by socialism. In the economic sphere, unfortunately, the Chilean process did not produce compensatory mechanisms capable of reducing short-term imbalances. As a result, critical problems developed. These included the progressive deterioration of the balance of payments, decreasing agricultural and industrial production, the appearance of scarcities and black markets, and, finally, inflation which was increasingly out of control. The impact of this inflation on the political and social base of the government is undeniable, especially since it led to a negative redistribution of income.

To summarize: the inability of the government to control the process of change in the short run began to undermine its future. The possibility of resolving the crisis, which, in essence, implied confronting the dilemma of state capitalism versus socialism, was reduced. The coalition's inability to find an answer laid the basis, during the final days of the first phase, for the emergence and evolution of a style of confrontation.

3. *The Reemergence of Old Problems in a New Context*

From a political point of view, the development of a system of confrontation between opposition and government was characterized by two fundamental, closely linked phenomena. Their evolution throughout the first phase determined the qualitative changes experienced by the system. The two were a) the relations between the coalition parties and the *Unidad Popular* government and b) the relations between the government and the opposition.

A) THE GOVERNMENT COALITION: INTERNAL POLITICAL STALEMATE

A fundamental characteristic of the *Unidad Popular* was its multiclass and multiparty nature. This basic trait also implied the existence of differing ideological and strategic positions within the alliance. Only the pragmatic character of the "basic government program" allowed the coalition to overcome traditional conflicts among its constituent parties. However, though these contradictions were minimized during the election campaign, once the coalition gained power they gradually returned to the fore.

The adoption of a quota system was a response to the need for representation of the ideological and immediate interests of coalition members. As a result, it became necessary to establish some form of combined leadership for directing the activities of both the *Unidad Popular* as a coalition and the individual parties in relations with the government and with the citizenry. Formally this function was assigned to the Political Commission of the *Unidad*

Popular, which was to plan, direct, and coordinate the program by means of permanent consultations. However, from the beginning the Commission was unable to fulfill its task, principally because the various coalition members lacked interest in the work and functioning of the *Unidad Popular* as a unit. On the contrary, they chose to concentrate on proselytizing and exercising political patronage. Most noteworthy was the struggle over eventual political hegemony. The relative power position of each group within the coalition took precedence over contributions to a common revolutionary effort.[32]

In the short run, this situation forced President Allende to function simultaneously as political leader of the movement and as arbitrator among competing partisan interests. The effectiveness of his leadership, somewhat impaired by his role as a disciplined socialist activist, was not sufficient to overcome these partisan differences. Consequently, the internal political stalemate continued, and the parties and movements of the *Unidad Popular* did not adopt a common strategy. This was particularly reflected in the *Unidad Popular*'s failure to expand its base of political support. Its efforts to woo middle sectors and incorporate them into the revolutionary process proved unfruitful. The entrance of the Christian Left Movement (MIC) into the coalition did increase its congressional bloc but apparently added little to its electoral base.

The Radical party—considered the middle-class party *par excellence* within the *Unidad Popular*—faced a series of internal problems as a result both of its precipitous decline in the 1971 municipal elections and, later, of its internal ideological divisions. These focused on the question of maintaining or reformulating the traditional ideology of the party. The most conservative faction of clear social democratic persuasion formed the Party of the Radical Left (PIR). After the resistance of those who opposed incorporating representatives of the bourgeoisie into the government was overcome, the PIR accepted the Ministries of Justice and Mining. Nevertheless, its presence in the government was brief. When President Allende refused to authorize PIR overtures in the name of the *Unidad Popular* to the Christian Democratic party—concerning vetoes of the constitutional reform on economic matters— the PIR abandoned the coalition. Thus an important base of support was lost.

As a result of the political stalemate, the *Unidad Popular* was unable to implement many important policies contained in its program. In general these were ignored or modified by partisan interests.[33] Finally, the nature of the stalemate and its causes also circumscribed the power of the government and its supporters *vis-à-vis* the opposition. As the system evolved toward confrontation and instability, these limits acquired particular importance.

B) RELATIONS BETWEEN THE GOVERNMENT AND THE OPPOSITION

The rapid course of events, the complex political, economic, social, and legal problems considered relevant to the process of change, and the ambiguity of the combatants' activities and decisions all make systematic analysis of government-opposition relations difficult. For the same reasons, it is not easy to select an analytical approach. In this essay I use a method in which I describe, in general terms, the problems and contexts which decisively influenced these relations and the composition of forces.

When Allende assumed power, the Chilean political situation was characterized by an environment of public anticipation, by an image of programmatic and strategic cohesion of the government coalition, and by a vigilant but barely visible opposition. The quiescence of the opposition resulted from at least three factors: the paralysis produced by the *Unidad Popular* victory, a general uncertainty as to the direction of government policies, and finally the assumption that similar programs would permit policy agreements between the Christian Democrats and the *Unidad Popular*.

Certain sectors within the Christian Democratic party—in general gathered around Radomiro Tomić—supported the ratification of Allende's victory and initiated negotiations to seek agreement on those points where the parties held similar views. The *Unidad Popular*'s rejection of or indifference to these advances contributed to the decline of the Tomić faction within the Christian Democratic leadership and to the subsequent hardening of that party's opposition to the government. Thus the Christian Democratic party moved gradually to the right, while the first signs of discontent emerged among party members on the left, who abandoned the party after the congressional by-election of Valparaíso. The dissident faction, known as the Organization of the Christian Left, adopted the original ideological banner of the MAPU, provoking in turn a division in the latter. The two groups then formed the Left Christian Movement (MIC), which joined the *Unidad Popular* and received ministerial representation in the government.[34]

The government's initial determination and energy in administering its program was confronted by opposition attacks on its goals and/or the mechanisms for their achievement. All this occurred in an environment beginning to reflect important changes in political style and practice, which augmented the unrest.

If at first the *Unidad Popular* had enjoyed the advantage in the ideological battle, it soon lost its ability to communicate with and mobilize the masses. At the same time the opposition, by appealing to the traditional symbols and values of Chilean political culture—democracy, liberty, the constitutional state, etc.—began to strengthen its own base of support. Its vitality became particularly noticeable after the April, 1971, municipal elections, in which the government received increased support. This stimulated unity among the opposition, which later took form in tacit agreements to enter by-elections in a united front that would permit victory over the government. The thesis that the "democratic forces" must band together before the "Marxist danger" was clearly articulated. In spite of the ideological, pragmatic, and strategic differences between the Christian Democratic and National parties, the political and economic implications of government policies pushed them toward a *de facto* alliance. The emergence of a united opposition helped to recreate a climate of tension similar to that which had existed immediately after Allende's election. Tension became increasingly severe as threatened national and international interests stepped up their propaganda attacks. As a result, the possibilities for coexistence and dialogue were gradually reduced.

By the end of the first phase the situation had reached a critical point. All of the various political groups agreed—although for different reasons—that a profound institutional crisis had developed. The stability of the system and the viability of the "Chilean road to socialism" would depend on its resolution.

The areas in which this conflict was most evident were a) political violence and *espontaneísmo*,* b) challenges to political institutions, and c) the definition of the economic sectors.

a) Political violence and *espontaneísmo:* In Chile's political development violence has not been unknown. On the contrary, it has always been used to influence policy, both by elites and by those who are marginal to the system.

---

* *Espontaneísmo*, for which there is no good English equivalent, was a political term invented in Chile to describe the "long and uninterrupted series of seizures and illegal occupations of farms, urban property, industries, and government agencies" which occurred throughout the Allende period. The goals of these activities varied, but they all involved direct mass political action to force rapid solution to real or imagined problems.

Through the so-called politics of persuasion, Allende hoped to lay a framework of peace and social harmony for government actions, making it unnecessary to resort to violence—whether institutionalized or not. To this end, the government, once in power, pardoned a number of extreme leftists imprisoned during the Frei administration. The move aroused the opposition, which feared that as a result the government would ascribe "legitimacy" to any group alleging "idealistic" political motives for their actions. Confronted with intense criticism, the government insisted anew that it intended to maintain public order within the existing legal system.

Nevertheless, by the end of 1970 one could already perceive the emergence of a new approach to violence: the use of assassination and crime as instruments of political action. The first victim was the Commander in Chief of the Army, assassinated in the hope of provoking a *coup d'état* that would prevent Allende from assuming power. Later, an ex-Minister of the Frei administration, Edmundo Pérez, was murdered by members of the People's Workers Vanguard (VOP), some of whom had been released by the presidential pardon. The VOP, an extreme left-wing organization, claimed to be seeking political vengeance against those whom it accused of "crimes against the people."

The assassination of Edmundo Pérez was unanimously condemned. In addition, it gave rise to a polemical battle whose accusatory language worsened tensions and further reduced the possibilities for dialogue. At the same time, Allende's increasing fear that extreme left-wing elements might also try to assassinate him led him to reinforce the group charged with his own personal security (the Group of Friends of the President, GAP), an illegal move which provoked bitter criticism from the opposition.

Political violence continued to occur on various fronts and with varying characteristics. The bitter political battle produced new victims, and both the right and the left organized extremist armed groups, which quickly proliferated. The presence and activities of these groups worsened relations between the government and the opposition.

Another element which contributed to the deteriorating situation was called *espontaneísmo*. This phenomenon took the form of continuous seizures and illegal occupations of farms, urban properties, industries, and government agencies. Such actions sought to quickly resolve long-standing problems, to effect the rapid transfer of industries or businesses to the Social Property Sector, or simply, in not a few cases, to take advantage of a context which offered immediate material benefits. As Radomiro Tomić commented in 1972:

Considered alone, each takeover could have a reasonable explanation and a "low social cost" (as has been in effect the case until now). But considered as a whole, multiplied by the hundreds and even thousands of cases which have occurred along the length of Chile, week after week and month after month, they end up having a cumulative effect on public opinion that is devastating for the government.[35]

The failure of Allende's politics of persuasion to resolve the problem of *espontaneísmo* created an image of social anarchy and of a government without authority. Problems of political and administrative leadership within the government only reinforced that image. For example, it was obvious that middle-level bureaucrats did not always act in accordance with the wishes and orders of the executive. The outcome could not have been worse for the government, especially in the area of relations with the opposition. It was at this point that the opposition initiated what would become an interminable series of constitutional censures against those "responsible for the disorderly situation in which the country finds itself."

b) Challenging institutions: In a political movement such as the *Unidad Popular*, which proposed profound changes in the Chilean system and its replacement with a qualitatively different system, it is only natural that the legitimacy and functioning of existing institutions be called into question. Nevertheless, once in control of the executive branch, the coalition became more restrained in its criticisms of the existing order. The need to change the system via its own institutions necessitated a strategy of gradually replacing the institutions themselves. A first indication of this strategy was the proposal to create the so-called neighborhood courts. The opposition, perceiving a double purpose, attacked the idea bitterly. On the one hand they feared that the government would use the courts to destroy the constitutional structure of the administration of justice in Chile—which, after all, was being seriously challenged. On the other, they saw in the bill the intention of creating a system of justice with a clear political bias—a Chilean version of "people's courts." The government was forced to abandon the plan, but not without attacking both the opposition and the Chilean judicial system. To the latter, it attributed a class bias that made it an instrument of interests other than those of the people.[36] The government's criticisms of the judicial branch touched off yet another battle with the political opposition—one which would become increasingly serious throughout the Allende administration.

An important part of the *Unidad Popular*'s attacks on institutions focused on the National Congress. The coalition questioned both the legislature's representativity and its legitimacy, regarding it, because of its composition and structure, as a major obstacle to change. In November, 1971, Allende sent to Congress a constitutional amendment designed to modify the structure of the legislative branch. In it, he proposed the creation of a People's Assembly, which would play a central role in the new state. Because of intense opposition, the proposal never succeeded. Its rejection by Congress made necessary a plebiscite, whose results and political implications were unforeseeable. As a result the government withdrew the proposal, choosing instead to pursue a strategy of gaining control of the Congress through elections.

Based on the results of a January, 1972, by-election, the *Unidad Popular* decided that the coalition should present a "united front" in the general elections of March, 1973. The idea was to profit from the Chilean system of proportional representation, which favored political units receiving greater numbers of votes by giving them greater representation in Congress than that to which their actual support would entitle them.[37] Paradoxically, opposition to this proposal surfaced within the *Unidad Popular* itself. No party wanted to risk losing its own political identity or its share of participation in political leadership. This was particularly true of the smaller parties, such as the PIR, which did not want to renounce their ideological positions.

The formula for a united front and serious discussion of it did not worry the opposition since, according to existing legislation, the *Unidad Popular* could have run as a single party in any case. Therefore a new round of consultations between the *Unidad Popular* and the Christian Democratic party commenced, in order to change electoral legislation so that in future congressional elections, all political actors would be subject to the same rules. As a result of these meetings, a bill unanimously supported by all parties was submitted to Congress. However, the bill's slow passage through committee threatened to impede the formation of electoral pacts within the permissible period. This led both the coalition and the National party to appeal to the Elections Court for a ruling on the articles of the elections law. These permitted parties to assume new organizational forms—e.g., federations and/or confederations with unified leadership. The court's favorable ruling opened the gate to the formation of pacts under existing legislation, without recourse to a new law.[38]

Thus the parties immediately coalesced into two opposing blocs. The opposition formed the Democratic Confederation

(CODE), joining the Federation of the Christian Democrats with the PIR, and the Federation of the National party with the Radical Democrats (RD). The *Unidad Popular* formed the Federated Party of Popular Unity, including all six parties in the government coalition. The Democratic Confederation opened up significant possibilities for the opposition. First, it gave them the opportunity to centralize leadership over the entire opposition and thus to campaign united in a wide variety of labor union and student elections during the following months. Second, unity presented another opportunity to mobilize the middle sectors (employees, small and medium industrialists, and businessmen) against the government's attempts to implement its program. The opposition interpreted the electoral decline of the *Unidad Popular*—confirmed in labor union and student elections—as highly favorable.[39]

In contrast, changing the electoral legislation did not help to unify government forces under federated direction. The problem of weak political leadership within the coalition continued unchanged.

The electoral reform and subsequent pacts had their most serious impact on the system itself. By legitimating the division of political actors into two opposing camps, despite internal ideological differences within each—particularly within the CODE—the reform established the legal basis for a political style of confrontation.

The government's efforts to shift from criticizing existing institutions to effecting concrete changes did not succeed. In the majority of cases, political debate reflected positions which were difficult to reconcile because of the nonnegotiable nature assigned to them by the combatants. Particularly during the first phase, the opposition employed constitutional censure to pressure and halt executive actions. Traditionally the mechanism of censure had been applied only at the ministerial level; now, as the conflict grew more serious, opposition legislators threatened to censure the President of the Republic himself. Their attitude reflected the conviction—shared by extremists on both left and right—that confrontation was inevitable.

c) Definition of the economic sectors: As implementation of the *Unidad Popular*'s programs advanced, relations between the government and the opposition deteriorated further. The irreconcilable nature of their positions was perhaps most clearly revealed in the definition of the economic sectors. Here the opposition attacked not only the government's procedures for achieving its ends but also the very goals themselves.[40]

For the *Unidad Popular*, the creation of the Social Property

Sector (SPS) was the crucial foundation in the construction of socialism. It was a goal to be achieved in the shortest possible time and with the fewest possible changes in the original conception. Control of the economic apparatus would permit the government to direct the proposed course of global changes. Hence the administration did not hesitate to initiate and expand actions to incorporate into the SPS a minimum of ninety-one firms which it considered crucial to the country's economy. Moreover, the government acted in spite of virtual approval by the National Congress of a constitutional reform, sponsored by the Christian Democrats, that was designed precisely to impede such incorporations.

Direct or indirect control of production would significantly increase the government's supply of political patronage and mobilized support. Thus, the opposition reasoned, the creation of the SPS was the first step in an escalation which would eventually lead to the destruction of Chile's democratic system. The opposition's argument can be simply summarized: without economic democracy there could be no political democracy. The notion had deep ideological roots among the groups in opposition, all of which rejected the idea of a central political, economic, or social role for the state. Although there were differences in the degree to which they would tolerate government intervention, they agreed in their basic rejection of "statist concepts."

The opposition's ideological stance rested on the assumption that acceptance of the government's model would give economic control to a governing coalition dominated by "sectarian parties with clear totalitarian tendencies." The government's intentions could be clearly seen in its effort to incorporate the National Paper and Carton Company (*Compañía Manufacturera de Papel y Cartones*) into the SPS. The move led to debates in which ideological questions took precedence over immediate economic interests. Thus it was argued that, with its high level of productive efficiency, the company guaranteed the supply of paper in Chile and, in particular, met the needs of newspapers. Freedom of the press and information was said to rest on a fair distribution of newsprint—a distribution not subject to political discrimination. The government's efforts provoked a powerful reaction because it was felt they hid an attempt at "the liquidation of the opposition press by means of a state monopoly of newsprint"—one more step in the totalitarian escalation.[41]

The opposition's criticisms of the government's economic policies combined both ideological and practical elements. Congressional approval of the constitutional reform sponsored by the

Christian Democrats was a political move which did not surprise the government. Constitutionally unable to reject the entire reform, the government announced its intention to modify it substantially by means of substitutive and suppressive vetoes.*

This conflict concluded the first phase of the *Unidad Popular* government; relations between the colegislative powers, the President and the Congress, had reached a critical point, as the opposing positions had become irreconcilable. On an institutional level, what was at stake was the presidential system itself and the prerogatives of the executive; on a political and economic plane, it was the viability of the model proposed by the *Unidad Popular*. *Mutatis mutandis*, at stake for the opposition was the survival of a democratic pluralist system.

In this manner the gap between the combatants became wider. During the second phase of the *Unidad Popular* government, this separation would affect events in such a way as to allow few real options to either side.

The Second Phase

1. The Background to Accelerating Crisis

In the development of every process of social change, some means must be found to resolve demands that are often contradictory; to succeed, such a program must enjoy wide social support and incorporate active political participation in its leadership. Unfortunately, wide support and active participation are not always compatible with the need to integrate and institutionalize the process of change itself.[42] Consequently, the search for some means to reconcile these diverse goals emerges as a fundamental political task. The *Unidad Popular*, recognizing the complex and critical nature of this problem, adopted a strategy which, ideally, would have permitted it both to expand its base of political support and to institutionalize its achievements, while maintaining direction and control of the process.

However, the strategy demanded that the coalition meet certain minimal requirements. First, there had to be a high degree of consensus with respect to goals and priorities. Second, there had to be a sufficient cohesion and internal discipline to allow the coalition to exercise rational political leadership consistent with

* Unlike the President of the United States, the President of Chile can veto or modify specific portions of legislation approved by the Congress.

the process of change. Third, within the limits of autonomy appropriate to any coalition, there could be no room for political *espontaneísmo*. Finally, *vis-à-vis* other participants in the political arena, the coalition had to act in accordance with the special rules of parliamentary democracy, but in such a way as not to sacrifice progress in the construction of a new society.

As has been shown above, the *Unidad Popular* revealed serious weaknesses in implementing its strategy. Its inability to meet the aforementioned requirements seriously hampered its efforts to obtain an institutional majority. The coalition's reduced support by the end of the first phase was a result of the *Unidad Popular*'s attempt to reconcile revolutionary goals with pragmatic measures, such as the quota system, designed to reduce the traditional friction among the coalition parties. In practice, the opposite resulted. Centrifugal tendencies developed, making it impossible to obtain the consensus and political leadership necessary to implement policies directing change.

While the coalition continued to insist upon its revolutionary goals—at least at the level of rhetoric—its base of political support gradually eroded. As a result, the coalition was less able to negotiate with an opposition which was not only increasingly strong and dynamic but also more flexible in dealing with the perceived "threat to democratic institutions." Similarly, the coalition's ability to create and implement policies which were not "populist" was also limited. In the context of growing confrontation, political conflict sharpened; the nonnegotiable nature of the government's goals and uncertain strategies only worsened the climate of political instability, generating feelings of frustration, tension, and social antagonism.

In this manner the broad lines of the various alternatives were drawn. For the government, the central choice was whether to consolidate its achievements or to radicalize the process of change. For the opposition, the dilemma rested in how best to confront the anti-democratic threat: by forcing a return to the traditional rules of the conciliatory parliamentary game or, more directly, by forcing the government's resignation through constitutional mechanisms. These alternatives shared one common trait; they all affected not only the stability of the system but also the viability of the process of change undertaken. In this context, the structure of a system of confrontation began to appear. In effect, it converted the Chilean political process into a chain of rapid, successive, and cumulative crises.

2. The Systemic Crisis and the Politics of Confrontation

In mid-1972 the emerging economic crisis and the growing political conflict between the government and the opposition forced the administration to modify its line of action. At the Lo Curro meetings, held in June, 1972, the government once again undertook to analyze the deficiencies in its economic policies and political leadership. These deficiencies threatened not only the coherence of the coalition—which was rent with internal conflicts—but also the political stability of the country.[43]

At these meetings the internal divisions within the *Unidad Popular* were clearly visible. On one side were the Socialist party, the MAPU, and the Christian Left (IC); on the other, the Communist party, the Radical party, and the API. The former supported continuation of the "Vuskovic Strategy": advancing, by whatever means possible, in the formation of social and mixed property sectors and opting for popular control of production and distribution. The latter favored consolidating the process, putting a brake on the mobilization of popular participation, and channeling that participation within the framework of state control.

The conflict was resolved with the triumph of the Communist party strategy, which included a policy of wage and price adjustments and a new attempt to negotiate a common definition of the Social Property Sector with the Christian Democrats.

Implementation of this moderate line had a variety of effects. First, inflation became more severe, reaching a rate of 99.4 per cent for the nine-month period up to September, 1972. On this basis, wages and salaries were readjusted. Second, as a consequence of the deepening economic crisis, the problem of scarcities, the black market, and the depletion of foreign reserves was exacerbated. The situation was worsened by the systematic international blockade of the traditional sources of external financing. The activities of the United States government produced effects which were not compensated for by the economic aid of the socialist bloc—the amount and usefulness of which were debatable.[44] At the same time, the application of the moderate line intensified the conflicts within the government coalition. The crisis of political leadership became more acute, given the logical consequences of *espontaneísmo* and confusion among government supporters. Thus the government's efficacy was further impaired.

Finally, the negotiations with the Christian Democrats failed because of profound disagreements over the Social Property Sector. These involved two problems: maintaining the National Paper Company outside the SPS, and creating a private banking sector. Failure of the talks led the Christian Democrats to adopt the strategy of blocking the government's efforts to consolidate the SPS. In effect, the Christian Democrats formed a strategic alliance with the National party. Thus, in practice, the economic policies adopted at the Lo Curro meetings weakened the government's position *vis-à-vis* an effectively coordinated opposition.

In this context the so-called October crisis began to develop. During the previous months there had been frequent strikes and confrontations of all kinds between the government and the opposition and, on not a few occasions, among the very actors that supposedly supported the government—particularly the Communist party and the MIR. The beginnings of a strong opposition within the coalition, demanding the radicalization of the revolutionary process at whatever cost, could be discerned. Opposition from the extreme left exacerbated contradictions within the alliance, polarizing the internal stalemate and seriously threatening to weaken the government's already limited capacity for centralized leadership.

The government's decision to create a state transportation company, together with the increased activities of the Supplies and Prices Committees (*Juntas de Abastecimientos y Precios,* JAP), precipitated a strike of truck owners. A national chain reaction rapidly developed. As the strike progressed, it gradually came to include a gamut of actors who glimpsed opportunity to articulate their demands and complaints. For numerous highly organized interest groups, which saw in the movement a last chance to defend their interests, the so-called middle sectors' strike became a decisive test.

The October movement tended to join all groups whose interests would be vitally affected by radicalization of the transition to socialism. It rapidly developed to the point where the opposition parties could no longer lead or control the strike. In essence, the parties could only react to a landslide of interest-group activities which, in effect, threatened their position as leaders of the political opposition.

The strike affected the government in various ways. As it had done before, the government sought to rally popular support through the masses under the political control of the central labor union confederation (*Central Unica de Trabajadores,* CUT). But the coalition proved incapable of responding flexibly and efficiently to new political strategies which went beyond the customary limits of battle. Internal disagreements on goals, strategies, and the specific means for responding to the strike enmeshed the government and limited its ability to act. While some groups desperately sought to negotiate through the regular mechanisms of political conciliation, others—especially those of the far left—saw the possibility of using the conflict to force open radicalization of the revolutionary process. For these groups, the strike exemplified the failure of bourgeois parliamentary democracy and was, more importantly, the last step in a "fascist escalation" designed to overthrow the popular government. This was the stiffest test that the coalition had faced since coming to power. Without guidance from a vacillating government, however, the mass base of the *Unidad Popular* was left to respond with spontaneous organization.

In this fashion a mass movement emerged and, as the conflict advanced, developed a series of organizations whose function was to offer base-level resistance to the opposition. The movement included new forms of popular organization, such as the Communal Action Commandos, defined as the "basis of popular power," the so-called industrial belts, and the Peasant Commandos, among others. Significantly, as was noted above, the parties of the coalition played a passive role in the formation of these groups and in their activities. Leadership and control tended to reside among those who, though supporting the government, rejected the traditional mechanisms for resolving political conflict.

The polarization of Chilean society which resulted from the strike—aggravated by the obvious "internationalization" of the opposition—produced major destabilizing effects. After October the ultras at both extremes of the political spectrum engaged in open confrontation which rapidly led to the point of violent conflict between the government and opposition.

The increasing severity of the conflict generated reactions which eventually led to its resolution. It was clear that if polarization were to continue, it would soon reach a point of no return. On the one hand, the "moderate" political parties—principally the Communist party and the Christian Democrats—approached one another and sought to agree on some formula for compromise. On the other, contrary to some expectations, the coalition developed increasing unity, overcoming partisan and/or ideological differences, as the government sought to defend itself. Finally, conscious of the strike's long-term implications, the government decided to bring the armed forces into the cabinet. From within the government, the military acted to bring the conflict under control and to reestablish order.[45]

For the opposition, incorporation of the armed forces into the cabinet was an indication that the government could be forced to negotiate—on the opposition's terms—critical political problems. For many important factions within the government coalition, the presence of the military was a grave, even inexcusable error by Allende, for implicitly it recognized a shift toward consolidation. Whatever the interpretation, given the particular context of October, 1972, the armed forces were the only group capable of restoring even minimal stability to a system facing seemingly inevitable confrontation.

Although the incorporation of the armed forces assured the survival and continuity of the administration, it also implied the strengthening of moderate policies. The military presence limited the executive's ability to expand the SPS and, in some cases, even forced a retreat from earlier decisions. This was shown by the implementation of the agreement resolving the October conflict.

The October strike accelerated the deterioration of the Chilean economy, already suffering from serious problems. The country's losses from the transportation strike and its impact on the productive and distributive networks, not to mention the tax system, were calculated at about $300 million. This in turn had a major impact on foreign trade and the precarious position of Chile's foreign reserves. Yet the strike did facilitate government efforts to expand the SPS, for it cleared the path to requisition of or intervention in a number of businesses. Although many of these were returned after the strike was settled, the government retained control of ninety-one firms which it considered crucial to its economic program. Nevertheless, the armed forces prevented legal completion of these interventions and requisitions. The military cabinet ministers refused to sign the Decrees of Insistence necessary to obtain definitive approval by the *Contraloría General de la República.**

The government adopted a conservative stance toward the organizational capacity of important working-class and popular sectors. Not only was popular mobilization neither taken advantage of nor institutionalized but, on the contrary, it was gradually dismantled. As a result, new conflicts between the Communist and Socialist parties appeared within the coalition, and these further paralyzed the government's attempts to remedy the already

---

* When the *Contraloría* questioned the constitutionality of these interventions, the government could override its objection only by Decrees of Insistence—executive decrees which required, by law, the signature of every cabinet minister.

serious administrative and productive deficiencies in the Social Property Sector.

The resolution of the October crisis led the opposition to abandon momentarily its extreme positions and accept Christian Democratic policies designed to hinder government action. The course of the political process was now seen as tied to the congressional elections of 1973. The opposition line immediately hardened, with its principal propaganda attack focused on the economic failure of the government. For the Christian Democrats, the military presence in the cabinet guaranteed the normal evolution of the electoral process.[46]

3. Elections in a Context of Confrontation

After the October crisis, political activity came to be centered on the March elections, which thus became a crucial institutional test for both government and opposition. Unlike earlier opportunities, however, this time only two actors participated: the Democratic Confederation (CODE), representing the opposition, and the Federated party of the *Unidad Popular,* representing the government. For the *Unidad Popular,* it was most important that the coalition obtain at least one third of the seats in Congress. This would allow them to control the legislative process through use of the presidential veto.

Having learned from experience, the *Unidad Popular* realized that the economic situation was the most serious obstacle in the way of its aspirations. Inflation reached 163.4 per cent in December; industrial production showed symptoms of decline; and agricultural production dropped no less than 7 per cent "in the best of cases."[47] The losses of nationalized firms reached fifty billion *escudos* (approximately one billion dollars at then current exchange rates). These were financed by loans from the State Development Corporation (*Corporación de Fomento a la Producción,* CORFO) and by uncontrolled currency emissions. The printing of money increased the fiscal deficit and expanded the amount of money in circulation by 166.3 per cent with respect to the previous year. This, of course, was one cause of inflation. Yet, in spite of everything, the unemployment rate remained at 2.8 per cent, the same as in December of the previous year.[48]

After October, the problems of scarcity, hoarding, and the black market became more serious. In various ways, these problems and their side effects were a result of the drop in agricultural and industrial production, the disorganization and corruption within the SPS, the activities of groups in the private sector, and the general panic buying among consumers. Finally, the depletion of foreign reserves, derived from falling export earnings, the drop in the international market price of copper, the need to service the external debt, and the importation of both consumer and capital goods all contributed to the crisis. However, it was somewhat alleviated by Allende's visit to the Soviet Union, where he obtained a loan of $300 million.

In light of this somber economic picture, the opposition defined the election as a plebiscite. The National party's goal was to obtain two thirds of the seats in both houses of Congress, in order to impeach Allende and "remove him constitutionally." For the Christian Democrats, revitalized by the return of ex-President Frei, the goal was to obtain an absolute majority which would demonstrate popular discontent with the government and force a drastic change in direction. In practice, however, the CODE was never solidly united. Beneath the common slogan of "beginning the reconstruction," each party adopted different tactics and sought to emphasize its own individuality. Consequently, there was no common program, nor even a united campaign. Electoral interests predominated and limited the alliance's ability to mobilize support. The alliance was based on weak premises, and its goal of "reconstruction" was vague. Moreover, it was fundamentally torn by the competition at the national level between ex-President Frei and Onofre Jarpa, president of the National party. Both were senatorial candidates for Santiago.

The primary goal for the *Unidad Popular* was to obtain a sufficiently large proportion of the vote to prevent the Democratic Confederation from controlling two thirds of Congress. However, in the search for a common strategy, the old conflicts within the coalition rapidly surfaced anew. The Communists, on the one hand, favored a moderate, defensive posture, similar to the line followed by the government after November, 1972. On the other hand, the Socialists, together with their allies (MAPU and the Christian Left), emphasized an aggressive stance. This earned them the support of the Revolutionary Left Movement (MIR).

The internal divisions inevitably affected government actions. For example, the socialist viewpoint was expressed in a speech by the Treasury Minister in January, 1973. He proposed a series of measures—described as an "economic war"—to deal with the problem of scarcities. The most important provided for rationing basic necessities. The emergency program was to be directed by the recently created National Secretariat for Distribution, while the

Committees of Supply and Prices and other popular and communal organizations were to assist in distributing the rationed commodities. The policy received only scant and formal support from other political actors in the government, however, and did not fare well.

In practice the task of redistribution was left to representatives of the military. Through the Ministry of the Interior, the functions of the Committees were clearly and rigorously defined. Although as the "base of popular power" the Committees had filled a central role in distribution during the October crisis, now their functions were dramatically curtailed. They were defined only as "advisory bodies" to those responsible for the distribution of consumer goods.

The tactics of moderation, advanced by the Communist party and its allies, were reinforced with the elaboration of a bill to regulate the Social Property Sector. The bill included various mechanisms for compensating owners of nationalized industries, provided for returning to private control the great majority of firms which had already been taken over or requisitioned, and, most important, took the first step toward returning some of the ninety-one firms previously considered crucial to the SPS.

The conflict between the Communist and Socialist parties required Allende's campaign presence to ameliorate the resulting political and electoral weaknesses. Without a doubt, Allende's activities during the campaign, and his defense not only of the government but also of the viability of peaceful change toward socialism, helped preserve the threatened unity of the coalition. He also helped to mobilize a left-wing electorate which, at this point, was thoroughly confused by the internal conflict.

Allende's campaigning, of course, did no more than postpone discussion of the old conflict between the actors in the government—"revolutionaries" versus "reformers" and, within the Socialist party, "extremists" versus "Allendistas." Although the coalition faced a united opposition that sought to block completely a weakened government, a movement emerged within the coalition itself which opposed the government's project for regulating the SPS. The movement centered on groups in the so-called industrial belt of Santiago and was led by the MIR, the left wing of the Socialist party and the MAPU. The conflict was in essence ideological, and the question under debate, expressed in an exchange of letters between the leaders of the Socialist and Communist parties, led finally to a major crisis. Moreover, all this occurred at a time when the system's stability had reached one of its lowest and most critical points.

In this context of confrontation, the 1973 congressional elections acquired special meaning. They came to symbolize a watershed in the evolving political conflict. On their results—all believed—would depend to a great extent the stability and survival of the Chilean system, as well as the viability of the *Unidad Popular's* project.

In some political groups expectations were pessimistic and contradictory. The efficacy of elections as a mechanism for resolving political conflict was seriously questioned. In any case, the legitimacy of the immediate results depended on the extent to which they served the specific interests involved. Even in the best of circumstances the victors would find themselves in a curious situation. Their triumph would not legitimate their past or future actions, for the losers would be tempted or forced to resist, by definition, through extraparliamentary means.

Perhaps this point best illustrates the nature and extent of the changes which had already occurred in the Chilean political system. The traditional mechanisms for resolving political conflict seemed to have lost their efficacy and legitimacy. The context was now qualitatively different. The March elections were a profound expression of the extent of the crisis. Despite their reservations, the political actors participated in the ritual of electoral battle with the blind hope of those afraid that the last chance for a democratic solution to the crisis would slip away.[49]

The Third Phase

1. Consolidation or Revolution—and a Military Coup as the Third Alternative

As might have been foreseen, the results of the election were far from what the combatants desired. To the surprise of the opposition, the government obtained unexpectedly high support—43.4 per cent of the vote. Any hope the opposition had of gaining control of two thirds of the Congress and attempting a constitutional "overthrow" disappeared.[50] When one notes the conditions under which the campaign took place, the election results seem even more surprising. The government, after all, confronted a situation of acute economic collapse, severe inflation, and widespread scarcities.

Different groups drew different conclusions from the results, which, in one way or another, accentuated the crisis of political legitimacy. For some sectors in the government they clearly indicated that the government should abandon once and for all its search for an understanding with the so-called progressive sectors of the opposition; the government's electoral support was "an order of the people to advance without compromise." In like fashion, for some sectors of the opposition, the results indicated categorically that it would be legally impossible to halt "the Marxist avalanche which seeks total power." They undertook simultaneously to denounce the "shameful intervention and electoral fraud" perpetrated by the government and to wage an open campaign of violent, extremist obstruction.[51] The post-electoral period ending in the military *coup* was thus one in which escalating confrontations, emphasizing violence and the economic crisis, impeded any serious attempt to avoid generalized conflict. The understanding among opposition sectors with common interests became obvious as never before. Their conscious effort to obstruct any and all government actions worsened critical social and economic problems.

The possibility of continuing to govern with the "coparticipation" of the military rapidly disappeared. The armed forces, doubting that they could exercise real power in the cabinet, preferred to avoid involvement and decided to resign from the government.[52] Their action was welcomed by the opposition, as well as by many sectors within the *Unidad Popular,* which saw in military participation a clear example of "reformist surrender."

Thus Allende was confronted with the withdrawal of the military and the gradually hardening positions of both the opposition and his own followers. In this situation he decided to name a clearly moderate civilian cabinet. Nevertheless, the government continued to show signs of internal weakness. As the chasm between the government and the opposition widened, so did the internal abyss between "reformers" and "revolutionaries." The schism of the MAPU only four days after the congressional elections was a classic example, reflecting the existing divisions in the coalition. One wing identified with the thesis of the Communist party. It argued for consolidating achievements and for continuing to seek expansion of the electoral base by appealing to moderate and progressive sectors of the opposition, while preserving above all the unity of the coalition—objectives which were in practice incompatible. The other wing adhered to the viewpoint of Carlos Altamirano and the more leftist Socialists. It favored radicalization of the revolutionary process and rejected any conciliatory position. In such circumstances the *Unidad Popular* projected the image of a coalition of incompatible partners, incapable of political leadership.

The opposition, in contrast, strengthened its consensus. It rejected out of hand every government project and measure. The government's decision to establish the Unified National School by administrative, regulatory law precipitated a new political storm. The incorporation into the Social Property Sector, by Decrees of Insistence, of forty firms occupied during the October strike did the same. Both actions, like those that followed concerning distribution of basic necessities and the roles of the JAP, the wheat monopoly, and the like, were interpreted by the opposition as part of a totalitarian escalation. It responded, as noted above, with concerned obstruction. Moreover, important opposition politicians had by this time arrived at clear and evident understandings with certain military factions. Their aims were obviously anti-constitutional. The "moderates" or "centrists" had become so isolated by both extremes of the political spectrum that they had no influence whatsoever over decisions.

In this manner the government's ability to act was dramatically reduced. The stability and legitimacy of the Chilean system were eroding. Violence, strikes, and constitutional censures became routine daily events. By May, 1973, it was clear that no political or administrative structure had escaped the effects of this process. As a result of the polarization, administrative decisions and the activities of the leaders of both opposing bands acquired almost independent dynamics—resolvable only with great difficulty. Allende found it increasingly hard to achieve agreement or reconciliation. Any action he took to moderate the conflict with the opposition did no more than deepen the problems within the government coalition. In his *Third Message to the Nation,* while recognizing the gravity of the economic situation, he dedicated an important section to the analysis of the dangers which threatened "democracy and civil peace." He announced that the government had prepared a project for a new constitution, which would be subjected to national public debate before being sent to Congress. By now it was obvious that, whatever merits the project might have, the opposition would reject it forthrightly.[53]

Allende's room for political maneuver was reduced still further by the election of Patricio Aylwin to the presidency of the Christian Democratic party. With his election the Frei faction consolidated its control over the party. Whatever possibilities had once existed for formulating an agreement that would not mean "surrendering the government program" to the Christian Democrats now disappeared forever. Frei seemed the person least interested in reaching "intermediate solutions."

The tremendous accumulation of events, actions, and decisions during this period tends to blur something even more important and decisive: a growing sense of the inevitable, a final collapse of the *Unidad Popular*'s basic project. It is very hard to avoid concluding that, whatever course Allende might have taken to evade direct confrontation, the original "model" for peaceful revolution would have had to undergo a profound transformation. As in the beginning, one question echoed insistently: consolidation or revolutionary advance? For either alternative, the immediate cost was the collapse of the coalition, the program, and the viability of the project. That price was seen as too high by all involved and led to continuing what had seemed the only internally acceptable form of political leadership: maintaining, in the name of ideological pluralism, the political stalemate and paralysis of all organized, political leadership.

Now, however, the opposition had no doubts about who held the political initiative, and it acted accordingly. Moreover, its concerted efforts to implant the idea that the government exercised power illegitimately began to bear fruit. The Supreme Court, for example, ruled that the administration was responsible for the imminent collapse "of the country's judicial process."[54]

In this atmosphere of tension and generalized violence, the head of the Emergency Zone for Santiago announced the arrest of a number of military officers involved in a plot against the government. A few hours later Colonel Roberto Souper, in an apparently isolated action, attempted to rescue one of those detained.

The *tancazo* left no doubt that pressure for a *coup* was rapidly building. In spite of the ease with which the "military adventurism" was suppressed, "the *coup*" was obviously now the central objective of major factions in the opposition, the military, and foreign interests. Foreign intervention, visible in the October strike, became more open every day.

In this context, the need to achieve minimal agreement among moderate sectors of the government and the opposition once again preoccupied political debate. It was obvious, however, that well-intentioned mediators no longer sufficed to make the combatants forget their immediate interests, fears, and suspicions. Thus the National Council of the Christian Democratic party rejected the government's request for a state of siege on the grounds that the government should not be given a weapon that could be used unfairly against the opposition. Their rejection automatically defeated the measure in Congress. Simultaneously, high officers of the armed forces, while formally supporting the government, were expressing serious reservations about returning to participate in a new civil-military cabinet.

At the same time that the new cabinet was being assembled, factions within the government intensified their efforts to incorporate into the Social Property Sector all industries which had been occupied by orders of the Workers Confederation (CUT) during the *tancazo*. The strains caused by these groups, acting in the so-called industrial belts and in other organizations of direct "popular power," once more divided the government.[55] While one part of the coalition declared its intention to negotiate with the opposition in search of consensus, another part directly subverted these attempts with actions which undermined their seriousness. Yet, given the circumstances, this situation seemed almost inevitable. The intensified political battle between actors with diametrically opposed interests and goals impeded any real negotiations. The most powerful actors in both coalitions sought the capitulation of the enemy. In the case of the government, it was clear that not all those involved in the conversations truly wanted a satisfactory solution to the conflict. Within the opposition, it was equally clear that some felt called to fill the "power vacuum" that would follow the government's fall. Consequently, they did everything possible to prevent any understanding. Few were really surprised when the negotiations finally failed.

From this point on, it was commonly taken for granted that relations between the government and the opposition would deteriorate. Early in July the Chamber of Deputies, reacting to the massive occupation of industries at the time of the *tancazo*, sent to the President a Congressional Resolution accusing him of continual and systematic violations of the law. This declaration joined a long list of statements by other political organizations, administrative institutions, and opposition leaders, all insisting on the illegitimacy of certain government actions. Since, they concluded, there was no legitimate government, they called on the armed forces to intervene and fill the power vacuum. Thus, ironically, the very actors on whom the possibility of dialogue depended came to desire and seek the alternative of a *coup d'état*.

Late in July, 1973, a strike very similar to that of October, 1972, began. In an effort which surprised equally the extreme left and right, the government was once more able to incorporate the armed forces into the cabinet. The achievement was undoubtedly a personal triumph for Allende and General Prats. Nevertheless, the move was greeted with general confusion. All were convinced that it was basically illogical. Unlike the previous year, this time no one seemed to understand or desire military participation in the government. The opposition was taken aback; considerable portions of the left felt betrayed. The former feared the strengthening of the government; the latter feared the strengthening of the counterrevolution. As before, the dynamic of events revealed both contradiction and vacillation, the logic of which, even now, is difficult to understand.

As the possibilities for violent confrontation increased, so did the call for creation of "armed popular power." Even the Communists began to drop their earlier reservations toward the idea. It is obvious, nonetheless, that any attempt to prepare for armed conflict by organizing the masses would not only have been irresponsible but would also have precipitated the end of the experiment. The crisis had reached peak intensity; to the economic collapse was added the ever weaker government and the ever more autonomous and direct actions of organized groups. For example, the extreme left increased its attempts to "infiltrate" the military and also accelerated the formation of armed groups to defend the government. As might be expected, these actions provoked reactions: the armed forces began a campaign against infiltration and the appearance of "armed, popular militias."[56] For example, it carried out a continuous search for arms. Overnight, the Arms Control Law became an important political issue between the military and the most radical sectors of the *Unidad Popular,* inevitably producing more problems for the government. Once more the administration found itself in a dilemma which could not be resolved by either evasion or eclecticism. As usual, its actions satisfied no one, while its scant authority was undercut.

The tenure of the second civilian-military cabinet was short but definitive. Relations with the armed forces progressively worsened as the possibilities of long-term political, economic, or social understandings were dramatically reduced. For many officers, the government had thrown away the only chance of collaboration when, months earlier, it had rejected the petition to reestablish national harmony.[57] Whatever the interpretation of the events, in retrospect it is evident that by this point there was no concrete basis for satisfying any of the allies "forced" to participate in the government. The resignation of General Ruiz as Minister of Public Works and Transport struck the final blow. Assuming that he had the authority to move as he desired to control the truckers' strike, he had acted in such a way as to make political problems with the subsecretary inevitable. When his decision-making ability was questioned, he presented his resignation as minister, because "he had not been able to achieve his objectives." Nevertheless, General Ruiz did not anticipate the reaction of Allende, who accepted his resignation not only as Minister but also as Commander in Chief of the Air Force. Allende's action evoked the protests of many officers who now did not dissimulate their anti-government sentiments.

The resignation of General Ruiz was important, inasmuch as it had immediate, catalytic effects. For one, his resignation precipitated the fall of the group of generals considered pro-Allende (Prats, Pickering, Sepúlveda). At the same time, it permitted those who favored a *coup* to gain the support of many officers who until then had maintained a cautious, constitutional attitude.[58] Their plans received a final blessing at the end of August when, from the floor of the Chamber of Deputies, the opposition called for a military *coup*. Not surprisingly, the second civil-military cabinet fell only a few days later. The Ruiz resignation also precipitated military moves to purge all officers suspected of *"allendismo."* At the same time, using the arms control law, they began to exercise open control over the southern provinces of the country.

By this time the government had reached its weakest point. Government power was, in fact, a mere fiction. The question was no longer whether a *coup* would occur, but when. Still the coalition was incapable of reaching any practical agreement. According to some sources, the meeting between Allende and the leaders of the *Unidad Popular* parties only three days before the *coup* was a complete failure. Other than agreeing to reject any plebiscite (which, it seems, Allende decided to support in the end), they were unable to agree on any common strategy for avoiding the *coup*. Allende, faced with circumstances in which any imposed decision risked breaking up the coalition, was authorized to seek solutions independently. In reality, given the conditions imposed by allies and enemies, even this alternative was closed.

Under the circumstances, and confident of receiving widespread support, the military saw no obstacle to the destruction of what they had come to consider a historical and cultural aberration. With the demise of the *Unidad Popular,* those who had placed their hopes for a better world on a program promising a peaceful road to socialism saw their illusions disappear in blood and fire.

THE CAUSES OF FAILURE

The list of what caused or, better, determined the failure of the Chilean road to socialism includes a wide variety of factors and nuances. The arguments emphasized by any particular author depend, in each case, on his ideological orientation and the theoretical and/or methodological framework he uses. In numerous cases the choice of crucial factors obviously reflects short-run, opportunistic purposes. In this section I limit myself to examining a few of the varied explanations offered in the literature. As much as possible, I omit those that are openly opportunistic.[59]

I will present the explanations in two general categories:

A. *Internal Causes or Factors*

    1. Nature and characteristics of the Chilean political system;
    2. Origin and composition of the coalition;
    3. Composition and orientation of the opposition;
    4. Errors of the coalition.

B. *External Causes or Factors*

    1. Isolation in Latin America;
    2. The invisible blockade;
    3. Weak support from the socialist bloc.

Internal Causes or Factors

1. Nature and Characteristics of the Chilean Political System

According to some, the major difficulties encountered by the *Unidad Popular* in its attempts to effect radical change stemmed primarily from structural factors. The Chilean political system was rich in institutional complexity. It included political styles which were accorded a high degree of legitimacy. The conciliatory nature of the system permitted the existence of social and political pluralism, which rested on the fact that new groups could be brought into the system without eliminating either the traditional actors or their privileges. Although this pluralism, in the long run, led to social stagnation and eventual political stalemate, it lent legitimacy to social and political structures and guaranteed a relatively high degree of systemic stability.

The Chilean conciliatory style, the incremental incorporating process which it implied, and the complex network of institutions, processes, and traditions all made significant changes involving brusque and radical transfers of power—whether economic, social, or political—impossible in Chile. By initiating an intensive process of radical change, the *Unidad Popular* altered the traditional rules of the game, and once these had been broken, the precarious legitimacy and stability of the Chilean system quickly broke down—especially given the severity of the economic recession. The battle in favor of or against change thus became open confrontation; moderate political actors (or those in the center) were pushed from the stage and replaced by dogmatic speakers for both extremes of the political spectrum. The breakdown of the Chilean system inevitably led to the collapse of the *Unidad Popular*'s project for change.[60]

2. Origin and Composition of the Coalition

In this category I include arguments noting a variety of factors of relative significance. These emphasize the importance of three intimately related elements: the character of the government coalition, its multiclass base, and its pluralist ideological content. According to the logic of the argument, Chilean history had consistently shown that the mechanics of coalitions forced the direction and implementation of government policy to follow the lines of the minimum agreement achievable within the coalition.

For the *Unidad Popular* the problem was particularly difficult. From the beginning the coalition included a mixture of diverse orientations, motivations, programs, and ideologies. While some key members believed that the electoral road and class and ideological pluralism were crucial to the construction of socialism, others—just as influential—remained skeptical of the model's virtues. The old, unresolved conflict between those who favored expanding the government's base of social support to include the progressive bourgeoisie and those who favored emphasizing the class-based nature of the process accelerated the process of internal polarization and led to political stalemate. Every possibility of developing adequate political leadership to confront the difficulties of the revolutionary process was frustrated. Every attempt to formally structure political leadership and control failed. In effect, Allende was the least common denominator, and the basic tasks were left to him. Yet, for the same reasons, Allende was denied the authority and legitimacy needed to meet those responsibilities.

Seen from this perspective, the failure of the Chilean experiment arises from the coalition's failure to overcome what were essentially predictable difficulties. Although the coalition was able to run an election campaign with considerable efficacy, it could not run a government—particularly one seeking radical change. This was particularly true because of the limited utility of the "model" offered by the program to direct so profound a process.[61]

3. Composition and Orientation of the Opposition

The arguments in this category seem to have received considerable support. They emphasize the possibility of reconciling "models" of development based on dissimilar schemes for distributing and exercising political, economic, and social power. The obstacle is that each "model" conceals social classes, or groups, with different interests.

Although in some cases these explanations admit the multiclass nature of the major Chilean political actors, they see the basic ideological orientation of the leadership (or dominant groups) as the key element: either the leaders favored a socialist model, or they supported a model of dependent capitalist development. It is clear, at least from this perspective, that the opposition's basic orientation was one of defense of the traditional socioeconomic system through the manipulation of existing symbols and political structures. The argument emphasizes the profound interrelation of objective interests among the so-called traditional sectors, the modern industrial bourgeoisie, and foreign investors— particularly North American. From the beginning these actors blocked government actions. Later they sought to capitalize on the discontent among the small and medium bourgeoisie, who were frightened by the incipient socioeconomic changes. Any attempt to establish a program involving the collaboration of opposing social classes (groups) would assume that, in practice, it was possible to overcome the differences in existing (or latent) interests. This assumption rested on a political impossibility.

According to this interpretation, the opposition was reacting rationally and consistently when, once it had overcome its post-election paralysis, it initiated concerted activities to block the policies of the government coalition. The opposition's task was facilitated by its majority in Congress, by its direct and indirect control over the state bureaucracy and the national economy, and by the unlimited support of foreign capitalists. The government meanwhile continued to insist on its initial "programmatic delusion," namely that socialism could be constructed by peaceful means.[62]

4. Errors of the Coalition

The importance attributed to government activities has led many analysts to concentrate on factors internal to the coalition in explaining its inefficacy and eventual failure. Without pretending to do more than survey the topic, I think it worthwhile to note some of the more important ideas.

First, this particular approach emphasizes the inability of the coalition to overcome its basic organizational problems and the difficulties it experienced in structuring leadership. The argument begins with the assumption that, because of the multiclass and multiparty nature of the coalition, it contained preexisting ideological positions and strategies. At first, the pragmatic nature of the coalition's program prevented open conflict among the rival parties, but it rapidly became obvious that the coalition could not operate efficiently without a centralized leadership capable of attaining consensus on goals and strategies. This limitation, for which various solutions were tried without success, precluded the leadership, coordination, and control needed in a process based on both political participation and institutionalization.

Second, the failure to establish a structure for political coordination and leadership—to replace the inert "Party of the Revolution"—derived from an even more significant problem: the existence of profound differences within the coalition over goals, strategies, and concrete development policies. As time passed, these internal divisions became so serious as to paralyze the coalition's ability to exercise leadership. Internal political stalemate gave way to sectarianism, *espontaneísmo*, and, eventually, political demobilization. The masses, treated with undisguised paternalism or suspicion, were left to act creatively on their own.

Third, as a result of these limitations, the *Unidad Popular* failed completely in organizing and leading the public sector. Continuing the time-honored custom of political patronage, the coalition opted for the division of the state administrative apparatus—in its broadest sense—according to a system of quotas. The "atomization" of public bureaucracy, combined with the government's scant capacity for centralized direction, impeded the establishment of an integrated system for planning, adopting, and implementing public policies. In a political process passing through a heavy emphasis on state socialism, this error had dramatic effects. The rebellion of middle-level bureaucrats, as it was called, the belief that partisan loyalty mattered more than technical competence, and the relatively passive attitude toward administrative corruption were only some of the results of the failure to understand that it is in organization that the theoretical and practical problems of a revolutionary process most often converge.

Equally important are those analyses that emphasize the critical impact of the government's economic incompetence. There seems to be a consensus that, during the first phase, the government's economic leadership was both appropriate and intelligent.

It revived the economy and, at the same time, emphasized political mobilization to expand its base of social support. This combination of objectives paid major dividends. But the insistence on prolonging a policy of economic expansion beyond the limits imposed by the emergency brought equally major economic problems and precipitated the crisis.

In spite of the apparent dominance of the Communist party, leadership of economic policy was also divided. As a result, government policies gave the impression that the coalition sought a revolution in consumption but not in production. Even those who consider foreign intervention and internal economic sabotage to be the critical causes of collapse recognize that the *Unidad Popular* committed serious errors. It failed to keep its economic policies in proper perspective; the unrestrained advocacy of state intervention reached such extremes that it alienated potential support. Similarly, the conviction that "economy is power" was not accompanied by recognition that the potential surplus of the "new economy" was crucial to the total project—particularly when the opposition undertook to blockade or boycott production and commerce. To the phenomenon of political *espontaneísmo* was added economic *espontaneísmo*.

Finally, the majority of these analysts agree in placing special importance on the *Unidad Popular*'s failure to control the extreme left. The combined effects of a rhetorical style and political activities which at times were deliriously provocative placed the government in a paradox: unable to reject categorically the extreme left-wing groups because of the internal effects such action would produce, neither could it support their activities. Unquestionably the government's vacillation had higher costs than benefits. From this perspective, the three years of the Allende government seem a constant ebb and flow of contradictory actions by the major actors within the coalition. The political stalemate was often broken as a result of actions by the extreme left, which thus surfaced as the most dynamic force in the process. The hardening of both internal and external coalition relations was conditioned to the end by the ideas set forth by the extreme left.[63]

External Causes or Failures

As was noted above, three elements in this category have been considered critical: the isolation of the Allende experience in Latin America, the invisible blockade directed and supported by the United States, and the lack of political support from the socialist bloc. In general, few works have explored these problems, and they tend to be openly polemical in character. My presentation will try to link the three themes through economic logic.

When the *Unidad Popular* came to power, the international environment made it seem an unpropitious moment for a new socialist experiment on the continent. Given the basic policy proposals of the government, there were undoubtedly many areas of potential conflict. Anticipating some of these problems, the government quickly sought to achieve certain specific goals: to minimize the potential conflict with the United States, to avoid hemispheric isolation, and to establish tight links with the socialist bloc and the Third World. Spokesmen repeatedly proclaimed that the government did not wish to be a continental leader of revolution. On the contrary, its policies would be based on the principles of nonintervention and the self-determination of all peoples. They denied the validity of the thesis of "ideological frontiers" put forth by Brazil and shared to some extent by Argentina.

There is no doubt, of course, that the *Unidad Popular* government achieved some of its objectives. It certainly obtained what at first seemed impossible: to avoid hemispheric isolation. In fact, with the implicit reservations of Brazil—and later Bolivia—Chile emerged as one of the spokesmen for regional interests seeking to break the framework of dependent capitalism. The same was true in the Third World, where Chile assumed an important role.

In other areas, the failures were obvious. In the case of relations with the United States, it was clear that breaking with the tradition of political and economic dependence would be the decisive test. As much as Allende wanted to avoid a conflict, he could not. As has recently been shown, North American intervention had begun even before the people's government assumed power. As time passed, it gradually increased until it provoked, to a great extent, the final collapse. In spite of those arguments denying the existence or importance of the invisible blockade, it is obvious that the United States used a variety of means to produce the economic and financial strangulation of Chile. One need not enter into details to demonstrate the decisive impact of these actions—coordinated domestically through representatives of the national opposition. They became particularly damaging after the Chilean economy began to experience serious problems with international commerce (caused by the fall in copper prices). Given the pressures to import food and other goods, the effects on the balance of payments became a problem of major proportions. Thus the blockade had a long-term impact which impeded economic recuperation even after credit again became available.

In its relations with the United States, the government erred in its belief that Chile would reach some agreement in the long run. As many analysts have suggested, the problem did not lie in an implacable defense of the interests of North American companies that were nationalized or threatened with nationalization. At heart, Washington was convinced that the Allende experience must fail. The "domino effect" of a successful experiment would have been disastrous for North American interests, since the constitutional achievement of socialism could serve as a major demonstration not only to the rest of the hemisphere but also in Western Europe—e.g., in Italy and France.

In her relations with the socialist bloc, as was suggested above, the *Unidad Popular* government encountered unforeseen difficulties that, to some extent, affected the viability of the socialist project. According to some observers, the Soviet Union was not interested in extensively supporting any new socialist experiment in Latin America for at least two reasons: a) it wanted some guarantee that the Allende government could achieve a relatively stable domestic position—that is, both within the coalition itself and *vis-à-vis* progressive sectors of the opposition; b) it did not wish to endanger possible terms of accord with the United States, which had unquestioned priority on the Soviet agenda at that time. Whatever the case, the economic and financial aid of the socialist bloc was simply not enough. Its inadequacy aggravated the economic situation; the latent crisis had begun to worsen, and the possibilities of constructing a socialist society and economy were condemned to final failure.[64]

*   *   *

Everything I have discussed leads, of course, to the interesting question of whether the failure of the Chilean experiment was inevitable. The answer is unclear. Examination of the experience suggests the possibility of other roads and strategies just as readily as it does the certainty that the experiment was condemned to failure by definition. As has so often occurred in historical processes of global significance, it is possible that the certainty of an answer reflects more a subjective viewpoint than a scientific truth. The important thing seems to be to explore the lessons which can be derived from the Chilean experience—which is the central purpose of this volume.

NOTES

1. In this article I have made use of certain central ideas which I developed together with Luis Quiróz Videla in previously published interpretive essays. See "El Gobierno de la Unidad Popular: El Difícil Camino de Transición Hacia el Socialismo," in James Petras (ed.), *América Latina: Economía y Política* (Buenos Aires: Editorial Periferia, 1972), and *Cambio Político y la Elección Parlamentaria de Marzo de 1973: Antecedentes de una Elección Crítico-limite* (Santiago: ICP/Univ. Católica de Chile, 1974). The errors of fact and/or interpretation which may exist in this essay are obviously the exclusive responsibility of the author.

2. Jorge I. Tapia Videla and Charles J. Parrish, *Clases Sociales y la Política de Seguridad Social en Chile* (Santiago: INSORA, 1970), p. 4.

3. It is illustrative to mention the statistics on the distribution of national income by occupational stratum. During the period 1940–1960, for example, while lower-class sectors saw their participation reduced from 33.7 per cent to 26.5 per cent, upper- and middle-class sectors increased their share in a clearly advantageous manner: 45.9 per cent to 47.0 per cent, and 20.4 per cent to 26.5 per cent, respectively. See CIDA, *Tenencia de la Tierra y Desarrollo Socio-económico del Sector Agrícola* (Santiago: Talleres Gráficos Hispano-Suiza, Ltda., 1966), p. 30.

4. Jorge I. Tapia Videla and Luis Quirós Varela, "El Gobierno de la Unidad Popular . . . ," p. 100.

5. See, among others, Maurice Zeitlin, "Los Determinantes Sociales de la Democracia Política en Chile," *Revista Latinoamericana de Sociología* 2, 2(July 1966), pp. 234–235; F. B. Pike, "Aspects of Class Relations in Chile, 1850–1960," *Hispanic American Historical Review* 43, 1(February 1963), p. 27, *et passim,* and Aníbal Pinto, S. C., *Chile: Un Caso de Desarrollo Frustrado* (Santiago: Editorial Universitaria, S. A., 1962), p. 182, and *Chile: Una Economía Difícil* (México: Fondo de Cultura Económica, 1964), pp. 60–61.

6. Luis Quirós Varela, "La Evolución Política de Chile, 1951–1971," *Mensaje,* nos. 202–203 (September–October 1971), p. 414.

7. See, among others, Sandra Powell, "Elections and the Radical Left: The Rise of Salvador Allende, 1958–1970" (mimeo, 1973); Norbert Lechner, *La Democracia en Chile* (Buenos Aires: Ediciones Signos, 1970), and Federico G. Gil and Charles J. Parrish, *The Chilean Presidential Election of September 4, 1964* (Washington, D.C.: Institute for the Comparative Study of Political Systems, 1964).

8. Jorge Ahumada, *En Vez de la Miseria* (Santiago: Editorial del Pacífico, 1958).

9. Arpad von Lazar and Luis Quirós, "Chilean Christian Democracy: Lessons in the Politics of Reform Management," in A. von Lazar and R. R. Kaufman (eds.), *Reform and Revolution: Readings in Latin American Politics* (Boston: Allyn and Bacon, Inc., 1969), pp. 338–339.

10. Eduardo Frei, "Perspectivas y Riesgos en la Construcción de una Nueva Sociedad," in Hernán Godoy (ed.), *Estructura Social de Chile* (Santiago: Editorial Universitaria, 1971), p. 552.

11. On the agrarian reform see CORA, *Reforma Agraria Chilena, 1965–1970* (Santiago, 1970), and on communitarian organizations, Kalki Glauser, "Crisis Social del Capitalismo en Chile," *Mensaje,* nos. 202–203 (September–October 1971), pp. 388–403, and F. Castillo, R. Echeverría, and J. Larraín, "Las Masas, el Estado y el Problema del Poder en Chile," *Cuadernos de la Realidad Nacional* 16(April 1973), p. 8.

12. In practice, the origin and growth of important Chilean labor organizations had occurred under the tutelage and control of specific political parties. Nevertheless, the pressure from their bases to adopt moderate, nonideological, but effective economic demands often led these organizations to take stands contrary to those of the parties by which they were supposedly controlled—whether because of similar doctrinal inspiration or because of the partisan affiliations of their highest leaders. Though different levels of conflict followed, this phenomenon was present during the Alessandri, Frei, and Allende governments.

13. Luis Quirós, "Chilean Agrarian Reform and Political Processes," in Ken Medhurst (ed.), *Allende's Chile* (London: Hart-Davis-McGibbon, 1972), pp. 148–175.

14. See David Cusack, "The Politics of Chilean Private Enterprise under Christian Democracy" (Ph.D. dissertation, University of Denver, 1970), especially pp. 289 and 234–281.

15. Cf. *Política y Espíritu,* nos. 323(July 1971) and 324(August 1971).

16. "Chile: Programa de Radomiro Tomić: Tarea del Pueblo," *Política y Espíritu* 317(August 1970), pp. 15–42.

17. Julio César Jobet, *El Partido Socialista de Chile* (Santiago: PLA, 1971), vol. 1, p. 130.

18. Cf. Julio César Jobet, *op. cit.;* and Robert Moss, *El Experimento Marxista Chileno* (Santiago: Editora Nacional Gabriela Mistral, 1973).

19. Cf. Sandra Powell, *op. cit.;* James Prothro and Patricio Chaparro, "Public Opinion and the Movement of Chilean Government to the Left, 1952–1972," *Journal of Politics* 36, 1(February 1974), pp. 2–41, and Robert Ayres, "Political History, Institutional Structure and Prospects for Socialism in Chile," *Comparative Politics* 5(July 1973), pp. 507–511.

20. "Programa Básico de Gobierno de la Unidad Popular," in Hernán Godoy (ed.), *op. cit.,* pp. 562–581.

21. See, *inter alia,* Renán Fuentealba, "Análisis de la Situación Económica del País" (Santiago, 1971), p. 9, and Jorge Pina, "El Acuerdo Decisivo," *Ercilla* 1843 (October 14–20, 1970), pp. 8–12.

22. Salvador Allende, *Primer Mensaje al Congreso Nacional* (Santiago: Talleres Gráficos del Servicio de Prisiones, 1971), p. xi.

23. Concerning the economic policies of the *Unidad Popular* government during its first year, see "Cuatro Opiniones sobre el Primer Año de Gestión Económica del Gobierno de Allende," *Panorama Económico* 266 (February 1972), pp. 15–28; Emilio Sanfuentes, "La Política Económica de la Unidad Popular," in Tomás MacHale (ed.), *Visión Crítica de Chile* (Santiago: Ediciones Portada, 1972), pp. 132–133.

24. Concerning nationalization of basic resources, see, among others,

Law no. 17.450 of July 16, 1971 (reforma constitucional); *Panorama Económico* 263 (August 1971), pp. 6–7; "Nacionalización: Las Platas del Cobre," *Ercilla* 1890 (October 6–12, 1971), pp. 17–18, and "Contralor: Indemnización a las Compañías del Cobre," *Ercilla* 1891 (October 13–19, 1971), p. 10.

25. The government's doctrinal basis for nationalizing banking is found in Allende, *Primer Mensaje, op. cit.*, pp. 387–389. In response to the government's strategy, the Christian Democrats presented a bill in Congress which, although supportive of the government's basic intent, included provisions impeding political use of the banking system and insuring fair assignment of resources and participation of bank workers as well as users in the system. It failed to win approval.

26. As in the previous case, government actions provoked opposition resistance. The government's reluctance to submit a bill to Congress for regulating and defining property sectors led the Christian Democrats to present their own bill for constitutional reform. This placed major limitations on government policies for achieving socialism; parliamentary approval of the bill and its subsequent veto by the Executive precipitated the first constitutional crisis of the Allende administration.

27. Luis Quirós, "Chile: Agrarian Reform and Political Process," *op. cit.*

28. "Programa Básico de Gobierno de la Unidad Popular," *op. cit.*, pp. 567–569.

29. See the interesting articles by N. Chinchilla and M. Sternberg, Kyle Steenland and Brian Loveman, published in the special edition of *Latin American Perspectives* 1, 2(Summer 1974), pp. 106–155.

30. *Los Acuerdos del Arrayán* (Santiago: Editorial Horizonte, 1972).

31. Allende reiterated his political perspective after six months in power, when he declared before the National Congress, "Our legal system must be modified. This is the great responsibility of the Congress at the present time: to contribute to the reduction of the barriers to change in our judicial system. To a very great extent it depends on the realism of Congress whether Chile can move from a capitalist legality to a socialist legality in accordance with the changes we are carrying out, without a violent break in our legal order opening the doors to arbitrary actions and excesses which we—in a responsible manner—wish to avoid." *Primer Mensaje al Congreso Nacional, op. cit.*, p. xi.

32. It is interesting to note that some of the parties in the government were themselves divided. In Congress, "more than one authorized its representatives to vote against the government on bills in which they were interested, or to abstain from voting." Radomiro Tomić, "Actual Situación Política y Económica de Chile" (an edited version of his intervention in the round table on the Chilean Road to Socialism, organized under the auspices of *Odeplán* and the University of Essex, 1972), p. 8.

33. The closed defense of partisan interests weakened the ability of the *Unidad Popular* to appeal to sectors which would have had decisive electoral and political importance. Thus the coalition did not attract, but gradually lost, the support of women and youth. Another example of its failure can be seen in the discussion of the first draft of a law to create a

Ministry of the Family—considered a key proposal in the development of government policy. The lack of initiative and will to ensure an efficient institutional base stands out both in its conception—timid if not conservative—and in its debate.

34. The *Unidad Popular*'s confidence that it could expand its base of political support without formalizing contacts with "yesterday's enemies," along with its rejection of any measure which could be interpreted as "selling out," explains in part why these negotiations failed.

35. Radomiro Tomić, *op. cit., loc. cit.*

36. "La Justicia, al Estrado," *Ercilla* 1848(1970).

37. See Jorge I. Tapia Videla and others, "Electoral Procedures and Political Parties in Chile," *Studies in Comparative International Development* 6 (1970–1971).

38. See *El Mercurio*, editions of March 3, 5, 8, and 16, April 21, and June 10, 11, 14, 16, 19, and 30, 1972.

39. In reality, however, an unstable situation was the result. In some worker, student, and community elections neither federation was united. In others, one or the other, or even both, were able to present a united front, as was the case in the congressional by-election in Coquimbo.

40. See Renán Fuentealba, *op. cit., passim.*

41. The increasing political use of state resources by the *Unidad Popular* (a practice in which it was not a pioneer) accentuated fears in the opposition, which rejected the government's proposal. About this time the attacks directed at the "constant" gap between the government's promises and plans and their distorted practical application increased significantly.

42. Cf. Samuel Huntington, *Political Order in Changing Societies* (New Haven: Yale University Press, 1968), especially Chapter One.

43. "Entre Lo Curro y la CUT," *Ercilla* 1925(June 7–12, 1972), pp. 7–8.

44. See pp. 68–69.

45. Until that moment, the role of the armed forces in the revolutionary process had been guided by the so-called Schneider Doctrine. Broadly, military actions had followed a "conception" tying the external security of the country to internal order, national unity, and the encouragement of development within the existing institutional and legal framework. Within this framework, their role as arbitrators and stabilizers of the system had been implicitly recognized. During previous governments, and in less conflictive situations than that of October, 1972, the armed forces had acted to "maintain the equilibrium" when political stability was threatened. This tradition made the call for military participation in the cabinet and its acceptance seem natural. All actors interested in maintaining (or restoring) the traditional mechanisms of political conflict resolution accepted military participation in the light of that tradition.

46. Claudio Orrego, *El Paro Nacional* (Santiago: Editorial del Pacífico, 1972), pp. 42–43.

47. The principal analyses of the Chilean economy during 1972 are Departamento de Economía (Sede Oriente), *Comentarios sobre la Situación Económica, Segundo Semestre de 1972* (Santiago: Universidad de Chile,

1973), and Instituto de Economía y Planificación, *La Economía Chilena en 1972* (Santiago: Universidad de Chile, 1973).

48. "Síntesis Estadística," *Panorama Económico*, 225(February 1973), pp. 32–33.

49. On the election campaign of March, 1973, see the interesting study by Carmen Barros and Patricio Chaparro, "La Campaña de las Elecciones Parlamentarias de Marzo de 1973: Un Estudio de Caso" (Santiago: ICP/ Universidad Católica de Chile, 1974).

50. For a summary of the different positions and opinions expressed during the campaign, see Barros and Chaparro, *op. cit., passim.*

51. On the accusations of electoral fraud, see R. Moss, *op. cit.*, pp. 188–189.

52. *Ibid.*, p. 195.

53. See *Tercer Mensaje Presidencial* (Santiago: Talleres Gráficos del Servicio de Prisiones, 1973).

54. The Supreme Court's declaration stimulated an uninterrupted string of similar pronouncements by institutions and individuals of varied importance and significance. It is interesting to observe the agreement on this point among actors of supposedly opposing interests. Polarization on the issue of institutional legitimacy became increasingly severe.

55. *Punto Final* and *Chile Hoy*, if kept in perspective, give the most complete panorama of opinions on the question of "popular power" during this period.

56. See the article by Kyle Steenland, *op. cit.*, pp. 13–14.

57. See R. Moss, *op. cit.*, p. 195.

58. K. Steenland, *loc. cit.*

59. In each category I will limit myself to indicating the author's name and/or the work in which pertinent ideas are developed. The citation is merely for illustrative purposes and does not pretend to be a complete summary of the work cited.

60. See, among others, the articles by J. Tapia and L. Quirós, previously cited, and Arturo Valenzuela, *The Breakdown of Democracy: Chile* (Baltimore: The Johns Hopkins University Press, 1978).

61. See, among others, R. Moss, *op. cit.;* Norma Chinchilla and W. Bollinger, "Theoretical Issues of the Chilean Experience," in *Latin American Perspectives, op. cit.*, pp. 3–8; Jaime Muñoz, "New Tactics for the Left: MAPU Analysis," in IDOC/NA., *Chile under Military Rule* (1974), and Paul Sweezy, "Chile: The Question of Power," *Monthly Review* (December 1973).

62. See, for example, the series of articles included in the section "Counterrevolution," in IDOC/NA., *op. cit.;* the articles by Norma Chinchilla and W. Bollinger, Kyle Steenland, Richard E. Feinberg, Victor Wallis, and R. E. Ratcliff in *Latin American Perspectives, op. cit.;* Fernando Alegría, "The Fall of Santiago," *Ramparts* 12(December 1973); and the series of articles in Les Evans (ed.), *Disaster in Chile* (1974).

63. See, among others, J. Tapia and L. Quirós, *op. cit.;* the articles by N. Chinchilla and M. Sterberg, Kyle Steenland, and Brian Loveman in *Latin American Perspectives, op. cit.;* R. Moss, *op. cit.;* the articles by Gary MacEoin and others and by Paul Rosenstein-Rodan in IDOC/NA., *op. cit.;* Alvaro Bardon and others, *Itinerario de una Crisis: Política Económica y Transición al Socialismo* (1972); Alejandro Foxley (ed.), *Distribución del Ingreso* (1974); Carmen Barros and Patricio Chaparro, *op. cit.;* Arturo Valenzuela, *op. cit.;* Pablo Hunneus and others, *El Costo Social de la Dependencia Ideológica* (1973); Francois Bourricaud, "Chile: Why Allende Failed," *Dissent* (Summer 1974); Andy Zimbalist and Barbara Stallings, "Showdown in Chile," *Monthly Review* (October 1973); and the various documents of "self-criticism" subscribed by the coalition and/or its parties during the period 1971–1973.

64. On this topic, see, among others, R. Moss, *op. cit.;* the articles in the sections "Counterrevolution" and "Chile in the U.S. Congress" in IDOC/NA, *op. cit.;* Paul Sigmund, "The Invisible Blockade and the Overthrow of Allende," *Foreign Affairs,* (January 1974), pp. 322–340; the articles by R. E. Feinberg and Victor Wallis and the final chapter, "Review," in *Latin American Perspectives, op. cit.;* NACLA, "Chile: Facing The Blockade" (1973) and "Chile: the Story Behind the Coup" (1974).

The Foreign Policy
of the Unidad Popular Government

CLODOMIRO ALMEYDA MEDINA

OBJECTIVES OF THE FOREIGN POLICY

The principal objective of the winning forces in the presidential election of 1970 was to promote structural changes in Chilean society, thus beginning the development of a socialist state.

This fundamental objective focused on domestic matters, but it necessarily had international implications. The intended social and political changes in Chile affected the international situation, especially in the Americas. The victory of a clearly anti-imperialist, socialist political force in an important Latin American country changed the balance of power on the continent, and was inevitably linked to the general political process in Latin America and the hemisphere. This in turn had ramifications, at least to some extent, in the world political arena where the East-West conflict overshadowed and still overshadows every event. Indeed, important actors in the *Unidad Popular* had participated in that world conflict and saw the Chilean experience in a larger context.

On another level, the proposed domestic changes threatened powerful North American interests, with strong ties to the political establishment in the United States. This made it necessary for the *Unidad Popular* to formulate a foreign policy consistent with its proposed internal policies.

The program of the *Unidad Popular*—formally approved by each of its member parties—sought to define that policy, in order to guide the future government in its international actions. These were not only to be consistent with fundamental domestic objectives but also to facilitate their fulfillment. Moreover, the relationship between the social process which the *Unidad Popular* sought

76

to initiate in Chile and experiments in other countries seeking to escape from backwardness must be recognized. And the link between the Chilean process and the international socialist movement, interested in weakening imperialism and its influence throughout Latin America, cannot be ignored.

The aims of the *Unidad Popular*'s foreign policy can be summarized as follows:

1. To reaffirm and strengthen Chilean national sovereignty and political and economic autonomy; to break the legal, political, and economic rules which limited Chilean independence.

2. To respect the self-determination of all peoples and the principle of nonintervention. To reject, therefore, any attempt by any state to pressure or interfere in the internal affairs of any other state.

3. To maintain diplomatic and economic relations with all countries regardless of their domestic political systems. Therefore to expand Chilean foreign ties in accordance with national interests, particularly with socialist countries and the developing countries of Africa and Asia, with whom Chile had no relations.

4. To criticize and denounce "Pan-Americanism" and its institutionalization in the Organization of American States as one more element in the system of North American domination of Latin America. (Note that the program did not advocate Chile's withdrawal from the OAS.)

5. To affirm the Latin American presence on the world scene; to promote the creation of institutions which would genuinely represent Latin American interests; to promote Latin American integration on the basis of policies that would eliminate dependence on the United States, the imperialist metropolis; to simultaneously develop bilateral relations with other Latin American states, always in accordance with Chilean interests.

6. To search for negotiated solutions to existing border problems.

7. To support national liberation movements struggling to break colonial or neocolonial bonds; to exhibit solidarity with the Cuban Revolution and with the people of Vietnam; to support the anti-imperialist battles of the Arab peoples and a peaceful solution to the Arab-Israeli problem; to condemn anti-Semitism and racial segregation.

The text of the program made no explicit references to support for international cooperation in pursuit of goals common to all nations or specific subgroups of nations. Nevertheless, from official declarations made by responsible government authorities, one can conclude that the *Unidad Popular* intended to support all initiatives in favor of international *détente* and disarmament, as well as all those designed to restructure international relations in favor of the developing nations. Similarly, in accordance with Chilean tradition, the *Unidad Popular* subscribed to the principle of the sanctity of freely subscribed treaties, a point not explicitly included in its program but repeatedly emphasized by officials in the new government.

This complex of propositions was the natural outgrowth of the political experience of the *Unidad Popular* and of the political actors which had come to form it. It represented a firm consensus. In discussions during the elaboration of foreign policy, there were no significant disagreements. This was distinctly different from what occurred in the discussion of domestic policy, where there were major disagreements among the various parties.

The "third force" positions, which once were shared by many actors on the left—particularly the Socialist party—had been abandoned by most of them several years before. They were replaced by an international perspective focusing on the battle between progressive and renovating forces, on the one hand, and imperialism and its allies, on the other. The former included the world socialist system, national liberation movements in dependent countries, and working-class and progressive sectors in the advanced capitalist nations.

Not even the special relationship between Chilean radicalism and the Socialist International—which had culminated in the formal membership of the Radical party—gave cause for disagreement. The Radical party did not share the anti-Communist viewpoint of most affiliates of the International, and it condemned the pro-imperialist attitudes of some members.

The perspectives from which the Communist party, on the one hand, and the other parties in the *Unidad Popular,* on the other, interpreted certain specific international events, such as the Soviet intervention in Czechoslovakia, did not create bitter polemics, either before or after the *Unidad Popular* took office. On the contrary, these differences gave rise to debates both within the coalition and in public, in which each side always respected the position of an allied party. All kept in mind that in matters of international politics much more united than separated them. Moreover, their differences dealt with questions which had no practical implication for government policies and were therefore, at least in the specific context of the moment, of more theoretical than practical importance. This consensus was the result of a long and difficult process of unification and understanding among the parties of the left. In its course many sectarian misunderstandings had been left behind.

In its evaluation of the previous administration, the *Unidad Popular* always noted those elements in the Christian Democrat foreign policy that the left considered progressive and that it intended, while in power, to pursue more vigorously. Among these were the reestablishment of relations with the Soviet Union and the majority of the socialist countries of Eastern Europe, the relative independence that Chile had occasionally demonstrated with respect to the United States in international conferences and organizations, and the Frei administration's favorable attitude toward the formulation of unified Latin American policies, particularly in the areas of international and hemispheric economic affairs. Among the negative aspects of the Christian Democratic foreign policy, the *Unidad Popular* noted its refusal to establish relations with Cuba, the People's Republic of China, and the German Democratic Republic; its hesitation to formally join the movement of nonaligned nations; and its compromises with North American imperialism, both in the Organization of American States and in its bilateral ties with the United States.

From this brief summary of the *Unidad Popular*'s policy objectives, one can conclude that, fundamentally, they accorded priority to the principle of nonintervention as a basic guide for international conduct and to seeking negotiation rather than confrontation to resolve conflicts which might arise with other states.

Underlying these objectives and the principles that inspired them was a theoretical framework which gave meaning and coherence to the *Unidad Popular*'s foreign policy. Because it determined the nature of that policy, and ultimately its results, let us consider this framework in greater detail.

From an examination of the international program of the *Unidad Popular* and the later conduct of that program, it is clear that through its foreign policy the government pursued two objectives: a) to create external conditions favoring the development of a domestic program of social change directed toward the construction of socialism, and b) to contribute to strengthening groups struggling in the international arena to transform the worldwide capitalist system into a socialist system. This double objective rested on the assumption that the fundamental characteristic of our era, overshadowing the daily events of world politics, is that we live in the epoch of transition from capitalism to socialism. This led to the conclusion that the Chilean revolutionaries faced a double task: to work for the construction of socialism in their own society and to contribute to the building of socialism for all humanity.

The specific nature of revolutionary foreign policy depends on the way in which both tasks are dialectically articulated. From a strategic point of view, the long-term goal of contributing to the world socialist revolution is the fundamental aspect of any socialist foreign policy. This is because the successful construction of socialism in any one society depends on the construction of socialism in the entire world, while the construction of world socialism does not depend on building socialism in any particular society. However, from a more short-term perspective, taking into account the present international balance of power between capitalism and socialism, the best way to contribute to constructing world socialism is, in most cases, for the revolutionary forces in a particular country to promote socialism in that country. And from the moment when promotion of domestic social change is defined as the principal short-term objective of the revolutionary forces in any given country, their foreign policy, particularly if they are in power, should be to create the most favorable international conditions for internal social change.

In the context of the Chilean revolutionary process, in which the *Unidad Popular* obtained control of the government, it was obvious that the best way for Chilean revolutionary forces to participate in the global transformation from capitalism to socialism was to direct themselves to the task of constructing socialism at home.

Although this argument may seem obvious, it was pregnant with consequences. In effect, it led to the conclusion that, under existing conditions, the general strategic objective of promoting worldwide revolution should be subordinate, for tactical reasons, to the more immediate objective of transforming Chilean society. The latter thus became the principal strategic objective, and policies designed to achieve it assumed a tactical character. That is to say, arguing dialectically, that under given conditions the Chilean revolutionary movement could best contribute to the world revolution by working to build socialism in Chile itself.

It follows that any direct support and stimulation the Chilean revolutionary movement could give to the world revolutionary process came to have secondary importance. Such aid could be given only insofar as it did not compromise the achievement of the principal objective, which was the success of the internal revolutionary process. In other words, direct support for the world revolution was subordinate to the achievement of domestic objectives.

There was a limit beyond which such support would affect or compromise the principal objective and become dysfunctional to the progressive unfolding of the process.

This, from a theoretical point of view, fully justified the priority which the *Unidad Popular* gave in its foreign policy to the creation of international conditions enhancing the viability of the domestic revolution. However, there was a political cost: solidarity with and support for other revolutionary forces in the world were limited by pursuit of the principal objective.

This theoretical orientation found empirical expression in attempts to minimize the intervention of international actors which had an objective interest in the failure of the Chilean revolutionary process. For this purpose, it was necessary to emphasize nonintervention as the fundamental norm of foreign policy. Strict Chilean observance of nonintervention would create favorable conditions for demanding similar respect from other states.

The effort to minimize intervention by hostile foreign actors also implied abandoning confrontation and, even more important, provocation as means for resolving conflict. Under existing conditions, the balance of power between ourselves and our potential external enemies was, by any measure, negative. The only way to restrain our adversaries from using all of their potential resources of power against us was to try to neutralize them, divide them, negotiate with them; to compromise and even retreat tactically in order to avoid a collision or confrontation, which could only have a negative outcome for Chile.

Of course, it was absolutely impossible to prevent foreign intervention in our affairs completely. To its enemies, the threat of the *Unidad Popular* was too great; its power was sufficient to make it utopian to hope that they would remain immobile, mere spectators. The only way to achieve their absolute passivity and nonintervention was to renounce the revolutionary project, compromise the program, and turn back to 1947, when the government of President González Videla abruptly abandoned the leftist program under which it had campaigned and, under the pressure of imperialism, assumed a frankly reactionary domestic and international demeanor. The development, maturity, consciousness, and unity of the left in 1970 made repetition of this move unthinkable. Moreover, Salvador Allende was not Gabriel González Videla. Their later destinies make further comment unnecessary.

Attempting to minimize the possibility of foreign intervention, scrupulously observing the principle of nonintervention, and avoiding confrontation by all means, so long as we did not com-

promise the essential content of the *Unidad Popular*'s program—
these were the only solutions to the problem of making the revolutionary process viable.

The foreign actors potentially hostile to the *Unidad Popular*
were many and powerful. The most important of these were the
representatives of North American imperialism, among whom
were those interests directly affected by the government's nationalist policies—specifically, the owners of the large copper mines
and other transnational monopolies. Not to be discounted was the
U.S. government itself, which saw its entire hemispheric policy
threatened if the *Unidad Popular* were successful and reacted accordingly. The United States feared that Chilean success would
have negative repercussions even outside the hemisphere, particularly in France and Italy, where the political scene was similar
to that of Chile. Henry Kissinger commented explicitly to this
effect, leaving no doubt that the United States feared a successful
Chilean construction of socialism by democratic means. Yet the
old arguments used by American propaganda to malign other socialist experiments, labelling them "dictatorial" or "totalitarian,"
could not be used against Chile. Intervention by the Central Intelligence Agency, the hidden, powerful arm of official North American banking and private economic groups, as well as by international and hemispheric credit institutions themselves, could easily
be foreseen. This threatened serious credit and supply difficulties
for the future *Unidad Popular* government. Another U.S. agency
concerned was the Pentagon, which, for reasons not always identical with those of the North American government, also saw its
geopolitical and military plans strategically menaced by the victory of the *Unidad Popular*. The obvious influence of the Pentagon on the Chilean armed forces was a mine field of problems and
difficulties in the path of the popular government.

Intervention by the financial and economic powers of Western Europe and Japan, in coordination with their North American
counterparts, could also be very damaging to the Chilean government. Hostile policies of these countries, coordinated with the
policies of the United States, could result in a financial blockade,
as well as difficulties for Chilean foreign trade. Chile was in
danger of finding herself isolated within the capitalist world.

Other potential enemies of the *Unidad Popular*—no less dangerous than the above—were the governments and conservative
sectors in other Latin American nations, particularly Chile's
neighbors. In this respect, the panorama was discouraging. Argentina was ruled by a conservative government, profoundly suspi-

cious of what was occurring in Chile. We had an active, angry border dispute with Argentina, involving sovereignty over islands in the Beagle Channel, which for fifty years had proved impossible to resolve. It was a powder keg which Argentina could use at any moment to provoke, pressure, or intimidate Chile. The significance of our economic relations with Argentina only increased her ability to apply pressure on us.

Bolivia was another potential adversary. Traditionally hostile toward Chile because of the question of access to the Pacific, Bolivia had no diplomatic relations with us. The progressive character of the military government in Peru might have provided important political support for the Chilean government, but there were weighty factors working against friendly ties. The traditional suspicion of the Peruvian military toward Chile, and the notorious anti-communism of some sectors within it, neutralized whatever good will toward Chile might have existed in the more advanced and progressive sectors of the government.

Brazil, the most powerful Latin American country, was controlled by a fascistic military government. Rabidly anti-Communist and anti-Marxist, she was another certain antagonist of the new Chilean government, with a particular interest in its failure. Colombia, Venezuela, and Ecuador, all controlled by conservative or moderate governments, were hardly potential allies either. Our isolation within Latin America was a very real danger. The ominous doctrine of "ideological frontiers," recently formulated to legitimate external intervention in the domestic affairs of other states, loomed as an available option for our adversaries.

The already negative balance between the *Unidad Popular* government and its potential was further aggravated by Chile's unfavorable geographic location. Situated in the western hemisphere, our country lies within the U.S. sphere of influence, tacitly recognized by the Soviet Union in the negotiated solution to the Cuban missile crisis. Geographically distant from the sphere of influence of the socialist states, we were surrounded, or almost surrounded, by potentially hostile countries. Thus, without a very careful, subtle foreign policy, Chile could not hope to counterbalance adverse geographic factors and make the revolutionary program viable.

Cuba's defiant socialist society, only one hundred miles from its great adversary, had served to put imperialism on the alert, and the United States was determined to prevent at all costs a repetition of the Cuban experience in the hemisphere. The so-called Johnson Doctrine epitomized the North American understanding of the lessons of the Cuban socialist triumph.

Strategically, in spite of this disquieting general perspective, the historical moment was and is encouraging to the progressive forces in Latin America and the world. Although it was no longer possible to take imperialism by surprise, neither could imperialism repeat with impunity its conduct in the Dominican Republic. During a crisis there in the 1960s the United States had intervened militarily to forestall a revolution.

The growing influence of the socialist system in world politics, the success of national liberation movements in the Third World, the now-visible failure of the economic blockade against Cuba, the internal reaction within the United States against the Vietnamese war, and the slowly emerging climate of *détente* all formed a favorable strategic backdrop to the Chilean political experiment. These circumstances, along with the undeniably legitimate and democratic origins of the *Unidad Popular* government, practically prohibited any direct, armed intervention by the United States in Chile. Imperialism would have to find other than military means to create difficulties for the disquieting Chilean political experience.

This brief overview of the general situation and the immediate circumstances which greeted the *Unidad Popular* government makes clear why it was necessary to adopt a policy that embraced the principle of nonintervention and avoided external confrontation by negotiating. This was the policy which had already been designed and which was, indeed, followed.

Although this realistic orientation was widely shared in the *Unidad Popular,* a small minority believed differently. Its members argued that sharpening the conflict with the United States could bring political results insofar as an open break with imperialism would stimulate greater internal political support for the government. Behind their position was the primitive battle instinct which, without reflection, sees every conflict as a test of strength and as a quick resolution of the struggle between imperialism and the Revolution. They ignored or did not recognize that although the confrontation between imperialism and the Revolution is real and unavoidable, particularly as these are considered mutually exclusive wholes, at any given time and place the battle does not necessarily lead, nor can it lead, to a definitive resolution. Any one battle is only a limited episode, the outcome of which, from the revolutionary point of view, depends on the objective circumstances. The link between what is won or lost in that moment with what is won or lost in all the other episodes that make up the fragmented Revolution is what gives a limited conflict its transcendental revolutionary significance. The minority in the *Unidad Popular* saw unjustifiable surrender in every negotiation and compromise. It was incapable of understanding that when the balance of forces in a given context is unfavorable, tactical retreat is the best way to avoid predictable defeat. Only thus can strength be accumulated to attack the enemy when and where available power resources can be used most effectively. Only thus can the possibilities for victory be maximized.

The logical way to implement this theoretical perspective was, as I have said, for the *Unidad Popular*'s foreign policy to give priority to the principle of nonintervention. This permitted Chile to demand respect for her revolutionary program, for by advocating nonintervention in general, she was in a good position to demand that no intervention take place against herself. At the same time, it obligated Chile to refrain from intervening in the affairs of other states.

Such a definition of Chilean foreign policy seemed even more necessary because our enemies were seeking to associate the Chilean government with Cuba's, judging the former by the conduct of the latter. At that time the memory of Cuban counterattacks to defend herself against imperialist intervention in her internal affairs was still fresh. These had included Cuban support for revolutionary forces in other countries, which, given the context which imperialism had imposed upon Cuba, was a legitimate defense against the avowed U.S. intention to destroy the Cuban revolution—a purpose shared by North America's Latin American allies.

From the beginning the practice of nonintervention made any foreign intervention to block the *Unidad Popular* illegitimate. Yet, even before Salvador Allende assumed the presidency, intervention was already a reality—as was later made absolutely clear by the confession of the participants. I refer particularly to the well-known plans of the ITT, with the assistance of the CIA, to obstruct the *Unidad Popular*'s assumption of power, and to the terrorist act which resulted in the assassination of General Schneider, Commander in Chief of the Army.

Thus it was necessary to gain a step on hostile foreign actors by placing on the side of Chile the weight of legitimacy of the basic principle of international coexistence. This was facilitated enormously by the clear constitutional, electoral, and legal origin of the government of President Allende. In other words, adherence to the basic principles of international coexistence, which inspired the Charter of the United Nations and which have been observed by Chile throughout her history, was not only compatible with the interests of the Chilean revolution but also a necessary condition for the viability and success of that revolution.

If, to the basic orientation just described, we add the desire to maximize advantages accruing from the support of socialist countries and the favorable disposition of the progressive forces of humanity, we have a fairly clear picture of how the foreign policy of the *Unidad Popular* was designed to contribute to its ambitious program for structural change in Chilean society.

In the next section we will examine the ways in which these principles were put into practice.

EVOLUTION OF THE FOREIGN POLICY

During the three years of the *Unidad Popular* government, I can affirm that its objectives were fully achieved.

For the purpose of examining Chilean foreign policy in practice, I will analyze separately the international activities of Chile in each of the political-geographic areas that concerned her during this period.

Latin America

The Chilean Foreign Ministry was well aware of the fundamentally adverse predisposition toward Chile of most governments on the continent. It sought to avoid the isolation of our country within the region. From the beginning, therefore, the popular government was preoccupied with defining the doctrine of ideological pluralism as the basis for peaceful and constructive coexistence in Latin America. In April, 1971, I, as Foreign Minister signed a joint communiqué with my colleague from Colombia in which the doctrine was explicitly formulated and contrasted with that of "ideological frontiers," backed by Brazil shortly before. The doctrine of ideological pluralism, a Latin American version of nonintervention, came to be central to all joint declarations signed by those responsible for Chilean foreign policy with their counterparts throughout Latin America. Thus was created a virtual network of bilateral agreements on principle. Among these were the aforementioned documents signed by Chile with Colombia and others with Argentina, Ecuador, Mexico, Cuba, and Venezuela. The fact that a number of these countries were ruled at the time by conservative governments contributed to the importance of the agreements. These declarations to some extent led to an initiative to include the principle of ideological pluralism among reforms in the Charter of the Organization of American States. In this fashion the *Unidad Popular* government efficiently and promptly checked any move to use the pretext of Chile's political coloration to isolate her politically on the continent.

The Chilean Foreign Ministry gave particular attention to relations with Argentina. Special effort was made to reach some accord in the old, potentially explosive fight for sovereignty over islands in the Beagle Channel. The long-postponed agreement to submit the matter to the arbitration of the British Crown was finally put into practice, while not discounting the traditional Chilean point of view. Thus an old and vexing problem was resolved. The *Unidad Popular* not only found the means to fix Chile's national borders once and for all, but also eliminated a dangerous dispute which could have been manipulated by external and internal enemies of the *Unidad Popular* to create difficulties between Chile and Argentina.

Friendship between the two governments was consummated by President Allende's visit to Salta and President Lanusse's return trip to Antofagasta. Although inspired by different ideologies, both realized that only on the basis of absolute respect for the principle of nonintervention could they further integrate their two economies—economies which in so many ways were complementary. That this accord went beyond mere declarations is shown not only by the growth which occurred in Chilean-Argentine trade during the three years but also by the considerable short-term credits that Argentina provided to help Chile overcome balance of payments difficulties. The Argentine government's political approval of these credits was crucial. Thus, on its most vulnerable front, Chilean diplomacy successfully achieved her goal of cementing friendly relations with Argentina. The danger of political and economic isolation was decisively eliminated.

Nor was the popular government slow to respond to the problem of Bolivia's traditional demand for sovereign access to the Pacific. During General Torres' administration in Bolivia the first constructive steps toward solving the problem were taken. These were inspired by the spirit of Latin American cooperation contained in the foreign policy of the *Unidad Popular*. Unfortunately a military revolt overthrew Torres and brought to power a reactionary, fascist coalition which was firmly anti-Chilean. This interrupted talks and put an end to the growing mutual confidence between the two nations—an indispensable requirement for the successful conclusion of such delicate negotiations.

The popular government also paid great attention to the process of Andean economic integration. For a time the Cartagena Agreement was viewed with suspicion by the Chilean leftist political parties, which were instinctively worried by the lack of guarantees that the expanded market created by the pact would not work primarily to North American advantage. Shortly after the government assumed power—in December, 1970—the so-called Decision 24, relating to a Common Andean System for Treating Foreign Capital, was approved with emphatic Chilean support. Approval of Decision 24 removed the basis of the left's doubts. In effect the statute, which regulated foreign investment, not only guaranteed that the advantages of an expanded market would accrue primarily to the economies of the signatories but also provided for the progressive recovery by member countries of their principal productive activities under foreign control.

For the *Unidad Popular,* the political implications of Andean integration were even more important than its economic effects, particularly given the existing international environment. By increasing reciprocal ties the Cartagena Agreement made any attempt to separate Chile from the other Andean countries that much more difficult. Moreover, if the Andean Pact was to function effectively, its members would have to accept the principle of ideological pluralism. Nevertheless, in some member countries there were entrepreneurial groups which questioned whether the institutions created in the Cartagena Agreement could function adequately if one of the members adopted socialist economic policies. Happily, these doubts did not prosper. In fact, to a greater or lesser extent, statist policies were being applied not only in Chile but in all the member countries. This was particularly so in the case of Peru. It was difficult to argue that only Chilean economic policy was incompatible with the Andean Agreement.

The Chilean government made every possible effort to further Andean integration, and its efforts were crucial for winning approval of the first agreement on economic planning, that for metallurgical industries. Even in Chile, however, there was at times opposition to certain provisions of the agreement. For example, there was strong resistance within the government to complying with obligations to spend foreign exchange on imports from the subregion. Many felt that, given the difficult Chilean balance of payments situation, this was unwise. The opinion of the Chilean Foreign Ministry, which eventually carried the day, was that at that moment the economic sacrifice involved in observing the Andean commitment was a price which had to be paid. It was judged important to maintain an active and visible Chilean loyalty to the process of integration. Nevertheless, the increasing severity of the balance of payments crisis during the last months of the *Unidad Popular* government forced Chile to resort to certain escape clauses included in the integration treaties and to withdraw temporarily from the common system of intraregional trade.

President Allende's trip through the Andean countries (with the exception of Bolivia, then undergoing political turmoil) provided an excellent opportunity for him to reaffirm his government's dedication to the Latin American idea, its adhesion to the doctrine of ideological pluralism, its backing for Andean integration, its determined defense of a country's sovereign right to control its natural resources, and its condemnation of foreign attempts to use economic pressures and other illicit means to prevent the full exercise of sovereignty over these resources. Bilateral statements signed during this trip by President Allende and the leaders of Chile's sister nations testified to the wide consensus achieved on these points.

Mexico's growing interest in Latin America and the Third World, which had become manifest during the second year of President Echeverría's administration, created an opportunity for Chile to strengthen political, economic, and cultural ties with that nation. These were eloquently affirmed by the results of President Allende's visit to the Mexican capital in late 1972.

Only a few days after assuming power, Chile reestablished full diplomatic, economic, and cultural relations with Cuba. This implied, of course, that Chile withdrew her support of the OAS sanctions which had obliged members to cut ties with the Castro regime. Chile's desire to develop closer relations with Cuba was clearly shown in the numerous and varied agreements signed by both countries and in the exchange of visits by President Allende and Prime Minister Castro.

As was foreseen, the *Unidad Popular* victory in Chile was ill-received by Brazil, which first did nothing to hide her antagonism toward the new Chilean government. One can assume that at the time Brazil would have been inclined to support any attempt to isolate Chile within the hemisphere. Nevertheless, the care with which Chile conducted her relations with Brazil and the success of the Chilean Foreign Ministry in neutralizing potential hostility in other Latin American countries caused the Brazilian government to abandon its earlier aims. In Latin America the doctrine of ideological pluralism vanquished that of ideological frontiers. While political relations between the two countries remained cold, economic ties—financial and commercial—did not deteriorate. On the contrary, during the last year of the *Unidad Popular* government the two countries achieved substantial economic agreements. These demonstrated the relative friendliness that still characterized their economic relations.

Although relations between Chile and both Paraguay and Uruguay—nations with notably reactionary governments—were chilly, at least publicly they did not become qualitatively worse.

The United States

The basic goal underlying the *Unidad Popular*'s policy toward the United States was to minimize the spread of conflicts which were necessarily going to emerge when the government's program was put into practice. In other words—as noted above—the Chilean government sought to avoid a severe confrontation between the two countries, which could only have a negative outcome for Chile. The policy became manifest when, only a few days after Allende assumed power, the North American government unilaterally and without the prior knowledge or approval of Chilean authorities withdrew scientific and paramilitary installations from Easter Island. The incident gave Chilean officials an opportunity to expound to North American representatives exactly what the parameters of Chilean conduct *vis-à-vis* the United States would be.

During the course of the three years the Chilean government was particularly careful in its relations with the United States. At every occasion it was ready to negotiate problems arising between the two countries rather than promote an internal or international public dispute. Only when, at the end of 1972, it had become undeniably evident that the North American government was promoting a financial blockade and trying to hinder Chilean bilateral trade, and there were unequivocal signs that transnational companies and even agencies of the United States government were intervening in Chilean affairs, did the government of Chile present to the United Nations, in President Allende's memorable speech, a measured denunciation of the immoral objectives and methods of North American policies toward Chile.

The principal reason for the difficulties between the two countries, at least according to official U.S. spokesmen, was the nature of the Chilean government's nationalization of the large copper mines. In the view of the United States, the nationalization

had violated international law. Chile argued the opposite, affirming that international doctrine, formalized in Resolution 1903 of
the General Assembly of the United Nations, made its actions
completely legal. Nevertheless, the Chilean government recognized that it would be useful to find some legal means to moderate
and channel the conflict through a structured framework. Therefore it proposed to invoke the only legal instrument existing between the two countries, a treaty which called for procedures of
conciliation in case of conflict. In spite of Chilean insistence on
submitting the conflict to the judicial procedure described in the
Treaty of 1916, the United States government resisted to the last,
under the pretext that the procedure contemplated in the treaty
did not guarantee any rapid, practical solution to the problem.

Chile's sovereign conduct in the nationalization of copper
brought into effect North American legislation providing, in cases
of that nature, for a series of reprisals, particularly financial. The
Unidad Popular government denounced these sanctions as a violation of explicit provisions in the Charter of the United Nations and
in other multilateral juridical treaties—including the basic statute
of the OAS. Both the OAS and the United Nations recognize the
sovereign right of states to make free use of their natural resources, and both condemn the use of economic pressures to force
changes in relevant policies.

Chile also favored extending territorial waters to 200 miles,
recognizing at the same time that maritime sovereignty must be
compatible with the needs of international commerce and travel.

The Organization of American States

At the very first opportunity to speak in an Ordinary Assembly
of the Organization of American States, the representative of the
new Chilean government questioned the nature of the existing
inter-American system. Chile saw the OAS as a structure designed
to maintain the hegemony of the United States over the continent
and inspired by "cold war" ideology—a world view no longer
appropriate for guiding international conduct among states. Chile
warned that, if the inter-American system were not adequately
modified, it would soon become so discredited as to cease functioning. Chilean criticism gave rise to a number of initiatives for
transforming the inter-American system, which were considered
in Washington at the Ordinary Assembly of April, 1973.

There the Chilean delegate maintained that the inter-

American system rested on two false assumptions: that all its members were equals, and that there existed an identity of interests and ideology among all American states. Reality was and is different. In effect—Chile argued—there exists a series of prob- lems and conflicts between the United States and Latin America as a whole. There were economic problems, such as the unjust terms of trade working against Latin America and the increasing debts of the southern region. There were legal problems, such as the different positions of North and South with respect to territorial seas and nationalization of foreign investments. There were political problems, such as the Panama Canal and the use of economic pressures by the United States to deform the sovereign will of countries trying to defend or recover their natural resources. If the inter-American system was to have any meaning—Chile maintained—it must become an institutional forum where these questions could be discussed and resolved bilaterally; that is, an arena in which the United States could be forced to deal with Latin America as a whole.

This conception of the inter-American system assumed a prior agreement among the Latin American states. The seeds of such agreement could already be seen in the functioning of the Special Committee on Latin American Coordination (*Comisión Especial de Coordinación Latinoamericana*, CECLA) and the Special Commission on Consultation and Negotiation (*Comisión Especial de Consulta y Negociación*, CECON) and even in the activities of the Latin American group at the United Nations. Intergovernmental agreements on hemispheric economic relations were articulated for the first time in the so-called Consensus of Viña del Mar, in which the Latin American countries criticized North American economic conduct toward Latin America. As Chilean Foreign Minister, I handed these criticisms to the U.S. President.

In the 1973 OAS debate Chile also argued that, for identical reasons, it was necessary to modify the Inter-American Reciprocal Assistance Treaty, a similarly obsolete product of the Cold War. Recently, the OAS has begun to consider the Chilean initiatives for modifying both the nature of the inter-American structure and the Inter-American Reciprocal Assistance Treaty.

The Western Countries

From the beginning, the predictable hostility of the United States led the *Unidad Popular* to give special attention to maintaining friendly ties with other Western nations. There were two reasons for this. One was the potential importance of economic relations with Europe in case of a blockade promoted by the United States. The other was the general political influence of Western states on the international community. The latter could be decisive in frustrating any attempt to isolate Chile internationally.

A friendly approach to Western Europe was possible because Chile had traditional ties in the area and because many European states were ruled at the time by left-leaning or Social Democratic governments. Thus they were predisposed to sympathize with the new Chilean regime. Moreover, the open, honest, and democratic election of President Allende, and the *Unidad Popular*'s goal of building a socialist society which would be "democratic, pluralist, and free"—as the Chilean president was accustomed to saying— made the Chilean political experiment particularly interesting to European public opinion.

Reality did not belie expectations, for in spite of the pressures of North American financial circles and the U.S. government itself, the Western European countries maintained friendly, cooperative, and favorable attitudes toward the *Unidad Popular* regime. Economic and financial relations continued to evolve normally. The friendship attained in Chilean relations with Western Europe is clearly shown in joint communiqués and agreements for economic, technological, and cultural cooperation, which resulted from my European visit as Chilean Foreign Minister in 1972. Similarly, following the *coup d'état*, the frank hostility of the majority of Western European countries toward the military *junta* can be attributed in large part to the friendly ties the *Unidad Popular* was able to maintain and reinforce with that important group of nations.

The Socialist Countries

We have already noted that the *Unidad Popular* government established relations with the German Democratic Republic, which demonstrated from the first a cooperative attitude toward Chile. In like fashion Chile established relations with Albania, thus showing unequivocally her intention to maintain ties with all nations, regardless of their ideological or political colorations. The previous government had already established relations with the other socialist countries in Europe.

My visit as Chile's Foreign Minister to Eastern Europe in mid-1971 initiated a series of important meetings on the financing of Chilean industrial, mining, and agribusiness projects. The meetings also sought to increase reciprocal trade, technological aid, and cultural bonds among the states involved. Certain long-term projects negotiated with the Soviet Union were particularly important. That country also gave considerable financial aid when Chilean balance of payments problems were most severe.

From the moment when the *Unidad Popular* assumed power, the Chilean government supported admission of the People's Republic of China to the United Nations, and shortly after Allende took office, relations were established with that country. Later a number of important economic agreements were signed. These were expanded following my visit to China. There was no evidence at this time that China would subsequently adopt a policy of friendly coexistence with the military *junta*.

Chile established relations with the People's Democratic Republic of Korea and closed its embassy in Seoul, although without breaking relations with the South Korean regime. Chile supported proposals demanding the withdrawal of United Nations troops from Korea and favoring the political reunification of that country.

Responding to the broad international movement of solidarity with the Indochinese defense of their national independence and sovereignty, Chile established relations with the Democratic Republic of Vietnam and recognized the Provisional Revolutionary Government of South Vietnam and the National Unity Revolutionary Government of Cambodia.

The Third World

In view of common interests and international objectives, the program of the *Unidad Popular* proposed close links with other developing nations. This policy took form in the expansion of relations in different areas of the Third World. Thus we exchanged ambassadors with Guayana and Zambia and established relations with a number of African states—Nigeria, Guinea, the People's Republic of the Congo, Madagascar, and Tanzania.

In international organizations the *Unidad Popular* supported the demands of the Arab countries for a Middle East solution in line with Resolution 242 of the United Nations and for recognition of the rights of the Palestinian people. Chile added to Third World efforts against racial discrimination and *apartheid* and supported decolonization in general—in particular, the independence of the Portuguese colonies. In international organizations and forums Chile worked with the developing countries to change the prevailing, unjust pattern of international economic relations and to organize a system by which the developed nations would contribute to the efforts of the poor countries to overcome their economic and social backwardness. This policy acquired special importance during the Third Conference of the UNCTAD, which was held in the Chilean capital. That conference symbolized the understanding and stimulus given to Chile by the international community during the *Unidad Popular* administration.

In an action consistent with its general foreign policy, Chile formally joined the Movement of Non-Aligned Countries, in 1971, and thereafter participated resolutely in its activities and forums. In this way Chile emphasized the Third World dimension of its foreign policy. In response, Chile received solid support from the Non-Aligned Countries, which, in a meeting of heads of state held in Algiers just before the military *coup*, unanimously approved a resolution by the Foreign Minister of the host country, backing the *Unidad Popular* government against all internal and external attempts to overthrow it.

EVALUATION OF THE FOREIGN POLICY
AND ITS INFLUENCE ON THE COUP D'ETAT

I am perhaps not the most appropriate person to evaluate the results of the foreign policy of the Allende government. Nevertheless, I feel that our success is objectively recognizable. The goals which the program and the strategy of the Chilean left assigned to foreign policy in implementing the *Unidad Popular*'s revolutionary project were completely achieved.

Chile successfully avoided isolation in Latin America and was able to maintain and develop friendly cooperative ties with her most important neighbors. In accordance with the program, she successfully advocated a policy which favored Andean integration and Latin American unity and was critical of the inter-American system. Chile was able to minimize the consequences of predictable difficulties with the United States, and that country was denied numerous pretexts that might have served to justify a more open obstruction of the revolutionary policies of the Chilean government. In addition, Chile was able to separate the United States, with respect to its conduct toward us, from its Western allies and from Japan. With the latter Chile maintained satisfactory political and economic relations throughout the *Unidad Popular* period. Relations of all varieties were expanded with the socialist countries, and Chile succeeded in establishing tight links with the Third World, particularly with the non-aligned nations. This gave our country an audience within the international community far greater than that achieved at any other moment in our history.

These results were no more than consequences of the Chilean Foreign Ministry's general strategy for confronting the difficult international circumstances encountered by the new government. In effect, by emphasizing and practicing the principle of nonintervention, by eluding a direct confrontation with North American imperialism and its allies, by removing the rationale for more open intervention in our affairs, and by trying to divide and neutralize potential antagonists through timely and reasonable concessions, the government was able to prevent external factors from causing insuperable difficulties. It was also able to maximize external economic and political support for the Chilean revolution— no easy task, given the difficult conditions under which it evolved.

All this leads us to reflect on a number of points. First, the strategy followed by the popular government in foreign policy differed from that which seems to have predominated in facing internal political problems. In domestic matters, in my opinion, there was a distinct tendency to overestimate our own power and underestimate that of our adversaries. This led us to elaborate a mistaken strategy, following which electoral, legislative, propaganda, and even labor union standoffs and defeats encouraged the antagonists of the *Unidad Popular* and permitted them to gain the support of undecided actors, thus gradually eroding support of the government. The resistance to tactical agreements with those adversaries which might have been most easily neutralized and the never-abandoned idea that a final social or even military confrontation could be won by the left were both factors preventing the design of any reasonable, consistent strategy for domestic policy. A strategy built on the basis of objective, existing conditions—and not on simple subjective desires, naively perceived as real—could have gradually cleared the road for uninterrupted, revolutionary advance.

In the conception and implementation of domestic policy, this mistaken perception of reality and the balance of power of the combatants had a negative effect. In the area of international policy, in contrast, a more objective appreciation of existing external conditions prevailed from the first. This made it possible to design and apply adequate, consistent, and efficacious strategies and tactics.

Within the *Unidad Popular* our foreign policy enjoyed the

support of a broad majority. Those who disagreed did not, for whatever reason, attack it in public, a fact which made it much easier to implement. In addition, the President gave complete and constant backing to the Foreign Ministry. Finally, we established within the Ministry a pattern of centralized decision making, free from partisan interference and disruptive pressures. These factors permitted us to give the government's foreign policy unity, consistency, and boldness.

Only one important question remains: In light of our analysis, what was the relative weight of external factors in creating the political crisis which culminated in the fascist military *coup* of September 11, 1973?

There are some who believe that the frustration of the Chilean revolutionary experience was determined by external factors. They insist especially on the importance of the United States' financial blockade, the economic and technical aid given by the CIA to the adversaries of the *Unidad Popular,* and the North American influence and infiltration in the Chilean armed forces. In their view, these tipped the balance of power in favor of a counterrevolutionary *coup.*

Is that opinion realistic? To answer, it is first necessary to define an appropriate analytical criterion for assessing the situation and weighing the reciprocal influence of endogenous and exogenous factors which conditioned the success of the *coup d'état.*

There are two possible ways for foreign actors to impede and even destroy a revolutionary process in a given country. One consists of attacking that country economically, politically, or even militarily in such a way as to make it impossible for the revolution to succeed. This directly provokes a "destabilized" internal situation of such intensity that it produces failure and political collapse. In this case, external agents act directly to stimulate the actors and tendencies which determine the defeat. An external military attack, a blockade which directly results in economic crisis, political isolation induced from outside which weakens domestic support for the government to the point where its continued rule is no longer viable—these are examples of this first situation.

A second form of external interference consists of foreign influence on internal factors harmful to the government which have already developed independent of those external factors. In this case the external element intensifies already existing instability until it produces an irreversible political crisis and the fall of the government. The financial blockade and the North American-inspired obstacles to United States-Chilean trade aggravated the balance of payments crisis and aggravated certain supply problems, but we cannot say that they provoked or caused these difficulties. The origins of such problems must be sought in the internal dialectic of the Chilean process. Here the decisive roles were played by the economic policies of the government and the consequent reaction of the dominant social classes.

It is obvious that aggravating the balance of payments and supply problems played an important role in creating the climate of scarcity and in worsening inflation. In turn, scarcity and inflation generated and extended discontent among significant social sectors, particularly those of the middle class, and this again facilitated the success of the military rebellion. But we cannot conclude that the role of the middle class in promoting the *coup* would have been radically different had the deterioration of the economic situation not been so severe. Their hostility toward the *Unidad Popular* government was not determined by the aggravation of the economic situation stemming from external factors. Essentially, it was the result of a counterrevolutionary posture adopted in reaction to the gradual success of the government's revolutionary program and to the sensation of irreversibility that the process was slowly acquiring. In contrast, a direct consequence of the economic crisis and its external aggravation was the spread of hostility to other social sectors, which became, for these reasons, more susceptible to manipulation by those promoting the *coup*.

The same argument can be made with respect to the importance of the CIA's financial aid to the opposition parties, to the right-wing press, and to the subversive activities of interest-group leaders behind the truckers' strikes of October, 1972, and August, 1973. External aid increased the efficacy of their activities, but one cannot say that it caused them. Still, through the CIA's aid the right obtained more votes, its organs of mass communication acquired more influence over public opinion, and the owners' strikes were led with greater confidence and success by their leaders.

North American intervention in the Chilean armed forces—particularly by the U.S. military intelligence service—had greater importance. It had to play an important role in order to convince the officers to stage a *coup d'état*, and it did so by providing technical and professional support and contributing to unity behind their subversive designs. Yet, even in this case, foreign activities had the impact they did because they occurred in a military environment which prodded the officers to respond favorably to the idea of subversion. In effect, because of the reactionary political subculture in which Chilean officers were immersed, the enormous majority could not be won over to the side of the government and naturally tended to resist and question revolutionary policies. From their point of view, the *Unidad Popular* was attacking the very basis of social order and their sense of nationality. Only the professional tradition of the Chilean armed forces—a tradition formed in historical periods when the social system was never profoundly threatened—and their corresponding habitual obedience to the legally constituted branches of government counterbalanced their opposition to the *Unidad Popular* administration. Without this anti-government predisposition, the Pentagon's encouragement of rebellion would never have been successful.

While noting that this political attitude of the Chilean armed forces predated their direct encouragement by North American counterinsurgency, I do not wish to imply that the systematic anti-Communist indoctrination of hundreds of officers, during years of courses in Panama and in the United States, had no importance. On the contrary, it reinforced and updated the reactionary political subculture already existing in the Chilean military.

In addition, the *Unidad Popular* government made no effort to place sympathetic officers in command posts. Thus, the North American encouragement of insurrection encountered a military leadership whose composition had not fundamentally changed. This government policy, unanimously judged suicidal *a posteriori*, was without doubt a crucial factor facilitating sedition.

In other words, although it would be absurd to deny the significance of North American intervention in Chilean military affairs, that intervention occurred in an environment where the most important aspects—the political attitudes of officers and the composition of leadership—were of endogenous origin. Unfortunately, the government made no effort to affect these—even to the extent that it could, which was probably considerable.

The absence of any significant "military project" in the *Unidad Popular* government's program appears clear. It was of even greater importance than the government's economic plans or its foreign policy. A policy should have been set forth regarding the entire problem of violence in the revolutionary process. It should have particularly emphasized the need for dependable military support for the government and the need to combat and neutralize the influence of North American counterinsurgency doctrines in the Chilean armed forces.

To summarize my argument, I believe that North American activities designed to "destabilize" the *Unidad Popular* government—activities which have recently been admitted by responsible United States officials—did not create the factors which produced the downfall of that government. They did, however, increase and intensify their efficacy.

Whether the marginal increase in the efficacy of subversion brought about by foreign intervention was sufficient to tip the balance of power in favor of the insurrection's success is, of course, another matter. Unfortunately, it is a question that is impossible to answer. Clearly, however, the impact of intervention on the political, economic, and military situation in the country shortly before the *coup* was substantial, and it most affected those factors which determined the behavior of the armed forces. I personally believe that even without external support the subversive attempt would have occurred. I am less certain that, without such support, it would have achieved the same success.

The next question is whether Chilean foreign policy could have prevented or significantly diminished North American intervention and its "destabilization" of the *Unidad Popular* government. To this I reply that I am certain it could not. To justify my assertion, let us consider two possibilities.

First, could the Chilean government's foreign policy have eliminated or diminished the range of causes and pretexts for North American intervention?

If we begin with the assumption that the *Unidad Popular*'s program could not be abandoned and that the government was not willing to compromise its sovereignty, we can state that the Chilean Foreign Ministry did everything possible within these parameters to eliminate provocations of North American action. To do more would have meant renouncing Chilean sovereignty in the question of indemnification of the copper companies. That sovereignty had been constitutionally expressed by the Chilean Congress in a unanimous decision establishing a procedure for determining the amount of indemnification. This procedure was followed by the *Unidad Popular.*

We can go even further. It is highly likely—even certain—that had the Chilean government, at great political cost and unjustifiable injury to national sovereignty, reached an agreement with the copper companies over indemnification, North American intervention would still have been maintained without change. The U.S. government would have continued to use the CIA and the intelligence services of its armed forces in clandestine attempts to "destabilize" Chile, to provoke riots, to strengthen the opposition, and to incite the Chilean armed forces to rebellion. Moreover, it was in these areas that intervention had greatest impact on the balance of power which determined the final outcome. Even had we resolved the question of indemnification by some despicable agreement and this had led to a relaxation of the financial blockade, the balance of power would not have been significantly altered to increase the *Unidad Popular* government's ability to resist a military *coup*.

I am led to this conclusion because it was the political dangers inherent in the possible success of the Chilean revolution which motivated North American intervention. For the United States, the problem of indemnification for the copper companies was really secondary, although publicly the U.S. government insisted that this was the most important obstacle to friendly relations between the two countries. In essence, North American diplomacy sought a pretext to justify its anti-Chilean policies, which took the form of clandestine "destabilizing" activities. It is naive to think that these would have ceased with indemnification to the copper companies, since their ultimate origins lay in a counterrevolutionary perspective which inspired and continues to inspire North American foreign policy. Before the greater danger, the question of compensation was less than transcendental.

To summarize: I am certain that greater care in managing relations with the United States—even assuming that it was possible—would not have significantly changed the impact of U.S. intervention on the success of the military *coup*.

The second possibility which must be considered is whether a more hard-line policy toward the United States could have prevented or diminished that country's intervention in Chilean affairs. Could it have improved the balance of internal power in favor of the government?

To have taken a harder line in its foreign policy toward the United States, Chile would have had to:

a) denounce at an earlier date and/or more vehemently, before the international community and Chilean public opinion, actions of the United States;

b) refuse to negotiate a legal solution to the disagreement over indemnification for the U.S. copper companies;

c) break diplomatic relations, following denunciations of North American intervention in our country.

I do not believe that any of these alternatives to the actual conduct of the government, whether adopted separately or jointly, would have eliminated or diminished in any way the danger or intensity of intervention.

Neither an international denunciation prior to President Allende's speech before the Assembly of the United Nations nor more stridency or violence in the language of that denunciation could logically have changed the course of events in Chile's favor. Nor, given the constitutional framework within which the government had to operate, could refusing to negotiate over the problem of compensation have favorably modified what was occurring. On the contrary, the only possible outcome of such refusal would have been negative. We would have been unable to parry—as we did before the international and hemispheric communities and, above all, before the Western European nations, worried observers of the Chilean-North American problem—the charge that Chile had acted in violation of international law. In contrast, we were able to argue powerfully that Chile desired and was doing all it could to obtain a juridical solution to the problem, by invoking the only existing instrument for resolving such questions, the Treaty of 1916.

It is possible that the Chilean government could have conducted relations with the United States so as to justify either side's breaking diplomatic relations, but such a break would not have altered the situation in favor of the Chilean government. On the contrary, the political climate prevailing in Chile in 1973 was such that a rupture in relations with the United States would have diminished public support for the government. One must keep in mind the attitude of the middle class at the time. Reduction of middle-class support could not have been compensated for by an increase among those who were already followers of the *Unidad Popular.* Yet these were the only sectors which, because of their greater anti-imperialist consciousness, would have responded favorably to a break in relations with the United States. Moreover, this kind of hard-line policy would have been neither understood nor supported by the great majority of Latin American governments. As a result, it would have helped to isolate Chile on the continent—exactly what the Foreign Ministry wished to avoid at all cost.

Breaking relations with the United States would certainly have precipitated the military insurrection. Such a break would have made it easier to persuade the officer corps to join the counterrevolutionary plot, and it would have led the military to implement that plot even sooner, among other reasons because of Chilean dependence on the United States for its military hardware. Thus it would have served as an excellent pretext to justify the sedition on the grounds that a break in relations with the United

States would seriously weaken the power of the armed forces and that this, in turn, would injure national security, for which, in the officers' view, the armed forces were most responsible. From the moment that Chile broke off relations with the United States, the vacillations and conflicting loyalties still present within the armed forces would rapidly have disappeared.

Thus, in my judgment, neither a policy of exercising greater caution in the conduct of relations with the United States nor one of taking a harder line would have significantly modified North American behavior toward Chile. The nature of the U.S. policy of "destabilizing" the *Unidad Popular* government would have remained unchanged.

In conclusion, I affirm that, within the parameters in which it had to evolve, the foreign policy of President Allende's government was successful in its principal task of facilitating the Chilean revolutionary program—at least to the extent that this depended on the international context. Moreover, recognizing the strategic priority accorded to the domestic program, Chilean foreign policy attained its objective of supporting, throughout the world, progressive movements struggling for peace, democracy, socialism, and the political and economic emancipation of dependent peoples.

The Interrelationship
between Economics and Politics

SERGIO BITAR

When one uses conventional economic indicators—essentially of a
financial, monetary, and fiscal sort—to study the period from 1970
to 1973 in Chile, the initial conclusion is obvious. There emerged
a variety of tremendous economic imbalances—imbalances which
are difficult to justify from a purely economic point of view. To
find an explanation for these that transcends the simple assessment of technical error or incompetence, with which economists
are all too often content, it is necessary to explore the interrelationship between the economic events of those years and the political process in which they were immersed.

This interrelationship must be examined as a dynamic process; that is, one must study its gestation and evolution over time.
Otherwise one runs the risk of simply enumerating factors, without capturing their relative importance during different phases of
the process.

To analyze the course of events and to identify critical moments, it is first necessary to distinguish between periods. These
can be classified according to the particular economic measures
applied and to existing political conditions. Thus we begin with a
chronological analysis of the three years of the *Unidad Popular*, in
order to finally arrive at more general conclusions.

What economic conditions existed when the *Unidad Popular*
government began to implement its program?

To answer that question, it is necessary to go back to the final
years of the previous administration. Following 1967, the moderately redistributive and expansionist policies begun in 1965 had
suffered a significant change. In that year the Frei government

implemented a number of measures to restrict public spending and to contain the rise in salaries. Although the growth rate of the economy was reduced significantly, inflation continued to accelerate, and the initial aim of gradually reducing the rate of price increases was not achieved.[1] Thus 1970 saw the culmination of a process which had been gathering speed since 1967. Simultaneously, the partial reforms and the stimulus given to organization of the peasantry and to workers in general created growing pressure on the government. One indication of this phenomenon was the number of striking workers, which reached its peak in 1970.[2] In synthesis, the predominant trends affecting the initial days of the Allende government were a growing demand by workers for a better standard of living, a slow economic growth rate, and increasing inflation.

To these was added the brusque economic recession which followed the presidential election (September to November, 1970). Economic contraction was essentially the result of political activity, which provoked a change in the economic behavior of various social groups. The crisis had two manifestations. The first was the so-called run on the banks, which could have been particularly serious, perhaps even leading to the collapse of the banking system, had the financial apparatus not been able to respond to the greater demand for liquidity. The second was a contraction in sales. It resulted from a drop in the demand for durable consumer goods, principally among middle- and higher-income groups, and from a precipitous drop in construction. In that area, the private sector, desiring to maintain a high degree of liquidity, drastically reduced investment. One important result was an immediate increase in unemployment in construction.[3]

These phenomena showed that political problems could have a strong impact on the functioning of the economy and on the behavior of the bourgeoisie. It was not a stable system in which one could apply specific economic measures and obtain the results predicted by theory. On the contrary, there were serious disturbances in the economic system that aroused great uncertainty as to whether the altered behavior would ever return to normal and, if so, how long it would take.

Thus the initial stage of government, which in my judgment extends from November, 1970, to the end of 1971, began with an economic recession of unknown duration, a phenomenon with potentially important political repercussions. The government could not remain passive, particularly since new national elections would be held in April, 1971. If the *Unidad Popular* was to promote social change, it was important that the government strengthen its position in those elections.

These initial circumstances served to reinforce the government's decision to expand its base of support through policies of redistribution and economic expansion. Thus there was a logical connection between reactivation (particularly given the post-election recession), the expansion of the government's base of support, and the initiation of structural change.

THE INITIAL STAGE: NOVEMBER 1970 TO LATE 1971

The most decisive characteristic of the initial stage was the implementation of policies designed to reactivate the economy. The resulting expansion surpassed all predictions.

It is worth reviewing briefly the assumptions underlying economic policy during this phase. The design for stimulating reactivation, which the *Unidad Popular* had begun to elaborate even before the election and which became more important as a result of subsequent events, was framed within a hyper-Keynesian model which underestimated the importance of monetary phenomena. The initial analysis was based on four assumptions that, it was believed, would permit a significant increase in supply: 1) idle capacity, 2) unemployment, 3) international reserves, and 4) a high level of copper production in 1971 (estimated at about 900,000 tons). These factors would make possible a response to the increased demand.

In the area of fiscal policy, the model assumed that profits from the Social Property Sector would compensate for the increase in public spending, thus reducing the inflationary impact of the deficit caused by reactivation and salary increases. There were also a number of hypotheses about the short-term effects of structural reform, although these are more difficult to identify. For example, it was implicitly assumed that an increase in the pace of agrarian reform would not necessarily bring about a drop in production; that nationalization of copper, with its concomitant organizational problems, would not result in less copper production than planned in the short run; and that the creation of the Social Property Sector would not affect the supply of goods produced in enterprises which passed to state control. These assumptions concerning the impact of structural reforms on the functioning of the economy were, in my judgment, overly optimistic. The disequilibria typical of transition periods were underestimated.

Events evolved differently. To understand why, it is useful to distinguish two periods: one before and the other after the April, 1971, elections. Between November and April the government concentrated its efforts on economic reactivation, seeking to reduce the insecurity which had followed the presidential election and to expand its electoral base of support. The period was characterized by increased public spending and salaries, increasing demand, and a reduction of unemployment. The state used the mechanism it controlled to stimulate economic activity.

Following the April elections, the results of which favored the *Unidad Popular,* the government rapidly initiated creation of the Social Property Sector, intensified the agrarian reform, and completed the nationalization of copper. Up to this moment the sequence was clear: reactivation, elections in which popular support increased, and structural reforms. Nevertheless, the policies of economic expansion continued to be applied after the election. In the following months, through the end of the year, the imbalance between supply and demand increased spectacularly. The amount of money in circulation and the fiscal deficit reached high levels, which indicated the presence of potentially unmanageable disequilibria.

These trends far surpassed the objectives of the government's economic team. For example, while the government proposed that salaries be raised in 1971 by about 35 per cent, they increased by about 50 per cent.[4]

The resultant economic conditions favored opposition activities, particularly those of a subversive nature. The so-called March of the Empty Pots, at the close of 1971, was a political manifestation of the impact of two factors: reaction to the process of structural change and articulation of the discontent over initial maladjustments in the supply of consumer goods. The right, supported by agencies of the United States, also found expression in a specific conflict: the question of compensation to the large copper companies. The Chilean decision to deduct excessive profits created a useful pretext for further reduction of credit from North American banks and international agencies. As a result, internal economic problems became even more acute.

A review of the *Unidad Popular's* three years leads to the conclusion that this first stage (1971) was decisive. After 1971 there were no real relevant options in economic policy. It was the year in which the interaction of political and economic variables left the greatest margin for maneuver. During the next two years, the limitations imposed by political factors would impede implementing any economic program coherently. Moreover, such implementation would become secondary to the maintenance of immediate political stability and the daily struggle over tactical problems, and there would be stubborn refusal to modify the general line of the economic program.

FACTORS EXPLAINING THE INTERNAL ECONOMIC MALADJUSTMENTS

How can we explain the divergence between objectives and results? It is possible to identify a number of fundamental economic and political factors. First, there was uncertainty as to the functioning of the system under conditions of structural change and social conflict. How long would the recession last? How and when would private sector investment begin to behave normally again? This uncertainty limited the precision with which policies could be designed. The lack of knowledge and the worry that the private sector might withdraw even more led the government to overstimulate expansion. Moreover, the government's analytic capacity was weak and thus tended to be superseded by interpretations in which ideology played a major role.

A second factor was the delay between the application of policies and their results. If we put ourselves in the specific context of each decision—and this is an important perspective for understanding the evolution of events—we see, for example, that in June and July of 1971, when economic problems were already growing, the available statistics on unemployment and levels of economic activities still showed only a slight recuperation. Delays occurred at three points in the policy process: a) between the appearance of financial disequilibria and their impact on productive activity; b) between the surge in production and its statistical measurement; and c) between the statistical demonstration of economic activity and its political evaluation.

The last two points acquired growing importance, for throughout the first period the gap between economic and political leadership persisted. Perhaps worse, one could argue that in the initial design of economic policy economists made political assumptions that were inconsistent with those of the political leadership. For example, the idea of creating favorable economic conditions and increasing general welfare, in the very short run, so that a plebiscite that would authorize modification of the existing legal system could then be held was not necessarily compatible with the idea of a gradual advance in which every card need not be played at once.

A third factor was the dynamics of a process which, though stimulated by the government, gradually and increasingly acquired an independent momentum. In a political context which favored their immediate and medium-range interests, the workers logically increased their demands. In the public sector and in enterprises whose ownership had passed to the state, salaries rose far more than intended. The same occurred in the private sector, though for different reasons. On the one hand, the workers now could count on the support of political parties in the government. Hence their negotiating power increased. On the other hand, owners wished to avoid conflicts which could generate pressure to transfer their businesses to the Social Property Sector. Moreover, the traditional practices of the leftist parties could not be changed significantly in so brief a period. The left was accustomed to backing workers' demands and struggling to strengthen workers' organizations, and it was still essential to do so in order to increase support for the government. However, because there was no adequate control of these demands, they rapidly outstripped the short-term possibilities for increasing production. Political support for workers' demands was further encouraged by the competition among the various parties within the *Unidad Popular* and by the competition between the coalition and the Christian Democrats.

Finally, the deficiencies in the design and implementation of economic policies bear repeating. The design of policy presented major theoretical and practical difficulties because it dealt with an economic system experiencing significant structural reforms and within which behavior would vary in ways that could be predicted only with difficulty. In addition, the resulting short-term economic disequilibria were underestimated. The conceptual orientation of the economic team was overly structuralist and administrative.

The Chilean capitalist system continued to function as such, even after changes in the ownership of strategic means of production. The system operated according to long-established rules that could not be abruptly changed, and it had a series of automatic regulatory mechanisms that, when impeded, generated severe imbalances. Somehow these mechanisms had to be replaced by new means of control, born of the expanded power of the state and of popular organizations. If capitalist regulatory mechanisms were dismantled more rapidly than they could be replaced, it would necessarily provoke the disarticulation of the market. This was in effect what occurred.

THE INTERMEDIATE STAGE:
FROM LATE 1971 TO NOVEMBER 1972

The next period, from late 1971 to June, 1972, was characterized by considerable restriction of the government's maneuverability in terms of economic policy. In my opinion, it was a time of waiting, of inaction in economic matters. The most important event was the meeting at *"El Arrayán,"* at which two positions began to take shape. One recognized the existence of major financial disequilibria, which, it argued, had to be corrected. This position was held by the majority of the government economists and by representatives of the more moderate political parties. Those who held this view did not articulate any concrete policy propositions, but it was clear that correction of these imbalances would signify slowing down if not halting the process of redistribution and expansion.

The second position, apparently more coherent but actually of limited technical and political viability, suggested two principal actions. First, it argued that the greatest possible quantity of liquid capital should be extracted from high- and medium-high-income sectors. In this way the government could prevent the burden inherent in any policies to control inflation and reduce fiscal deficits and the deficits in the Social Property Sector from falling on workers and employees of low and moderately low income. Otherwise the progress which had already been achieved would be diminished. Second, it argued that more rapid expansion of the Social Property Sector was necessary to control the market disequilibria which had emerged in 1971. Particularly important was inclusion of producers of essential consumer goods and firms engaged in distribution.

In spite of this argument, the period was characterized by relative inaction. It was questioned whether the government had the political capacity to advance along the two lines suggested and whether, in practice, it possessed the means to extract enough resources from high-income groups to maintain the initial redistribution.

To realize the gravity of the last difficulty, one must remember that during the first stage redistribution was not based so much on transferring resources from one group to another as on differential expansion of incomes. In other words, overall consumption increased, but the increase was differentiated by strata; the poorest sectors gained proportionately more than others. By mid-1971, however, internal productive capacity had reached its peak, and foreign exchange was limited. As a result, the battle over consumer goods became more intense, taking the forms of inflation, partial scarcities, and other failures of market functions.

A system which has existed with high rates of inflation over considerable periods of time usually develops mechanisms to conserve and recover the income of its most powerful and best-organized groups, which belong to the middle- and high-income strata of society. Other sectors are unable to use these mechanisms; e.g., the purchase of equity shares, or real estate. The increasing inflation in Chile, therefore, had begun to diminish the real earnings of the lowest-income sectors. Although the government struggled to maintain its advances, it was unable to extract sufficient resources from middle- and high-income sectors. This led to increasingly frequent government-decreed salary raises, with the result that financial disequilibria constantly worsened.

These circumstances made it increasingly easy for the political and economic right to appeal ideologically to the middle sectors and to begin articulating the organization that would combat the government. On the economic front, its principal objective was to intensify the economic crisis.

The situation of relative immobility was finally overcome by June, 1972, giving way to a third period during which the government sought to effect some sort of economic adjustment. The period began with a new set of economic policies; it ended with the October strike. The new measures sought a financial adjustment; they permitted a general rise in price levels while attempting to correct relative distortions in the market, particularly in the Social Property Sector and in the exchange rate.

However, the level of accumulated imbalances was now so great that the major result of the new measures was a rapid acceleration of inflation. Rising prices had to be compensated for by salary readjustments, thus reinforcing the inflationary cycle. It can be debated, of course, whether the timing and sequence of the new measures was correct. Should prices in the private sector have been readjusted first and those in the social sector later? Should the price of the dollar have been attended to first and then the prices of essential consumer goods?

I think that, in any case, it was too late and that changes in the sequence would have had at best only minor effects on the inflationary spiral. Whatever might have occurred, the policies were not even fully implemented. Their application was halted by the strike of the transportation workers and merchants, the first great reactionary attack. It became a strike seeking to paralyze the economy.

By the time the October strike was resolved, the opposition

had attained at least one of its objectives: it had deepened Chile's economic crisis. The economic disequilibria had become even more severe. It was now very difficult to maintain control through administrative mechanisms. Without doubt, the Social Property Sector gave the state greater administrative capacity, and this compensated somewhat for the loss in the regulatory capacity of the market. In 1972 there were rapid advances in the creation of the social sector, in agrarian reform, in the sector of foreign commerce, and in distribution. But the rate of advance was inferior to that of the disarticulation of the market and to that which the right organized to intensify the crisis.

MILITARY PARTICIPATION IN THE CABINET: A POLITICAL TRUCE

From November, 1972, through March, 1973, the Chilean military participated in the cabinet. From an economic point of view, the period was static; events seemed frozen. The new cabinet perceived that any major change in economic policy might have unpredictable results. The political consequences of any action could be significant, given the precarious equilibrium among political actors. As a result, the cabinet decided to make only the marginal adjustments that were necessary to resolve the most acute short-term problems. The impasse between the Executive and Congress with respect to the creation of the Social Property Sector continued. Although the new cabinet proposed a formula to open the door for new negotiations, it too was frustrated, this time not only by the opposition but also by the internal differences within the *Unidad Popular*. Internal tactical disagreements over how to confront an opposition determined to overthrow the government had by now been defined more clearly. In effect, as the situation became more complex and the road narrower, two tactical lines were drawn with respect to whether the government should seek to broaden its base of support. In summary, it was a period in which the conflict was contained, a truce in which all efforts were turned to the electoral battle of March, 1973.

THE FINAL STAGE

With the election and the resignation of the military from the cabinet the last period began. From a strictly economic point of view, there were no significant changes between April and September. Efforts were concentrated on creating a system for the direct distribution of essential goods, in order to guarantee a supply to the poorest sectors of the population and to partially contain the effects of the widespread black market. However, these efforts were minor in comparison with the magnitude of the problems. It was a struggle for daily survival, with an exhausted political and economic leadership. The intensity of both national and international opposition had reached its peak. The enemies of the coalition continued to seek to aggravate the economic crisis and to paralyze the state bureaucracy, thus creating optimal conditions for encouraging a military *coup.*

The opposition launched two great attacks. The first began in April and culminated in June. It consisted of a series of strikes, the most important of which was at *El Teniente* copper mine. The objective was to expand the base of the October strike to include new groups of employees and workers with some impact on critical economic activities. This attack ended with the military uprising of June 29. The second great attack began in July and culminated with the *coup d'état* on September 11, 1973.

Economically, the tactics of insurrection revealed two lines of action. The first was to create panic and scarcities. While the government made an enormous effort to supply the market with normal quantities of goods, the press announced future scarcities. As a result, shoppers went out and bought what was needed for fifteen days instead of smaller quantities which might last for one or two. It was, in short, a self-fulfilling prophecy. The second line was to encourage strikes and economic paralysis. Given the rapid inflation, it was quite easy to raise the banner of higher wages. Strikes were especially directed toward activities which would disrupt distribution (transport and commerce). It was in this area that inadequacies were most resented by the middle sectors.

THE INTERACTION OF POLITICS AND ECONOMICS

In synthesis, the above chronology of events brings into relief the existence of a clear division in the evolution of the Chilean process. In 1971 the government held the political initiative and, as a result, enjoyed considerable room for economic maneuver. It encouraged economic expansion and the creation of the Social Property Sector. It advanced in the areas of agrarian reform, the nationalization of copper, and the nationalization of banking. In other words, the government attempted a rapid and simultaneous advance on all fronts. It was the critical year. After 1971 the initial favorable effects were gradually displaced by major economic problems and disequilibria. From the second half of 1972 until the *coup d'état* the situation changed. The right moved from a phase of defense and organization to one of attack. In its economic policies the government gradually assumed a defensive attitude, reacting to the activities of the opposition rather than initiating a broad search for some alternative model.

This is not to say that no alternative model was debated. There were two general proposals for dealing with a major imbalance between global supply and demand. The first, traditionally applied by governments of the right, consisted of raising prices, freezing salaries, and diminishing public spending—that is, forcing a reduction in demand in order to bring about a new equilibrium. The greatest impact of such a strategy would necessarily fall on the income of salaried workers. Hence, almost by definition, this alternative was not considered. The second proposal was to consolidate advances in the distribution of income. This assumed that the role of the state would be extended to include direct control over the distribution of essential products. Whereas traditionally the state had played a regulatory role, relying on the use of financial mechanisms, this solution suggested that the state should act directly in critical areas of the economy. Yet to some extent this debate was academic. The process had advanced and fundamental decisions had been postponed; the political conditions necessary to impose this option no longer existed.

THE SEQUENCE AND INTENSITY OF STRUCTURAL CHANGES

One of the government's most important tactical errors was its attempt to implement all contemplated structural changes rapidly and simultaneously. From the beginning it advanced with equal rapidity on all fronts. Basically the disarticulation of the market was caused by the intensity of economic expansion and redistribution, but the superimposition of changes in property ownership generated effects which were difficult, if not impossible, to control with the available means.

The existing system had a certain inertia and was regulated by certain mechanisms. Redistribution and expansion modified the functioning of these mechanisms, as did the changes in ownership, particularly at the level of supply. The combination of the two was difficult not only to predict but also to regulate.

Each of these policies generated effects that, though favorable or neutral at first, later became damaging. Once the limit of productive capacity was reached, deficiencies in one enterprise or sector rapidly spread to others. The exhaustion of Chile's international monetary reserves and the resulting balance of payments difficulties eliminated one way of dealing with the problem. Yet the relatively complex nature of the Chilean economy—measured in terms of the density of intersectoral relations—made rigorous management necessary. Moreover, in an electoral context, mismanagement of the economy would have major political implications. Many important social groups evaluated the *Unidad Popular*'s strategic objectives in terms of the immediate, short-term results of government actions.

The simultaneous implementation of policies on three fronts, reflected in the rapid expansion of demand, the drastic agrarian reform, and the deficiencies in the management of the large copper companies, was a clear example of incompatibility among government actions. Advances at once on the three fronts adversely affected the balance of payments, and the scarcity of foreign exchange increased Chile's vulnerability to the North American financial blockade. In the final stages of the process the scarcity of exchange forced the government to reduce the rate of advance and to diminish the overall food supply.

To overcome these problems it would have been necessary to accelerate progress in certain critical areas (ownership of the means of production), while moderating the intensity of redistributive measures. Priority could have been shifted to the latter in later stages.

However, a question immediately arises. Could the government effect changes in the ownership of the means of production without expanding its base of political support? If not, were redistributive policies necessary to expand that base? This line of reasoning underlay the *Unidad Popular*'s approach to the April, 1971, elections, and on that occasion the government expanded its base of support considerably. The improvement of economic conditions had a positive effect, but we should not forget that the support of the incumbent party has traditionally tended to increase in elections subsequent to the presidential.

Moreover, in the congressional elections of March, 1973, in the midst of the economic crisis, the *Unidad Popular* obtained greater support than it had in the 1970 presidential battle. Since by then the economy was showing obvious symptoms of decline, these results could not be attributed to economic improvement. The reason should be sought in the growing political consciousness of the workers, stemming from the conflict itself. Thus it is not possible to establish a direct connection between electoral support and a context of economic improvement.

Here emerge some of the principal economic and political questions regarding any process of change within a democratic, electoral framework. Is the use of redistributive measures to obtain immediate improvement intrinsic to the process? In other words, is a major dose of populism necessary? Is so, how can it be made compatible with an attitude of disciplined effort and with rapid organizational advance among the workers, both of which are necessary to sustain changes in ownership and to neutralize the strong bourgeois reaction? Finally, if the disarticulation of the market is inevitable, what impact does it have on the political behavior of the middle sectors?

THE ECONOMIC PROGRAM AND THE SOCIAL ALLIANCE

One basic assumption of the *Unidad Popular*'s program was that the government could build an alliance between the proletariat and the middle sectors: workers, peasants, employees, intellectuals, professionals, and sectors of the small and medium bourgeoisie. Such an alliance was compatible with the program's central objective and would have permitted isolating the owners of the major means of production. That alliance was not achieved. On the contrary, the government's economic program affected the behavior of the middle sectors and facilitated their ideological penetration by owners' associations and their principal political organization, the National party.

To understand this phenomenon we must remember certain political assumptions implicit in the government's economic actions. First, it was assumed that eliminating the economic power of the large owners, through nationalization of their productive resources, would lead directly and rapidly to a decline in their political power. In reality, however, the Chilean bourgeoisie preserved considerable economic power, increased their liquidity, received outside support, and continued to control the most important communications media. Their attack on the government and its program, emphasizing the ideological axiom that property is a requisite for liberty, gradually increased its scope of operation to medium owners and then to small. While the goal of the *Unidad Popular* was to isolate the large owners politically, the upper bourgeoisie sought to break that isolation by seeking allies among small entrepreneurs, self-employed workers, professionals, and highly paid employees.

Another widespread assumption was that the increase in the profits of medium and small entrepreneurs, derived from the economic expansion, would guarantee their neutrality. Yet, even at the moment when their earnings were greatest, they worried that their ownership of productive means was insecure. This affected their behavior. The political and ideological appeals of the right were most important, but the government failed in its tactical response. For example, it did not clarify until late in the process the list of firms to be expropriated. Nor did it give concrete guarantees of security to firms not included, or condemn, in any meaningful sense, factory seizures which went beyond government policy. These failures contributed to pushing the middle sectors into the arms of the opposition.

The disarticulation of the market, the resulting inflation, the scarcities, and the black market also affected principally the middle-income groups, which saw their relatively advantaged standard of living threatened.

There were also subjective factors which contributed to the radicalization of the so-called middle sectors. Among these were the *Unidad Popular*'s inability to project a clear image of its intended "model," its verbosity, the announcements of inapplicable or premature measures, the careless discussion of the character of the revolution and its reach, and the permanent emphasis on the hegemony of the proletariat.

Nor did the social alliance between the proletariat and the middle sectors receive coherent political treatment from the *Unidad Popular*. Its eminently sociological and structural analysis of the Christian Democrats emphasized their multiclass character. Its conclusion was that it would be possible to attract the Christian Democratic base through measures which favored workers and employees. The *Unidad Popular* thus underestimated the contribution of ideological factors to partisan cohesion. One result was that conservative sectors within the Christian Democratic party found it far easier to push the party toward an alignment with the right. This blocked the institutional road and made it virtually impossible to achieve the minimum legal changes necessary to direct the revolutionary process.

Finally, and characteristically, the economic right was very quick to reorganize and take the offensive. On the one hand, the right's perception of the risks involved led it to seek the widest possible alliance. On the other hand, though the organization and support of the workers by and for the government increased, they did so at a slower pace. One perceives most quickly and intently what one already has, meanwhile losing that which one does not yet have, though one might have gotten it. Too much attention to the bird in hand may permit those in the bush to escape.

ECONOMIC LEADERSHIP AND POLITICAL LEADERSHIP

To manage a situation of such complexity, effective economic and political leadership was required. To begin with, the task of creating a new and expanded state administrative apparatus had to be confronted. The state would have to surpass its conventional role of regulating the economy through indirect means and take direct control of the systems of investment, foreign trade, and distribution and management of the great state firms. It would take time and tremendous effort to create and consolidate the required administrative mechanisms. However, movement from a regulatory state to a producing and planning state, with workers' participation, must keep pace with the breakdown of traditional regulatory mechanisms and the consequent economic disequilibria.

The link between economic leadership and political leadership was never adequate. Indeed, until late in the process there was only a weak tie. To a large extent the problem could be attributed to the particular individuals in the positions of policy leadership. The economists did not make sufficiently explicit the political effects of their measures, nor did they make clear, once the principal imbalances had appeared, the political requirements for changing earlier policies. On the other hand, the political leadership underestimated the importance of economic phenomena, particularly during the first phase. One reason was that many of the *Unidad Popular*'s leading cadres had limited technical and administrative experience. Their formation was eminently parliamentarian.

Economic leadership also suffered from a lack of unity. The administrative hierarchy was compartmentalized by quotas through which positions were distributed among the coalition parties. Thus the struggle to maintain the internal balance of power in the coalition led to partisan interference in administration. The confusion between technical and political responsibilities led to the marginalization of technical personnel, who were replaced by political appointees. The left did not have adequate numbers of trained followers. On the one hand, the political parties displaced those it did have. On the other, they did not take advantage of the technical skills available within the state bureaucracy.

The dynamics of events also demanded unified political leadership. There arises, of course, the question whether coalition government is compatible with a need for unified, rapid, and efficacious leadership. The procedures for decision making within the coalition delayed important measures. Tactical disagreements had a similar effect, and there was no energetic effort to mediate differences.

On a theoretical level, the Chilean experience also showed that the economists of the left did not possess an analytical structure capable of integrating immediate, day-to-day phenomena with long-term models of structural change. Nor was there a conceptual framework for integrating economic and political variables at a level sufficiently specific to direct government functions. Both problems provide fertile terrain for the study of the processes of change.

Finally, the government confronted the political problem of the transformation of institutions. On the one hand, it had to achieve active, widespread popular mobilization. On the other, this mobilization had to be carefully directed. Success depended on the political maturity of the workers and on partisan organization, both of which had achieved a high degree of development in Chile. They were, however, insufficient to control opposing forces and reconcile them within the existing restrictions on power. Strengthening these capacities is the principal requirement for the success of other processes which evolve under similar historical conditions.

NOTES

1. The rate of growth in the expenditure of gross geographic product was 2.9 per cent in 1968, 3.3 per cent in 1969, and 3.1 per cent in 1970. *Odeplán.* See R. French Davis, *Políticas Económicas en Chile* (Santiago, 1973), p. 252, table 34. The inflation rate (CPI) rose from 18.1 per cent in 1967 to 26.6 per cent in 1968, 30.6 per cent in 1969, and 32.5 per cent in 1970 (annual averages). Instituto Nacional de Estadísticas.

2. The number of strikers rose from 225,480 in 1967 to 656,170 in 1970. Instituto Nacional de Estadísticas, *Síntesis Estadística,* various issues.

3. The unemployment in Greater Santiago in December, 1970, reached 8.3 per cent, the highest level in the period from 1965 to 1970. Instituto de Economía y Planificación, Universidad de Chile.

4. The readjustment was supposed to be equivalent to the rise in prices for 1970, which was 34.9 per cent. For the poorest strata, the readjustment was supposed to be greater. The index of wages and salaries elaborated by the Instituto Nacional de Estadísticas showed an increase of over 50.0 per cent for 1971. See *La Economía Chilena en 1971,* Instituto de Economía, Universidad de Chile, Santiago, 1972, p. 260.

Problems of Collective Land Exploitation in Chilean Agriculture*

DAVID BAYTELMAN

> Agrarian Revolution turns into an empty phrase if its victory does not presuppose the conquest of power by the revolutionary masses. Without this last condition, it will not be an agrarian revolution, but a peasant revolt. [Lenin, Speech on the Agrarian Question, Stockholm, 1906]

LAND, POPULATION, AND LAND TENURE

Chile has 11 million hectares of cultivable land of varying quality.†
In addition there are 20 million hectares which can only be used for pastures and 21 million suited to forestry. There are about 22 million hectares which are not usable for agriculture, cattle, or forests. This adds up to 74 million hectares, the total surface of the country.

If we take into account only the 5 million hectares which can be classified as good land and apply Roger Revelle's coefficients,[1] Chile should be able to feed a population of about 100 million inhabitants. If one considers only the 1.3 million hectares actually irrigated, the quality of which is among the world's best, it should be able to feed about 25 million inhabitants, two and one half times the present population of the country. (See Table 1.)

In 1965 most of this land was occupied by the latifundia. If we use a realistic definition of the term and not that established in the Agrarian Reform Law,[2] this was particularly the case.

---

*The author dedicates this essay to Juan Bruna, popular poet and peasant leader of the valley of Choapa, "assassinated by the Chilean nazis, because he wrote poetry for his people."

†Trans. note: A hectare is 2.5 acres.

TABLE 1   *Soil Usability Based on Agricultural Capacity (Millions of Hectares)*

Category	Area	Per Cent
Cultivable (Arable)		
I	4,987	6.7
II	1,937	2.6
III and IV	4,155	5.6
Subtotal	11,079	14.9
Uncultivable (Nonarable)		
V	4,290	5.8
VI	15,519	20.9
VII	21,363	28.8
Subtotal	41,172	55.5
Not Suitable for Agriculture		
VIII	21,926	29.6
Total	74,177	100.0

Source: Ministry of Agriculture
Note: Roman numerals indicate levels of quality, with I being the highest.

In 1965 some 80,000 peasant families resided on latifundia as defined by the law. This included tenants (*inquilinos*) and supplementary laborers (*obligados*).[3] (See Table 2.)

TABLE 2   *Social Strata in the Countryside*

Category	No. Families
Minifundistas	185,000
Small owners	27,000
Medium owners	8,500
Latifundistas	8,000
Employees	11,000
Tenants	90,000
Subtenants	80,000
Total	409,500

Derived from the Agricultural Census of 1965.

The demographic distribution of the peasantry in Chile was the same as in every country where there are latifundia. Density on large properties was very low, while the vast majority of the peasant population were forced to live on minifundia. These tiny operations provided the reserve labor force for the large and medium properties. They contributed to maintaining rural salaries at a disgracefully low level and offered a temporary labor force for periods of planting and harvest. In 1965 the 80,000 families which resided on latifundia constituted slightly more than 20 per cent of the total number of peasant families. The largest sector was that of the *minifundistas*—about 185,000 families, or 44 per cent of the total.

NEW FORMS OF LAND OWNERSHIP

The Policy of the Christian Democrats

From the above, it is obvious that rural Chile presented a number of difficult problems. For some political actors, however, the dilemma did not seem too serious. Their goal was to increase the area in small properties at the expense of the latifundia, while ensuring the survival of a large sector of medium-sized properties of sufficient size to develop highly efficient agriculture. The solution was relatively simple. Sooner or later—in three to five years according to the law—expropriated land would be subdivided into so-called economically viable units and distributed among those peasants who had previously lived on the property and shown sufficient entrepreneurial ability to take charge of the land.[4] The rest of the peasants—those without land—were excluded by definition. Similarly, all hope of benefit from agrarian reform was denied to the *minifundistas*, whose precarious situation obviously derived from the latifundia and whose poverty was as great as and perhaps greater than that of the rest of the peasantry.

It goes without saying that to expand the social stratum of small owners would tend to increase significantly the political base of whatever movement promoted such expansion. If that expansion were accompanied by an increasing flow of credit and financing toward existing small owners, there would be no political power capable of challenging the rural domination of those who proposed this line of action. This must have been the tactical thinking of the Christian Democrats as during the Frei administration they became active in the countryside. In their Program for Government they proposed to create a hundred thousand new landowners. They also proposed to expand the activities of the Institute of Agrarian Development (INDAP), an agency designed principally to provide credit to small owners.

The internal contradictions which later appeared in the Christian Democratic policy permitted them to expropriate land for only some 25,000 families. And they were not able to convert these into private owners, in part because not all peasants wished to own land individually and in part because the cost of subdividing the land was high. On the other hand, the large landowners' near monopoly of credit made it difficult to finance activities geared to the minifundia and small properties. As a result, exemplary initiatives such as that of Marchigüe, in the province of Colchagua, became relatively insignificant actions given the magnitude of the national problem.[5]

All of the above tended to lead the peasantry away from the Christian Democrats. It contributed to a massive rise in their "consciousness" of the need for a more rapid and profound agrarian reform, and it contributed significantly to Allende's triumph in 1970.

The Policy of the Unidad Popular

The *Unidad Popular* viewed the problem in a considerably different manner. From the first it was fully aware that expropriation was not an end in itself. The low productivity and underutilization of land characteristic of the latifundia would, if remedied, permit the extension of the benefits of land reform to all the peasantry, at least in the long run. Table 3 shows the extent to which the "Usable Agricultural Area" was exploited by each stratum of agriculture in 1965. The situation did not vary significantly during the rest of the decade. It is worth noting that, among the minifundia, proportionately seven times more land was cultivated than by the latifundia, and among small and medium holdings, 3.5 times more. The remaining soils were used for pastures or left fallow, even when they were irrigated. Since the latifundia encompassed 78 per cent of the irrigated land and 65 per cent of the cultivable area in the country, this acute underutilization of land had fundamental importance.[6] It meant that not only was there a wide margin for increasing productivity of land already under cultivation but also that sufficient good land was available to greatly increase the area being cultivated.

TABLE 3 *Use of Land According to Land Tenure Pattern (Thousands of Hectares 1965)*

	Latifundia	Per Cent	Medium Properties	Per Cent	Small Properties	Per Cent	Minifundio	Per Cent
Annual Crops	258.7	2.4	494.8	12.7	257.0	17.1	325.0	43.31
Artificial Pastures	490.5	4.6	447.0	11.4	70.2	4.7	23.0	3.07
Fruit and Grapes	29.1	0.3	79.0	2.0	46.4	3.1	39.7	5.29
Total Cultivated	778.3	7.3	1,020.8	26.1	373.6	25.0	387.7	51.67
Natural Pastures	7,762.4	72.5	1,670.3	42.8	556.5	37.2	161.8	21.56
Fallow Land	580.5	5.4	740.1	18.9	389.8	26.0	160.0	21.32
Uncultivated Potentially Productive Land	1,581.21	14.8	474.2	12.2	177.6	11.8	40.9	5.45
Total Usable Agricultural Area	10,702.41	100.0	3,905.4	100.0	1,497.5	100.0	750.4	100.0

Source: René Billaz. From 1965 census data.

By July 30, 1972, the *Popular Unidad* government had expropriated 58 per cent of the irrigated area and 52 per cent of the cultivable area without irrigation in properties larger than 40 "basic irrigated hectares." This was equivalent to 43 per cent of the irrigated and 24 per cent of the dry-farmed surface in the country. Approximately 75,000 peasant families had received land. This, however, was only the beginning of the process for the *Unidad Popular*. The agrarian reform would not be complete until the land was used more intensively. This was to be promoted through state investment, thus permitting absorption of the rest of the peasantry into the productive process.

Expropriated properties generally formed single productive units with centralized infrastructures—alone sufficiently powerful reason to maintain their unity. Chile already had an example of the excessive cost of subdivision in the *Colonia John Kennedy,* previously the *Hacienda Hospital,* to the south of Santiago. The farm had been expropriated from its owners, the *Beneficiencia Pública,* and then subdivided into small parcels under the agrarian reform law of Alessandri. As a result, the central infrastructure— the stables, barns, silos, and the like—was made obsolete. It became necessary to erect miles of fences. Houses, as well as barns and other buildings, were built for each of the beneficiaries. The irrigation system had to be redesigned, with a net loss in available water. In sum, if this experience had been extended to the rest of the country, it would have rapidly led to economic collapse, for it would have been materially impossible to finish the entire task. Thus, in spite of the Christian Democrats' declared policy of developing individually owned property in the reformed sector, they did not do so. The economic constraints were simply too great.

As a result, the simple financial interests of the *Unidad Popular* were sufficient reason to maintain the unity of the latifundia. It was similarly in the government's interest to improve the use of existing installations in order to increase the production of all peasants to whom land had been given.

The *Unidad Popular* had announced long before assuming power that it would favor the collective exploitation of land. Its intention was seconded by the peasant leaders of syndical organizations sympathetic to the government and by a fraction of those who followed the Christian Democrats. Peasants who had become disillusioned with the Christian Democratic experience because they had failed to benefit from the agrarian reform accepted the land as it was given to them. Their greatest desire, the dream which their own experience made seem a concrete possibility, was to escape from the tutelage of their *patrón*. They still had had no contact with the deformations which developed within the *asentamiento* system. To a great extent these had contributed to disillusionment with collective exploitation of land, discouraging the peasants who had placed their hopes in the *asentamiento*. Of course, the objective conditions of rural Chile, within which life on the *asentamiento* evolved, accentuated the deformations intrinsic to the *asentamiento* concept. All these problems contributed to the formation of a new kind of peasant, who, in the absence of other alternatives, defended his privileges against those who were still without land.[7]

Deformations of the Asentamiento

The agrarian reform law defined the *asentamiento* as a transitional form of organization. In fact, however, under the Christian Democratic administration its duration had become indefinite. The *asentamiento*'s formation, organization, control, and management had been products of paternalism, and it created two basic impediments to the development of collective enterprise. First, the *asentamiento* was prohibited from incorporating more peasants than had lived on the farm at the time of expropriation, even when there was growing demand for labor. On the contrary, the opposite idea, that the land was not sufficient for all the peasants, was officially propagated on the majority of farms expropriated during the Frei administration. The conclusion was that a number of peasants would have to be evicted once the transitional period had passed. These would receive compensation as established by the law. If more labor were needed, it would be obtained from salaried workers. Moreover, on many *asentamientos* the peasants preferred to continue extensive methods of cultivation, in order to avoid contracting workers who might later dispute what the peasants considered their exclusive right to the land.

The second great defect of the *asentamiento* was its system of remunerations. This consisted of anticipatory payments to the peasants by the Agrarian Reform Corporation (CORA). These were made on the basis of the farm's future earnings, to be calculated at the end of the agricultural year. The absence of an adequate accounting system and the resulting lack of realistic balances of credits and debts converted anticipatory payments into virtual salaries. The fact that salaries were identical for every peasant in the reformed sector had a serious impact on the productivity of labor and tended to disillusion the best workers.

Considering the high cost of subdividing the large farms, avoidance of such division was the best alternative for any government. However, the *Unidad Popular* considered that the advantages of maintaining large agricultural units were even more important. Intrinsic to large farms were economies of scale that would facilitate introducing the advanced technologies necessary to resolve the chronic Chilean food deficit in the shortest possible time—a deficit which was aggravated by the immense jump in demand following 1971.[8] In addition, large farms would facilitate educating the peasantry, thanks to the free time which collective farming would permit. An educated peasant would be able to manage the new technology. Learning such skills in a relatively brief period of time would not be possible for the small owner, whose job is one of the harshest and most absorbing known to man.

The Choice of a New Form of Collective Organization

It was necessary for the government to define the kind of collective organization it would seek to create in the countryside. The law permitted formation of Production Cooperatives, in which each peasant would receive a title of cooperative domain as well as a small plot of individual property. However, these could only be formed after a transition period of three to five years. It was also possible to form *Centros de Producción* (CEPROs), or state *haciendas*, if the peasants so desired. CEPROs could be formed without first passing through a transition period, and a number were organized in different parts of the country, particularly among the immense latifundia of Magallanes.

The positions taken during the debate within the *Unidad Popular* were not many, but they were distributed across a wide spectrum. On one extreme was a faction which favored the formation of CEPROs. On the other were those who, while admitting the obvious advantages of collective exploitation, felt it necessary that each step taken by the peasantry be based on the peasants' own experience, their free will, and their complete participation in all decisions concerning the form agricultural organization would take. Consequently, it was also necessary to respect their desire for individual property, though this might seem mistaken. Only in this manner could the government guarantee massive peasant support.

If we take into account the objective conditions in which the

Chilean revolutionary process was evolving, perhaps the debate lasted longer than it should have. More expropriations were taking place every day. Millions of hectares were passing into the hands of the peasants. Yet the agrarian sector of the *Unidad Popular* still had nothing to propose to the new landowners on the question of organization. The debate continued. The enemies of the *Unidad Popular*, both within and outside of Chile, effectively took advantage of this period to sow doubt and suspicion within a significant sector of the peasantry.

The easiest solution would have been to reach some agreement with the peasants on the already existing *asentamientos*, correcting the deformations there. In addition, some system could have been instituted whereby debts to the state could be paid in produce. This would have avoided a national conflict—provoked by the right—over what to call the transitional form of collective organization. It would also have avoided the subsequent confusion among the peasantry. However, the right wing of the Christian Democrats, which controlled the board of the National Confederation of *Asentamientos*, was so virulently opposed that, after the initial break in conversations, it was impossible to reopen negotiations in the short run. As a result, the *Unidad Popular* chose to move toward a new form of organization in the reformed sector.

The CERAs

Agreement was finally reached on the creation of what were called Agrarian Reform Centers (*Centros de Reforma Agraria*, CERAs), transitional organizations as provided for in the law whose internal constitution and bylaws would be formulated by the council of the Agrarian Reform Corporation (CORA).

The CERAs represented true progress, but only on paper. In spite of some errors and idealistic mistakes which slipped into their constitution, they were a model for flexible action in the countryside and were much more democratic than the *asentamientos*. For example, new peasant members could join the CERAs under equal conditions with the old, but only when more intensive use of the land justified a larger labor force. In practice, however, the CERAs' formation was tainted by the same paternalism as that of the *asentamientos*. There was no wide debate among the peasantry before the statute was approved by the CORA council. To paternalism was added the old vice of anticipatory payments.

The *Unidad Popular* did not have sufficient time to discuss an alternative to them, and their negative impact was transferred to the CERAs. Moreover, there were many who were tenaciously opposed to such economic incentives, arguing that they would develop "petit bourgeois tendencies" in the peasantry. At the moment of decision, there was no alternative. A new debate would have been interminable.

The CERAs were not accepted by the peasantry. Enemy propaganda and our own errors destroyed any chance for their success. In spite of all the efforts of political parties, allied peasant organizations, and agricultural technocrats, no more than one hundred CERAs were organized. Yet almost 4,000 farms were expropriated. On the majority of the rest, another kind of transitional organization, known as the Peasant Committee, was formed to direct production. Thanks to the opposition's propaganda, the peasants were convinced that the CERAs were state *haciendas,* in which they would be subject to arbitrary rule by impersonal *patrones.* What is curious is that each time the regulations governing the CERAs were described, without mentioning the name, these were approved unanimously. But when the name of the organization was mentioned, peasant opposition would resurface. Doubt had been sown and was bearing fruit.

The exploitation which the peasant has suffered for centuries and the continuous bitter lessons of experience, as well as the ignorance to which he has long been condemned by the latifundia, cause him to reject anything new about which he feels the least shadow of doubt. He prefers to keep what he has and what he knows, even if that is insufficient to meet his needs. This is not simply a Chilean trait; peasants everywhere in the world react similarly.

On August 13, 1972, Luis Corvalán, secretary-general of the Chilean Communist party, in a speech before the party's Central Committee dedicated entirely to the agrarian problem, said:

> We can draw some conclusions from evidence collected in the countryside itself. Neither the *asentamientos* established by the Christian Democrats nor the CERAs created by the present government satisfy the peasants completely. Nor do they constitute, as they now stand, the most appropriate forms of transitional organization for the reformed sector. Lately a new form of transitional organization, the Peasant Committee, has emerged as a way to begin the educational process and avoid the conflict over whether to create CERAs or *asentamientos.* It seems to us fundamental and urgent to review all these organizational forms, ever bearing in mind the opinion and interest of

the peasants. Only in this way can we count on their support for our efforts in the great tasks we face in the countryside. This does not mean that we favor accepting any idea or interest that emerges in the peasantry, and less so since the enemy is active in the countryside. Our obligation is to help the peasants clarify their own problems and to elevate their level of political consciousness. It does mean, we repeat, listening at every moment to their opinions and searching with them for the most appropriate solutions—solutions which are also in the interest of the country. For example, the peasants do not accept that their surplus production go to a common fund. Nor do they accept that grazing fees are set arbitrarily without considering the real situation of individual farms in the reformed sector. We believe the peasants are right. It would be lamentable to impose upon them rules which are contrary to their interests and to those of the nation. The contribution that the peasants must make to the country today is fundamentally to increase production and reimburse the credits and investments they have received. Tomorrow, with a more developed agriculture, there may be other forms of contributions.

THE POLITICAL BATTLE AND THE FORMS OF COLLECTIVE PROPERTY

The year 1971 was a year of action and intense political effort to ascertain what was needed for Chile to move forward. It was natural, therefore, that the *Unidad Popular* should debate the problems it needed to confront in agriculture. That debate occurred, however, in the midst of an implacable political battle in which the majority of communications media were controlled by the opposition, particularly in the agricultural provinces. Moreover, agriculture was only a part—perhaps the least important—of the entire economy. This, of course, did not prevent the *Unidad Popular* government from trying to benefit the lowest-income groups.

Both internationally and nationally, it was the large companies in the copper-mining sector that took priority. Then came the great industrial and distributive monopolies and banking. As a result, during the first stage a great portion of the coalition parties' attention was concentrated in these areas. The agrarian sector was left almost completely in the hands of specialized commissions, high government bureaucrats, and peasant organizations affiliated with the *Unidad Popular*.

During the first two years of the government great advances were achieved, and these were hailed by all the parties in the *Unidad Popular*. This was particularly so at the full meetings of the Central Committees of the Socialist and Communist parties, held in August, 1972. For the first time in the history of either party, the meetings were dedicated exclusively to the agrarian sector. As Luis Corvalán said in the first part of his report:

> The government of the *Unidad Popular* has not exactly moved at a snail's pace [literally: the speed of a tired ox]. We have realized Chonchol's maxim, which was adopted by the Christian Democrats during their administration but which they could not put into practice. I refer to that which says that agrarian reform should be a rapid, massive, and drastic process of redistribution of land and water. With this government a great advance has been achieved, a truly historical change in the pattern of land tenure. The latifundium, the principal obstacle to the expansion of agriculture and to the dignity of the peasant, has been basically eliminated. This is one of the great conquests of the Chilean Revolution.

Later, however, Corvalán noted the reasons that led his party to dedicate a Central Committee meeting to the agricultural problem:

> The reformed sector is the fundamental base for organizing the new agriculture to meet the tasks of production. Since this is so, what should be done? There is no alternative but to move forward. And in this respect, we firmly submit that the principal error lies not with the peasants, but with us, for having considered the agrarian reform as a task only for peasants and for agricultural institutions. It is not. It is a national task, for the entire country, for all the people and above all for the working class of the countryside and the city. I can tell you that the principal goal the Communist party pursues at this meeting of the Central Committee is to produce an about-face in this sense; that is, to get into our heads and our hearts the revolutionary content and the decisive character of the battle for production in the countryside, and the idea that, to guarantee an advance toward socialism, we must weld ever more tightly the workers-peasants alliance. And this we must do not with words and good intentions, but with concrete deeds.

The Attacks of the Opposition: The Right and the Christian Democrats

Virulent attacks against the agrarian policy of the *Unidad Popular* came from both the right and the extreme left—an absolutely normal phenomenon in a process of change as profound as that pursued in Chile. The right spread suspicion and, at times, terror. It called collective exploitation a new form of slavery in which the state would be the *patrón*. In essence, the tactic consisted of the same propaganda which the right had used against the Christian Democratic administration and its agrarian reform. The activities of the right might easily have been neutralized if those concerned with agriculture in both the Christian Democratic party and the *Unidad Popular* had acted together from the first to implement a program capable of quickly achieving the goals of the agrarian reform law. To this end the *Unidad Popular,* early in its administration, approached the Christian Democratic peasant organizations, both in the reformed sector and in the peasant labor unions. However, even before the end of 1971, the first attacks of the right wing of the Christian Democratic party had begun to appear in the opposition-controlled press. Initially, these sought to portray the popular government as simply another demagogic political group, one that had promised to carry forward a rapid and profound agrarian reform but in practice had done nothing. Its promises had been merely empty words. The peasantry was betrayed, for in the first two months of the government "not one single square meter of land had been expropriated."[9] Events quickly neutralized this line of attack, for only a few days after the statement was made, the administration initiated the process of taking legal possession of nearly one hundred latifundia, according to a plan developed by the previous government. These would be given to the peasants. One week later, on December 31, 1970, the *Unidad Popular* began its swift agrarian reform with the expropriation by the CORA council of one of the largest latifundia in the world, a farm of more than 600,000 hectares owned by the *Sociedad Ganadera de Tierra del Fuego.*

This was sufficient to make the right change its tactics. It began to make the same criticisms of the *Unidad Popular* that it had used against the Christian Democrats during their administration. These consisted basically of attacks on collective forms of exploitation in the reform sector and were focused particularly on the new structures. These were the most important points, but the right also sought to identify expropriation with plunder. It tried to instill fear in small owners by claiming that the *Unidad Popular*'s final objective, far from supporting them, was "sooner or later" to expropriate their tiny plots of land. Similar attacks rapidly followed from most Christian Democratic peasant leaders. This contrasted notably with the position of the great majority of Christian Democratic professionals and bureaucrats, particularly those in the CORA, who firmly believed that the best way to continue the effort begun by their own government was to help the people's government achieve its own goals in completing the process of expropriation and improving the organization of the reformed sector.

The Struggle for the Political Support of the Peasantry

Confronted with the *Unidad Popular*'s drive to change the entire structure of society—particularly in agriculture—each political actor naturally sought every possible way to challenge the government for control of the peasantry.

Through their peasant leaders—particularly those at the head of the National Confederation of *Asentamientos*—the Christian Democrats very early adopted a belligerent attitude. Their attacks grew even stronger during the hard-fought municipal election campaign of April, 1971. This seems to have been the major cause of the breakdown of the negotiations begun in 1970; that is, talks were halted so that each side could challenge the other for the vote of the peasantry.[10]

It was understandably important to the Christian Democrats to maintain at least the number, if not the proportion, of their peasant following. In 1967 a Law of Peasant Syndicalization had been promulgated. From then until 1970—that is, during the last three years of the Christian Democratic government—the *Unidad Popular*-affiliated federation, *Ranquil*, had grown by 300 per cent, although it still controlled only a minority of the peasants. *Triunfo Campesino*, affiliated with the Christian Democrats, had split and grown by only 140 per cent. If one further considers that an important portion of the *Confederación Libertad* sympathized with the coalition, then it is reasonable to assume that the *Unidad Popular* had the support of about 70 per cent of the organized peasantry. (See Table 4.)

The unfortunate assassination of Pérez Zujovic, only two months after the April elections and when the wounds of the campaign had not yet healed, eliminated any hope of reopening negotiations. An understanding was no longer even remotely possible. Thus the assassination paved the way for national political collaboration between the National party and the Christian Democrats.

The Tactics of the Cold War

The nature of the attack on collective forms of organization was not new, original, or particularly Chilean. It continued the long campaign against such organization begun after the Russian revolution and intensified during the Cold War which followed the Second World War. It coincided with the awakening of the peasantry throughout the countries of the Third World.

TABLE 4 *Peasant Syndical Confederations*

	Membership in 1967	Per Cent of Total	Membership in 1970	Per Cent of Total	Per Cent Growth since 67	Membership in 1972	Per Cent of Total	Per Cent Growth since 70	Per Cent Growth since 67
Ranquil Unidad Obrero Campesina	10,961	20.6	43,867	31.3	300	105,990	47.8	142	867
Triunfo Campesino	26,827	50.4	64,003	45.6	39	44,901	20.3	-30	67
Provincias Agrarias Unidas	—	—	1,097	0.8	—	1,219	0.5	11	—
Sargento Candelaria	—	—	2,194	1.6	—	2,241	1.0	2	—
Libertad	15,411	30.0	29,132	20.8	89	34,715	15.7	19	125
Total	53,199	100.0	140,293	100.0	164	221,618	100.0	58	317

Note: one confederation (*Unidad Obrero Campesina* / *Triunfo Campesino*) shows 1972 membership of 32,552 (14.7 per cent of total).

Source: Ministry of Labor, Syndical Department.

The strategy consisted simply of a campaign of terror directed at the peasantry in underdeveloped and dependent countries. It sought through constant repetition to convince them that collective forms of exploitation of the land are a synonym for communism, loss of liberty, state control of property, and insecurity. The technique was to introduce the idea that at any moment the peasants could be expelled by the *"patrón* state," denied their rights, and condemned to starvation.[11]

It cannot be denied, of course, that the detractors of collective organization sowed in fertile soil. To the natural tendency toward anarchy present in some sectors during periods of rapid and profound change was added a peasantry which had only recently been introduced to organization and the fight for economic demands. The Chilean peasantry had only begun its massive growth in political consciousness. It was no more than ten years, and perhaps less, since Chile had witnessed the beginnings of mass peasant organization. This was true even though the political parties of the left, throughout almost the entire century, had made intense, difficult, and frequently futile attempts to unite the peasants, particularly among leaders from agrarian communities in the provinces to the north of Santiago. The peasants' struggle had been initiated with their first, stumbling steps in the fight for higher wages. When they realized that unity would permit victory and their first hopes were converted into reality, they added to their battle the dream of owning land. But it was impossible to ask that their imagination move beyond frontiers and encompass the experiences of their brothers in other countries as well. Even to think in terms of provinces often meant to overcome the solitude, isolation, and the ignorance of generations. The exploitation that they had suffered in the past naturally made them suspicious of all new forms of organization. While this did not mean that they rejected all new forms out of hand, it did mean that experience had taught them to demand, tacitly, a demonstration that the efficacy of a proposal was superior to that which life had already shown them. The Chilean peasantry asked nothing more nor anything less than peasants elsewhere in the world.

The attacks of the right were well aimed. A high proportion of the population of the underdeveloped world lives in the countryside. This has made the peasant a principal political target of the Cold War, though that war has gradually waned over the last thirty years. Because of the special circumstances in which peasants live, they are extraordinarily vulnerable to propaganda, particularly that which centers on policies and events which may change their traditional pattern of existence. Well-directed propaganda can induce peasant suspicion of revolutionary and even reformist governments. Thus it can help the right to maintain and reinforce, even if only temporarily, the various forms of neocolonialism and the *status quo* within the underdeveloped world. In other words, in the struggle of the underdeveloped nations to advance toward higher forms and structures, a large proportion of the population—the peasantry—is susceptible to being effectively neutralized.

In some ways Chile does not typify the underdeveloped world. Slightly more than 70 per cent of its population is urban. Nevertheless, within the dynamic process evolving in Chile, agriculture became the Achilles' heel of the revolution.

The *Unidad Popular* had to increase its political support from the peasant masses. It did so and gained significant ground. It was the peasantry and women, traditionally the least politically mature sectors, who transferred significant portions of their vote from the National party and Christian Democracy to the left in the congressional election of March, 1973.[12] Nevertheless, though the peasant vote for the *Unidad Popular* was without precedent in Chilean electoral history, the majority of peasants continued to vote either for the right or, more likely, for the Christian Democrats.

The Political Battle and Production

It was important for the *Unidad Popular* to finish the process of expropriations and organization of the new agriculture rapidly in order to concentrate its efforts on achieving higher rates of growth in production. Production was a principal target of the attacks of the right, which argued that output was decreasing because of the agrarian reform and collective forms of exploitation.[13] Perhaps someday there will be statistical data sufficient to compare the levels of production before and after expropriation of the latifundia. The general impression is that previous production levels, which were very low, were at least maintained. It is clear, however, that throughout the country in 1972–1973, the production of some crops, particularly wheat, did decline. The natural reaction of the opposition was to blame this drop entirely on the process of agrarian reform.

A number of obstacles specific to the Chilean case prevented the peasants from maintaining normal productive operations. Most important were the following:

1. There was a sizeable reduction of capital investment in the expropriated farms. This resulted from a provision in the agrarian

reform law permitting expropriation of the land and infrastructure but not of the operating capital—machines, animals, etc. This factor produced its greatest impact during the 1971–1972 agricultural year. Later a special fund was set up that allowed purchase in cash or on terms negotiated with the owner of any item not included in the law.

2. There were a number of farms—though not many—that, as a result of legal impediments erected by their old owners, were not expropriated. Despite specific prohibitions by the Judiciary, many of these were able to begin production with credits they received in the name of other farms whose legal status had been resolved.

3. During the period after possession was taken, agricultural credit from the *Banco del Estado* often functioned irregularly, largely because no adequate method of operation had been devised. This was particularly true during 1972–1973.

4. The withdrawal of the *patrón* left a vacuum in entrepreneurial capacity. With respect to this problem, at the meetings of the Communist party dedicated to the agricultural problem, Corvalán said the following.

> The latifundio, with all its vices, and in spite of the injustice and criminality which accompanied it, was still a centralized and hierarchical institution. It represented a certain entrepreneurial capacity, with its owner, administrator, foreman, and accountants, who managed production on the farm and controlled banking and marketing operations. When a farm was expropriated and possession was taken, that organization disappeared almost entirely. In part this resulted from the understandable tendency of the peasants to refuse to continue to work with these administrators—even the most modest employees—because they were, or appeared to have been, tied to the peasants' exploiter.

5. Problems were also created by the Irrigators' Association (*Associaciones de Canalistas*). More than 50 per cent of all irrigated land, with its respective water rights, passed to the reformed sector. Nevertheless, the old Irrigators' Associations continued to function as previously constituted, and the directors continued to be the representatives of the latifundia. During 1971 and 1972 dues were paid punctually by the new owners, yet in the 1972–1973 agricultural year very few of the principal canals were cleaned. As a result, at the end of spring and through the summer there was a serious water shortage, particularly in the north central region. This caused major crop losses. The problem was most serious in the central and lower reaches of the Aconcagua Valley.

6. Many medium and small owners, and even *minifundistas,* feared that their ownership of the land was insecure, and, indeed, some of their farms were occupied, although very few. Traditionally, a substantial part of the country's agricultural production was concentrated among these strata. (See Table 5.) Their fears seem to have begun to diminish by the end of 1972 when the process of expropriations was for a time declared to be complete.

7. The price of all meats rose sharply on the black market. As a result, farmers, including those in the reformed sector, dedicated ever greater quantities of cereals, especially wheat, to animal feed. Cereals were used in particular to feed fowl. The price of wheat destined to this end often rose to a level many times higher than that paid for the production of flour, a price that was officially set. At the same time, the ever greater gap between the price of meat and the price obtained for milk in the dairy centrals led to an appreciable drop in the production of milk for human consumption. Milk was increasingly used for raising calves, since, per liter, the return in meat was far higher.

8. As the inflationary process gained momentum, farmers and intermediaries tended increasingly to acquire stocks of nonperishable or slightly perishable agricultural products while awaiting better prices. As long as pastures were sufficient, whether these were owned or rented, cattle simply were not sent to the market.

9. The rate of illegal slaughter of beef cattle was very high, in spite of its absolute prohibition by the people's government. On the property of the *Ganadera de Tierra del Fuego,* Magallanes Province, immense numbers of sheep were slaughtered in the period prior to expropriation.

10. About 200,000 beef cattle were smuggled illegally into Argentina, where the beef could be sold at prices far higher than the official prices obtained in Chile.

11. During the wheat harvest numerous fields were burned maliciously.

12. In 1972 torrential rains resulted in slightly more than twice the normal amount of rainfall. This caused a drop of almost 50 per cent in the area sown with winter cereals, which, because of the duration and amount of precipitation, could not be replanted immediately.[14]

13. The final cause for the drop in production was the transportation strike of October, 1972. To a great extent the losses from the torrential rains of late fall and winter could have been replaced by spring planting. Spring crops are grown primarily on irrigated land, and the indications were that the supply of water

TABLE 5 *Value of Agricultural Production by Category of Land Tenure (Millions of Escudos 1965)*

	Latifundio	Per Cent	Medium Property	Per Cent	Small Property	Per Cent	Mini-fundio	Per Cent	Total	Per Cent
Wheat	72.30	28	114.64	44	37.70	15	33.57	13	258.21	100
Corn	11.24	20	26.67	47	6.84	12	11.75	21	56.50	100
Potatoes	9.66	10	32.70	35	18.21	20	32.33	35	92.90	100
Beans	6.05	14	12.36	28	5.10	12	19.70	46	43.21	100
Sunflowers	3.51	19	10.05	55	2.65	14	2.19	12	18.40	100
Rape	7.42	24	15.84	52	5.65	19	1.49	5	30.40	100
Sugar beets	5.64	16	21.73	63	4.84	14	2.39	7	34.60	100
Vegetables	10.98	5	32.98	16	40.25	20	119.13	59	203.34	100
Fruit	16.54	14	38.06	31	31.49	26	35.51	29	121.60	100
Wine and grapes	26.69	16	90.57	54	35.69	21	13.84	9	166.79	100
Others	19.75	16	48.43	39	23.22	19	32.90	26	124.30	100
Total Crops	189.78	16	444.03	39	211.64	18	304.80	27	1,150.25	100
Beef	75.61	28	111.48	41	39.57	15	42.28	16	268.94	100
Sheep	60.73	67	15.48	17	7.06	8	6.79	8	90.06	100
Pig	6.35	8	18.54	22	18.04	22	39.50	48	82.43	100
Fowl	2.84	4	35.21	47	14.02	19	22.53	30	74.60	100
Milk	42.45	26	83.76	51	19.50	12	18.19	11	163.90	100
Wool	51.49	81	7.59	12	2.55	4	2.17	3	63.80	100
Eggs	5.59	4	82.66	61	27.14	20	21.01	15	136.40	100
Total Livestock and Livestock Products	245.06	28	354.72	40	127.88	15	152.47	17	880.13	100
Total Production	434.84	21	798.75	39	339.52	17	457.27	23	2,030.38	100

Source: René Billaz. From 1965 census data.

would be excellent, basically because of the accumulation of snow in the Andes. However, the truckers' strike prevented the arrival of inputs for planting, precisely at the moment when they were necessary. When the strike was finally settled, it was just too late. Thus the strike had disastrous effects.

The thirteen factors all influenced, in different degrees, the drop in production during the agricultural year 1972–1973. Of the thirteen, it would seem that the two with the greatest impact were the heavy rains and the October transportation strike.

As Table 6 shows, there were similar declines in the production of annual crops during 1968–1969 and 1972–1973, even though the two were caused by diametrically opposed climatic phenomena.[15] The first was the result of an extreme drought; the second of torrential rains, in addition to the transportation strike during the critical period of spring planting. In the second period, the total area planted was fundamentally affected by the losses suffered in winter wheat, which is entirely dry-farmed. The October strike then prevented the sowing of spring wheat in irrigated areas. In contrast, since wheat is a product which can reach harvest with much less water than the majority of cereals, the earlier drought had acted as an incentive to planting wheat in irrigated areas, where it was substituted for other crops. The same occurred in dry-farmed areas.

For almost all other crops the acreage in production was higher in 1972–1973 than during the period of drought.[16] It is important to exclude from the analysis both potatoes and peas, since, as can be seen in Table 6, both tend to have a production cycle in which the area sown fluctuates greatly, a well-known phenomenon in Chile. The fluctuations result from variations in supply and their consequent impact on market prices. The variations in rape and sunflowers stem from the varying demand of the single purchasing firm—a subsidiary of a multinational corporation. The two crops are used for the production of vegetable oil, and demand for them depends on their availability in the international market. Finally, sugar beets seem to be the only product to have been greatly affected by the distortions produced in the Chilean economy in general and, specifically, by the process of agrarian reform.[17]

Among the remaining crops, it is interesting to call attention to the area sown with corn during 1972–1973, a record in Chilean agricultural history. This too has an explanation. Corn in Chile has become a crop which is cultivated with a high level of technology. It is produced particularly by medium owners. Planting occurs almost entirely in the month of September. Since it was practically

TABLE 6 *Areas Cultivated for Principal Crops*
(in Thousands of Hectares and as Percentage of 1964–1965)

	1964–65		1965–66		1966–67		1967–68	
	Hectare	Index	Hectare	Index	Hectare	Index	Hectare	Index
Wheat	727	100	780	107	718	99	700	96
Oats	70	100	66	94	68	97	108	154
Barley	38	100	39	103	50	132	72	189
Corn	88	100	81	92	92	104	88	100
Rice	27	100	37	137	33	122	32	118
Beans	58	100	65	112	68	117	53	91
Chick Peas	8	100	9	112	9	112	16	200
Lentils	24	100	11	46	7	29	7	29
Sugar Beets	18	100	21	117	29	161	30	167
Potatoes	91	100	76	83	77	85	80	88
Rape	58	100	62	107	45	78	37	64
Sunflowers	32	100	42	131	22	67	29	91
Peas	7	100	11	157	8	114	9	124
Rye	7	100	7	100	6	86	7	100
Total	1,253	100	1,307	104	1,232	98	1,268	102

(Continued on next page)

TABLE 6 (*Continued*)

	1968–69		1969–70		1970–71		1971–72	
	Hectare	Index	Hectare	Index	Hectare	Index	Hectare	Index
Wheat	743	102	740	102	727	100	712	98
Oats	81	116	73	104	75	107	84	120
Barley	44	116	47	124	52	137	67	176
Corn	58	66	74	84	77	87	84	95
Rice	16	59	25	92	27	100	26	96
Beans	47	81	57	98	69	119	79	136
Chick Peas	9	112	11	137	16	200	20	250
Lentils	14	58	17	71	18	75	18	75
Sugar Beets	27	150	40	222	35	194	31	172
Potatoes	76	83	72	79	80	88	79	88
Rape	48	83	54	93	49	84	56	96
Sunflowers	25	78	20	62	15	47	15	47
Peas	11	157	7	100	10	143	13	186
Rye	8	114	8	114	9	129	9	129
Total	1,207	96	1,245	100	1,259	100	1,293	103

(*Continued on next page*)

TABLE 6 (Continued)

	1972–73		1973–74		Average 1965–70		Average 1971–74	
	Hectare	Index	Hectare	Index	Hectare	Index	Hectare	Index
Wheat	534	73	700	96	735	101	668	92
Oats	70	100	95	136	78	111	81	116
Barley	67	176	71	186	48	126	64	168
Corn	108	123	75	85	80	91	86	98
Rice	18	67	14	52	28	104	21	78
Beans	65	112	73	126	58	100	72	124
Chick Peas	19	237	11	137	10	125	17	212
Lentils	18	75	24	100	13	54	20	83
Sugar Beets	26	144	43	239	28	156	34	189
Potatoes	70	77	80	88	79	88	77	85
Rape	40	69	50	86	51	88	49	84
Sunflowers	13	41	13	41	28	87	14	44
Peas	10	143	18	257	7	100	13	186
Rye	9	129	10	143	7	100	9	114
Total	1,067	85	1,277	102	1,250	100	1,225	98

It is important to note, in addition to the commentaries included in the text, the average areas sown in 1965–1970 and 1971–1974, one affected by drought and the other by the rains and transportation strike. One can see that the differences in area sown are minimal. The area sown to wheat decreases during the *Unidad Popular* period, but the majority of crops for consumption show spectacular increases. Even in the case of sugar beets, in which there were a number of problems, the area sown increased by 21 per cent.

the only crop that was not affected by the transportation strike, which occurred the following month, inputs for planting corn arrived on time. To this advantage was added the certainty of an abundant supply of water.

In 1969 no one claimed that the steep production drops were a result of the Christian Democratic agrarian reform, although at various moments there were those who tried. At that time, of course, the general economic situation did not have to contend with the strong pressures of rapidly rising demand. In 1972 this parallel phenomenon was caused by the unprecedented growth of real income enjoyed by the lowest-income sectors under the people's government.

Collective Exploitation of the Land: A Socialist Monopoly?

As we have said, the myth that collective forms of exploitation are found exclusively in socialist countries is a result of the Cold War. On all continents, through all stages of history, and in every social system there have been collective forms of organizing the men who work on the land. The objective conditions of agriculture forced such organization upon society long before it occurred to anyone that socialism would appear in the world. Moreover, there are in the modern world a number of capitalist countries which have developed advanced forms of collective agriculture. Among these are Israel and Tanzania. Erich Jacoby describes the problem:[18]

> There is no doubt that collective farming as a tenure system should not be treated as a monopoly of the socialist countries; it is a rational means for increasing agricultural production and creating a less-depressed society in underdeveloped countries. Provided that there is no discrimination against collective farming, it can happily coexist with individual tenure types as is the case in Israel and Tanzania. . . . The time when individual tenure types could monopolize agriculture is at an end. The continued subdivision and fragmentation of holdings and the growing rate of landlessness is making millions of peasants increasingly aware of their state of isolation and frustration. Working their minute plots with outdated implements for returns hardly exceeding mere subsistence, they are becoming increasingly less susceptible to the argument that collective farming will reduce them to a state of still greater frustration and exploitation.

Of course, one can increase the productivity of labor and land on small individual plots, but the effort and investment necessary to do so on a massive scale seem infinitely greater than that necessary to obtain more far-reaching objectives on large collective properties. To improve productivity on small plots, each item of investment, from the construction of fences for subdividing the land to the multitude of technicians and experts giving aid to each individual owner, must be multiplied many times over.

It follows clearly, therefore, that the arguments and attacks on collective forms of land exploitation, as an ideological weapon of the Cold War, have no logical foundation. Collective forms exist, subsist, and prosper as much in the capitalist world as in the socialist. In the former, of course, they take the form of a capitalist enterprise, since their character is determined by the relations of exchange. It is curious that, while "ideological axioms" argue the need for small individual units in agriculture, immense national and even multinational enterprises are defended for industry and the rest of the economy. And it is more curious that, while it has been argued that in the underdeveloped world small individual property is necessary to safeguard the security and integrity of the family and the liberty of the peasant, millions of impoverished small owners in the developed countries have been forced to abandon their lands and join the proletariat in order to survive.

The hidden objective behind these arguments has been to permit, in an era of technological revolution, the maintenance of properties of the most efficient size for adopting new technology and competing in the market. What alternative is there for the small farmers of the underdeveloped world, who are every day poorer? In truth, the alternatives seem few, for in the underdeveloped nations industrial expansion is insufficient to absorb those who find themselves forced to migrate to the city.

The Activities of the Ultra-Left

At the other extreme, the ultra-left attacked the *Unidad Popular* from every possible angle, particularly in the countryside. It maintained that government measures were "reformist and not revolutionary," that the *Unidad Popular* was simply one more populist government, and that its professed goal of leading the country to socialism was mere rhetoric which did not correspond to practice. In agriculture, the ultra-left began by emphasizing the slow pace of expropriations. For example, in October, 1971, the leadership of the MIR accused the government of having limited the process of expropriation in Cautín Province to "only 1,300 latifundia," while there existed 3,800. By July, 1972, when the government had completed expropriation of almost 4,000 large farms, the ultra-left had changed its line. It began to argue that the *Unidad Popular*'s strategy for the development of agriculture essentially sought to reinforce the capitalist mode of production.

Early in 1972 the ultra-left finally realized that the government was effectively liquidating the latifundia, as these were defined by law, and that this would be a reality within a period of a few months. They responded by demanding that the government expropriate without compensation, that it not allow owners to keep a "reserve," even where they met legal standards, and that expropriations include everything—that is, operating capital as well as land and infrastructure.

There was also a minority opinion within the *Unidad Popular* which sincerely maintained that it was necessary to form the maximum number of state *haciendas* within the reformed sector and that, to do so, the maximum number of properties should be brought together into single units. Small owners and *minifundistas* would not have access to this collectivized sector, since they pertained to the "little bourgeoisie," and the government should not run the risk of "contaminating the socialist sector with capitalist tendencies." This argument was accompanied by the thesis that economic incentives would destroy the principle of equality and deform the objective of a socialist agriculture, which was to form a "new man." Therefore, such incentives should not be applied under any conditions. There were even some who proposed the total elimination of money in the reformed sector.

The most damaging activity of the ultra-left was its organization of indiscriminate occupation of farm properties, many of which, according to the law, would not have been subject to expropriation. The best justification the extremists offered was that their action was taken "to maintain the revolutionary combativeness of the peasantry."[19] These occupations produced an extremely negative impact on small owners and *minifundistas,* pushing them in great numbers to seek political refuge under the wing of the right. This was so even though the total number of farms occupied was small.[20]

It is only natural that, in any country, during any process of rapid and profound structural change, small minorities develop viewpoints which place them on the extreme left or right. To understand this, however, is not to underestimate the impact of their actions on the evolution of events. On the left, their arguments tend to influence the least mature political sectors, and on the right, the opportunists. They view every process with marvelous simplicity. They are convinced that a revolution in their minds will be transferred automatically to the masses. Terms like "the balance of power" or "the action and experience of the masses" have no meaning for them. History begins when they first became conscious of the injustices of this world—injustices which "it is necessary to eliminate immediately." Many act consistently with their principles and are ready to give their lives for what they believe. But in most cases their acts of terrorism and indiscriminate activities only serve to push the same impoverished people they seek to defend— social groups whose interests should be those of workers and peasants—toward the most reactionary sectors.

Collective Exploitation and Socialism

Although collective forms of land exploitation cannot be considered a socialist monopoly, it is impossible to consider the development of socialism without coming, sooner or later, to collective exploitation of the land. Expressed in very schematic form, socialism implies the parallel development of all sectors of the economy, from an initial point which is usually underdevelopment. The goal of the socialist state, within its planned economy, is to raise the income of the people as quickly as possible, a process obviously limited by the availability of the consumer goods necessary to improve their standard of living. For this process to be rapid, it is necessary to organize large enterprises in all sectors of the economy, and the only way to organize large enterprises in agriculture, without causing unemployment, is through collective exploitation of the land. Just as it makes no sense to organize artisans into a great industrial enterprise if they have to continue working with their traditional tools—unless it is to profit from economies of scale in marketing—similarly it is senseless to organize large agricultural enterprises unless they are accompanied by adequate investment in productive capital. Only thus can they take advantage of economies of scale. Large socialist farms can evolve most successfully when their growth is coordinated with the ability of industry, perhaps with international help, to provide them with the means of production and inputs necessary for the development of large-scale, modern agriculture. Nor will the collective enterprise be successful if the participation of the peasantry results from pressure and not of their own free will. This can be achieved only through example and demonstration.

The Free Will of the Peasantry

All this has been argued from the earliest theoretical elaborations of Marx and Engels. Yet to maintain that forming state farms or collective units of any kind is sufficient to form a socialist agriculture is to deny a basic principle of economics. In the capitalist state, collective units behave as capitalist institutions, as in Israel and Tanzania. Similarly, it is not enough to amalgamate large farms into larger enterprises to accelerate the incorporation of peasants into the "socialist" sector. Soil cannot be eaten, and the demand for labor does not depend only on farm size. It also depends on the level and manner of capital investment in both the socialist and capitalist systems. To see the expansion of socialism as dependent on the development of collective rural enterprises only repeats the idealistic mistakes of the nineteenth-century utopian socialists who wanted to arrive at socialism through the gradual evolution of collective forms of production. On the contrary, only when socialism has been solidly established can the next step forward be taken—that is, the organization of collective land exploitation. And only then can there be the confidence and approval of the participants in this higher stage of organization of mankind.

To cross this threshold is to increase the productivity of labor to the limits permitted by technological advance and the consciousness, culture, and organization of the peasantry. Moreover, it is increased at the lowest cost. In this manner, the progressive reproduction and accumulation of capital are guaranteed. On small properties, in contrast, not only are surpluses minimal, if they exist at all, but also, because of the continuous subdivision of the land, future generations are irremediably condemned to misery. Shortly before his death in 1884, Friedrich Engels described the problem in his essay, "The Agrarian Problem in France and Germany":

> The main point is and will be to make the peasants understand that we can save, preserve their homes and fields for them only by transforming them into cooperative property operated cooperatively. It is precisely the individual farming conditioned by individual ownership that drives the peasants to their doom. If they insist on individual operation they will inevitably be driven from house and home and their antiquated mode of production superseded by capitalist large-scale production. That is how the matter stands. Now we come along and offer the peasants the opportunity of introducing large-scale production themselves, not for the benefit of the capitalists but for their own, common benefit. Should it really be impossible to make the peasants understand that this is in their own interest, that it

is the sole means of their salvation? . . . We of course are decidedly on the side of the small peasant; we shall do everything at all permissible to make his lot more bearable, to facilitate his transition to the cooperative should he decide to do so, and even to make it possible for him to remain on his small holding for a protracted length of time to think the matter over should he still be unable to bring himself to this decision.

In his writings and speeches Lenin constantly repeated that the only way for the peasants to escape from backwardness was by organizing collectively. This was to be done, however, with the absolute agreement of the peasants and with their conviction that they were adopting a higher form of organization. Perhaps where Lenin best expresses these ideas is in his speech of November, 1918, to the delegates of the Committee of Poor Peasants from the Moscow region:

> The workers have helped and are helping the poor peasants in their struggle against the Kulaks. In the civil war which has broken out in the countryside, the workers are on the side of the poor peasants as they were when they passed the Socialist Revolutionary law on the socialization of the land. We Bolsheviks were opposed to the law on the socialization of the land. Yet we signed it because we did not wish to go counter to the will of the majority of the peasantry. The will of the majority is binding on us always, and to oppose the will of the majority is to betray the Revolution. We did not desire to force on the peasants the idea that the equal division of the land was useless, an idea which was alien to them. We considered it better if the toiling peasants themselves, as a result of their own experience and their own suffering, came to realize that equal division was nonsense. Only then would we be able to ask them what, then, was the way of escape from the ruin and Kulak domination that followed from the division of the land.

In the Eighth Congress of the Soviet Communist Party, in 1919, he added the following:

> You cannot create anything here by coercion. Coercion applied to the middle peasants would cause untold harm. Here coercion would ruin the whole cause. Prolonged educational work is required. We have to give the peasant, who not only in our country but all over the world is a practical man and a realist, concrete examples to prove that the *"communia"* is the best possible thing. . . . On this question we must say that we do encourage communes, but they must be so organized as to gain the confidence of the peasants. And until then we are pupils of the peasants and not their teachers. Individual property does not in any way harm socialism if power is held by a government

of workers and peasants, if control by workers has been introduced, if banks have been nationalized, if a supreme economic council of workers and peasants has been established to regulate the nation's economic life.

Finally, in his essay on cooperatives, written in 1923, he made the following points:

> It is one thing to draw up fantastic plans for building Socialism by means of all sorts of workers' associations; but it is quite another thing to learn to build it practically, in such a way that every small peasant may take part in the work of construction. . . . Strictly speaking there is "only" one more thing we have to do, and that is to make our people so "civilized" as to understand all the advantages of their all taking part in the work of the cooperatives, and to organize this participation. "Only" this. We now need no other cunning devices to enable us to pass to Socialism. But to achieve this "only," a complete revolution is needed; the entire people must go through a whole period of cultural development. . . . But it will take a whole historical epoch. At best we can achieve this in one or two decades.

This is not the place to debate the form that collectivization of agriculture took in the Soviet Union. Agriculture was a problem that the USSR had to confront in its own way, taking into account its specific needs. We can state, however, that the special historical circumstances faced by the USSR explain the process which evolved there during the 1930s. Moreover, that process seems to have been the only road open in that context. The objective was to produce an accumulation in agriculture sufficiently great to finance growth throughout the economy. Thus agriculture would form the base allowing the first socialist country in the world to escape from underdevelopment. All the evidence seems to indicate that the policy of using agriculture as the source of capital affected Soviet agriculture until the end of the fifties, when, for the first time, financial resources were transferred from other sectors of the economy to agriculture.

In Bulgaria, the harmonious development of collective agriculture, accompanied by massive, voluntary peasant participation, was aided by the work of Dimitrov and Kolarov, who studied the alternative paths to collectivization. The Bulgarian experience was repeated in the German Democratic Republic and in North Vietnam, where the road taken followed the conditions enunciated by Engels and Lenin so long ago. It goes without saying that the initiation of collectivization, when accompanied by the participation of the peasantry, has required a minimum of a decade to prepare.

Although collectivization is the only way to increase the productivity of labor and land to the limits permitted by technological advance, it is equally true that, if peasants are to accept collective enterprise as superior, they must have access to sufficient farm equipment to use the land efficiently. However, in Chile as elsewhere there must first be organization. Even without sufficient equipment, the Chilean peasants on expropriated farms were accustomed to communal labor, whether under the orders of their foremen and *patrones* or on their individual plots. In the majority of cases they accepted collective labor with enthusiasm, until the absence of material incentives caused the hardest workers to refuse to participate in collective efforts.[21] The existing small owners had, of course, a different attitude toward collective organization, although there were some who favored it.

The Need for an Understanding with the Christian Democratic Party

In spite of the position of the ultra-left in the countryside, there is no doubt that the critical point of the transition to socialism was not in agriculture, and much less in its collectivization. During the three years of the *Unidad Popular* government, the truly decisive factors were the struggle for power—the power to control the economy—and the struggle to exercise this control and leadership freely through the government.[22] For this reason it was necessary to expand the *Unidad Popular*'s base of support to include additional workers, peasants, and others. Unavoidably this implied the need for some combined action with the Christian Democrats that would permit incorporating PDC worker and peasant support into the popular government's struggle on their behalf. The power of the Christian Democratic labor and peasant bases could have counterbalanced those factions in the party that did not want the process to advance.

In addition to the numerous minor errors that were impossible to avoid, we made one fundamental mistake in our agricultural policy. This was to fail to have the flexibility, as a government, to permit the peasants a wide variety of forms of association and of exploitation of the expropriated land. We could have shown such flexibility without ceasing to encourage collective exploitation. The only condition we should have established was prohibition of the useless subdivision of farms, even if the peasants had decided to exploit the land individually. Thus the peasants' own experience, the example of the CERAs, the *asentamientos* and cooperatives which they organized voluntarily, and the continual contributions of capital from the state would have helped to create conditions for the voluntary incorporation of all the peasantry. Of course, we understand that the right of choice would have allowed the peasant to withdraw from the collective unit, under certain conditions, if after a given time he was dissatisfied. Flexibility would also have allowed us to extend the reach of our policies to *minifundistas*, small farmers, the Mapuche Indians, temporary workers, and the communal villagers of the regions north of Santiago.

Flexibility in the agrarian policy would have facilitated common actions with the Christian Democrats, so necessary to strengthen the government for the unequal fight against the internal and external enemies of the Chilean revolution. Postponing final decision on the definitive character of Chilean agriculture would have allowed the peasants in each region to participate effectively in the debate over that choice. Finally, it would have permitted us to carry forward more easily our plans for increasing production.

Capital Investment and Collective Exploitation

Much happened in Chilean agriculture during the three years of the *Unidad Popular*, even though when speaking of agriculture one should talk in terms of decades. Many of the proposals described in this essay were being debated, and application of a few had already begun, shortly before the military *coup*. These included policies relating to credit and to payment in produce at the end of the agricultural year, as well as those relating to the introduction of material incentives for labor. Hard experience is the best university. The agrarian reform was only the launching pad for the development of Chilean agriculture. It was constructed, moreover, on the remains of the most serious obstacle to that development—the latifundia. There was insufficient time—in agricultural terms—to show how decisive this could be for the growth of Chile and the dignity of the Chilean peasant.

The revolution, which had only just begun in Chile, sought to develop all sectors of the economy simultaneously. A solid base for coordinated action in the industries of the Social Property Sector and in large mining already existed and would have created a tremendous boom in the demand for labor. Indeed, the phenomenon was already visible. In contrast to the peoples of other unde veloped countries, a relatively small proportion of Chileans live in the rural sector. Hence the new perspectives opening in industry would have accentuated peasant migration to the city, especially by the *minifundistas* and the temporary workers. For this reason it was necessary to promote large collective enterprises within the limits noted above. It was also necessary to mechanize and industrialize the countryside, in order to promote more intensive use of the soil. The great reserve of land for Chile was the expropriated latifundia (see Table 3), while on the minifundia and small properties was the great reserve of labor.[23]

THE PROCESS PRODUCED BY THE MILITARY DICTATORSHIP

Today the peasantry of my country is living through a bitter and silent experience, imposed by the force of arms. From the limited data we have, we can state without fear of error that, in terms of basic irrigated land, more than half the area expropriated has been returned to the old owners, though this represents only 25 per cent of the physical total. In other words, the best land in the country has been returned. Under the popular government of Dr. Salvador Allende the peasants had begun to live with new hope. Now, under the military dictatorship, a multitude of reserves have been granted or extended, leaving the peasants with narrow, tiny strips of land. Credit has been suspended to all those with unpaid debts, meaning that the measure has been applied to all that remains of the reformed sector. To subsist, the peasants have been forced to sell a large part of their machinery and animals. The interest rate of state credit has increased to 200 per cent. Usurious credit has appeared. The prices of inputs, fertilizers, pesticides, and the like have increased to such an extent—30,000 per cent through March, 1975, for certain fertilizers—that those without state credit—that is to say, most of agriculture—have ceased to use them. Production of fowl and pigs has been completely ruined. Official statistics speak of the slaughter of 670,000 head of beef cattle during 1974; that would represent 25 per cent of the total in the country. This would mean the liquidation of the cattle industry in four years. Yet meat is nearly all either consumed by the highest-income sectors or exported. The agricultural worker, with his unions suppressed, has seen his earning power reduced to a sixth or seventh of what it was under the popular government. Where once his salary sufficed to purchase forty-four kilos of wheat per day, in December, 1974, it would buy only six kilos of wheat. That is to say, the impact on the salaried peasant of Chile has been even greater than that on the population in general, whose income has been reduced by 35 to 40 per cent from what it was under the popular government.

NOTES

1. Roger Revelle, "Food and Population," *Scientific American* 231, 3 (September 1974), pp. 161–70.

2. The Agrarian Reform Law 16640 defined expropriable latifundia as all those properties whose area surpassed 80 hectares of "basic irrigated land" (land of the best quality). There were about 5,000 such *haciendas*. From the beginning of debate on the law, the *Unidad Popular* considered that latifundia should include all properties with more than 40 hectares of "basic irrigated land," a total of about 8,000 properties.

3. *Obligados* were supplementary laborers demanded by the landowner and provided by the tenant. The *obligados* were either members of the tenant's family or came from the available labor force on nearby minifundia.

4. Whether a unit is "economical" depends on a number of factors: the prices of inputs and products, investments, productive efficiency, distance from the market, etc. It is a dimension that can vary widely over time.

5. In Marchigüe the Christian Democrats implemented a development plan for the centralized, industrialized production of poultry. The project was administered by a Small Owners Local Cooperative. It created very favorable conditions for improving the standard of living and the entrepreneurial skills of the small owners.

6. Latifundia used about 35 per cent of their cultivable surface compared with almost 70 per cent on small properties. It is unbelievable that so much validity was given to the propaganda of the Chilean right, which maintained that, as a result of the agrarian reform, the peasants were exploiting only half of the cultivable land. As can be concluded from the data, if half of all cultivable land had been put to use, it would have been a success without precedent in the annals of agrarian reform in world history.

7. At the end of 1970 I attended an assembly of the Federation of *Asentamientos* in the province of Osorno. At that meeting various leaders declared that no more money should be spent on expropriations and that everything should now be invested in the already existing *asentamientos*.

8. When I speak of resolving Chile's chronic food deficit in the shortest possible time, I do not mean increasing domestic production by enough to meet the increase in demand during the three years of the *Unidad Popular* government. This would not have been possible even in the total

period of six years, had the government been permitted to rule until 1976. In Chile between 1970 and 1971, slightly more than five million inhabitants, or one million families, increased their real income by about 40 per cent. About one half of that income was spent on foodstuffs. In terms of aggregate supply (production plus imports), it was necessary to increase the supply of wheat by 9 per cent, rice by 13 per cent, meat by 15 per cent, chickens by 17 per cent, cooking oil by 12 per cent, etc. Real income continued to rise in 1972. There is no agricultural system anywhere capable of attaining such annual growth in the production of most crops, even under the optimum conditions where development results from a serious, planned process of investment—hardly the case in Chile. Nevertheless, there were important leaders in the *Unidad Popular* who placed a kind of mystic faith in Chilean agriculture's ability to produce a miracle in a short period of time.

9. *Las Ultimas Noticias*, December 16, 1970.

10. Initial contacts with the leadership of the National Confederation of *Asentamientos* were friendly, and it seemed that no problems would impede close collaboration. Later, during the first skirmishes of the campaign for the municipal elections of April, 1971, those leaders began to demonstrate unprecedented aggressiveness. They seemed determined to provoke the collapse of the talks, whatever the pretext. As meeting followed meeting, there appeared no way to convince them that the land would not be "nationalized" (*estatizada*). Finally, they organized a limited strike on the *asentamientos*. Its purpose, according to the peasant leaders, was "to prevent the nationalization of the land and to keep the peasants from becoming dependents of the *patrón* state." The Federation of Workers of the CORA negotiated in our name with provincial leaders, invited to Santiago expressly for that purpose, and was able to reach a solution. The Federation was controlled by the Christian Democrats.

11. During the last week of December, 1970, upon taking possession of *El Tránsito* farm near Santiago, Jacques Chonchol and I found it difficult to convince the peasant women that their houses would not be confiscated by the Allende government, as they had been told by the *patrón* of the farm, and that the agrarian reform would, on the contrary, be the beginning of their liberation.

12. When one compares the presidential elections of 1970 with the congressional elections of 1973, one observes that the vote for the *Unidad Popular* in the agricultural provinces grew by 31.9 per cent, and in the agricultural provinces with light industry by 28.6 per cent. In contrast, in Valparaíso and Santiago it grew by only 19.3 per cent, in the mining provinces by 15.1 per cent, and in the mining and manufacturing provinces by 10.6 per cent. In the national voting totals, the *Unidad Popular* increased its share by 20.4 per cent with respect to 1970. In the national elections of the CUT, the coalition obtained its highest proportion of the vote in the agricultural provinces.

13. The propaganda of the right called Chonchol "Attila," after the proverb which says, "Where Attila walks, the grass ceases to grow."

14. In the April 3, 1974, issue of the English magazine *New Scientist*, there is an article entitled "Climatic Clues from Tree Rings" by Professor

Valmore LaMarche, an investigator in dendrology at the University of Arizona. In it the author presents a diagram (see Table 6) recording rainfall over a period of 972 years—from 1010 to 1960—for the region of Santiago. The diagram presents average rainfalls for one-hundred-year spans, derived from the examination of the rings on a type of Chilean cyprus which grows in the region. In that period the highest index of rainfall occurred in 1600 and totaled about 530 mm. The total rainfall in the Santiago region in 1972 was about 650 mm.—i.e., 120 mm. greater than the heaviest annual rainfall in a period of 950 years.

15. One could argue that we are blaming nature for phenomena that had other causes. What is certain is that in 1972 a number of countries in the world suffered severe consequences from adverse climatic conditions. These produced a worldwide crisis in the supply of cereals. In general, the countries which are most sensitive to the fickle nature of climate are those in which there is a low level of capital investment in agriculture. This is the case with dry farming in Chile. The most heavily capitalized sector of Chilean agriculture is that with irrigation, where farmers can plant and cultivate almost without worry about climatic variations. However, that sector suffered the effects of the strike at planting time.

16. The area cultivated with wheat dropped in 1972–1973 by 25 per cent with respect to the previous year. In contrast, in 1968–1969, the production of rice dropped in comparison with the year before by 50 per cent, of corn by 34 per cent, and of barley by 38 per cent.

17. Because the National Sugar Industry was the only purchaser of sugar beets, these could not be found on the black market. Moreover, the cultivation of sugar beets requires a great input of labor. Consequently the problem became a question of relative advantage, and the tendency in all of Chilean agriculture, including the reformed sector, was to shift land and labor to other crops. For its part, instead of mechanizing operations, the National Sugar Industry continued to consider the problem as if there were considerable unemployment in the sugar beet sector, a fact which no longer corresponded to reality.

18. Erich H. and Charlotte F. Jacoby, *Man and Land: The Essential Revolution* (New York: A. A. Knopf, 1971).

19. A concrete example can serve in part to illustrate the problem. In January or February, 1972, while I was in the province of Cautín, I received directions from President Allende to go immediately to the province of Colchagua, where events of grave importance were occurring. I boarded a plane and a few hours later was in the city of San Fernando, the provincial capital. At the airport I was informed of what was happening. A few months earlier, peasants on a farm of vineyards had occupied the "reserve" which had been left to the old *patrón*. Conversations between the CORA and the peasants had had no effect. The peasants insisted that they would remain on the reserve, and the *patrón* had appealed to the courts. Finally, the Supreme Court had ordered the police (*"cuerpo de carabineros"*) to evict the peasants from the reserve, by force if necessary. The deadline for eviction would arrive at 7 p.m. on the following day. Meanwhile, confronted with the unexpected arrival of the police, more than three hundred peasants from the area had gathered and erected barri-

cades on the reserve. They obviously intended to resist, though the fight would be unequal, and all feared that lives would be lost unnecessarily.

That afternoon I met with the leaders of the peasants. I explained that their general argument about the reserve was just and that the President and the political parties in the *Unidad Popular* agreed with them. Nevertheless, a reserve was authorized by the agrarian reform law, and we still did not have a majority in Congress with which to change that law. We had already done as much as possible by not giving reserves of eighty basic irrigated hectares. Indeed, their own *patrón* had received a far smaller plot of twenty-eight basic irrigated hectares. It would be of no use to provoke a confrontation with the police, and their lives were worth too much to be wasted. I promised, in addition, that if they gave me authorization, I would speak with the ex-*patrón* to see if I could convince him to agree to a reduction in the area of his reserve. I told them that sooner or later the representatives of the latifundia and foreign interests would probably seek a confrontation to overthrow the people's government. The situation was so tense that this local event could contribute to precipitating events of national impact. I argued that it was already a victory to have obtained practically the entire farm. If they had shown the patience to wait for more than four hundred years, they should save their lives until it was truly necessary to offer them for their cause.

The leadership agreed, and we set out for the farm, dodging barricades and road blocks. The assembly lasted until 2 a.m., gathered on a bridge under the light of a marvelous moon. I repeated the same arguments, but the reply of the assembly was absolutely negative, and I listened with consternation as the leadership, after having voted that they agreed with me, now pledged loyalty to the position of the assembly. I pleaded with the peasants once more, this time addressing the women, who had come with their children. I begged them to prevent this useless sacrifice of lives, which would contribute nothing to the revolution. I was only repeating the express request of the President of the Republic, of a government which had shown that it was on the side of the workers and peasants and in which they had already declared their confidence. At that moment some ten young men, seemingly university students, stepped from the shadows and, shouting "reformist," threatened to beat me. The leadership formed a circle around me and the other peasants defended me. The president of the peasant organization then addressed the students, firmly but calmly, informing them that they were not peasants and that, if they touched a hair on my head, the peasants would kill them.

The next events passed quickly. We agreed that the leadership would meet once more to reconsider the situation. The following day I would receive a reply. As I left, I added that if their reply were negative, although I disagreed, I would remain on the farm to share their fate. The following morning I received word that the peasants had expelled the students from the district and that I was authorized to negotiate with the ex-*patrón*. The conversations lasted several hours. He agreed to reduce his reserve to approximately twenty-two hectares and to permit the current year's harvest on the reserve to be kept entirely by the peasants. At six in the afternoon, in the office of a notary in San Fernando, the agreement was signed by the peasants, the ex-*patrón*, and myself, while a police colonel stood anxiously in the doorway.

20. To convey how easy it was to turn landless peasants against small owners and *minifundistas,* it is worth relating an event that occurred in 1971. I was attending, with students from the Agronomy School of the University of Chile, the official ceremony of the takeover of a farm in the province of Nuble. After the peasants had officially received possession, they asked us to help resolve a problem they had with a "rich man" whose lands bordered their farm. We went and discovered, to our consternation, that the "rich man" was in reality an extremely poor *minifundista* whose only wealth, in addition to his heavily eroded and impoverished bit of earth, was a team of oxen, a horse, and his guitar. Of course, this conception of the world resulted from the isolation and ignorance in which the peasants had been maintained by the latifundia.

21. In January, 1973, a pilot project applying certain rules to labor was begun at a CERA in the province of Coquimbo. The CERA produced primarily grapes. A study of the project was to serve as a thesis for one of my students. The rules were approved in a day-long assembly that all the peasants attended. The results were surprising. For most products the productivity of labor was doubled and in some cases tripled. After the military *coup* the farm was returned to the old owners, the student was arrested, and the president of the CERA, along with other peasants, was executed by a firing squad, without any charges having been formulated.

22. We must not forget, though it almost goes without saying, that the process of change in agriculture was not isolated from other processes. It occurred in an environment in which the government's agricultural policies were opposed by Congress and the Judiciary, which systematically blocked budgets and laws advanced by the President and in which foreign intervention, besides cutting off external credit, led to the assassination of the Commander in Chief of the Army and to the transportation strike.

23. During the agricultural year 1971–1972, about ten thousand tractors were imported. This practically doubled the number of machines in the country. Unfortunately they arrived too late for the year's agricultural labors. There were powerful objections to their importation, among them the traditional argument that machines produce unemployment in the countryside. However, this was not applicable to the conditions evolving in Chile. On the contrary, the intensification of agricultural production through mechanization, fertilizers, agro-industry, and centralized national and regional marketing, in addition to the expansion of the area under cultivation, would have contributed rapidly to extending benefits of agrarian reform to the entire, relatively small, peasant population and to solving the deficit in foodstuffs.

The Social Property Sector: Its Political Impact

PIO GARCIA

INTRODUCTION

The alliance known as the *Unidad Popular* was formed in mid-1969 amidst intensifying contradictions throughout Chilean society. In particular, the battle for nationalization of copper had become a mass movement, rejecting the so-called "Chileanization" of the mines proposed by the reformist government then in power. This antecedent reveals the depth of the problems to which formation of the *Unidad Popular* responded and the profound political process that permitted its composition. Certainly the breadth of the coalition (which included the Communist, Radical, Social Democratic, and Socialist parties, the Movement of Popular United Action, and Independent Popular Action) evinced the growing integration of the left. It particularly reflected the unity between Socialists and Communists, which had existed since 1956, the growing strength of the United Workers Confederation (*Central Unica de Trabajadores,* CUT), and the Communist party's policy of seeking broad coalition. Above all, however, the *Unidad Popular* responded to the need for structure in a vast popular movement, waxing in response to the general crisis of the Chilean system and to the failure of the palliatives of the Christian Democratic government's "revolution in liberty." The Chilean masses, in constant ferment, demanded an effective revolutionary alternative.

For these objective reasons the *Unidad Popular* was able to incorporate dissident factions of the Christian Democrats, which only a few months before had been part of the party in power, and the Radical party, which had resumed its progressive stance. Only the exigencies of a difficult situation could lead to unity among

160

such widely differing parties, which had long been separated by disagreements and differing perspectives.

This explains why the first goal of the Coordinating Committee of the *Unidad Popular* was to elaborate the coalition's Basic Program. The final document began with the following description of national reality:

> Chile is in a state of profound crisis. This may be seen in our economic and social stagnation, in our general poverty and in the neglect suffered on all fronts by the workers, peasants and other exploited groups, as well as in the increasing difficulties facing clerical workers, professional people and the smaller businessmen, and in the limited opportunities existing for women and young people.
>
> What has failed in Chile is a system that does not correspond to the needs of our time. Chile is a capitalist country, dependent upon imperialism and dominated by sectors of the bourgeoisie allied to foreign capital. These sectors are unable to solve the fundamental problems of the country, which are derived precisely from class privileges they will never surrender.
>
> Furthermore, as a result of world-wide capitalist development, the contribution made by the national monopoly bourgeoisie to imperialism grows progressively greater, while their dependent condition further emphasizes their role of junior partner to foreign capital.
>
> In Chile the "reformist" and "developmental" formulae supported by the Alliance for Progress and adopted by the Frei government have not caused any important changes.... This has shown once again that reformism is incapable of solving the problems of the people.
>
> The development of monopoly capitalism prevents the spread of democracy and encourages the use of violence against the people.
>
> The fighting spirit of the people rises as reforms collapse, in turn hardening the attitudes of the more reactionary sectors of the ruling class, which, in the last resort, have no other recourse but to violence.[1]

The specific proposals for construction of the social sector followed from this general analysis.

THE SOCIAL SECTOR: GENERAL BACKGROUND

Formulation of the Basic Program

During preparation of the basic program, "the Radical and Social Democratic Parties suggested formation of three sectors within the new economy of the country. . . ."² This version is consistent with the fact that perhaps the first mention of a "social sector" in the restructuring of the Chilean economy was made by economist Alberto Baltra in 1968. At that time Baltra was one of the chief spokesmen of the progressive wing of the Radical party. He argued that Chilean economic development required—together with private and mixed sectors—the strengthening of a social sector to reinvigorate the traditional state role of propelling economic growth.³

Nevertheless, the basic program's proposals for restructuring the economy and forming a social sector far surpassed the limits of a statist renovation of capitalist development. In effect, their substance was determined by the general definition of the character of the Chilean revolution and by the tasks thus suggested for the people's government. Debate during elaboration of the program revolved around this fundamental question, and at times the discussion became so heated as to threaten the sought-after consensus. The positions in this controversy generally reflected those of the parties of the working class, the Communists and Socialists, which together represented more than three quarters of the *Unidad Popular*'s voting strength.

The position of the Communist party corresponded to that of its own program, according to which "the Chilean revolution, in its essence and its objectives, is anti-imperialist, anti-monopolist and agrarian, and *looks forward to the construction of socialism.*"⁴ The Communist party held its XIV National Congress in November, 1969, at a time when discussion of the *Unidad Popular*'s program had already begun. The report of the secretary-general reiterated that "the popular power which we wish to generate and the revolution which we must make are, in their essence and their objectives, anti-imperialist and anti-oligarchic, and *look forward to the creation of socialism.* Thus, it may be said in passing, those often-heard arguments that the revolutionary process we must effect should be given an immediate socialist character seem to us not serious and lacking in scientific rigor. The road to socialism must first pass through anti-imperialist and anti-oligarchic stages." But, he added, "the step from the anti-imperialist and anti-oligarchic revolution to the socialist revolution can be very rapid and constitute a single, continuous process, as occurred for example in Cuba."⁵

In contrast, the Socialist party had gradually evolved a different position. In the political resolution of its XXI General Congress (1965), it was expressed in the following manner:

[The party] rectifies in its entirety the line of a Workers' Front, a policy based in theory and practice on the class struggle in backward countries, in which the bourgeoisie emerges linked to the creole oligarchies and to imperialism. As a result, it is the mission of the working class, united with the exploited masses, *to liberate the country from its backwardness and vassalage at the same time as it implants the socialist regime.*[6]

The Socialist party later described the debate in this way:

The difference between our position and that of the others was that we demanded that the initiation of socialism be a task for this government and not simply an historical perspective. . . . We argued the need for implementing a policy that would rapidly create, during the course of this administration, the conditions for changing the capitalist character of the existing system.[7]

These strategic and tactical discrepancies among the organizations in the *Unidad Popular,* and between the Communist and Socialist parties in particular, were resolved in an original compromise contained in the text of the basic program as approved unanimously on December 17, 1969. With respect to the character of the revolution and the consequent objectives of the people's government, the program concluded:

The only really popular alternative, in fact the basic task which the government of the people has before it, is to end the rule of the imperialists, of the monopolies, of the landed oligarchy, and *to begin the construction of Socialism in Chile.*[8]

This statement reflected a conviction that the system, with its dependent capitalist economy, was suffering from a general crisis. Its essential traits—structurally interconnected—had been uncovered in numerous scientific studies. Thus the anti-imperialist, anti-monopoly, and anti-oligarchic goals of the program formed an important part of an anti-capitalist policy and hence of the transition to socialism. The basic program proposed not reforms that would only modify the functioning of the system but rather a qualitative change in its character. It proposed not to resolve the problem within the system's limits but to replace that system. The task of *beginning the construction of socialism* belonged to the period referred to by the program—that is, to the six-year administration of the people's government.

The transition to socialism presupposed the *conquest of power,* and to this end the program stated:

In order to stimulate and direct the mobilization of the people of Chile for the conquest of power, we shall establish committees of the

Unidad Popular everywhere. They will be set up in every factory, farm, village, office and school. . . . *This new form of power,* which Chile so needs, *must begin to take shape now.* . . . The revolutionary changes that the country needs can be brought about only if the Chilean people take power into their own hands and wield it in a real and effective way. . . . The popular and revolutionary forces have not united to fight merely in order to substitute one president of the Republic for another, nor even to replace one party by others in government, but to bring about the basic transformation that the national situation demands. These changes will be effected by *transferring power from the old ruling groups to the workers, peasants and progressive elements of the middle class in the city and in the country.* . . . The problems of political structure that will concern the government are: to preserve and make more effective and far-reaching the democratic rights and the triumphs of the workers; to transform the existing institutions in order to establish a new state where power will truly belong to the workers and to the people.[9]

Thus the program's economic proposals assumed a revolutionary socialist character. They were designed to resolve what Lenin called "the fundamental problem of every revolution . . . the problem of State Power."[10]

This revolutionary character was emphasized in the part of the program dealing with "construction of the new economy." It began with the following statement: "The central objective of the policy of the *Unidad Popular* is to replace the present economic structure and end the power of monopoly capitalism, together with that of the landowner, in order to begin the construction of socialism."[11]

For these reasons the economic reforms proposed in the program had a revolutionary content, especially the formation of a social property sector. "The process of transforming the economy begins with a policy aimed at establishing a dominant public sector, composed of forms already owned by the state and also others that will be expropriated."[12]

In general terms, the economic program proposed the following:

a) establishment of a social sector through nationalization of basic resources, principally the copper, nitrate, iodine, iron, and coal mines; nationalization of the financial system, of the large distributive enterprises and monopolies, of strategic industrial monopolies, and, in general, of all activities directly affecting the social and economic development of the country;

b) maintenance of a private property sector, corresponding in general to artisanry and small and medium production, and of a mixed sector, in which state and private capital would be joined;

c) deepening and extension of the agrarian reform;

d) establishment of a *national* planning system;

e) redistribution of income, ultimately affecting the orientation of production, reactivation of the economy, employment, monetary stability, and sustained economic growth.[13]

The decisive step—that with which, according to the program, the transformation of the economy would begin—was the formation of the social sector. It was conceived basically as the sector to which, by virtue of its extent and significance, the general functioning of the economy would be subordinate. On this basis, economic planning would extend over the entire economy, including the sector of private property.

Preparations during the Presidential Campaign

The basic program's statements on the economy and the social sector were essentially political. Certainly they corresponded to scientific analyses of the country's economy—its development, present situation, and perspectives for the future—but they were directed fundamentally to a general definition of the historical revolutionary project. The essentially political treatment of national questions, directly linked to the conflicting positions of the various social sectors, was characteristic of the 1970 presidential campaign. On the left, the debate was conducted in nontraditional terms, calling for the "immediate" mobilization of popular power to nurture the revolutionary project. The *Unidad Popular* articulated its respective intentions in an appendix to the program, entitled "An Agreement on the Leadership and Style of the Campaign."

With regard to the preparation of plans and government policies, there was a significant departure from Salvador Allende's previous presidential campaigns. Particularly in 1964, the professionals and technocrats in the so-called Central Planning Office (OCEPLAN) contributed heavily to the elaboration of specific programs. These were published in two thick volumes. In 1970, in contrast, the emphasis was on the political battle, while references to the fundamental content of the program were limited. Indeed, it was hardly mentioned until, late in the campaign, the so-called First Forty Measures of the People's Government were tersely defined. In general, the essence of the campaign was activism—the continuous mobilization of the masses, land occupations, and strikes by workers and peasants.

On another level, it is worth noting that since 1964 there had been considerable progress in economic and social investigation, both by academic institutions and by the government, most of which reflected a Marxist theoretical orientation. More importantly, the left had gained considerable power, including institutional control, in some of the universities, and since 1967 it had promoted a vigorous university reform movement. Particularly interesting was the influence acquired by the left in the School of Economic Sciences of the University of Chile. In 1969 Pedro Vuskovic, then a high official in ECLA, was elected director of the Institute of Economics.

Following approval of the *Unidad Popular*'s basic program, a small group of investigators in the Institute of Economics began, on its own initiative, to examine the economic program in depth, particularly the proposals for a social sector. It profited from past studies and the enormous body of existing data on the national economy. The group gradually expanded to include investigators and students from other university departments and leftist professionals working in various government agencies. Its work led to a meeting in mid-1970 of professionals and technocrats, all partisans of the *Unidad Popular,* to discuss the left's specific economic and social plans for governing. This meeting, held at El Quisco, resulted in the formation of several permanent working commissions under the coordination of Vuskovic.

Throughout the campaign period, the political parties were notably absent from this preparatory labor. That is, from the beginning independent and party militants collaborated as equals and individuals. The meetings at El Quisco were inaugurated by Salvador Allende himself, and the parties, through the presence of their members, were kept informed of developments; but there was no regular mechanism for participation by the parties as such in the debates or general resolutions. The leaders of the Central Labor Confederation (themselves party activists) participated more directly in the early design of the industrial sector than did the political parties as such.

Between September 4 and November 4, following the election victory, the activities of these working commissions were considerably broadened and intensified. Vuskovic was officially named economic coordinator for the government, with the explicit responsibility of countering maneuvers by the right designed to produce financial chaos and panic. Even some high officials in the Frei administration were involved in these.[14] At this point the parties were given official representation on the central technical commission.

Around the time of the El Quisco meetings, a general definition of industrial and distributive enterprises to be included in the social sector was devised. There were four principal criteria for inclusion. One was ownership by certain clearly identified economic groups which exercised a virtual monopoly over the Chilean economy. Among these were the so-called Edwards and Matte "clans," the "piranas" and others.[15] Another criterion was the proportion of production and sales controlled by the principal enterprises in a given branch of industry. Third was the importance of particular enterprises in intersector transactions, and last was the size and degree of control of foreign capital. Using these criteria, a list of about 140 basic enterprises was amassed by the time the people's government assumed power. Other larger estimates undoubtedly existed, but there was a general consensus on these 140. Nevertheless, no official political pronouncement was made.

In addition, with the collaboration of prominent jurists, the commissions worked to develop legal procedures that, given the institutional constraints of Chilean democracy, would permit formation of the Social Property Sector. In similar fashion they outlined appropriate mechanisms for economic control. Specifically, they constructed plans for transforming the Corporation for the Development of Production (CORFO) into a kind of Industrial Ministry, based on the use of so-called Sector Committees to direct different industrial areas. Finally, in general accordance with the basic program,[16] the commission considered specific mechanisms to structure workers' participation in the administration of enterprises in the social sector and in general economic planning. Again, these plans were developed by technical commissions with no official political pronouncements.

Following the election, the commissions established, in accordance with their conception of structural change, general lines for conducting economic policy during the first phase of the people's government. The three principal objectives, discussed in an unpublished document, were to promote economic expansion and employment, reduce the rate of inflation, and initiate the redistribution of income to benefit the lowest-income sectors. These would satisfy the legitimate immediate interests of the masses and create the political conditions necessary for the government to fulfill its program. The association between both elements—the restructuring of the economy and expansion linked to redistribution—was later summarized by Pedro Vuskovic, Minister of Economics in the first cabinet of the people's government, as follows:

> The two policies are necessarily interdependent: they cannot be conceived in isolation, one from the other. It is not possible to undertake

profound substantive changes without expanding the government's base of political support. Therefore the problems of expansion and redistribution of income are crucial if we are to be able to carry out more profound transformations. And, vice versa, we could not follow a policy of expansion and redistribution without simultaneously undertaking structural modifications in depth, because such a policy could not be maintained.[17]

THE PEOPLE'S GOVERNMENT AND THE SOCIAL SECTOR

Basic Considerations

Once the people's government assumed power, it rapidly initiated the formation of the Social Property Sector. The first expropriation of an industrial firm, *Panos Bellavista Tome*, took place on December 1, 1970. That same month the government granted a monopoly on the importation of fuel oil and lubricants to the *Empresa Nacional de Petróleos*. It also acquired stock in the country's only steel mill, the privately owned *Compañía de Aceros del Pacífico*, thus reestablishing state ownership in an enterprise originally created by the state. The administration also intervened in the industrial enterprises of NIBSA, principal property of the North American consortium NIBCO, and Purina Foods, controlled by the North American Rockefeller group in combination with the Edwards "clan." A proposal for reforming the Constitution to permit nationalization of the copper industry was sent to Congress, and the coal mines were nationalized. Finally, a bill to nationalize banking was announced, simultaneously with the alternative of stock purchases.

Salvador Allende had declared on the night of his victory: "I want all to know without doubt . . . we will fulfill the historical commitment that we have undertaken, that of making the program of the *Unidad Popular* a reality."[18] From the start the intense activity of the people's government bespoke this commitment. In his first message to the National Congress, on May 21, 1971, President Allende said, "The working class knows that its battle is to socialize the principal means of production. There can be no socialism without a social property sector."[19]

In effect, formation of the social sector was vital to the revolutionary strategy of the *Unidad Popular*. Advances in its creation did not assume the prior existence of socialism nor even a period of transition to socialism.

In a strict sense, the transition to socialism corresponds to the period in which the dominant capitalist (or even precapitalist) modes of production are replaced by socialist modes. The very nature of this transition first requires the proletariat to gain control of state power. Social ownership of the fundamental means of production does not emerge spontaneously from the growing socialization of the productive forces in capitalism. It must be politically imposed, and only then can the government plan for the economy as a whole, no longer in the interest of capitalist profits but in the name of social benefit.

The uniqueness of the Chilean experience resides in the left's pursuit of power in a situation where it governed and yet was still constrained to act within a bourgeois legal and political superstructure. Chile is perhaps the most advanced historical example of an attempt by the left to gain power by using the most privileged bourgeois institution, the Executive, as a means for accumulating strength. This is why many have cited the Chilean case as an archetype of revolutionary strategy, designating it "the Chilean road."

Under these circumstances, the government's activities were defined in relation to this struggle to control state power. This was particularly true of all policies—not simply those designed to produce structural change. The character of economic policy was thus *eminently* political. More precisely, the unique situation resulting from the formation of the people's government was that fulfillment of its program would force it inexorably toward breaking the economic, political, and ideological system of domination. At the same time, accomplishing its policy objectives would strengthen the revolutionary forces and facilitate the formation of a real, alternative power, which in turn would permit confronting the system of domination from an objectively strengthened position.

In this respect, the formation of the social sector was the key to the entire program. Control of the government, given the powers inherent in the Executive and the presidential nature of the political system, would permit advances in the creation of social property, with a double political effect. On the one hand, it would dismantle the economic base of the dominant classes and imperialist interests in Chile, progressively eliminating capitalist ownership (or control) of the fundamental means of production. On the other hand, it would foster the material and objective conditions for strengthening the working class and its allies. Advances in the nationalization of strategic areas of the economy would aid in establishing workers' control and guarantee a dominant economic role to the social sector. Finally, it would contribute to establishing general principles of socialist leadership and, in the long run, to socialist planning.

Referring to this dual task, simultaneously destructive and constructive, President Allende commented, "Our first job is to take apart this restrictive structure, which only generates a deformed development. But it is necessary at the same time to build the new economy . . ."—and here he added a warning against the convulsion that might follow—"in such a way that one follows the other without a break in continuity, build it while conserving to a maximum the productive and technical capacity that we have obtained despite the vicissitudes of underdevelopment, and build it without crises artificially induced by those who will see their ancient privileges proscribed."[20]

Nevertheless, the reaction of those whose interests were affected would impose a different course upon events, culminating in the *coup d'état*. As was later revealed in detail, the government of President Allende faced a conspiracy of national reaction and North American imperialism even before it took office.

Because of its nature, the people's government not only had to strive to achieve its program but also had to do so immediately. Among the few observers who have commented on this situation is economist Oscar Lange, who writes:

> But the problem of transition from capitalism to socialism presents some special problems. Most of those problems refer to the economic measures made necessary by the political strategy of carrying through the transformation of the economic and social order. But there are also some problems which are of a purely economic character. . . . The socialist government must start its policy of transition immediately with the *socialization* of the industries and banks in question. . . . A program of comprehensive socialization can scarcely be achieved by gradual steps.
>
> To be successful, the socialist government must put itself at the head of a great mass movement against monopoly and restrictionism, against imperialism and the concentration of economic control by a few, against social and economic instability and insecurity. Only under the impetus of such a mass movement, embracing the majority of the population, will it be able to carry out speedily a bold program of socialization. In the absence of such a mass movement, there is little a socialist government in office can achieve. For, as we have seen, if socialization cannot be achieved by a great and bold stroke, the government has to give up its socialist aims altogether.
>
> For there exists only one economic policy which we can commend to a socialist government as likely to lead to success. This is a policy of revolutionary change.[21]

There certainly existed in Chile economic problems that limited any possibility of achieving initial, short-term economic goals. Cumulatively they made the need for structural change overwhelming. Among others, these problems included the diminution of foreign exchange reserves, the exhaustion of idle productive capacity, and the inflationary pressure that increased deficit public spending would provoke. To compensate, it would be necessary to appropriate the surplus enjoyed by monopoly capital. For the people's government therefore, rapid formation of the social sector was both a political and an economic imperative.

Our argument to this point—the decisive importance of the social sector and the necessity for its rapid formation—emphasizes the interrelation of politics and economics perceived by leadership of the revolutionary government. The original composition of the government, however, reveals the inconsistencies that would later arise. In effect, the principal responsibility for basic structural changes fell on the Ministers of Economics and Agriculture and on the Copper Corporation. The first Minister of Economics, Pedro Vuskovic, was an independent technocrat, as was Max Nolff, the first executive vice-president of the Copper Corporation. The first Minister of Agriculture, Jacques Chonchol, was an activist in the MAPU, a party with an incipient popular base. Gonzalo Martner, Directing Minister of the Office of National Planning (ODEPLAN), was also an independent technocrat.

In practice, the Ministry of Economics undertook to form the social sector in the areas of industry and distribution, as well as in banking and foreign trade. It was also responsible for general economic leadership. Following the precedent set during the campaign, Vuskovic acted in collaboration with a team of technocrats, the majority of whom were also independent. In any case, they had little weight or influence in their parties. Not until well into 1971 did the parties begin to designate political leaders to hold ministerial positions, a procedure that entailed more delay than efficiency. Although Vuskovic constantly reiterated that economic policy had a political character and needed to be developed by the masses themselves, under these circumstances the idea encountered structural obstacles. It demanded a direct effort by the bureaucrats and the minister himself to mobilize the necessary base.

The lack of coordination between the development of economic policy and the exercise of political leadership was equally exposed during the municipal elections of April, 1971. In spite of restrictions on the government's freedom of action, particularly in the formation of the social sector, the administration had achieved considerable success in diverse areas, particularly in satisfying the immediate economic interests of the masses. These successes were reflected in the elections, the first nationwide balloting since the presidential vote the previous year. Support for the parties of the left increased significantly, and if we consider all left-wing groups, they received an absolute majority. At this time it was suggested that the government hold a nationwide plebiscite; but the Socialist party foresaw circumstances that would be even more favorable, and the idea was rejected. Thus an opportunity was lost which, though it would not have led to any definitive resolution of the struggle for power, might well have increased the government's margin for maneuver. This in turn might have advanced the achievement of the government's economic goals and consolidation of its majority support.

Some Comments on Formation of the Social Sector

Although the *Unidad Popular* did not renounce the possibility of modifying the legal framework through a future plebiscite, for the moment it accepted that framework as it stood. As a result, the government was limited in the measures it could take to advance formation of the social sector by the legal powers available to the executive. The only exception occurred in the nationalization of the large copper mines, which was based on a constitutional reform unanimously passed by the Congress. The principal procedures used to form the social sector were expropriation (in certain exceptional cases allowed by law), purchase through direct negotiation, requisition, and intervention.[22] In the first two procedures the state assumed directed ownership; in the latter two it assumed administrative control for an indefinite period, while legal ownership did not change.

Decrees of requisition and intervention and, more narrowly, of expropriation were issued in response to specific economic crimes by a private employer, such as improper cessation of economic activity, production halts, hoarding, or speculation. They were also issued to prevent disturbances in normal economic activities, caused, for example, by supply shortages or labor conflicts. Thus the social sector was formed in three ways: first, as a result of negotiations to purchase or to create mixed enterprises, as in the cases of the private banks and the Chilean subsidiary of R.C.A.; second, in response to illegal actions by owners, as occurred particularly in the cases of *Panos Bellavista Tome*, NIPSA, and Purina Foods; and third, from the workers' own struggle to create favorable conditions for government intervention, as occurred most notably in the case of the textile monopolies, "intervened" in May, 1971.

In practice, then, the formation of the social sector followed a path quite different from that originally envisioned. Either the political determination or the ability to mobilize the workers behind rapid formation of the sector was absent, above all during the first phase of the government. As a result, many of the enterprises originally planned for inclusion remained under the control of monopoly capital. It is worth noting that the bourgeoisie did not immediately counterattack; indeed, its initial reaction was one of retreat and terror. In late 1971, for instance, Agustín Edwards, head of the "Edwards Clan," was fleeing to the United States to collaborate in North American plans for intervention, while his representative in Chile, Fernando Léniz, was negotiating with high government officials to transfer Edwards' properties to the state. Léniz later became Minister of Economics under the military *junta.*

At the same time, however, the government was forced to assume control of enterprises that it had not planned to include in the social sector. It is too simplistic to attribute this fact, which affected medium-sized and even smaller firms, to mere extremist political agitation, although this certainly existed. More fundamentally, the unplanned expansion of the social sector resulted from management actions, such as lock-outs or the simple abandonment of enterprises, or worker reactions, including the seizure of firms, to management's withdrawal of investment, hoarding, speculation, or abusive treatment of labor. Such managerial behavior came to be used increasingly as a weapon in the political battle, culminating in the October, 1972, owners' strike. The workers found that, under the people's government, they could for the first time successfully rebel against abuses they had long suffered in silence. Consequently they fought to have firms guilty of abuses included in the social sector, even though the government had not originally intended to do so. They also struggled against abuses with the declared political intention of undermining the government. The delay in suppressing private monopolies, however, decisively influenced the course of events, permitting the great bourgeoisie to maintain its domination over medium and small owners. Another problem was the failure to develop mechanisms for worker participation in the administration of firms in the private sector.

The inability to incorporate firms on the original list into the social sector and the unplanned expansion of that sector to other enterprises are revealed in the following statistics. In mid-1972, only 7 of the 90 enterprises originally planned for the social sector had become state property. Another 29 had been requisitioned or intervened. Yet 113 firms not on the list had been requisitioned or intervened.[23] As late as July, 1973, 32 of the 90 were still in private hands. Of these, 22 were industrial firms, and the value of their production alone was equal to the total production of all enterprises which had been requisitioned or intervened.[24]

During the government's first year, through the *Contraloría*, the courts, and Congress, the opposition gradually increased its institutional obstruction, its political agitation, and its propaganda against executive initiatives.

As the Under Secretary of Justice noted:

> The above reflects the relative exhaustion of the political conditions that have permitted the government to act. Those hurt have reacted, and they have done so in the name of the Constitution and the law. For this reason it is necessary to obtain *clear juridical norms* that will permit the government, once copper has been nationalized, to build the social property sector with the necessary vigor and speed. This does not imply, of course, abandoning the use of the methods employed until now.[25]

In October, 1971, the government presented to Congress a bill to define the limits of the economic sectors. The government hoped to reach an agreement with the Christian Democrats, on the basis of negotiations already begun, that would enable it to obtain the majority necessary for congressional approval of the bill. In essence, the proposed legislation would have given the President authority to nationalize all enterprises whose capital was greater than 14 million *escudos* on December 31, 1969—a total of "253 firms in the most diverse areas of production." Of these, "at the moment when the bill was submitted, 37 were already under state control. There was some foreign investment in more than 56 per cent of the 253, and in 43 per cent foreign investment held an absolute majority."[26]

Christian Democratic Senators Hamilton and Fuentealba presented their own bill for constitutional reform almost simultaneously, and, with the support of all opposition parties, it was duly approved by the full Congress in February, 1972. In essence, this bill nullified all the legal methods the President had used to form the social sector, returned to private hands all firms transferred to state control after the bill was presented, and created an additional requirement that in the future a specific bill be presented for each case of nationalization. It has been estimated that, even had the government enjoyed the collaboration of Congress, it would have required at least twelve years for the bills representing planned nationalizations to complete their path through Congress.[27] This calculation is based on a precise list which the government had meanwhile appended to its own bill. Late in 1971, during the debate in Congress, President Allende announced that the administration intended to include in the social and mixed sector some ninety firms, corresponding to the industrial, commercial, electric, gas and water, transport, and communications sectors. In February, 1972, the government began to purchase stock in these firms through CORFO, and in April it introduced a detailed list in its veto of the Christian Democratic constitutional reform.

While the administration was preparing its veto, negotiations with the Christian Democratic leadership were renewed. At that time the PDC was controlled by its most progressive sectors, and in mid-1972 a virtual understanding was reached. The government submitted new proposals to Congress and withdrew certain vetoes of the constitutional reform. Nevertheless, incipient agreement was successfully blocked by the determined opposition of the Christian Democratic right wing, inspired by Eduardo Frei. Definitive ratification of the constitutional reform was then delayed until after the elections in March, 1973. By then constitutional debate over the size of the majority necessary to impose the reform on the administration had become a full-blown conflict between the branches of government, in which the opposition's position was supported by the *Contraloría* and the Supreme Court. The conflict evolved amidst evident seditious activity, and it served as a pretext for the *coup d'état*.[28]

In January, 1973, the administration introduced yet another bill reaffirming its decision to include the ninety enterprises in the social sector and adding the National Distributing Company. It also proposed the immediate expropriation of 44 of those firms and five others deemed strategic but originally excluded from the list. The only real consequence of these initiatives was to aggravate the existing differences within the government. The administration was angrily attacked by the Christian Left, the MAPU and the Socialist party, and there were demonstrations against the proposal by the workers.[29]

In general, the government assumed that the social sector would exercise control over different areas of the economy, particularly industry. Unfortunately, we lack quantitative estimates of the impact the sector would have produced had it been formed as originally conceived. By the end of 1971, however, there were various conflicting estimates. A study by the secretariat of CIAP, in March, 1972, noted that "the process of socialization of the means of production in Chile has thus far been characterized by its limited achievements." Based on information from the Ministry of Hacienda and the Secretary of the OAS, the study estimated that the enterprises in the social and mixed property sectors (SMPS) "together represented 13 per cent of the gross value of production in the manufacturing areas *where the SMPS have been expanded during 1971.*"[30] The calculation submitted by the Institute of Economics at the University of Chile was significantly greater. It included state enterprises formed prior to the people's government and can be considered more accurate. "Considering the entire industrial sector, one can estimate that the SMPS generate approximately 23 per cent of total gross production. With respect to employment, more than 18 per cent of the population employed in industry work for firms in the SMPS."[31]

The Institute of Economics evaluated the impact of the ninety firms as follows:[32]

Sector	No. of firms	% of total sectoral production	% of total sectoral employment
Industry	74	14.6	9.9
Commerce (sales)	6	8.6	1.1
Transportation and communication	6	n.a.	4.2
Electricity, gas, water	4	n.a.	n.a.
Total	90		

In light of the above, the following declaration of the Society for the Advancement of Industry (*Sociedad de Fomento Fabril*) seems grossly exaggerated. "The 91 enterprises [including the National Distributing Company—author's note] represent 55 per cent of total national industrial production. Adding the 25 per cent that is already produced by state enterprises, the state-controlled area rises to 80 per cent of industrial production. The remaining 20 per cent is produced by enterprises dependent in one way or another on the above firms. That is to say, the final result will be that 100 per cent of industrial production will be controlled directly or indirectly by the state."[33] Nonetheless, the frankness with which the right, in declarations such as these, recognized the domination of a handful of large monopolies over more than 30,000 small and medium-sized industrial firms is surprising.

Late in 1972, on the basis of information from ODEPLAN and the Industrial Office of CORFO, the Institute of Economics published new figures that were generally accepted. The total number of industrial firms in the SMPS was then 103, of which 30 had been state property before the people's government came to power, 8 had been created during the government, 7 had been expropriated, and 58 had been acquired by some other means. Together they represented 12.7 per cent of all employment in the industrial sector and 13.4 per cent of the total value of production. Ninety-nine industrial enterprises had been requisitioned or intervened, representing 6.9 per cent of industrial employment and 8.5 per cent of the value of production. Thus altogether there were 202 industrial firms under state control, representing 19.6 per cent of sectoral employment and 21.9 per cent of total production.

Of the 74 industrial firms on the original list of ninety, 24 remained to be incorporated into the SMPS, and nine others were being negotiated. Together, these 33 enterprises accounted for 4.0 per cent of the employment in industry and 10.0 per cent of production value. In this fashion, the total number of firms under state control, plus those that the government sought to integrate into the social sector, would have reached 235, accounting for 23.6 per cent of sectoral employment and 31.9 per cent of sectoral production.[34]

The above statistics (which did not vary significantly in 1973) permit a number of observations. First, the government was unable to establish state control over nearly one-third of the seventy-four industrial firms included on the original list of ninety great monopolies. This already represented a substantial reduction in the original conception of the social sector. Second, because of the political conditions under which the process evolved, a large number of additional enterprises were intervened or requisitioned. This distorted the planned composition of social property and required an administrative effort far out of proportion to the sector's economic significance. The great monopolies whose inclusion in the social sector was not achieved were, in general, those with the largest capital investment. The value of their production was almost half the total production of all firms under state control.

At the same time, the control achieved by the state over different areas of industrial production was very uneven: " . . . it dominated, in general, the internal production of intermediate industrial goods in the metal, petroleum, rubber and chemical sectors . . . but not in wood, furniture, paper and leather; it was less important in the production of capital goods and durable consumer goods . . . and even less in the production of light consumer goods, particularly foodstuffs and tobacco."[35] Early in 1973, Pedro Vuskovic, then head of CORFO, referred to the "surviving bases of bourgeois economic power" and evaluated the situation as follows:

> In the first place . . . we have not yet completed the creation of the social property sector as we envisioned it. In the second place, the social sector has not become effectively dominant, capable of imposing limits on the operation and administrative decisions of those forms that—according to the program—remain, and will continue to remain, in the private sector of the economy. Nor have we been able to establish effective forms of workers' control in the private sector. For these reasons, a broad sector dominated by the bourgeoisie continues to function, but in no way consistent with our general policies for production and the use of surplus value. The profits that it generates are used to purchase scarce consumer goods, without injury to the sector's privileged ability to obtain greater financial resources from the banking system. The private sector effectively resists cost and price controls; it eludes its tax obligations, maintaining high rates of evasion; it engages in speculation more or less with impunity and impedes strengthening state mechanisms of wholesale distribution; it contributes to financing the ideological campaign of the reaction and even certain openly seditious activities. In the third place, we have not been able to impose any real, definitive redistribution of income in favor of the workers and the process of accumulation.[36]

In this manner Vuskovic summarized the economic conditions on which the continued political ability of the bourgeoisie to resist was based. Yet to assume that these obstacles could be removed completely *before* the definitive resolution of the struggle for power is equivalent to assuming that the transition to socialism could be achieved through a process of structural reforms without *first* altering the character of the state itself. The essential problem could not be reduced to a question of sequence in the achievement of economic reforms *but rather* lay in the conceptions of the state and the revolution. Debate on the general political orientation of the *Unidad Popular* and on the particular proposals for the social sector reflected strategic disagreements on these broader questions.

Conceptual Disagreements within the Unidad Popular

From the very beginning of the government, there were general disagreements over the breadth and rapidity of the social sector's formation. As government actions generated ever more organized resistance by a united opposition, they also created economic difficulties; but these were not sufficient to create the conditions necessary to overcome them. As this process evolved, differences within the coalition reemerged, roughly corresponding to the earlier positions of the Communist and Socialist parties concerning the preparation of the basic program. The debate had then been framed in terms of a theoretical analysis of Chilean social development leading to the definition of revolutionary goals for the people's movement. Now it referred to evaluations of the concrete situation and the relation, at each moment, between the advance toward the program's objectives and the existing balance of social forces. The opposing positions taken with respect to formation of the social sector in industry and distribution were cast in these terms.

On the one hand, Orlando Millás, a member of the Political Commission of the Communist party, offered this analysis:

> From our point of view, the characteristic of the present situation is that the balance of power has shifted against the working class and the People's government. It would be disastrous to further increase the number of our enemies. On the contrary, we must make concessions in order to neutralize at least some sectors and specific social groups. We must correct tactical errors.
>
> Under such circumstances it does not help the revolutionary process to emphasize what we will do in the future when conditions are more favorable. Before seeking to take over new capitalist enterprises, it would be wiser to take advantage of the incorporation into the reformed sector ... of the enterprises already expropriated or intervened and use the resources already available in order to establish realistic worker and popular leadership. On the basis of what has been done we can and should complete ... construction of the social sector of the economy. And we can do so within the framework enunciated in our government's basic program, that is with respect to the great enterprises of strategic importance. But this requires isolating those who plot sedition, shoring up the government, consolidating its accomplishments and modifying in its favor the balance of social forces.[37]

Others argued that the existing balance of forces permitted giving a substantial, immediate stimulus to the construction of the social sector—that, indeed, the only way to modify that balance, to make it more favorable to the government and the attainment of its objectives, was to intensify the process of change. This would permit confronting existing problems and strengthening the development of popular power, without, of course, obviating necessary corrections in the government's leadership and its administration of enterprises in the social sector.

In mid-1972 this polemic, reflected in such simplistic slogans as "Consolidate in order to advance" and "Advance in order to consolidate," led to the meeting of the *Unidad Popular* known as the "conclave of Lo Curro." The results were important modifications in the government's economic policy.

After Lo Curro the gradualist concept of the revolutionary process, represented by Millás and others, became frankly predominant within the leadership of the government and the *Unidad Popular*. It called for the pursuit of anti-imperialist, anti-latifundist, and anti-monopolist reforms that would amplify the bases of democratic support for the state. The progressive adaptation of state institutions to basic socioeconomic reforms was to eventually permit the transformation of the state's class character.

For Millás, "the social sector now became decisive in the national economy,"[38] and he insisted that its formation had not been adequately accompanied by appropriate mechanisms for workers' control and economic planning. In practice, the application of norms for worker participation in the administration of social enterprises (formulated in an agreement between the CUT and the government), like economic planning, suffered considerable delay. During the later course of the government, however, considerable advances were made in both areas. At the time of the *coup* workers throughout Chile were involved, under CUT leadership, in a debate on "complementary or necessary changes in the Basic Rules for Participation and . . . the establishment of efficacious mechanisms to permanently control their application and adaptation to economic leadership at all levels."[39] Workers were also involved in discussing the Economic Plan for 1974.

On these issues, too, there were important disagreements linked to different strategic conceptions within the *Unidad Popular*. Factions disagreed on the role of workers in the leadership of social enterprises and on the role of labor unions. Both questions were tied to that of the meaning of the people's government and the character of the state. There was also disagreement over planning mechanisms, specifically their impact on the relation between the social, mixed, and private sectors. In effect, the different factions understood the domination of the social sector in different ways.

On one side were those who argued that the social sector could regulate the entire economy; thus the private sector would be subject to conditions imposed by the social sector. On the other were those who saw the new economic order as emerging from a kind of competition between the social and private sectors. Compare the following statements:

> It is a life and death matter for the revolutionary process that the nationalized mines, the industries incorporated into the social sector, the reformed sector in agriculture and the nationalized banks work more and better, with greater efficiency and productivity, than under their previous masters. The superiority of the People's government must be proven with its economic successes.[40]

> The battle is being joined between the capitalist and social sectors of our country's economy to see who conquers whom, which places the other at its service. With proper use of the state's administrative apparatus, together with mobilization of the popular masses, there is no doubt that the social sector can be victorious. But for this to be so, production in the social sector must grow more rapidly. This implies investment, creation of new enterprises, expansion of existing ones and application of new and more modern methods of production. In short, there must be a permanent increase in the productivity of labor. This is the decisive indicator. In this fashion the production of the social sector will have greater weight in the economy as a whole. This will become the dominant form of production in the country.[41]

To summarize, within the *Unidad Popular* there were different strategic conceptions with respect to the state and the struggle for power and concerning the role of economic transformations in relation to them, especially in industry and distribution, strongholds of the monopolist bourgeoisie and keys to control of the economy. These disagreements were expressed in different positions on the extent and speed of the formation of the social sector, on the modes of worker participation in management, and on the terms of the social sector's domination of the economy as a whole.

$$* \quad * \quad *$$

In the formation of the social sector, the people's government revealed serious weakness. It allowed important bases of the economic power of the monopolist bourgeoisie to survive and, with them, the bourgeoisie's ability to manipulate the middle sectors and disrupt the economy for political reasons also survived. Certainly this contributed to creating conditions propitious for the *coup d'état*.

Yet, in spite of everything, advances in the formation of the social sector were the principal factors propelling and sustaining the revolutionary process. In the struggle over the social sector and the administration of the enterprises within it, the workers offered lessons in consciousness, sacrifice, strength, and creativity. Moreover, it was on the basis of the social sector that the principal forms of popular power, such as the industrial belts and the communal commandos, were organized.

NOTES

1. "Programa del Gobierno de la Unidad Popular." There are various editions. Here we have used the translation included in the anthology edited by Joan E. Garcés, *Chile's Road to Socialism* (Baltimore, Md.: Penguin Books, Inc., 1973), pp. 23–24.

2. Eduardo Labarca, *Chile al Rojo,* Juan Pablos (ed.) (Mexico, 1971), p. 219.

3. In 1968 the magazine *Punto Final* reprinted a speech by Baltra. Unfortunately I do not have a copy of the issue and am quoting from memory. Publication of this speech in a magazine linked to the extreme left is symptomatic of the breadth of debate within the popular movement. As is known, Baltra was advanced by his party as the *Unidad Popular*'s candidate for the presidency. Later, when Allende was in power, he joined the party's dissident right wing, paradoxically known as the Party of the Radical Left, which passed to the opposition.

4. *Program of the Chilean Communist Party,* 1969, p. 3. (My italics.)

5. Luis Corvalán, "Unidad Popular para Conquistar el Poder, Informe al XIV Congreso Nacional del Partido Communista, 23 Noviembre 1969, " in *Camino de victoria* (Santiago: Editorial Horizonte, 1971), p. 323. (My italics.)

6. Quoted by Julio César Jobet in *El Partido Socialista de Chile* (Santiago: Editorial PLA, 1971), vol. 2., p. 112. (My italics.)

7. Partido Socialista de Chile, "Informe del Comité Central al Pleno de Algarrobo, Febrero 1972," in *Cuadernos Socialistas*. Documentos del Partido. Resoluciones, Declaraciones, Informes y Discursos, 1971–1973, p. 10.

8. "Programa del Gobierno de la Unidad Popular," *op. cit.,* p. 29. (My italics.)

9. "Programa del Gobierno de la Unidad Popular," *op. cit.,* p. 37.

10. V. I. Lenin, "Uno de los Problemas Fundamentales de la Revolución," in *Obras Escogidas* (Moscow: Editorial Progreso, n.d.) vol. 2., p. 284.

11. "Programa," *op. cit.,* p. 37.

12. *Ibid.,* pp. 37–38.

13. See *ibid.,* pp. 37–42.

14. The alarmist speech a few weeks after the elections by Andrés Zaldívar, then Minister of Economics, stands out.

15. A detailed discussion of the property of these monopolistic groups can be found in the MAPU's publication, *Las Empresas Monopólicas y el Area de Propiedad Social de la Economía Chilena: El Libro de las 91* (Santiago: Eds. Barco de Papel, 1972), pp. 47–58.

16. See "Programa del Gobierno de la Unidad Popular," *op cit.*, pp. 30–38.

17. Pedro Vuskovic, "La Política Económica del Gobierno de la Unidad Popular," in *La Vía Chilena al Socialismo*, J. Ann Zammit, ed. (Mexico: Siglo XXI, 1973), p. 10.

18. Salvador Allende, "Discurso ante el Pueblo de Santiago," delivered on September 5, 1970, in *Allende, Su Pensamiento Político* (Buenos Aires: Granica Ed., 1973), p. 10.

19. From "Primer Mensaje del Presidente Salvador Allende al Congreso Pleno," May 21, 1971, in *ibid.*, p. 127.

20. *Ibid.*, p. 114.

21. Oscar Lange and Fred M. Taylor, *On the Economic Theory of Socialism* (Minneapolis, Minn.: The University of Minnesota Press, 1938), pp. 121–129.

22. For a succinct discussion of the available legal instruments see Reinhard von Brunn, *Chile, con Leyes Tradicionales Hacia una Nueva Economía?* (Santiago: Instituto Latinoamericano de Investigaciones Sociales (ILDIS, 1972), pp. 14–25.

23. Data are from *El Mercurio* as cited by Reinhard von Brunn, *op. cit.*, p. 38. In the chart he presents, the sum of the partial totals does not coincide with the totals we have reproduced here.

24. *Chile Hoy*, No. 59 (July 17–August 2, 1973) (Santiago), p. 11.

25. José A. Viera Gallo, "Sobre la Legislación que Define las Tres Areas de la Economía," in *Cuadernos de la Realidad Nacional*, No. 11 (January 1972) (Santiago), p. 196. (Italics in the original.)

26. Reinhard von Brunn, *op. cit.*, p. 30.

27. *Ibid.*, pp. 36–47.

28. For a legal and constitutional discussion of the controversy which emerged, consult Reinhard von Brunn, *op. cit.*, pp. 47–51.

29. See *Chile Hoy*, No. 34 (February 2–8, 1973), pp. 4 and 14–17.

30. CIAP 541: "El Esfuerzo Interno y las Necesidades de Financiamiento Externo para el Desarrollo de Chile" (Washington: March 20, 1972), p. 33.

31. Claes Croner and Oriano Lazo, "El Area de Propiedad Social en la Industria," in *La Economía Chilena in 1971*, publication of the Instituto de Economía of the Universidad de Chile (Santiago, n.d.), p. 426.

32. Based on Claes Vroner and Oriana Lazo, *op. cit.*, pp. 461–462.

33. *La Economía Chilena en 1972* (Santiago: Instituto de Economía de la Universidad de Chile, 1973), pp. 87, 89, 90, 93, 134, and 135.

34. *Ibid.*

35. *Ibid.*, pp. 138–139.

36. Pedro Vuskovic, Dos Años de Política Económica del Gobierno Popular," in *Revista de la Universidad Técnica del Estado*, Nos. 11–12 (November–December, 1972, and January–February, 1973) (Santiago), p. 62.

37. Orlando Millás, "La Clase Obrera en el Gobierno Popular," *Cuadernillo de Propaganda No. 4* (Santiago: Partido Comunista de Chile, 1972), pp. 32–33.

38. *Ibid.*, p. 21.

39. *Ibid.*

40. Orlando Millás, "Hay que Ganar la Batalla en el Terreno de la Economía," in *Revista de la Universidad Técnica del Estado, op. cit.*, p. 10.

41. José Cademártori, "Perspectivas y Tareas Revolucionarias en el Frente Económico," in *Revista de la Universidad Técnica del Estado, op. cit.*, p. 110.

Commentaries

Some Clarifications
of Certain Historical Facts

RADOMIRO TOMIC

I will permit myself some comments on the very thorough exposition by Jorge Tapia Videla, since it contains a few facts and opinions on which I have a slightly different perspective.

For example, it seems to me excessive to call Jorge Alessandri "the candidate of the middle class" in the 1958 presidential election. I think that Frei, the Christian Democratic candidate, and Bossay, of the Radical party (the most genuine representative of the Chilean middle class), received more votes from that social stratum than did Alessandri. Between them they obtained 37 per cent of the vote, while Alessandri's 31 per cent included the vote of the traditional right, which at that time still controlled a large sector of the peasantry, dependent on its *patrones*.

Nor do I share Tapia's evaluation of the Christian Democratic candidate in 1970—who was myself—as the candidate of the center. That characterization undoubtedly facilitates a methodological presentation, but it sacrifices what is perhaps the most significant phenomenon in Chilean politics during the last twenty years: the transformation of a significant—at times even dominant—portion of the Christian Democratic party into a force which, by ideological inclination, stands on the left.

Today the PDC receives the majority of its support from workers and peasants. No doubt because it is not an "electoral" phenomenon, this leftward movement by a party with essentially Christian roots has decisive repercussions in a country such as Chile—and a continent such as Latin America. Some say the process began in 1941, when a group of party leaders resigned because they considered it too "leftist." Others see the beginning at the 1946 National Congress, where Bernardo Leighton called

187

for a platform in support of "proletarian democracy" and lost by a scant two votes.

In any case, the dilemma was formulated in concrete detail in the National *Junta* of 1963—one year before the next presidential election. There it was proposed that the Christian Democratic party seek "an agreement with all the political and social forces of the left," thus to establish the basis for the replacement of the capitalist system in Chile. Although at the time the thesis labeled "our own road" prevailed, the internal confrontation continued. It became more acute when, in the 1965 election of new leadership, Aylwin ("our own road") defeated Jérez ("people's unity") by a very narrow margin. It was again underscored in 1966, when the Christian Democratic National Congress adopted as the basis for its program the leftist thesis of a "noncapitalist road of development."

In 1967, 1968, and 1969 the tendencies clashed democratically, each winning and losing respectively the control of the party. In May, 1969, the "people's unity" platform, proposed for the 1970 presidential election, lost by fifteen votes in a National *Junta* of 540 delegates. In August, however, it won overwhelmingly when the National *Junta* proclaimed the Tomić candidacy and elected a new National Council (which included representatives of the minority). An official document entitled "Fundamental Political Declaration and Programmatic Bases for a Second Christian Democratic Government" stressed that the essential task was the "replacement of capitalism in Chile." This objective could only be achieved through the "political and social unity of the people." Precisely, explicitly, and without evasion, the document stated that unity implied seeking a pragmatic—though not doctrinal—agreement among the Christian Democrats, the Socialists and Communists, and labor unions and popular mass organizations—not to mention social, professional, and technocratic forces disposed to support radical change: churches, universities, and the like.

All this was developed systematically in the presidential platform of the Christian Democrats. Our agreement with the program of the *Unidad Popular* on fundamental questions was manifest. It was vehemently denounced by the right in the slogan "A vote for Tomić is the same as a vote for Allende."

I repeat: this definitively anti-capitalist stance, favoring agreement with all other forces on the Chilean left, did not originate with the Christian Democrats in 1970. Nor did it have a purely electoral purpose. It began much earlier, as a result of a gradual but ultimately revolutionary revision of the mission of Christian laity to constructing "a new socialist, communitarian, pluralist and democratic society in Chile."

I also disagree with some of Tapia's observations on the military participation in the two key cabinets Allende organized in October, 1972, and August, 1973. The October cabinet resulted from an agreement with the Christian Democrats. Its final objective (at least for the PDC) was to ensure that the congressional elections of March, 1973, would be impartial. For the opposition, impartiality was fundamental.

The origins of the August cabinet resided in public advocacy by the Chilean Episcopate of a "truce which would avoid armed confrontation among Chileans; a truce which, while not the solution, would allow time to search for that solution." The Aylwin National Committee ceded to the moral pressure of the Episcopate and agreed to a dialogue with the government. As a prior condition, however, it requested the formation of a new cabinet, "with the participation of the armed forces at the highest institutional level." This meant the commanders in chief. Initially Allende refused, and Aylwin proceeded to state publicly that the dialogue had ended. Three days later, nevertheless, Allende incorporated the four commanders in chief into his cabinet. Although this produced some transitory vacillation in the anti-government position of the Christian Democratic leadership, the dialogue had been declared officially dead. The new military cabinet—without the backing of the Christian Democrats—lost all political significance. Two weeks later the four military ministers had resigned.

Finally, I would like to express one last, important reservation. For the left wing of the Christian Democrats, it was not obvious in September, 1973—nor is it obvious now—that the military *coup* was inevitable. What was clear to us was that the *Unidad Popular* government had exhausted all of its options. Allende and his government had lost control not only of the country but also of the *Unidad Popular* as such. The coalition parties were divided and fighting for different and contradictory objectives. Some were committed to the development of "parallel power," advocated by the MIR and the extreme left, outside and against the *Unidad Popular*. The end of the Allende government was inevitable, but outcomes other than the military *coup* were possible. One was Allende's resignation, prior to a national plebiscite called by the President himself. We know now that this was his intent. Another possibility was the simultaneous resignation of the President and the entire National Congress, to be followed by combined elections. This was actually proposed at a plenary session of the Christian Democratic provincial presidents. Both roads—alien to the military *coup* and to dictatorship—could have been followed and were in fact under consideration.

Other topics which deserve clarification are those of "the two roads" and the transformation of *tripolarity* into *bipolarity*.

The problem of the two roads, violent and peaceful—which some on the left scoffingly call the "railroad problem"—is perhaps the greatest challenge faced by socialism in Latin America. Is there a "second road to socialism"? How does it differ from the classic, well-known road?

Julio Silva argues that the *Unidad Popular* did not elaborate this point theoretically. Unfortunately he is right, perhaps because to probe deeply into the question would raise the possibility of a second socialist model, one without a prior armed clash and its corollary, the dictatorship of the proletariat. It is not strange that such theoretical elaboration was not attempted by the *Unidad Popular*. It would obviously have been too explosive a theme.

With respect to *why* and *how* the tripolarity of Chilean politics in 1970—represented by the *Unidad Popular*, the Christian Democrats, and the right—was transformed into the bipolar antagonism between the *Unidad Popular* in the government and the Christian Democrats and right in opposition, I disagree with the interpretation which has predominated here. I lived through the process personally, and I believe that I can summarize its substance in a single sentence: The strategy of the *Unidad Popular* was *never to collaborate with the Christian Democrats,* but to divide and destroy them.

To explain this transformation from tripolarity to bipolarity—for which, erroneously, the Christian Democrats are more often blamed than the *Unidad Popular*—it has been argued that the Christian Democratic left wing "only controlled the party until December, 1970" and that Narciso Irureta "was the representative of the tendency which opposed the *Unidad Popular*."

In this fashion history is written! Andrés Zaldívar, ex-Treasury Minister in the Frei administration, was the candidate of the current within the PDC opposed to the *Unidad Popular*. Frei not only attended the National *Junta* meetings but actually spoke. However, Zaldívar was not elected, and Irureta emerged victorious. In that same *Junta* a new National Committee was elected, and the left wing obtained eight seats to four for the opposition. Two days later the entire leadership (*Mesa Directiva*), led by Irureta, met officially with Allende and told him, "We come to greet you, because we have been elected leaders of the largest political party in Chile, and to tell you that we interpret our responsibility as an obligation to help you govern." In continuation they added these words, which today seem almost incredible: "Help us to be good *Allendistas.*"

This astounding offer, which would have permitted the government to consolidate its position as had no other Chilean government in a hundred years, was contemptuously ignored—at that moment and in the days, weeks, and months that followed.

Irureta's election did not put an end to the thesis of the Christian Democratic candidate in 1970—i.e., that of "political and social unity of the people." Exactly the opposite occurred. In December, 1970, Irureta responsibly attempted to put that policy into practice. He tried again following the April, 1971, municipal elections (despite Allende's unnecessarily aggressive verbal intervention in the polemic between Irureta and the Minister of Mining over the intervention of the "riflemen" in an attempted copper sale). And in June, 1971, he attempted one last time, following the congressional by-election in Valparaíso. On each occasion he asked me to help him contact Allende; each time I did. And on each of these three occasions where the Christian Democratic leadership took the initiative, it was the *Unidad Popular*—if not Allende himself or some Minister acting in his name—which refused to seek an agreement and to initiate or continue the negotiations.

The Program
of the Unidad Popular

JULIO SILVA SOLAR

In my judgment, any analysis of the *Unidad Popular* government and the leadership of the Chilean process during the triennium 1970–1973 would be incomplete if it did not refer to the circumstances surrounding the birth of the "Program of the Alliance of People's Parties."

The debate on the program was not easy, and in it the dual orientation or dual line, which the *Unidad Popular* was never able to resolve, was already apparent. I remember very well (because I participated in the discussion) that the differences were manifest on two particular points: a) the problem of socialism and b) the problem of power. The representatives of the Socialist party persisted in emphasizing the socialist character of the program, insisting that with it the construction of socialism in Chile had already begun. In contrast, those of the Communist party preferred to describe the program in terms of anti-imperialism, anti-latifundism, and anti-monopolism. For the Communists, these were tasks that had to precede socialism. They would create the conditions or clear the path for socialism, but they did not constitute the transition to or construction of socialism itself.

In every debate, this disagreement was latent. At times, it seemed almost an academic discussion, whose theoretical and practical importance was unclear (although later it would become painfully obvious). The Communist position was that the transition to socialism would become possible only when the working class had gained control of state power as a whole; that is, when the dictatorship of the proletariat had been established. This had not happened in Chile, even after the victory in the presidential election. The socialists wanted not a reformist program but a revo-

192

lutionary one; they thought it immediately necessary to assume the tasks of socialism and "People's Power." They felt that by advancing more radically and quickly—by making the process more profound—they would awaken the masses and win support among the people, from forces that were still under the influence of the bourgeoisie and its parties (the National Party, Christian Democrats, etc.).

On the question of power, the Communist party argued that, regarding the balance of competing forces, an institutional strategy was the most favorable to advance the people's movement. As part of this strategy, the specific policies adopted by the people's government should be accompanied by vast, mass mobilization. Both intimately linked factors would generate institutional change and alter the balance of forces in favor of the working class. This, however, would necessarily be a relatively gradual process. For the Communists, the program's objective was not to establish class power by suppressing, by whatever means, the power of the bourgeoisie in Congress, in the Judiciary, in the communications media (radio, television, press), in the public administration, or the armed forces. Naturally, the Communists sought "power," but only through an institutional process. What was not sought was to move beyond Chilean "democratic" institutions to a direct, armed confrontation with the forces of the bourgeoisie, for it was felt that to pass from an institutional struggle to open confrontation would in practice, given the existing balance of forces, favor the bourgeoisie. For example, it seemed obvious that no sector in the armed forces, not even the most progressive, would support the government in an unconstitutional confrontation designed to win power for the dictatorship of the proletariat. To attempt such a confrontation, the *Unidad Popular* would have had to organize its own paramilitary force. This would have meant an immediate break with the armed forces, which had an explicitly constitutional monopoly over the use of arms and armed force within the country.

In contrast, the Socialist party insisted that it was necessary to achieve total power. Revolutionary change could not be achieved in any other fashion. Institutions had to be transformed and a new state inaugurated in which the workers and people would exercise real power. Without openly proposing to abandon the institutional road, the Socialist point of view was that the dynamics of the process, and the reaction it would engender, would very quickly surpass institutional limits. Therefore, it was necessary to prepare in advance popular and military power sufficient to dissuade the opposition from confrontation or to defeat it if confrontation occurred. Hence the Socialists emphasized moving beyond the program objectives. Programmatic goals and even the people's government were not ends in themselves but means for gaining total power, for radicalizing the struggle and for gaining ground in it. The end was always to decide or define, immediately, the problem of power.

Anyone who analyzes these points of view with the least attention will understand how numerous and how serious were the problems of government and leadership of the Chilean process. It would be of no use to detail all of them here.

The difficulty could not be resolved during discussion of the program. Both sides presented coherent and extensive arguments, but debate was not an effective way to reach a solution. In the end a compromise, in some ways containing both points of view, was accepted. Instead of resolving the conflict, this ambiguity aggravated it and justified a dual orientation and dual leadership within the people's forces.

It is necessary to add only one last point. In this compromise the Communist point of view was expressed in far more concrete terms than the Socialist. Thus, for example, the measures designed to transform institutions (workers' participation at different levels, the creation of a unicameral legislature, etc.) were given considerable conceptual specificity, while the new "Workers' State" was no more than another abstraction. This does not invalidate, however, the points made above.

Although the debate in question occurred during the program's elaboration, it had many earlier antecedents. One must remember that the Socialist leadership had questioned the electoral road and later the idea of a broad front (*Unidad Popular*). They judged the first as unlikely to lead (in Chile) toward a people's (proletarian) government, and the second as only a new version of earlier experiments—reformist-populist (the Popular Front) and social-democratic—which did not guarantee revolutionary change. They specifically objected to the presence of the Radical party, the sector known as *Tarud,* and other elements. In contrast, the Communists had pressed for a broad front, claiming that if it were not formed, they would present a candidate from their own ranks (Pablo Neruda) and would not support a candidate from another party (that is, a Socialist candidate).

Campesinos, Land, and Employment under Unidad Popular

JOHN STRASMA

DIMENSIONS OF THE REFORM: LAND AND CAMPESINOS

No doubt about it; although Chilean agrarian reform began in earnest under the Christian Democrats, it was during the *Unidad Popular* that it fulfilled the criteria stated by Jacques Chonchol: it was "massive, drastic and rapid."

Figures alone (see Table 1) are insufficient, of course, without something to indicate their significance. For example, the total area of Chile is about 74 million hectares, of which 11 million are suitable for crops, 19 million only for grazing, and 22 million for forests; 22 million more have no potential agricultural use whatever (Baytelman, 1975). Public Law 16,640, Frei's land reform, was used by Allende because it was impossible for him to get congressional approval of an acceptable revision. The law allowed most owners to

TABLE 1 *Expropriation under Christian Democrats and Unidad Popular*

Period	Farms expropriated	Area expropriated (hectares)		
		Irrigated	Nonirrigated	Total
Nov. 1964– Nov. 1970	1,408	290,000	3,275,000	3,565,000
Nov. 1970– Dec. 30, 1972	3,780	309,000	5,259,000	5,568,000
Totals	5,188	599,000	8,534,000	9,133,000

Source: Agrarian Reform Corporation (CORA)

195

retain "reserves" of up to eighty "basic irrigated hectares"[1] (B.I.H.), although as a rule the *Unidad Popular* functionaries managed to trim the owners' reserves to forty B.I.H. or less. As of July 30, 1972, 58 per cent of the irrigated land and 52 per cent of the nonirrigated agricultural land in farms larger than 40 B.I.H. had been expropriated—that is, 43 per cent and 24 per cent of Chile's total area in each category. About 75,000 families were benefitting (Baytelman, 1975), a figure which probably rose to 80,000 by 1973 (Chonchol, 1975).

As candidates in 1964, Frei and Allende promised that they would include 100,000 families as land reform beneficiaries. Frei reached only some 24,000, so it is obvious that Allende came closer to that original goal. Nevertheless, 100,000 families was merely the initial goal, since the total *campesino* population in the 1965 Agricultural Census turned out to be much larger than that (see Table 2). Toward the end of 1972, the government announced that the process of expropriation under Public Law 16,640 was essentially completed. There were scarcely twelve properties left in the country large enough to be taken, and these had not been for special reasons—typically, because they were too remote, subject to flooding, or otherwise of no interest to *campesinos*. Still, only some 75,000 to 80,000 families participated in the agrarian reform—about a fifth of the rural population—and many more were left with a sense of frustration and hopelessness, seeing that the process was completed and they hadn't benefitted in any way.

WAS THERE ENOUGH LAND?

Chile is a far cry from the Peruvian *Sierra*, where the population density is so great that agrarian reform cannot ensure every *campesino* enough land to achieve a minimum living by international norms for calories and proteins. In Chile there are at least eleven million hectares of crop land plus nineteen million more suitable for grazing. That is, there is more than a hectare of cropland per Chilean—man, woman, and child—and in any case almost 70 per cent of the population lives in the cities, so there are about three hectares available for everyone living in the country. Moreover, a good part of this land is as rich as that of California, suitable for very intensive cultivation in vegetables, fruit trees, and other crops highly valued for processing. On the face of it, there is no geographic reason why every *campesino* who wants it could not have an opportunity to work and to participate in agrarian reform.

TABLE 2   *Social Categories in the Campesino Population (1965)*

Social Category	Families	Labor Force
Minifundista	185,000	462,000
Small holders	27,000	54,000
Medium landowners	8,500	8,500
Large landowners	8,000	8,000
Farm managers, etc.	11,000	11,000
Resident year-round workers	90,000	90,000
Temporary resident workers	80,000	80,000

Source: Baytelman, 1975

Unfortunately, from the very beginning Chilean agrarian reform has been the victim of a slogan of its promoters: "Land for the tiller." The reform was understood by most people to mean throwing out the landowner and turning the land over to the *inquilinos*, those resident laborers with year-round employment who had been working the land under the direction of the former owner. Many functionaries of the Agrarian Reform Corporation (CORA) saw the need to include landless *campesinos* as well and the grown children of the resident laborers, but only in a few cases did they succeed in persuading the initial beneficiaries to allow more families to enter the projects. In those cases the *inquilinos* normally only accepted their own grown children or other old laborers from the farm that were well-known but had not had guaranteed year-round work with the former owner.

Indeed, in many cases during the Frei administration, CORA functionaries accepted petitions from reform beneficiaries claiming that there were already too many of them on a given farm (which was called an *asentamiento* during a transition stage). In response, the CORA staff spoke of moving some of them to other farms, thus leaving the original farm finally to an even smaller number of workers. This happened only in a few isolated cases, for obvious reasons. Few existing reform projects were willing to receive more families or to divide the land among more participants when they reached the final allocation of property to beneficiaries.

To understand the process, it is useful to have in mind the concept of capacity (*cabida*) used by CORA functionaries during the Frei administration. In essence, they sought to estimate the amount of land necessary for a typical *campesino* family to earn a net cash income on the order of three times the legal minimum wage of Santiago. With this income, they believed, migration to the city would be slowed, reducing social costs, because the level of living in rural areas would be raised substantially above what *campesinos* could expect if they moved to the city. Unfortunately, the CORA functionaries took as "givens" the existing levels of farming know-how, productive capital, and intensity of cultivation in each area and hence came up with several times as many hectares per family as would be possible if reform were to give land to all who sought it. The planners began with an income standard, rather than comparing the available land with the number of claimants.

To be sure, the demographic pressure on the land varied among provinces, as did the quantity and quality of available land. And much of the man/land problem came directly from distortions in the Table of Equivalencies, which indicated the quantity of land of each soil type, in each zone, equal to the eighty basic irrigated hectares used in the law to define the area which owners could retain as a "reserve," the rest being subject to expropriation. Obviously, with a terrain as varied as Chile's, this kind of equivalency table was indispensable.

One basis for such calculations was available already, but it was rejected in the process of drafting the Christian Democrats' agrarian reform law. Between 1961 and 1964, a detailed cadastral study had been carried out for almost the entire agricultural area of Chile. The boundaries, soil types, exact size, and current and potential production of every farm was determined by aerial photogrammetric techniques and three-dimensional photo interpretation, verified with more than 60,000 soil samples and field visits. This study served as the basis for almost every effort at regional, agricultural, transportational, or other kind of planning carried out from 1965 on, as well as providing the fundamental basis for the reassessment of farm land for the real estate tax, which was implemented in 1965. As a participant observer in that process, I saw that a very high degree of "horizontal" equity was attained. Any given property was likely to be assessed at exactly the same value as any other property of similar soil type, distance to the market, availability of irrigation water, etc. (Improvements built after 1954 were exempt from the tax, so assessed values reflect essentially the soil and only to a small extent include barns, stables, houses, etc.) On this basis, Table 1 can be rewritten as in Table 3 to show the land expropriated by each government in relation to its assessed valuation.

Are the equivalencies of Public Law 16,640 used in the land reform valid? There are various reasons for skepticism. For in-

TABLE 3   *Assessed Valuations of*
Expropriated Farms

Period	Number of Farms	Assessed Valuation (in 1972 *escudos*)
1965–1970	1,324	E°634,300,000
1971 and 1972	3,535	1,219,400,000

Source: Gimeno, 1975. A few farms are missing because of delays in the exchange of data between CORA and the Internal Revenue Service.

stance, in the soil classification used for the 1963–1965 tax reassessment, there are twelve classes (four of irrigated land and eight for nonirrigated land), and each class has various subclasses. But the Table of Equivalencies in Public Law 16,640, of 1967, only distinguishes two classes of irrigated land and two of dry land in each province. In each zone, this favors the owners of the best land and hurts owners of poorer land within each of these broad classes since both are allowed to reserve the same number of hectares.

Another relevant fact is that in order to obtain votes from certain Conservative party legislators, urgently needed to enact his bill to "Chileanize" the copper mines, President Frei made a deal with them to alter the land reform Table of Equivalencies, especially for provinces to the south of the Bio-Bio River. The amount of land legally defined as the equivalent of eighty hectares of the Maipo River Valley, the basis for Public Law 16,640, was raised substantially over the quantity in the first version of the bill, which had been prepared by agricultural technicians. With some reason, then, the *Unidad Popular* and the Christian Democrats agreed later on to reduce the "unaffectable" area to forty B.I.H., although they could also simply have restored the Equivalency Table of the first version of Frei's bill.

Without claiming that the fiscal valuations are perfect, or even close to perfect, I do believe they reflect differences in the potential agricultural value of Chilean farmlands much more accurately than the figures in the Table of Equivalencies of Public Law 16,640. In a study prepared by the Internal Revenue Service and the Institute for Agricultural and Livestock Development (INDAP), an irrigated hectare in the *comuna* of Buin (assessed on average, in 1970, at E°4,692), was compared with the area which would be its equal according to the land reform Table of Equivalencies in three other *comunas*. According to the Table, it would be equal to 2.5 hectares of irrigated land in Ovalle, assessed at E°5,589; to 3.1 hectares of irrigated land in Temuco, assessed at E°4,805; and to 6.9 hectares of crop land in Puerto Montt, assessed at E°6,003 (Gimeno, 1974). The size of an owner's reserve in Puerto Montt was 28 per cent greater than it would have been if tax assessments had been used as the basis for defining affectability and reserves.

THE UNEMPLOYMENT PROBLEM

The "class selfishness" (*egoísmo de clases*) of the agrarian reform beneficiaries, who threw out the owners and managers but refused to admit other members of the *campesino* classes, is sharply reflected in the figures for the amount of land which wound up in three distinct sectors as of late 1972 (see Table 4).

TABLE 4   *Division of Agricultural Land in 1972*

Subsector	Units	Per Cent	Assessed Value(1972)	Per Cent
Reform units	4,859	1.7	E°1,851,060,000	30.8
*Minifundist**	258,013	92.0	1,297,502,000	21.6
Commercial farms	17,703	6.3	2,852,447,000	47.6

*Units with assessed value below E°47,000 in 1972, considered the "family unit," capable of producing incomes of 3.9 times the legal yearly minimum wage for white-collar workers in Santiago. Also includes landless peasants and *minifundia,* usually merely houses with gardens of fewer than 0.5 hectares. Source: Internal Revenue Service, CORA, and INDAP. (See Gimeno, 1974.)

The commercial farm sector consisted of small and medium-sized farms, the legal reserves left to expropriated owners, and farms broken up via private division in 1966 to escape expropriation. It was still in excellent health in 1972, with almost half of the agricultural land in the country. According to what was written and said about this commercial farming sector by the partisans of agrarian reform under Frei and Allende, it would be supposed that this sector had mechanized everything possible and hence would provide fewer jobs in relation to the land than the other two sectors. Nonetheless, the figures in Table 5 bring surprises.

In short, agrarian reform in Chile left its beneficiaries with more land apiece (valued by its potential output) than the average worker in a commercial farm. There was a misallocation of land

TABLE 5   *Allocation of Land and Workers in 1972*

Subsector	Workers	Per Cent	Assessed Value (1972)	Value of Land per Worker
Reform units	106,000	12.1	E°1,851,060,000	E°17,463
Minifundist	548,311	62.4	1,297,502,000	2,366
Commercial farms	224,407	25.5	2,852,447,000	12,711
Totals; average	878,718	100.0	6,001,009,000	6,829

Source: Same as Table 4.

and labor resources, possibly almost as bad as that which characterized the latifundia before the reform.

The leaders of the agrarian reform process realized this problem and spoke of it even before Allende's election in 1970. Nonetheless, the parties in *Unidad Popular* failed to agree on a solution either before or after his election, at least until the middle of 1971. Expropriations went ahead, accompanied by endless debates within the *Unidad Popular* coalition about the future organization of the reform sector. While the intellectual debate went on, the *campesinos* themselves organized expropriated farms into *asentamientos* much like those of the Frei reform, because at least this model existed legally and thus they could begin to work, get credit, and function.

The first important attempt by the *Unidad Popular* to resolve the problem was baptized "Centers Agrarian Reform" (CERA); the basic idea was to merge two or more adjacent farms into a single larger unit. The pretext was that the boundaries of the expropriated farms were historic accidents and inappropriate for rational planning of an efficient operation. Along the way, the government hoped to incorporate not only all the people living on the expropriated farms but also others who typically live on tiny plots along the road between those farms. The basic idea was thus to include many *campesinos* who formerly had only precarious or tenuous ties to the expropriated farms (working occasionally, when called), through the simple trick of setting up a single unit with new boundaries that included them. The *Unidad Popular* leaders also announced that all persons over eighteen, including women, would be automatic participants in the new units, in spite of the fact that women and young people coming of age were generally excluded from decision making in the *asentamientos*.

It is impossible now to determine the degree to which the general rejection of the CERA model was due to its effort to "blanket in" many more families with the resident permanent workers on the expropriated farms, as opposed to *campesino* rejection of egalitarian participation of young people and women; both factors appear to have been influential. No more than a hundred CERAs were ever formed in the entire country, in spite of an enormous effort by CORA personnel in late 1971 and 1972 (Baytelman, 1975). Another effort to tackle the man/land problem used a tax approach. Existing tax laws exempted the land in agrarian reform projects from property taxation. During the transition period it was state property, and after assignment to beneficiaries it was usually property of a cooperative, exempt as the result of an old incentive intended to encourage the formation of production cooperatives. Even if the land had been divided equally among the beneficiaries, much of it would have remained exempt as the result of the minimum exemption in the real estate tax law.

Exemptions of this sort matter little when little land is involved; when almost half of the agricultural sector becomes exempt, it's quite another matter. An F.A.O. expert, José Gimeno, studied the taxation in various socialist countries as a project of ODEPA (the Chilean sectoral planning office for agriculture) and discovered that in general some kind of agricultural taxation exists in those countries. For this reason, even before discovering the low employment density in the reform sector, the Minister of Agriculture (Jacques Chonchol) created a Mixed Inter-Ministerial Commission on Agricultural Taxation.[2] This Commission worked during 1971 and 1972 and presented recommendations that could have helped in four ways:

First, by taxing land in the reform sector just like all other land, it would have pressured for higher output and thus perhaps led to the acceptance of more workers. The land reform beneficiaries usually tried to avoid hiring additional workers out of fear that these workers would then demand a permanent participation in the farm and eventually in any assignment of the land. The Chilean land tax, since 1965, was 2 per cent per year on assessed values.[3]

Second, the Commission recommended elimination of the employer's contribution to the social security tax, replacing it with a higher rate on agricultural land to yield the same revenue. This contribution, about 40 per cent of the legal minimum wage, was collected from *asentamientos* and CERAs just as from private employers and tended to discourage taking on more workers. By converting it into a fixed tax on the land, the proposal would remove a genuine disincentive to create more jobs.[4]

Finally, I proposed and the Commission recommended that the land tax should be increased or reduced according to the employment intensity with which the property was farmed. Basically, the idea was to divide the total land available by the number of *campesinos* in the labor force, which came out to about E°6,800 of assessed value of land (at 1972 prices) per worker,[5] and then adjust the tax according to the actual ratio of land to employment.

In other words, if a commercial farm or an *asentamiento* gave itself the luxury of employing only one worker for E°13,600 worth of land, twice the national average ratio of these two key resources, then that farm would have to pay the land tax with a surcharge of—say—25 per cent (a rate of 2.5 per cent instead of 2.0 per cent on assessed values). On the other hand, if more employment were created through intensification of land use and the hiring of abundant laborers, the tax would be lowered. The precise scale of surcharges and reductions could have been worked out later with the *campesino* organizations, but the concept involved making those who refused to accept more participants in the reform pay for the privilege. The government said it would not force more workers into reform projects, against the will of the initial beneficiaries, but it could at least give tax incentives for doing so. By collecting more taxes from those who refused, it could finance the creation of other jobs outside the sector, perhaps in processing or other industries related to agriculture.

Fourth, most or all of the land tax revenue would have gone to the *Consejos Comunales Campesinos*, organizations which represented reform beneficiaries, farm laborers, and small commercial farmers in each *comuna* and which served, in theory, as advisors to the Ministry of Agriculture.[6]

SUMMARY AND CONCLUSIONS

Agrarian reform ended the latifundia in Chile but failed to solve the problem of rural unemployment or to respond to the need to intensify agricultural production. In the reformed sector, many farms were left with fewer workers than before. The resident permanent workers (*inquilinos*) threw out the owner and his foremen and did not let anyone else move in, so each would get a larger share in the eventual land assignment. The parties of the *Unidad Popular* coalition had no real consensus as to the ideal organization of the sector, so the expropriation process was completed without resolving the issue. Two attempts to reach a technocratic sort of solution failed: one sought to create larger units in order to "blanket in" more workers. The other—which did not even reach the party chiefs or the cabinet before the forced resignation of the Minister of Agriculture who had ordered its study—proposed the use of tax instruments to create pressures and incentives for increasing rural employment. The tax would also have increased fiscal revenues and given the *Consejos Comunales Campesinos* a genuine role in rural Chile.

Other authors have analyzed the political problems of the reform, as well as the ups and downs of production (Barraclough, 1974; Baytelman, 1975; Chonchol, 1975). In general, it could be concluded that the *Unidad Popular* government came into power with an agrarian reform already under way but with no consensus as to how it should be modified. As a result, the reform was accelerated but not adjusted in any substantial way until it was too late.

After more than a year of philosophical debate on the organization of reform units and the division of profits to be earned in the reform sector, it was discovered too late that there *were* no bookkeeping profits to be divided. That happened because the *campesinos*, distrustful of CORA because its accounting was sloppy and often two years behind, quit reporting sales and sold products outside government controlled channels. They also refused to pay back credit received from CORA or even, in many cases, from the *Banco del Estado*, and most refused to permit the entry into reform projects of other *campesinos*, of still lower, landless classes. Far from there being a simple *campesino* class, of the sort described by the theoreticians of agrarian reform ten years earlier, there were various subclasses whose members had very little solidarity. By the time the man/land problem was perceived clearly, the dominant problems were obtaining more production and facing the threat of civil war.

In the end, the Chilean agrarian reform appears to have reduced the intensity of labor use in agriculture rather than raising it. Production rose (Smith, Stanfield, Brown, 1974) in both the reform sector and commercial farms, but employment did not. It is to be hoped that future land reforms can learn from and avoid a repetition of this experience.

NOTES

1. A standard unit based on a hectare of irrigated land, class III, in the Maipo River Valley near Santiago. All other agricultural land was con-

verted into B.I.H. by means of a Table of Equivalents included in Public Law 16,640.

2. I participated in that Commission, representing the Institute of Economics and Planning of the University of Chile, where I taught public finance during most of the period 1960–1972.

3. The reassessment was promulgated in 1965. In 1966 two students and I did a field study of assessment ratios to market in four *comunas* of central Chile, using personal contacts to detect underdeclaration of transfer prices, and concluded that with 99 per cent confidence one could say that the assessment ratio for those *comunas* was between 40 and 60 per cent of market values. After 1966 there were legal barriers to the free sale of large farms, so genuine market prices were not available to update this study. Given deficiencies in the index adjustment system, I suspect that the ratio by 1972 was somewhere between 20 and 30 per cent of what land prices might have been in a free market, or as capitalized values of the earning power of land in uses typical of each zone—the theoretical base of the 1963–1965 reassessment.

4. This was an old idea of José Gimeno's; he had proposed it to ODEPA back in the Alessandri and Frei administration as well, with no results.

5. About 1.3 B.I.H. per worker.

6. Minister Chonchol created 186 Councils in 1971, but they never had any real resources to administer or clear tasks to carry out. My tax proposal would have given them funds to invest in each *comuna* according to their own best judgment. *That* would have been a decentralization and a participatory form of planning.

BIBLIOGRAPHY

Barraclough, Solon. "The State of Chilean Agriculture Before the *Coup*," Land Tenure Center *Newsletter*, no. 43, January–March 1974.

———. "After Land Reform, What?" Paper presented at the Land Tenure Center's International Seminar on "Agrarian Reform, Institutional Innovation and Rural Development," Madison, Wisconsin, 1977.

Baytelman, David. "Some Problems of Collective Farming in Chile's Agriculture," paper prepared for delivery at the Group Farming Conference, June 10–12, 1975, jointly sponsored by the Research and Training Network of the Agricultural Development Council and the Land Tenure Center, University of Wisconsin-Madison.

Chonchol, Jacques. "Reflections," paper prepared for the same Group Farming Conference.

Comité Interamericano para el Desarrollo Agrícola (CIDA), 1964, *Tenencia de la Tierra y el Desarrollo Agrícola de Chile*. Santiago, 1964.

Gimeno, José M. "Incidencia de la Tributación en el Desarrollo Agropecuario, con Especial Referencia a la Experiencia Chilena." Santiago, mimeographed, 1974. (A treatise studying agricultural taxation in some depth and incorporating many of the findings and recommendations of the Inter-Ministerial Commission on Agricultural Taxation, which worked in Santiago in 1971 and 1972. A further study on the Commission's work is available from the Land Tenure Center, University of Wisconsin-Madison. Madison, Wisconsin.)

Lagos, Ricardo, and Kurt Ulrich. *Tributación y Agricultura*. Santiago, Instituto de Economía, Universidad de Chile, 1965.

Lehman, David. "Political Incorporation vs. Political Stability: The Case of the Chilean Agrarian Reform, 1965–70," in *The Journal of Development Studies*, London, July, 1971.

Pistono, Jose Luis, *et al. Tributación Agrícola*. Santiago, Instituto de Economía, Universidad de Chile, 1958.

Strasma, John. "Property Taxation in Chile," ch. 9 in Arthur Becker (ed.), *Land and Building Taxes*, Madison, University of Wisconsin Press, 1969. (A Conference Book of the Committee on Taxation, Resources & Economic Development.)

———. "Compensation in Land Reform," ch. 2 in the *Fourth Report on Progress in Land Reform*, United Nations Secretary General, 1967.

———. "Las Técnicas de Tasacíon y la Planificación Fiscal; Estudios Catastrales v. Auto-tasación por los Dueños de Predios en Chile, 1961–64," in García and Griffin (eds.), *Ensayos Sobre Planificación*. Santiago, University of Chile Press, 1967.

———. "El Financiamiento de la Reforma Agraria Chilena," *Boletín Informativo*, Santiago, Sociedad Chilena de Planificación y Desarrollo (PLANDES), no. 17, September, 1966.

———. "The Economic Background to Allende's Reform," LTC *Newsletter*, no. 43, January–March, 1974. (Land Tenure Center of the University of Wisconsin-Madison. Madison, Wisconsin.)

———. "Agrarian Reform in Chile under Frei and under Allende: Some Problems in Evaluating Resources and Results," paper prepared for the October, 1975, conference of the Pacific Coast Council for Latin American Studies, and available from the Land Tenure Center, University of Wisconsin-Madison. Madison, Wisconsin.

PART TWO

Causes of the Outcome: Viewpoints Concerning the Failure

Christian Democracy and
the Government of the Unidad Popular

RADOMIRO TOMIC

I was the Christian Democratic candidate for President of Chile in 1970. Our program defined its goal as the replacement of capitalism and its means as an agreement between the Christian Democrats and the forces of the left, both Marxist and secular.

This program crystallized a long process of internal struggle within the Christian Democratic party, the root of which lay in the increasing disintegration of the prevailing system of values and institutions in Chile and in the need to build a new society. It was essential that Christian Democracy opt clearly for change, and our choice was clear: the "Political and Social Unity of the People."

Invited to participate in this prestigious seminar on "The Causes of Failure," I think the most useful contribution I can make is to present, with the greatest intellectual honesty, my own experiences in that process often called "the Chilean road to socialism."

"I awake once every hundred years, when the People awake," Bolívar says in a poem by Neruda. It is not an exaggerated comment for the Chilean drama, as we shall see.

The universal resonance of Allende's victory and his administration, and the global wave of repudiation unleashed by his overthrow, cannot be explained as a merely Chilean phenomenon. After all, no fewer than thirty countries change their governments every year, more than half of these by violent means; yet a few weeks later no one remembers even the name of the deposed administration. But Allende, two years after his death, continues to be a reference point for hundreds of millions of human beings in a hundred countries or more, and for many of these, a banner! So vast a projection cannot be explained simply by the drama of his death nor the works of his government. In itself, his administration was neither so revolutionary nor so exceptional. I think it not unworthy to add that its achievements were largely counterbalanced by the previously unheard-of inflation, the scarcities, and the general disorder and lack of discipline, both within the government and in the country as a whole. Indeed, that strange slogan that Allende himself quoted with good humor, "This is a government of shit, but it is *my* government," accurately summarized the sentiments of his followers in 1972.

How, then, can we explain why, for the last five years, the attention of the world has seemed so disproportionately focused on a country like Chile—small, distant, and of little international consequence—whose socialist experiment received lukewarm support at best from the nations with Communist governments? The answer is that the presidential election of 1970 and the subsequent government dramatically symbolized the same three elements that form the underlying reality of more than one hundred countries. In Chile these three elements were, first, the decision to abandon the capitalist system; second, the decision to replace it with the values, institutions, and leaders proper to a socialist system; and, third, the vague but reiterated and appealing pronouncement that it was possible to move from capitalism to socialism without resorting to either armed confrontation or the dictatorship of the proletariat.

Is this not the fundamental problem confronted by no fewer than one hundred sovereign states on five continents today? One hundred nations that *cannot,* in any way, find an answer to their basic problems in capitalism. And that, even if they could, *do not want* to seek an answer in communism. Herein originates the worldwide echo of the Chilean case.

Physically, the experience took place in Chile, but its potential had meaning for many other countries. Just as the Industrial Revolution, though born in England, was not only English; or the liberal revolution that originated in France, not merely French; or the Communist revolution in Russia, not only Russian; so the Chilean case echoed throughout the world. It is this latent historical potential, more intuited than articulated, that explains the tremendous international resonance of the Chilean experiment, entirely out of proportion to what the *Unidad Popular* was in fact.

There are anecdotes that express far better than rational arguments what we want to say. I remember, for example, an intimate dinner that Allende gave for an Italian delegation, visiting Chile during the so-called Operation Truth. Among those present were Giorgio La Pira, Marcela Glisenti, Father Turoldo, and Professor Corghi, all important personages in the political, spiritual, and intellectual worlds of Italy. For a long time, in vibrant silence—there is no other way to define it—Allende listened as this group of eminent Italians, none of them Marxist, described what they believed was at stake in Chile. Here is the gist of what they said:

"Mr. President, if you can show in Chile that a second road to socialism is possible, that it is possible to create a symbiosis of Christian *values* and socialist *institutions,* then the next country to advance along that road will be Italy, and very soon others in Latin America, and later, in one or two generations, half of the world."

This is what many people, in many countries, saw or thought they saw beginning in Chile with Allende and the *Unidad Popular.* It is this worldwide attitude of expectancy, and not the "international Communist conspiracy" alluded to so disparagingly by the military dictatorship, that has given the Chilean experience such a vast, deep, and persistent impact.

ANTECEDENTS AND PRIOR CRITERIA

Before attempting to interpret the "causes for failure," I believe it would be useful to locate unambiguously my position with respect to the Allende government, the *Unidad Popular,* and the so-called "Chilean road to socialism." I believe that in Chile in 1970 the need for a "new democracy"—an expression of humanist values, socialist institutions, and leadership more authentically representative of the Chilean majority—was more than a *legitimate option.* It was also an *historical necessity,* imposed by the evident and irremediable exhaustion of traditional capitalist society. From this point of view, the failure of the *Unidad Popular* and the Allende government is only an accident that does not itself alter the historical need for democratic socialism. Once the present military dictatorship falls, this need will reemerge in terms even more urgent, more demanding, and—what is more important—more promising than in 1970. To study the causes and errors leading to the collapse of September 11 and draw the appropriate conclusions is therefore an essential task in advancing toward that future.

One cannot understand what happened in Chile or learn its lessons if one ignores its primary cause: the exhaustion of the values and institutions of capitalism at all levels of Chilean life. Under capitalism Chile was a sick economy, the expression of a sick society, eaten away by internal disintegration and in continual international retreat. All basic indicators, economic as well as social, political, legal, cultural, and moral, reflected this fact.

It is true that, during the nineteenth century, the Portalian consolidation of the state permitted Chile, within the capitalist or precapitalist framework then prevalent in Latin America, to realize its actual advantages—racial homogeneity, national integration, the sense of authority and discipline developed by the lengthy war with the Araucanian Indians, good climate and fertile soils, its condition as a maritime nation, etc. In only forty years Chile transformed herself from one of the poorest Spanish colonies into the best-organized nation in Latin America. It is also unarguable, however, that after the revolution of 1891 the contradictions inherent in capitalism and the way these were resolved, both domestically and internationally, rapidly eroded the efficacy of the Portalian state. Following World War I this process was accelerated, and with the Radical governments (1938–1952) the system's capacity for constructive compromise was exhausted. The governments of Ibáñez, Alessandri, and Frei all struggled, in different ways but ultimately in vain, to surmount democratically the growing crisis created by these contradictions. The sophistication of Chilean democracy—civilized, tolerant, but limited to a minority of the population—was visibly stymied. By the end of the 1960s it was the entire system, not a specific government, that was collapsing.

WAS ALLENDE'S FAILURE INEVITABLE?

To facilitate analysis I will distinguish among three points: 1) was the failure inevitable? 2) internal causes; 3) external causes.

Was the failure of the Chilean road to socialism inevitable? Could Allende's program have been implemented within the political and institutional framework of Chile?

We know it failed. This is a fact. We do not know, however, if it *had* to fail. In other words, the decisive problem is to determine whether the causes of failure were insuperable or if failure was rather the result of errors that could have been avoided.

The dramatic aureole of Allende's death amidst the flames of the government palace has tended to suggest that the outcome was inevitable, that the Chilean road to socialism was from the first condemned to fail. We must resist the temptation to oversimplify the Chilean process in this way, so easy but false.

The attempt to move from one social order to another without the systematic use of violence is undoubtedly a very difficult and complex task. It is, of course, hard to generalize, for the concrete circumstances of a specific country at each specific historical moment are what make possible or impossible a transformation "from within," that is, the use of existing institutions to replace one system with another.

I believe, as did Allende, that such a move was possible in Chile. The *favorable* elements outweighed those that were *unfavorable*—at least initially. As we are dealing with a problem that is objectively very important, let me analyze this point in some detail. What were the principal favorable elements? I note seven, whose importance cannot be denied:

1. *A high degree of receptivity to the idea of socialism (but not Marxism-Leninism) in the minds of the majority of Chileans,* confronted by ever more severe basic problems and the objective failure of the Radical governments, the Ibañist experience, the "government of the bureaucrats" of Jorge Alessandri, and the Christian Democratic "revolution in liberty." In September, 1970, two thirds of all Chileans *voted explicitly in favor of advancing toward socialism* by voting for Allende or Tomić. Both candidates coincided in their support for the total nationalization of copper and other basic resources, an integrated agrarian reform, the nationalization of banking, the need for a new Constitution, the creation of a Social Property Sector, and a foreign policy open to all countries, "nonaligned" in the conflict between East and West.

In Chile in 1970 socialism was "an idea whose time had come."

2. *The determined position of the Christian Democratic party, under the dominance of its left wing,* in favor of the "Political and Social Unity of the People." Only thus could Chile be given a government capable of confronting its fundamental problems. The PDC proposed concretely, explicitly, and repeatedly—both before and after Allende's election, and with the party's full support in Congress—the need for an agreement between the Christian Democrats and the Socialist and Communist parties as well as the traditional secular left. The platform of "Political and Social Unity of the People" did not emerge by "spontaneous combustion" within Chilean Christian Democracy. Nor was it a casual electoral posture. It resulted from a process of internal confrontation, prolonged for more than ten years and increasingly explicit, reflecting the worldwide crisis in Christian orientations to power, capitalism, and dominant social minorities. In 1970 at least two

thirds of the Christian Democratic leadership, and a much higher percentage of the party's base, shared this vision of Chilean reality and the mission of Christian Democracy. It was the foundation of the Tomić presidential campaign, articulated without pause for more than a year. It resisted all pressures and maneuvers after September 4, 1970—both domestic and international—to block Allende's election in Congress. In October, 1970, the National *Junta* of the PDC, by a vote of two to one, ordered its congressional representatives to vote for Allende. The new National Council elected in December of that year reflected the same distribution of strength.

The determined Christian Democratic commitment to support the Allende government and the essential elements of its program could have permitted the *Unidad Popular* to enjoy a decisive majority in both branches of the National Congress, in worker and peasant labor unions, and in thousands of mass organizations, such as neighborhood councils and mothers' centers, as well as in the universities, student federations, and professional and technical associations. One must not forget that, in 1970, the Christian Democrats controlled 40 per cent of the Senate and Chamber of Deputies, 70 per cent of all peasant organizations, one third of the workers organized in the Central Labor Confederation, an overwhelming majority of neighborhood councils, mothers' centers and professional and technical organizations, five of the eight universities, and an important part of the communications media: newspapers, magazines, radio, and television.

3. *The social and economic situation in Chile at the close of the Frei administration.* We have already noted that the "revolution in liberty" was rapidly losing support in Chile. This was shown by the decreasing Christian Democratic vote, which fell from 43 per cent in 1965 to 36 per cent in 1967 and barely 29 per cent in March, 1969. The government thus found itself in a minority position both institutionally and in its social base, isolated between an ever more powerful, secular-Marxist left and a right resurging with great impetus. I am convinced that the failure of the "revolution in liberty" was inevitable, essentially because of the contradiction between its *program for economic development,* based on and reinforcing the capitalist structure of the Chilean economy, and its *program for social development.* The latter, mobilizing the people in defense of their interests, increased the many contradictions in Chilean society, particularly those related to the functioning of a capitalist economy in an underdeveloped country.

Nevertheless, apart from the failure of the Christian Democratic government's contradictory goals, there can be no question that it was one of the most homogeneous, highly motivated, and administratively efficient Chilean governments during the last fifty years.

In the social realm, the number of workers' and employees' unions doubled during the Frei administration, while the number of peasant syndicates was multiplied by *one hundred*. By the end of the administration, the agrarian reform had expropriated more than three million hectares and—very important for the predominantly Marxist administration that followed—had absorbed the initial psychological and physical shock of the landowners' resistance. "Popular Promotion" had helped to form thousands of neighborhood councils, mothers' centers, youth centers, and the like, with hundreds of thousands of participants, capable of being psychologically mobilized in support of a socialist program. It would be stubborn and unfair to deny the importance of this objective "inheritance," this massive preparatory labor—undertaken, no doubt, with intentions other than that of promoting socialism but nonetheless objectively valuable for the government of socialist orientation that followed.

In the realm of economics, the Allende government received the Chilean economy with an excess of industrial capacity of almost 15 per cent. Seventy per cent of all national investment was state investment, 40 per cent of the gross domestic product was produced by the public sector, and, as a consequence of high copper prices, there were $370 million in reserves in the Central Bank—a tremendous amount by Chilean standards.

How can we deny that these economic and social factors greatly facilitated, at least initially, the new government's program of advance toward socialism? To those on the left who would argue that this was "only state capitalism," we must remind them of Lenin's comment that "state capitalism is the most complete preparation for socialism, its hallway. Between it and socialism there are no other intermediate steps."

I am not claiming that the Chilean economy and society were "on the edge of take-off," as is argued by many Christian Democratic politicians and technocrats, ignoring contradictory evidence more profound than that reflected in these statistics. In 1970 the objective exhaustion of capitalist values and structures made Chile a sick democracy, *a sick society, and a sick economy.* The system's contradictions were simply strangling it from within. This was demonstrated not only by the high rates of inflation, monetary devaluation, unemployment, and foreign debt—which during the last fifteen years were literally among the highest·in the world—but also by the simultaneous rapid erosion of the prestige of norms and institutions ("the state of law") and the extreme polarization of political and social life. The rate of increase in the GNP, the essential goal of all "developmental governments," barely reached an average of 2 per cent per capita during the last thirty-five years and was declining. It was less, for example, during the Christian Democratic government than during that of Alessandri. In short, Allende took office under conditions substantially similar to those in which Ibáñez, Alessandri, and Frei had begun their respective administrations. *Contrario sensu,* to the extent that the government sought to justify itself on the basis of new and different policies, the existing political tensions favored it.

4. *The international situation.* In no area is a socialist experiment in Latin America more vulnerable than in that of international relations. While it is true that everything that occurs in this world in some way affects the interests of every nation, there are specific factors—geographic, historical, economic, cultural, and geopolitical—that differentiate the basic interests of each country. In this sense, Chile's international interest was linked, favorably or unfavorably, to *six spheres of relationships:*

a) the three countries with which Chile shared borders—Argentina, Peru, and Bolivia—each of which, for different reasons, could endanger Chile's military security and territorial integrity, and with which Chile had important commercial ties, particularly Argentina;

b) the entire block of Latin American countries, especially the South American republics and more particularly the six nations associated with Chile in the Andean Pact;

c) the United States, with formidable bilateral, continental, and worldwide influence;

d) the European countries, generically called "Western Europe," with traditional and important ties with Latin America and Chile;

e) the countries of the "Third World," with problems and interests similar to those of Chile and Latin America; and

f) the socialist countries.

Of these six "spheres of international interest for Chile," in only one—the United States—was the situation frankly unfavorable, even dangerous, for the Allende government. It is impossible to overestimate the negative effects, both open and hidden, of North American suspicion and ill-will. Nevertheless, two points should be considered. First, it was clearly impossible to avoid the hostility of a government such as Nixon's to a program of advance toward socialism. Yet, second, despite the CIA's intervention to prevent Allende's election, he was elected President of Chile. And despite its intervention, the large copper mines and other important North American investments were nationalized without interference, while diplomatic relations and formal commercial ties between the countries were maintained. Although commercial bank credits dropped from US$ 220 million to little more than US$ 20 million, and international agencies in which the United States had a dominant or important interest deferred and delayed loans to Chile, this North American refusal to finance the Chilean socialist experiment was both foreseeable and understandable. Moreover, although the financial impact was immense (equal to some US$ 200 million per year), it was not impossible for the new government, much more open to the socialist sphere, to overcome that deficit. After all, the GNP of the Chilean economy was some US$ 6 billion per year. In any case, in counterbalance to the disadvantageous situation *vis-à-vis* the United States, the *Unidad Popular* government encountered in the other five spheres of Chilean international interest an environment as favorable as had Ibáñez, Alessandri, or Frei and, in some, far better.

In the short run, for example, the most important element in Chilean foreign policy is its relations with its three neighbors: Peru, Bolivia, and Argentina. When Allende assumed power, both Peru and Bolivia had dictatorial governments with definite leftist leanings, committed to anti-capitalist and anti-imperialist programs—even "socialist," though not Marxist. These coincided on major points with the program of the *Unidad Popular,* and relations with both countries improved noticeably. At the same time, the Argentine government under General Lanusse, capitalizing on the obvious ideological distance between "the Chilean road to socialism" and Brazil, did more than any of its predecessors in half a century to build close ties with Chile. Cámpora later carried this desire for friendly Argentine-Chilean relations even further, reflecting very favorably on Allende. For a new government seeking to build socialism, one cannot overstate the importance of avoiding the most dangerous threats—insecurity on its borders, political and military isolation, and international incidents designed to provoke internal division and demoralize public opinion. Chile avoided these and, equally important, thus avoided having to spend a significant part of scarce available resources on the massive acquisition of arms.

In Latin America, in general, there was no hostility toward Chile. Even Brazil, knowing that her "hour" had not yet arrived, maintained correct formal relations in spite of obvious ideological differences. The six Andean Pact countries gave the Chilean government the same degree of backing and cooperation they had given to the Frei administration, which, with the government of Colombia, had been the principal promoter of the past. Mexico maintained outspoken solidarity with the Allende government, to an extent without precedent in its relations with Chile. The same was true of Cuba, with whom diplomatic relations were reestablished and trade was vastly increased.

Among the countries of Western Europe traditionally linked to Chile, all of the social-democratic governments, led by England, Germany, Holland, and the four Scandinavian countries, supported the new Chilean government at least as much as they had the governments of Alessandri and Frei. Indeed, the northern European countries, particularly Sweden, went further than ever before in their efforts to support the regime. Others, such as France, Italy, Spain, and Belgium, maintained official ties, credit policies, and previous levels of commercial and cultural exchange with no decrease in cordiality. The same was true of Japan.

For obvious reasons, the socialist countries, principally the Soviet Union and China, gave the Allende government far greater diplomatic, financial, commercial, and technological support than before.

Last, "the group of 77" (now more than one hundred) observed correctly that the Allende government supported the international objectives of the African, Asian, and Arab countries, all members of that vague but real association known as the Third World or the nonaligned countries. In practice, their attitude took the form of public solidarity with Allende and global recognition of his international position and prestige. Thus ties between the Third World and Chile were incomparably better than under any prior administration.

In sum, we may affirm that Chile's international situation was, when Allende assumed power, relatively better—or at least no worse—than it had been for any other Chilean government. This conclusion emerges even more clearly when we remember that, during the Frei government, Chile not only reestablished diplomatic relations with the Soviet Union and the majority of the East European socialist countries but also initiated substantial commercial contacts with Cuba and Communist China. This saved the so-called Marxist government of Chile from international accusations of "entering the Communist orbit." To use a Chilean expression, such campaigns would have "died in embryo," given that the Christian Democratic government, as well as Allende, had taken the initiative and made the principal decisions.

5) *The loyalty of the armed forces to the Constitution, reinforced by the assassination, by persons associated with the right, of the Army Commander in Chief, General René Schneider.* During the election campaign—as throughout the previous thirty-five years—the armed forces impeccably abstained from politics. In spite of right-wing provocations, General Schneider publicly reiterated that the military would faithfully observe the Constitution, even if the President finally had to be chosen by the Congress from between the two candidates receiving the most votes. The assassination of Schneider, directed by ex-General Viaux and physically perpetrated by individuals linked to the traditional and reactionary ultra-right, was the first political assassination in Chile since the death of Portales, almost 150 years before. It shook the entire army to the core and united it behind a repudiation of any identification with the assassins—linked to the right and to hatred for Allende. Schneider's death sealed for at least two years the neutrality of the army and its rejection of every attempt to involve it in a *coup d'état* against the *Unidad Popular* government. Throughout this period the garrisons offered no threat of any kind to either Allende or his policies.

6) *The political neutrality of the Church and its commitment to the people.* Although many years ago the Chilean Church ceased to be a decisive electoral factor or political power, 90 per cent of all Chileans continue to profess themselves Catholic. It is also clear that a major stumbling block for all socialist governments in the West has been the problem of relations with the Church, in both its domestic and international projections. Church opposition might have left Allende seriously vulnerable and created severe conflicts. However, the Church's refusal to identify with any candidate—even the Christian Democrat—was maintained throughout the campaign and continued with equal emphasis after the election. Although there were a few outbursts of anti-religious sentiment in the government press and in the Ministry of Education (particularly in the attempt to impose the National Unified School, ENU), the Cardinal and practically the entire episcopate firmly resisted all pressures to mobilize the Church in the "struggle against Marxism." For years—both before and after the fall of Allende—Cardinal Silva Henríquez has been attacked as the "Red Cardinal" by right-wing circles and press.

At the same time, the movement to identify the Church with the people in their struggle against the inherent injustice of the capitalist system—the "institutionalized violence" denounced by the entire Latin American episcopate in the Medellín Declaration—had gradually spread and deepened. The so-called Christians for Socialism movement came to include three hundred Chilean priests, pastors, and nuns. How can we forget that a significant number of priests were tortured to death and dozens of others expelled from the country or forced to seek exile following the September 11 *coup?*

7. *The active support of Freemasonry*. For a government led by a Marxist, whose program threatened the dominant groups in traditional society, Masonic support was particularly significant. If Allende himself had not been a Mason, we would most certainly have to add Freemasonry to the list of his enemies.

After more than a century of bitter struggle with the Church for influence over education, public administration, teachers, the armed forces, universities, liberal professions, the judiciary, etc., Masonry had finally acquired appreciable power in each of these sectors, as well as in banking, commerce, and industry. Given the traditional antagonisms of Chilean society, the cumulative effect of the *neutrality* of the Catholic Church and the *active support* of Masonry should not be understated—above all for a government of socialist leanings. Few previous governments had enjoyed this advantageous position.

*   *   *

Let us return to our essential point. Allende was right—as were those of us in the Christian Democratic party who argued for the "Political Unity of the People"—in maintaining that the "Chilean road to socialism" was not foolhardy in 1970. Nor was it demagoguery or merely a dream divorced from reality.

We have indicated a number of factors, all of them important and some very important, that favored the replacing of capitalism by socialist structures in 1970. Moreover, they suggest that it was possible to do so by peaceful means, using existing institutions, and without passing through a prior stage of armed struggle and dictatorship by the proletariat. Nevertheless, it did not work. Allende went to his death with great dignity as President, as a man, and as a socialist, but his program was not implemented and his government was destroyed in blood and fire. *However, that failure was not inevitable! In Chile the possibility of a second road to socialism did exist!* This conclusion is basic if we are to renew the socialist transformation of Chilean society on a more adequate basis in the near future. But for this to occur we must analyze with fraternal spirit, humility, and frankness the errors of omission and commission leading to the failure of an experiment *that did not have to fail.*

THE INTERNAL CAUSES OF FAILURE

To what can we attribute the failure? The agenda of this seminar suggests that we analyze the internal and external causes. Internal causes are those having to do, on the one hand, with the government, the *Unidad Popular,* and other Marxist groups and, on the other, with the conduct of the opposition, politically, economically, and socially. The external causes are foreign interventions, concretely North American.

Obviously I will limit myself to those I consider most important. I should add that, in the measure that this analysis includes those who were defeated and the direct victims of the *coup* and the military dictatorship, it is done only in that spirit that Kierkegaard called "with fear and trembling." There are so many who have paid with their lives and suffering! It is hard to forget that price when judging prior motives and conduct. I trust that I will be pardoned if I add that, on a somewhat less anguished plane, I too have suffered and that persons of my closest family have been affected.

If I were to summarize the *internal causes of failure attributable* to the Allende government and the *Unidad Popular,* the central protagonists of the process, I would choose the following four:

1) One of an *ideological nature:* the *Unidad Popular's* inability to define, even for itself as leader of the process, the "second road" or "Chilean road" to socialism and what this consequently required.

2) One of a *psychological and moral nature:* the lack at all levels, from the highest leadership to the base, of the degree of *revolutionary consciousness* necessary to motivate *revolutionary conduct* sufficiently exemplary and sufficiently shared to make the *Unidad Popular* the moral and psychological backbone of the Chilean people.

3) One of a fundamental *political nature:* the fatal error of not understanding that "the Chilean road to socialism" necessarily required the government to *have a majority both institutionally*

and in its social base, and rejecting repeatedly, both before and after the presidential elections, any agreement with the Christian Democratic party, which for two years was led by its left wing.

4) One of a tactical *economic nature* with irreparable political and economic effects: that of trying to "purchase" the support of 50 per cent or more of the electorate in 1971, through massive increases in salaries, monetary emissions, and the promotion of "consumerism," in order to call a plebiscite in the future and write a new Constitution.

The "Chilean Road" as a "Second Road to Socialism"

The Marxist-Leninist argument of the essentially class-based nature of the state is well-known, as are their beliefs concerning the systematic institutional coercion of the great national majority by the dominant minority in capitalist countries, the inevitability of armed confrontation between the exploiters and the exploited, and the necessity of a dictatorship of the proletariat in the advance toward socialism and then communism. In the course of this century these theses have been applied in at least fourteen countries. They form what, for the purpose of this analysis, I will call the classic road or the "first road" to socialism.

The ideological question raised by the enunciation of the "Chilean road to socialism" in 1970 can be posed in very clear terms. Was the "Chilean road" *a second road, based on assumptions and therefore a strategy* other than those of the classic road? Or was it purely a tactical diversion, designed to conceal fidelity to the first road and the destruction of institutions by violence (the "midwife" of history according to Marx) in order to impose the dictatorship of the proletariat? Perhaps it is worth formulating the dilemma differently. Did the socioeconomic, political, and cultural evolution of Chile, and of the world, permit a theoretical and practical reformulation of the requirements for the advance toward socialism? Or was the so-called Chilean road only a verbal artifice designed to impose the dictatorship of the proletariat by other means?

Although the terms of the dilemma are clear, in practice the real problem was different. The dilemma itself was simply ignored. There was no effort to clarify what was meant by the "Chilean road," what its goals and "potholes" were, nor what theoretical and practical demands the exercise of government would impose on the Communist and Socialist parties, etc. For my part, I believe that the admonition of the prophet Isaiah, "Where there is no vision, the people perish" (Proverbs 29:18), preserves its relevance. There can be no authentic revolutionary process if one does not know where one is going, or why, or how one proposes to arrive.

It is true that one can discover America without realizing it, particularly when one seeks—as Columbus did—not a new world but only a new way to reach India. But in doing what one does not seek to do, the difficulties and negative consequences are inevitably multiplied—as they were for Columbus. Here, in my opinion, lies the greatest omission of the experiment we are studying. It did not examine in depth the originality of this attempt to construct a socialist society under unknown circumstances. It was obvious that new intermediate goals, forms of action, and evaluations of Chilean reality were necessary, yet the *Unidad Popular* limited itself to reiterating the old denunciations of capitalism and imperialism, publicizing the "forty measures" and mouthing "revolutionary" speeches.

The experience of three years in power showed that it was a fatal error not to have clarified, even internally or at a purely ideological level, whether the goal was "a new world" or simply one more way to "reach India"—in this case, Cuba, the Soviet Union, or China.

Rhetorical comparisons aside, the lack of clarity regarding the political requisites of the proposed and unprecedented project was an insuperable weakness—although for many reasons an understandable one.

I mention this as a fact, not as an accusation. Perhaps they could not advance in this definition of a second or Chilean road without tearing apart the fragile edifice of the *Unidad Popular.* Perhaps those who could have debated this problem preferred not to do so because of its obviously explosive implications for Marxist orthodoxy.

The virulence of Lenin's denunciations of the "renegade Kautsky" and the "reformist Bernstein" still terrifies and paralyzes, though today's world has little in common with that of the early 1900s. Kautsky, Bernstein, and Lenin himself died many years ago, and socialism has evolved from a "book theory" to a concrete plan of power governing one third of the people, area, and production of the contemporary world.

Perhaps it was the variety of forms that Marxism has assumed—in Russia, China, Yugoslavia, Cuba, etc.—and the violence with which Marxist-Leninist parties and governments denounce each other for the crime of "revisionism" that prevented any creative debate on the political content of the "Chilean road."

No one is to blame. With this said, however, and given that the reasons for remaining on the periphery of the problem are obvious, the vacuum and ambiguity remain, as do the consequences. No revolutionary process can advance very far without a clear conception of what it is, what it proposes to do, and, to an important extent, how it proposes to do it.

Some will say—and not only people on the right—that my observations are naive, that such an omission or ambiguity did not exist in the minds of Allende or the Socialist and Communist leadership, that for them the Chilean road, or the "peaceful road," or the "second road," was never more than a tactical diversion to "divide the bourgeoisie" and gain time to better organize for a future armed confrontation between exploiters and exploited, the violent destruction of Chilean institutions, and the establishment of the dictatorship of the proletariat—in short, the first model. Those who so argue present some evidence. They use Allende's reply to Debray as to why he had accepted the Statute of Democratic Guarantees—"It was a tactical maneuver." Or they repeat the violent proclamations of the majority on the Socialist party's Central Committee or the more ambiguous declarations, though susceptible to the same interpretation, of the Communist party. They note the "direct action" impelled by the ultra-left and the government's notorious reluctance to deal with it, the slogans proclaiming the creation of "people's power" parallel to the power of the state, and the formation of the "industrial belts" as incipient expressions of future "factory soviets."

These are all facts that cannot be denied, but their meaning should not be exaggerated. There are other facts that more than counterbalance them, defining, limiting, and characterizing the nature and intentions of the Allende government and the *Unidad Popular* far more authentically.

For example, if Allende declared *once* to Debray that he had moved "for tactical reasons," on hundreds of other occasions he reiterated without the slightest qualification that he was bound to the democratic commitment represented in the Statute of Constitutional Guarantees. Moreover, some of these were occasions of the greatest international solemnity, such as his address to the United Nations, his annual message to Congress, his official speeches to the nation, and his press conferences. He repeated interminably that "although he himself was a Marxist, the *Unidad Popular* was not Marxist as such, nor were his presidential program and government."

The evidence is overwhelming that there was never, in the government or the *Unidad Popular,* any surreptitious plot to impose the dictatorship of the proletariat by surprise, by a *"coup d'état* from above." This, like the "Plan Z" (which included the assassination of Allende himself!), was an astute invention contrived and diffused by foreign interventionists and the Chilean right.

My intention, of course, is not to maintain that the Chilean Marxists were not Marxists or that they would not have preferred the dictatorship of the proletariat. Rather they *knew,* with a conviction born of obvious experience, that in the Chilean, American, and world contexts of 1970, an attempt to impose the dictatorship of the proletariat by force would have been insanity without the least chance of success—not one in a million! They knew that they did not have the necessary domestic power or the indispensable international support; the venture would be destroyed in blood and fire.

I might add some uncontested and incontestable facts. The Soviet Union never encouraged a "second Cuba" in Chile. China was more spectator than participant, so much so that it still maintains its ambassador to the military *junta.* And Castro, in his long visit to Chile, fully backed Allende's constitutionalist stance, though he probably held few illusions about the final outcome. All these are facts. They cannot be denied, and their weight overwhelmingly counters the significance of specific speeches or agreements among certain party leaders, and even the numerous illegal activities, almost all economic or administrative, that can be attributed to the *Unidad Popular* or the ultra-left.

In contrast, the evidence is irrefutable that the right and ultra-right opposition used every means within their reach—both legal and illegal—from September 4 on. Moreover, following the congressional elections of March, 1973—aided, although somewhat reluctantly, by the new leadership of the Christian Democratic party after May—they refrained from nothing, twisting the constitutional role of the Congress, the courts, the *Contraloría,* the armed forces, and the mass communications media they controlled, and using massive terrorism to attack the government and public order.

The object of this long digression has been to show that it was a fatal omission for the *Unidad Popular* and the government not to have clarified the ideological content of a "second road" to socialism, as well as its strategic and tactical requirements.

There Can Be No Revolution without Revolutionaries. Without Revolutionaries There Can Be No Revolutionary Conduct

It is impossible to imagine a more difficult, complex, and prolonged task than that of changing the values and structures of a given society. Although a revolutionary ideology is essential, as I have tried to demonstrate, in and of itself it is not sufficient. Like the seed in the hand of the mummified Pharaoh, the "truth" contained in a particular vision of reality will not germinate by itself. Thousands of men and women, possessed by a burning spirit of sacrifice and abnegation in the service of the revolution, are indispensable if it is to move beyond empty phrases and transform the lives of millions. In the words of Marx, "the task is not to interpret history, but to change it."

The decisive factor is *revolutionary spirit*, measured above all in terms of what the activist is disposed to *demand of himself* in the service of the revolution, and only then by what he demands of others. Individual advantages and appetites must be absolutely subordinated—in essence sublimated—to the pursuit of revolutionary interests. Certainly this can be asked of each and every one of us! But the decisive question is still whether the revolution is led by groups or individuals interested in using the advantages of power to pursue their own immediate interests or, in contrast, by those animated by a clear spirit of sacrifice and abnegation.

Although thousands of Chilean men and women fought generously for many years for the Socialist and Communist parties, and for Allende as their candidate, one cannot deny that after they won the 1970 presidential election, the very rationality of the party system, with its methods of recruitment and training, were counterproductive for an authentic revolutionary leadership of the country. The dominant preoccupation in the struggle for power—in unions, interest groups, municipalities, Congress, the presidency, student bodies, etc.—was the "hunt for votes," and this engendered the psychological deformity of seeking power solely to displace others from the tangible benefits inherent in its exercise. "The Left gives, the Right takes away" was one of its slogans. Another was "Now it is our turn!" I will mention in passing some of the devastating effects of this psychology, typically "establishment" and essentially anti-revolutionary:

1. The "quota system of government" among the *Unidad Popular* parties. Although it would be exaggerated to speak of a "federated government," the truth is that the feudalization of

power had disastrous consequences for the unity of both government efforts and the government itself.

2. At the base level—in public administration (both state and municipal), in the labor unions of workers and employees, in the neighborhood councils and other mass organizations with hundreds of thousands of members, in the peasant masses, and in youth, university, and student organizations—sectarianism in the exercise of power became general and acquired hateful forms. Millions of Chileans came to feel they were denied their citizenship and arbitrarily discriminated against in the exercise of their rights or legitimate options. As the *Unidad Popular* did not use, and couldn't use, arbitrary arrests, torture, or the machine gun, this sectarian harassment of the "conquered" by the "conquerors" ultimately provoked a wave of blind resentment in the Chilean populace against the new governors.

4. At the same time this psychology of tangible benefits and the "distribution of spoils" inherent in the slogan, "Now it is our turn," impelled millions of workers, peasants, and officials into an all-out race for massive increases in wages, salaries, and fringe benefits. This was not only consistent with the traditional style of economic demands with which the Marxist parties were identified but also with Allende's campaign promises, the "forty measures" and the like. The same psychology was also translated into extreme labor indiscipline in the public and state sectors. The middle-class groups, many of whom were not committed to the traditional bourgeoisie and had voted for the *Unidad Popular*, were demoralized and alienated.

Labor absenteeism in copper reached 29 per cent; the cost of production in *escudos* rose 50 per cent in six months. In *Chuquicamata*, the world's largest copper mine, the same workers who voted for Allende struck one hundred times in 1972. The losses in the nitrate industry rose from US$ 11 million in 1970 to more than US$ 20 million after the industry was nationalized. Agricultural production dropped in 1972, with respect to 1971, by more than 10 per cent, independent of climatic factors, etc. Similar or even worse effects of this *economicismo** could be noted in practically every sector of the Chilean economy controlled by the state.

Although for obvious reasons I would prefer not to say so, one of the more substantial weaknesses of the Chilean experiment was

*Trans. note. *Economicismo* is a neologism invented by the Latin American left. Essentially it refers to the pursuit of immediate economic goals. For example, demands for wage increases would represent *economicismo;* wage restraint in the interest of the revolution would not.

the early absence of this decisive *revolutionary spirit*. Without revolutionary consciousness, there is only the remedy of revolutionary conduct. And without either, what remains of a revolution is no more than a caricature. To repeat the words of Clodomiro Almeyda, describing the *Unidad Popular* in a recent interview in Mexico, "it was weak and inconsistent ideologically, politically and organizationally." In short, it was a frustrated attempt, condemned to disintegrate quickly.

The Fatal Political Error

Only 36 per cent of the Chilean electorate voted for Allende. His government—limited to the *Unidad Popular*—was a minority in the Congress, the Judiciary, and the *Contraloría* and controlled a minority of the communications media, organizations of professionals and technocrats, representative bodies of businessmen, the middle class, employees' and peasant unions, urban squatters, universities, youth and student organizations, etc.

Theoretically, the *Unidad Popular* confronted an impossible dilemma: either it had to destroy Chilean institutions, for which it did not possess sufficient force, or it had to use them to create new institutions, for which it needed a majority.

The first alternative—to attack and destroy the existing institutional structure of Chile—was absolutely beyond the government's reach, and the government knew it. However, the second alternative—to assemble a powerful government majority, both institutionally and in its base of support—was possible. Indeed, that majority, the greatest Chile would have known in the last hundred years, depended on a single, two-sided factor: the willingness of the Christian Democrats and the *Unidad Popular* to reach a pragmatic, though doctrinal, agreement. Although today, after the disaster, it seems difficult to believe, the Christian Democrats sought that agreement in both word and deed for more than two years, and for more than two years—from August, 1969, to June, 1971—first the Marxist parties and then the *Unidad Popular* and the government explicitly rejected, time and time again, this approach.

The Christian Democrats argued that "political and social unity of the People" was vital to real government in Chile, the replacement of capitalism, and the advance toward socialism. I have already explained how this gradual shift toward a rejection of capitalism and in favor of an agreement with the Marxists had taken place within Chilean Christian Democracy. I have also noted how, after various ups and downs, the Christian Democratic left had obtained an almost overwhelming majority in 1969. In reality, that majority within the party survived until 1971 or 1972.

In contrast, the *Unidad Popular*, particularly the Socialist party at its National Congress in La Serena, in January, 1971, defined an equally clear but opposite strategy. It can be summarized as follows: to force the Christian Democratic party to reach an understanding with the right, and to divide its leadership from its mass, peasant, and youth base. Naturally, this strategy was more than a mere caprice. It reflected a whole perception of Chilean reality: Christian Democracy and its multi-class nature, the content of the "Chilean road" to socialism, etc. In any case, the conclusion was categorical: *Divide the Christian Democrats and reach no understanding with them.*

Objectively, this was a colossal political error, a consequence of prejudiced and less than lucid information. Yet the strategy of dividing the Christian Democrats paid a number of important dividends to the *Unidad Popular.* In May, 1969, in the midst of the battle within the PDC over the platform and presidential candidate, it succeeded in pressing the so-called rebel faction to abandon the party, taking with it two senators and one deputy, and form the MAPU. In July, 1971, they produced a second crisis by inciting a direct confrontation between the *Unidad Popular* and the Christian Democrats in a by-election in Valparaíso, effectively forcing the latter to accept right-wing support for their candidate. As a result, nine deputies and a number of youth leaders resigned to form the Christian left and officially entered the *Unidad Popular* and the government. Thus, on two occasions separated by two years, the left effectively obtained the separation from the PDC of sectors valuable for their intellectual quality, doctrinal formation, and popular appeal. In the end, however, these were pyrrhic victories. On the one hand, they greatly weakened the left-wing faction in the Christian Democratic party, thus effectively favoring the opposite faction, an enemy of the *Unidad Popular* and the government. On the other hand, these divisive maneuvers were seen as a threat to Christian Democracy as such and created in the Christian Democratic base a legitimate resentment against the *Unidad Popular.* Inevitably, this strategy of the left denied all practical meaning or content to the Christian Democratic left's concept of "People's unity" and played a decisive role in shifting party leadership to its anti-Marxist faction, which fought the Allende government and the *Unidad Popular* without truce or pause.

The Economic Error: "Expand at Any Price the Unidad Popular's Electoral and Social Base in Order to Call a Plebiscite and Emerge Victorious!"

The fact that Allende had received only 36 per cent of the national vote, coupled with the rejection of any agreement with the Christian Democrats, led the strategists of the *Unidad Popular* to seek some other means to become a majority. The situation was presented with great frankness by Minister Vuskovic in March, 1972, at a round table in Santiago organized by ODEPLAN and the University of Sussex: "We had electoral support, but not enough; and we had support from the social base, but not enough." To win a plebiscite that could resolve the constitutional conflict between the administration and Congress, the government had to obtain 50 per cent or more of the vote. During 1971 economic policy was designed, without any doubt, with this political and electoral objective in mind. All other considerations, including the economic orthodoxy of contemporary socialist experiences, were sacrificed in the process.

To expand its electoral and social base, the government unhesitatingly applied a variety of measures designed to "seduce the people":

—making salary and income readjustments far greater than the increase in the cost of living;

—using US$ 370 million in Central Bank reserves to double the import of foodstuffs and other consumer goods;

—fixing official prices on almost two thousand articles, using subsidies and other direct or indirect means of compensation;

—issuing uncontrolled amounts of paper money by the Central Bank to stimulate the economy in the short run, even at the cost of creating severe disequilibria in the medium run.

—employing hordes of unnecessary personnel in the government bureaucracy, semi-state agencies, and the nationalized economic sector, with no consideration of productivity, etc.

In sum, policy was designed to shift a substantial part of the GNP toward the working class. In effect, according to technocrats of the *Unidad Popular,* the workers' share of the GNP, which had been on the order of 53 per cent in 1970, climbed to 65 per cent in 1971. Unfortunately, it was dedicated entirely to consumption.

The immediate effect of this massive stimulation of consumption was to permit the use of excess industrial capacity. Unemployment dropped from 8.3 per cent at the end of the Frei administration to 3.8 per cent in 1971. The growth rate that year reached

8 per cent, the highest in twenty-five years, and so on. But the seeds of disaster had been sown! This short-term policy essentially ran counter to the requirements of hard work, austerity, economy, and discipline, the indispensable bases for a transition to socialism. It ran counter to the need to channel a large portion of GNP toward new productive investments and to establish strict priorities in the use of scarce capital resources. And it contradicted the need to emphasize publicly the importance of deliberate austerity and to awaken in the entire nation, particularly in the masses, an awareness that we confronted a great historical test, laden with future opportunities but also fraught with immediate dangers.

The government's short-term policy failed on both fronts. It did not succeed in "buying" a sufficiently large or certain majority to win a national plebiscite (which the government never did hold), and it destroyed in advance, without later remedy, the prerequisites for an efficient socialist system capable of standing on its own.

THE OPPOSITION'S ROLE IN THE DESTRUCTION OF THE CONSTITUTIONAL REGIME

In the political arsenal of the Chilean right, the "fight against communism" has been the most important, dynamic, and effective weapon for mobilizing support and protecting the "established order" that ensures their interests and privileges. Even before the Communist party was founded in Chile, the great massacres of workers during the first three decades of this century—particularly in the North but also in other regions—were justified by denouncing the *ácratas*.*

The fleeting appearance of the "Socialist Republic" of 1932 deepened the hatred and fear of the traditional right. And in 1938, even though the new president—Pedro Aguirre Cerda—was a Radical tied by family and fortune to the traditional establishment, the right did everything possible to see that the armed forces would intervene against the Popular Front and invalidate the election. When they failed, they encouraged the *Ariostazo*, as the con-

---

* An *ácrata* was "a partisan of the suppression of all authority." The term used to designate individuals or groups who questioned not only established authorities but also the existing social order. It was a derogatory term used by conservative sectors to refer to Communists and anarchists in particular. (Eds.)

spiracy led by General Ariosto Herrera came to be called. Later they plotted against the government of Juan A. Ríos.

Democracy, constitutional government, and "civil liberties" have been valued by the Chilean right only as long as they have guaranteed—along with force—the *status quo*. Any possibility that they might lose control of the institutions of government, even within the purest democratic game and to men whom they could not accuse of personally being "Communists," makes the traditional Chilean right the mortal enemy of constitutional government. In 1969 the supposedly "respectable" right-wing press encouraged General Viaux in every possible way in his frustrated *coup* against the Frei government. In 1964 they unleashed a gigantic campaign of hatred, systematically fostering fears of Allende's candidacy in public opinion. As we know now, on that occasion they had colossal financial support from the CIA and various North American multinational firms with interests in Chile.

In 1970, sustained once more by the river of foreign gold and convinced that Alessandri would be victorious, they adopted a less frantic attitude. But when the results were known, they reneged on everything they had said and written committing themselves to "vote in the Congress of whomever came in first, even if by only one vote" and mounted a campaign that came to be called the "sodomization of the Constitution." On September 9 the citizenry were shocked to learn that Alessandri had offered "to resign immediately" if elected by the Congress (he had come in second). This would force a new presidential election in which the right, as they promised the PDC, would support "any Christian Democratic candidate" in order to defeat Allende.

When the Christian Democrats rejected this indecent proposal, the right unleashed a wave of financial panic in September. In October they planned and executed the kidnapping of General Schneider, Commander in Chief of the Army. He resisted and was assassinated. The monstrosity of this crime—as we mentioned before—repelled the armed forces, and for almost two years the right had to do without military support. But they continued, by every means within their reach, to seek to paralyze the government and destroy the very foundations of the constitutional order. This time the ferocity and persistence of their offensive responded directly to the double stimulus of the political support and enormous financial aid received from the United States. Soon the campaign assumed forms heretofore unknown in Chilean politics: the mobilization of women, for example, already underway in December, 1971, and later the mobilization of other sectors of the population. It was always possible to finance the eruption of "protest groups," facilitated—as I explained above—by the sectarian policies of the *Unidad Popular.*

The year 1972 was one of great offensives paving the way for the overthrow of the constitutional regime. Along with the legislative blockade, designed to asphyxiate the government's efforts by approving unfinanced laws (expressly prohibited by the Constitution), and successive censures against ministers of state, the subversive program was extended to other areas of national life. Two key sectors in which foreign funds could play a decisive role were chosen: small commerce and trucking. More than 2,200,000 small store owners and 50,000 trucks, in a country of rugged geography such as Chile, constituted vital centers of the economy, whose disruption would have an immediate impact on the masses. In October, 1972, taking advantage of errors by the government and the *Unidad Popular,* the two great strikes of commerce and transport were begun with carefully orchestrated street demonstrations in the centers of Santiago, Valparaíso, and other important cities. Within two weeks the tension was extreme, with a string of violent incidents between police and strikers that stirred up demonstrations by students, women, etc. These, in turn, generated new incidents, exploited by the right-wing press with maximum drama.

In October, 1972, negotiations between Allende and the Christian Democrats led to formation of a cabinet that included the military. The PDC supported that cabinet, although the party maintained its independence. Allende, for his part, promised that the cabinet, with General Carlos Prats as Interior Minister, would supervise the congressional elections of March, 1973. In this way the neutrality of the government was guaranteed.

Two factors contributed to ending the immediate conflicts. One was the influence of the Christian Democrats, not only in state institutions but also in the party's social base. The other was the opposition's illusion that it could obtain control of two thirds of the Senate and Chamber in March, permitting the constitutional overthrow of Allende. Thus began a relative truce that would last four or five months.

However, the congressional elections showed that the *Unidad Popular* had not been wiped from the people's consciousness! It might be a "government of shit" but given the alternative of Allende's fall and a right-wing government a large portion of the country continued to support the *Unidad Popular!* With 44 per cent of the votes it was still a minority, but in spite of everything—

inflation, scarcities, general disorder, etc.—the *Unidad Popular* had elected two more senators and eight more deputies. The position of the government was thus stronger than before, and the opposition's illusions of removing the President by constitutional impeachment were buried.

In March the slogan of the right had been, "We must get rid of Allende." Now its determination to destroy the constitutional regime was openly revealed. From March on, but particularly between June and the day of the *coup*, the country was overwhelmed by illegal activities, violence, and terrorist attempts such as Chile had never known before, and probably as very few other Latin American nations had known either—in any case, certainly never in the name of "democracy" and "freedom"!

On June 29, 1973, tanks from an armored regiment fired for two hours on the presidential palace of *La Moneda*. For the opposition, this premature uprising served as a dress rehearsal for September 11. (The same cannot be said for the government or the *Unidad Popular*, which learned nothing and were on September 11 even more helpless, if that is possible, than on June 29!) In the weeks and months that followed, the opposition, working through the National Congress, the Judiciary, and the *Contraloría*, literally paralyzed the state. At the same time, daily street riots transformed the center of Santiago and other cities into shameful spectacles of police impotence. The opposition sought—successfully—to show that the government had lost all control over public order. The miners' strike in *El Teniente*—the second largest copper mine—for an illegal and offensively unjust double increase in their salaries, was transformed into the "heroic strike" and exploited to the hilt, in an effort involving the student federation of the Catholic University, political parties, the National Congress, etc. A new transport strike, involving fifty thousand trucks for fifty days, paralyzed more than one million tons per day of food, primary materials, fuels, fertilizers, etc. Railroad bridges, gas lines, oil lines, and electricity towers were blown up, and civilians, police, and members of the armed forces charged with defending the President (Navy Commander Arturo Arraya) were assassinated. There was a paroxysm of terror. For months the government watched helplessly, and the country with astonishment, as the greatest acts of sabotage were perpetrated *every hour of the day and night!*

Those who executed and inspired this systematic crime wave knew what they were doing. Since earliest history, every time a nation has faced the sinister dilemma of choosing between anarchy and dictatorship, it has opted for dictatorship. The *coup de grace* for the destruction of Chilean democracy was the resolution of the Chamber of Deputies, late in August, proclaiming the "illegality of the government's acts." The original wording, proposed by the National party, denounced "the illegitimacy of the government," but the "legalists" representing Christian Democracy in the discussions preferred to avoid the moral responsibility implicit in so substantive a declaration. Their solution was to refer to "the acts" of the government but not to the government itself. Unfortunately, no one noticed or was interested in this fine legal point! Both before and after September 11 this declaration of the National Congress served to justify subversion and the *coup.*

Thus the last six months of the Allende administration offered the world the strange spectacle of a Marxist-led government desperately trying to preserve and protect itself with democratic principles and bourgeois institutions, while the forces of opposition, the self-proclaimed defenders of democracy, smashed the constitutional and legal edifice of the republic by every means within reach.

Although I am still convinced that the greatest responsibility for the institutional disaster at the end of the "Chilean road" must inevitably fall on the government and the *Unidad Popular,* for what they did and did not do as the principal protagonists, I am equally certain that an immense share of responsibility for the destruction of Chilean democracy belongs to the opposition.

However, although the events that form the background to the *coup* occurred in the civilian sector, the Chilean tragedy was not simply an "affair among civilians." The responsibility of the armed forces' high command and the police merits a chapter apart. Above all, the contradictory tenor of certain declarations by military spokesmen, including generals now members of the *junta,* should be examined. According to these, the "decision to overthrow the Allende government was made when we knew the results of the March elections." This would indicate six months of secret preparation and prolonged collusion with the right and those behind the right.

EXTERNAL CAUSES: FOREIGN INTERVENTION

In mid-1970, according to the North American press, the Nixon government had already chosen its policy toward the presidential election in Chile and the possibility of an Allende victory. On

June 27, at a meeting of the so-called Committee of the Forty, Secretary of State Kissinger said, "I don't see why we need to stand by and watch a country go Communist due to the irresponsibility of its own people." The comment has not been denied, and other personal witnesses as well-placed as President Ford and the director of the CIA have confirmed the active CIA intervention in Chile, as well as the distribution of $12 million during the presidential elections of 1964 and 1970. On both occasions the purpose of intervention was identical: to impede the election of Allende. (I wish to state officially that in 1970 the Christian Democratic candidate—myself—neither requested nor received a single penny from this source, directly or indirectly.)

This money certainly was not changed into *escudos* at the Central Bank but on the black market—at an average rate perhaps six or seven times greater. Hence its buying power (or corrupting power) was equivalent to 40 or 50 million dollars. In Chilean terms (and certainly in Chilean political terms) this was a flood of money. It was used with devastating effect, and most assuredly not only to "help finance the opposition press and radio."

In addition to the tremendous potential of such enormous sums for creating chaos, the CIA intervention introduced *ideas* and *experience* on how this money could be used with maximum efficacy. I am convinced, for example, that the "Plan Z" did not originate in Chile.

Nor was intervention limited only to encouraging those already willing to subvert the Constitution. Today we know that in October, 1970, the CIA backed and participated not only in the plan to kidnap the Commander in Chief of the Army, General Schneider, but also in a second plan, similarly designed to block Allende's election in the Congress. Nor did intervention cease with the evidence that a constitutional government in Chile had been elected with impeccable respect for the Constitution and the law. To "destabilize the Allende government" was the new task, and the right and the extreme right knew with absolute certainty that their efforts to fulfill it would receive the psychological and monetary support of the most powerful government in the world. It is impossible to exaggerate the multiplier effect of this support on the minds, actions, and numbers of the hard-core opposition. With the Congress, most of the press, and the judges in their favor, it is true that they were not risking much, and there would always have been some volunteers; but without the presence and stimulus of North America, these would have been far fewer in number. And had they had no more than the barest resources, their subversion of public order and massive corruption of institutional functions would have been reduced to the level of a minor irritant.

It is hardly worth adding that anyone with even the slightest knowledge of Chilean politics knew that Allende himself was not a Communist, nor had he ever been one, that the Socialists and Communists in Chile had a long history of serious disputes and distrusted one another profoundly, and that the Socialist party rejected outright the leadership of the Soviet Union. Whatever the course of events might have been, Allende would never have allowed Chile to become a satellite of the Soviet Union, nor would he have accepted a hegemonic Communist party—unless, perhaps, North American pressure had forced him to do so.

The CIA's intervention was not only *unnecessary to "save Chile from communism,"* but it also may prove dangerously counterproductive for the permanent interests of the United States and Chilean democracy—even more than on other occasions:

—In 1964 Frei would have won in any case. The support of the right was not "bought" by the CIA but rather resulted from the panic of the Conservative, Liberal, and Radical parties following the by-election of Curicó. In that election—only a few months before the presidential balloting—the left had received the vote of 40 per cent of the electorate. The right realized that if Allende had this much support in a rural province, he was assured of the large bloc of the national electorate. In contrast, the CIA-financed "campaign of terror" corrupted Chilean politics and weakened its very basis. The principal practical result was undoubtedly to cut all possible bridges between Frei and the left. The left's battle cry, "We will deny him salt and water," was not a spontaneous demonstration of hatred for Frei or the Christian Democrats; rather, it was the embittered reply of the left-wing parties to the "terror campaign" and the obscene maligning of which they had been victims. We know now that $3 million, provided by the CIA, were spent on that campaign. Its only result was *to destroy the tolerance* that until then had characterized Chilean political struggle and had permitted governments to coexist peaceably with their opposition. The seeds of failure for the Frei administration—isolated and incapable of breaking free of the suspicion generated during the electoral campaign— were sown by foreign advisors and money in 1964.

—The exorbitant financial support for Alessandri in 1970 did not prevent Allende from coming in first. At most it "bought" the votes of a few hundred thousand impoverished peasants and slum dwellers, who would otherwise have voted—not for Alessandri and the right, who had always been their exploiters—for the

Christian Democratic candidate. Without the suction of votes caused by the massive, foreign-financed fraud, the Chilean right would have received only about 21 per cent of the vote, rather than the 34 per cent that was cast for Alessandri. The Congress would have had to choose between Allende and Tomić.

—The frantic interval between the national election on September 4 and the election in Congress on October 24, during which General Schneider was assassinated, not only did not block Allende's election but guaranteed that for two years the armed forces would remain neutral and could not be used to pressure the *Unidad Popular*. The intervention of the CIA and various transnational companies destroyed the moral basis of civic debate and made political crime, which Chile had not known for a century, once more a weapon of struggle.

—In contrast, the scheme to "destabilize" the Allende government successfully accomplished its direct and narrow objective. It did accentuate economic chaos in Chile, and it did promote massive subversion and anarchy. Without doubt, it did shorten the duration of the Allende government. But if the CIA had not intervened, if there had been no CIA—as with the Popular Front triumph in 1938, while civil war was raging in Spain and shortly before the outbreak of World War II—the *Unidad Popular* would have disintegrated just the same, as did the Popular Front in the 1940s. Disintegration was a consequence of what the *Unidad Popular* was, of its different interests and its multiple contradictions. It might well have occurred more rapidly. (I speak of the *Unidad Popular* as a coalition of parties, not of the Allende government as such.) There is nothing that creates stronger unity than the existence of a powerful and implacable enemy. In any case, it is certain that there would never have been a *Communist dictatorship* in Chile, only a political process of attrition, internal division, and new attempts to rebuild majorities, just as during previous governments.

—Unfortunately, it is more than likely that Allende's overthrow and the immeasurable price in suffering, injustice, and abuse the military dictatorship has imposed on the immense majority of Chileans will become like "riding a tiger"—once begun there is no way to stop. In the Chilean people's struggle to retain their rights and achieve a new destiny, the final fruit of foreign intervention is more likely to be a strengthening of communism, as the only and most efficacious alternative to the machine gun in the service of privilege and as the result of the internationalization of the popular struggle.

Thanks to the admirable capacity of the North American institutional system for self-criticism and faith in the people, we know today that foreign intervention played a continuous and important role in the internal politics of Chile for more than ten years—from 1963 to 1973, at least. This had not occurred since the distant days of the Revolution of 1891, which overthrew Balmaceda and mutilated the destiny of Chile. This time, however, intervention was much more elaborate, sophisticated, and dangerous. The cruel and cynical idea of the "Banana Republic" whose destiny and government are manipulated from abroad now applies to the southern continent. Chile was neither respected nor immune to intervention, which was justified with the arrogant pretension that the Chilean people did not have the right to vote "irresponsibly" even though their elections were incontrovertably free, secret, and democratic—as in 1970.

What other Latin American nation can feel safe today? How can we avoid the horrifying prospect that actors in the political battle will be forced to obtain foreign "patronage" to finance their campaigns, win elections, reach power, and keep themselves there? Will the price inevitably be the mortgaging of national sovereignty? It is difficult to imagine a more counterproductive policy for the future of Latin America and Chile! Perhaps the "winners" are too quick to celebrate the success of intervention in Chile, to celebrate the fall of Allende at the price of having destroyed Chile's constitutional order and imposed immeasurable suffering upon millions of men and women. The march of time cannot be halted. There comes to mind that famous and challenging verse, "Death be not proud! Where is your victory?"

The Strategy and Tactics of the Chilean Counterrevolution in the Area of Political Institutions

LUIS MAIRA

THE COUNTERREVOLUTION AND ITS FRONTS OF ATTACK

The establishment of authoritarian regimes following the violent overthrow of modernizing or, in some cases, revolutionary governments has been a recurrent phenomenon since the end of the First World War. These regimes, fascistic to varying degrees, emerged following the Russian Revolution, which showed that the construction of a socialist society had become possible. After 1917 socialism ceased to be a utopian dream and became a concrete reality.

Since then a complex political framework has been created throughout the world—but particularly in the backward capitalist countries—to prevent this threat from materializing. Considerable energy and resources have been expended by those who feel threatened by socialism and are ready to react aggressively to experiments that, objectively or in their minds, contain the seed of a workers' society. On the one hand, the working class and its parties have sought to assault the bourgeois state, to capture it, destroy it, and replace it with a new structure that will ensure the hegemony of their interests. To this assault the defenders of the old and threatened order have responded with efforts to repress and eliminate workers' and mass movements and revolutionary organizations. As the lines of battle have become more sharply drawn and the contradictory interests of groups and social classes more clearly articulated, some rather lengthy periods of counterrevolutionary activity have given rise to the use of openly authori-

240

tarian methods. These go beyond and, essentially, contradict the model of nineteenth-century bourgeois democracy. The most extreme of these models is fascism.

It is often argued that the confrontations that have led to authoritarian regimes have been practically identical. Indeed, a quick glance at what happened in various countries where experiments in political change or social agitation were violently interrupted—as in Spain in 1936, Iran in 1953, and Guatemala in 1954, Brazil in 1964, Indonesia in 1965, Greece in 1967, and Chile in 1973—reveals many rough similarities. For this reason it is tempting to postulate a model of a typical counterrevolution. It would undoubtedly include the following principal elements:

Much of the responsibility for subversion falls on foreign governments or enterprises which, threatened by changes, support internal subversive forces. Proclamation of an imminent threat to democracy (embodied in the risk of a Communist regime) is used to justify an institutional breakdown. Varied and sustained attacks against the existing political and legal system prepare the way for that breakdown. The productive system is purposely dismantled in order to create problems in production and distribution. These, in turn, are exploited for political advantage. Religious feeling is manipulated in order to make an overthrow into a kind of "crusade." The middle sectors' expectations of a higher standard of living (equal to that of the highest-income groups) are used to isolate the popular sectors and parties. It is argued that the model of change is "alien" and that its liquidation is therefore demanded by "nationalism." An attempt is made to consolidate and extend the social and political alliance between a solidly unified bourgeoisie, wide sectors of the middle class—particularly producers (small and middle-sized farmers, industrialists, merchants, and professors) who provide services for the wealthiest groups—and the less conscious and less organized popular masses.

Almost all these elements were present in Chile, but this alone is not sufficient for analysis. We must move beyond a simple typology. We must ask what is unique in every counterrevolution and examine how each of the above objectives was pursued. The Chilean bourgeoisie and its foreign allies showed amazing creativity between 1970 and 1973 as they designed a variety of tactical operations to eliminate any possibility of revolution. They were also to organize a mass reply to working-class and popular mobilization, and they systematically used an institutional political conflict to divert the government from its chosen channel of action. They used the former to polarize the social conflict, thus guaranteeing gradual recruitment of the middle sectors to their cause. Through the latter they denied viability to the political project of the *Unidad Popular*, for that project assumed a stable political system and an unchallenged legality, the very base of the government's legitimacy.

I believe that much of the importance of what occurred during the Allende government lies in the originality and uniqueness of the internal confrontation. The traditional methods of destroying radical governments that had not yet attained effective political power but still refused to abandon their goals were updated in Chile. It will be useful to examine the events from the point of view of the antagonists, because it continues to be true that revolutions that falter and are defeated teach fundamentally through their errors and limitations.

Why did the working classes and their parties lose the battle to their enemies? How was the opposition able to eliminate any possibility of success for the *Unidad Popular*'s program? For what reasons did the political initiative pass to the counterrevolutionaries? The most adequate way to answer these important questions is to reconstruct the battle in its principal sectors. Obviously, the struggle for power forms a single conflict, and only for purposes of analysis can we isolate different arenas in which that conflict occurred—political, economic, social, military, and international. But keeping in mind the essential unity of events, we can sketch the outlines of these fundamental areas in order to better understand the behavior of the combatants. In this fashion we can better evaluate the power (in relation to the existing structures of Chilean society) of the masses and the bourgeoisie at different moments in the conflict, the objectives that both were pursuing at different stages, the manner in which they achieved or failed to achieve their goals, and the internal coherence and compatibility of their goals and projects.

What is important here is not the Chilean project in itself, considered *a priori*, but the concrete feasibility of putting it into practice. The Chilean case confirms the historical maxim that it is not the good "intentions" of a political actor that determine its success but rather its concrete capacity to administer resources and adopt decisions, to encompass strategic and tactical objectives, to make use of its potential strength and the groups and social classes that support it, and to reinforce and broaden its original class base by integrating all those who objectively should benefit from its programs. All or the majority of these were what the *Unidad Popular* did not know how to do in Chile. To defeat the neofascist model and plan for the future, it is indispensable that the Chilean left begin by learning from its own mistakes.

In this essay we will explore one scenario of the Chilean conflict—that of political institutions. The interest of the analysis resides in the basic incompatibility of two facts. On the one hand, the Chilean road to socialism was defined as the achievement of gradual change using the existing institutions. That is, it was a policy of change from within. At the same time, the traditional forces maintained a profound domination over the political system they had designed and then modified, which gave them important advantages. As we shall see, the Chilean right knew how to exploit these on its own behalf. For this reason—I believe—analysis of these events will shed light on the intense dispute over whether it is possible to advance toward socialism within an inherited legality and whether the *Unidad Popular* acted correctly in respecting the restrictions imposed by law on the achievement of its program and its attempts to consolidate power.

THE CHILEAN POLITICAL SYSTEM: ITS FORMATION, MODIFICATION, AND CRISIS[1]

Chile was one of the first Latin American nations to establish her political system upon a solid base. After the country achieved independence from Spain in 1818, there quickly emerged two competing factions, liberal and conservative, both of which advocated bourgeois-democratic forms of organization. These were originally tested in their "pure" forms but met with little success, meanwhile generating intense disorganization and open conflict. In 1830 a civil war broke out, which was resolved militarily in favor of the conservatives. Once solidly established in power, they sought some institutional format through which to channel their control. The result was embodied in the Constitution of 1833, inspired by one of the most important personalities of the incipient Chilean bourgeoisie, Diego Portales. (The present military *junta* considers Portales "one of the principal inspirations for their action.")

The political model set out in the Chilean Constitution of 1833 coincides with what historians have called the "Conservative Republic." It was, in many ways, a liberal and conservative hybrid. It drew substantially from the liberal political theory then in vogue, including Montesquieu's theory of the separation and balance of powers and Rousseau's idea of the general will, but at the

same time it proclaimed the need for a strong, impersonal government, subordinate to law and respect for presidential authority—
the keystone of the entire power structure. This formula effectively ended the influence of the military *caudillos* and assured
solid civilian control of power. The landowning and Catholic oligarchy ruled within the framework of a democracy with suffrage
restricted to those who paid taxes; the great mass of the population
simply did not participate. In practice, the political process in
Chile became one of control through a kind of legal dictatorship.
Power was greatly concentrated.

Not until the second half of the nineteenth century, with the
rise of liberal ideas and the appearance of a new mining bourgeoisie, was this political organization seriously questioned. The
1833 Constitution suffered its first modification in the liberal reforms of 1874. In 1891 President José Manuel Balmaceda, an
advanced liberal nationalist, tried to increase presidential authority for the purpose of introducing reform. The result was the
counterrevolution of 1891, in which conservatives allied with
British entrepreneurs in the nitrate industry overthrew Balmaceda and produced a second modification of the political model.
They imposed a pseudo-parliamentary system, particularly sterile
and negative, which survived until Arturo Alessandri was elected
President in 1920. Alessandri was a civilian *caudillo* whose populist and liberal administration sharpened the crisis. Within five
years new modifications of the 1833 Constitution had become
absolutely necessary. These were embodied in the Constitution
of 1925, a document that, with only slight changes, would remain
in force until September 11, 1973.

In 1925 the traditional sectors sought to modernize their political organization, redistribute roles and responsibilities within
the structures of the state, and return to a clearly defined presidential regime. In time this revised system would correspond to
what is technically called a "presidential regime with a strong
executive." The result, nevertheless, was more precarious and
contradictory than the Portalian project of almost a century earlier.
The first years of the 1925 Constitution were characterized by
institutional instability. From 1927 to July, 1931, Chile lived
under the dictatorship of General Carlos Ibáñez. For more than a
year after his overthrow there was not stable government. There
was even a fleeting Socialist Republic in June, 1932. Although its
only lasting imprint was a number of progressive laws which
would prove useful to the Allende government forty years later,
the Socialist Republic symbolized the growing importance of the

left on the Chilean political scene. This importance did not decline in the following decades.

Not until the end of 1932 did Chile finally return to constitutional rule, beginning an uninterrupted period of more than four decades of governments based on bourgeois democratic principles. These included the leftist Popular Front of 1938; the radical governments of 1942 and 1946, which aligned Chile with the United States in the context of the Cold War; the nationalist-populist experience in 1952, when General Ibáñez returned as a constitutional ruler; the orthodox liberal government led by an independent businessman, Jorge Alessandri, in 1958; and the Christian Democratic administration of Eduardo Frei in 1964, which closely followed the reformist inspiration of the Alliance for Progress and unsuccessfully proposed a "Revolution in Liberty." This was the immediate background to the *Unidad Popular* government.

The Chilean political model established in 1925 had clearly defined characteristics. It was a multiparty system in which the parties, though in constant competition, served at the same time to aggregate a broad and growing social organization. It sought periodic renovation of the incumbents in public office, and for this legislated separate general elections for congressmen, municipal councilmen, and President. As a result, Chile was always either anticipating a general election or feeling the aftereffects. The system provided for interdependent branches of government, although reaffirming the head of state as principal political actor. It sought to guarantee the neutrality and nonintervention of the military. It consecrated a broad statute of political rights, which were effectively applied and later complemented with recognition of economic and social rights as well. All of these principles were included in a semi-rigid Constitution that in four decades experienced only three or four important modifications.[2]

Nevertheless, from its origins the political model of 1925 was dominated by contradictions. Presidential hegemony was in many ways nominal. While legal norms stressed the presidential character of the system, the multiparty structure and its resulting alliances created a situation in which the President normally found himself with minority support. (One must remember that an absolute majority was not necessary to be elected President. Very simply, the task of choosing between the two candidates who had obtained the highest relative majorities was given to a joint session of the National Congress. Salvador Allende himself reached office in this way, after receiving 36.4 per cent of the vote.)

The contradiction between the structure of state power and

the party system sharpened with time and assumed an almost institutional nature. As the number and variety of parties multiplied, the political crisis became more acute. Although Chilean electoral legislation placed certain restrictions on the organization of new parties, these were clearly insufficient; in 1953, a record twenty-nine legal political parties participated in congressional elections. The number gradually decreased, but never below ten or twelve. This tendency was particularly felt on the left, where since the 1930s the working class had been represented by two principal parties: the Socialist and the Communist. Both enjoyed approximately equal support (about 15 per cent of the electorate), but their disagreements on domestic and international matters kept them from forming one large movement. As other political organizations moved to the left, they also tended to remain separate, as in the cases of radicalized groups of Christian and social democratic origin and of dissident Marxists. Indeed, when the *Unidad Popular* was established in 1969, it included six political parties, and one more, the Organization of the Christian Left, was added in 1971.

Thus, while political theory and the Constitution ascribed a long list of prerogatives to the President and assumed the primacy of his authority, the dispersion of political actors and their tendency to form varied and shifting blocs made it almost impossible for him to secure adequate support.

It is important to note that this conflict between the presidential character of the political regime and the complex structure of parties and alliances could not be resolved within Chilean institutional rules. While elections almost invariably left the President in a minority position, the Constitution provided for no mechanisms to resolve the numerous difficulties that derived from this fact.[3]

Above all, the problem resided in the particularly demanding structure of decision making. For the President to prevail, it was necessary that he control an absolute majority in both houses of the Congress. For the opposition to have its way, it needed an absolute majority in the Chamber of Deputies and two thirds of the members of the Senate, by virtue of the functioning of the legislative veto and constitutional censure—to be analyzed below. Obviously, a multiparty system, characterized after 1958 by a tendency toward party alliances in three loose blocs, worked in practice to keep either situation from emerging. In effect, after 1932 and increasingly over time, the President faced majorities in Congress which were numerically insufficient to impose their point of view upon him. Thus it became normal practice for the Chilean political system to function with a minority President confronting sterile but obstructionist congressional majorities.

This problem was the root of the increasing crisis in the political model of 1925, a crisis so paralyzing and obvious that Salvador Allende's two predecessors had both proposed constitutional reforms—Alessandri in 1964 and Frei in 1967. Each sought to reinforce presidential attributes and break the impasse that, in the political language of Chile, had come to be known as the "political stalemate." Neither, however, was successful. For this reason the political crisis constituted a given at the beginning of the *Unidad Popular* administration.

In the absence of adequate structural mechanisms, the conflicts between the President and an opposition majority could be resolved only through continual direct political negotiations, in which the head of state sought to compromise with sectors of the opposition in exchange for their support of specific presidential initiatives. This type of negotiated agreement became so important in Chilean politics that, if one analyzes the composition of partisan leadership following 1938, one quickly discovers that there were always leaders filling the specialized role of political negotiators. Their task was to find "the just middle ground" between apparently irreconcilable positions, thus amassing sufficient support to gain approval for new policies. It is easily understandable that this process worked—i.e., it was possible to find equitable solutions—only as long as the basic legitimacy of the existing political and social system was implicitly accepted. For this reason, as the gap between political blocs widened and the projects proposed by different actors became more antagonistic, the capacity of the political system to function normally—through negotiations based on fluid positions—gradually dwindled. Specifically, as the political power of the working class increased and as its desire for a new kind of state, incompatible with the existing one, was articulated, the political structure became more rigid and vulnerable. The crisis of the Chilean political system in the 1950s and 1960s, with open conflict between the three Presidents preceding Allende and the Congress, reflected the increasing polarization of Chilean society. The interests that underlay opposing conceptions of the political order were increasingly incompatible.

This tendency was reinforced by one additional factor, the growth of Christian Democracy. For years the important middle sector of Chilean society had found political expression in a strong center, equidistant from right and left, capable of defining alternative political options. From the 1930s to the end of the 1950s, the predominant force in this center had been the Radical party, characterized by a limited attachment to ideological schemes and a willingness to participate in coalitions with either side of the political spectrum. The only condition was that its immediate interests be protected.[4]

Following its creation in 1957, the Christian Democratic party rapidly replaced the Radical party as the major expression of the middle sectors. By 1963 it had become the most powerful political party in Chile, a position it did not lose until the *coup d'état* of 1973. However, unlike the Radicals, the Christian Democrats had a major ideological commitment—to social Christian thought—that played an important role in their political rise and greatly conditioned their decisions. They also cultivated a style of political "alternativism" that had led them to reject seeking alliances with other forces. The best expression of this political isolationism were the *"castillista"* theses of the first PDC Congress (1959) and the "our own road" policies of 1969.[5]

The policies of the Frei government also contributed to the growing tripolarity of the Chilean political system. Its program, perceptively characterized by British economist Nicholas Kaldor as "advanced in the countryside and conservative in the city," included an agrarian reform directed against the largest and most inefficient landowners, while compromising with North American copper firms and the powerful commercial and industrial enterprises owned by the national bourgeoisie or foreign consortia. In this way the Christian Democrats accentuated their isolation, alienating both the great landowners, who controlled the National party, and the workers' organizations, which had great influence in the Socialist and Communist parties, both openly opposed to the denationalization of the Chilean economy advocated by Frei.

The parties of the left perceived correctly at the time that the rigidity of the Christian Democratic party would prevent it from constructing a dominant and self-sufficient political center. Moreover, they realized that the maxim that multiclass and centrist political organizations, in periods of definition and conflict, tend toward dispersion would hold true in Chile.[6] What they did not perceive, in contrast, was the fragility of the tripolar structure and the advanced state of crisis in the political system. It should have been foreseen that if implementation of the *Unidad Popular* program suggested the viability of socialism in Chile, all the traditional mechanisms of political compromise would immediately be shut off. Yet the program designed in 1969 was based on the assumption that the political system would continue to function normally. The left did not realize that the rules of the game only applied under conditions of relative normality and could easily be blocked as soon as the established order was seriously questioned.

The tripolar structure and respect for political institutions were simultaneously conditions and consequences of the continued existence of a bourgeois-democratic model. The concrete development of policies of social change by the Allende government rapidly altered the political system. The *Unidad Popular* could not work within the same institutions as its predecessors. Instead, it had to confront a political system in a rapidly accelerating crisis, every day more unstable and irrational. Constant modifications eventually produced that system's definitive paralysis.

FIRST DEFINITIONS

As a logical result of the political process, the possibilities for negotiation were blocked by obstacles that could be removed only with great difficulty. No road remained open save that of confrontation. Although this process affected all areas of Chilean politics and society, its intensity was greatest in the area of political institutions.

Those most opposed to socialism initially thought that force would be the most adequate means to block Allende's assumption of power. The failure of their attempt to kidnap General René Schneider, and his assassination in the process, temporarily paralyzed these sectors and deprived them of the political initiative. After a brief pause, however, the extreme right, via its natural expression in the National party, was able to take permanent control of the institutional attack on the *Unidad Popular* government. In contrast, the Christian Democratic party showed itself absolutely incapable of escaping from the tactical framework imposed upon it.

The earliest proposal to use the political system as a means to impede the government's program was formulated by the right-wing Senator Raúl Morales Adriazola. He suggested creating "an institutional checkmate." Morales had been implicated in General Schneider's assassination when it was discovered that he had ties to Chilean financiers residing in Venezuela who had supported the plot by supplying arms and grenades of paralyzing gas. The government requested that his senatorial immunity be lifted, but the Supreme Court denied the request in December, 1970, in a ruling that could not be appealed. This decision, reflecting an opposition bias characteristic of the judicial branch, blocked any possible clarification of Senator Morales' participation in the attempt. At a social gathering with friends to celebrate his judicial victory, the senator delivered a speech pointing out that the Chilean Constitution fortunately offered sufficient resources to crush a socialist government by denying it the ability to realize its plans. The fundamental mechanism for doing so, he asserted, was a succession of constitutional censures, brought constantly against ministers, governors, and other close collaborators of the President. These censures required only an absolute majority in the Senate. The ideal, of course, would be to impeach Salvador Allende himself, but impeachment necessitated control of two thirds of the Senate. For that, the right would have to wait for improved political conditions after the general elections of March, 1973. Meanwhile, they could strike at the government by depriving the President of his most qualified aides.

Early in January, 1971, Sergio Onofre Jarpa, president of the National party, formulated a second proposal for confronting the government. Jarpa had left Chile shortly after the September elections, citing reasons of health, but had returned to the country at the end of 1970. He then quickly undertook to design a strategy for confronting the new government and its programs. He found a panorama laden with events, for President Allende had struck rapidly and in depth. In the first weeks of his administration Allende had sent to the National Congress a proposed constitutional reform to permit nationalizing copper, renewed diplomatic and consular relations with the government of Cuba, and established ties with the Chinese People's Republic, North Vietnam, and North Korea. He had initiated a program to nationalize private domestic and foreign banks by purchasing stock sufficient to consolidate public control, and he had intensified the agrarian reform, applying the legislation approved in 1967.

What Jarpa found, however, was more significant than simply the concrete implementation of the *Unidad Popular*'s policies. Throughout Chile there was a new political climate of change and social organization. None of the right's disastrous predictions of what would happen if a "Marxist President" reached *La Moneda* had been fulfilled. On the contrary, the economic crisis unleashed at the close of the Frei administration by panic among the wealthiest groups had given way to noticeable economic expansion. A process of income redistribution, accompanied by economic normalization, had clearly begun and would continue until the end of 1971. Abuses or violent acts by the people's parties or workers' organizations had not occurred. A climate of peace and tranquility reigned that was astonishing in a country which for ten years had witnessed convulsions, social conflict, and street agitation. It almost seemed that, after a long period of rejection and frustration, the majority had finally won the right to lead the country and had got down to work.

Onofre Jarpa was a man of tried political skills and vast conspiratorial experience. In his youth he had been an activist in the Chilean National Socialist Movement, and later he had participated in Jorge Prat's *"estanquerista"* organization.[7] He understood the danger for the right if the Allende government established a climate of normality. Particularly risky was the potential impact on mass sectors of the Christian Democratic party. Much of the younger and peasant membership of that party openly sympathized with the *Unidad Popular* program, which in any case was very similar to that proposed slightly earlier by Radomiro Tomić. It was therefore necessary to dig a chasm between the forces of the left and all other political organizations in Chile, replacing the tripolarity of Chilean politics with a polarized alignment of two blocks, one "democratic" and the other "Marxist."

To meet these needs, the National party defined its new tactic: a policy of appealing to the Christian Democrats, to whom Jarpa formally proposed the formation of a united opposition. The ultimate goal of this great center-right alliance would be to win the support of the Christian Democratic masses, which was indispensable if the anti-socialist effort were to have a popular character. The right felt that successful creation of a united front would facilitate the task of committing the PDC bases to overthrowing the constitutional government. This could be done through constantly escalating confrontations that would dissipate the initial support government policies had earned among broad Christian Democratic sectors. This, in effect, is what occurred. Through a long process, a single political opposition front to the *Unidad Popular* took shape, culminating with the official formation of the Democratic Confederation in July, 1972. Thus Nationals and Christian Democrats, as well as two small dissident Radical factions, were linked in a single federated political party.

During these first months of the *Unidad Popular* government, the Christian Democrats, for their part, underwent a laborious redefinition of leadership. During the presidential campaign a number of the closest collaborators of Radomiro Tomić, the party candidate and leader of its left wing, had reached high leadership positions. This did not reflect any change in the correlation of forces within the party, which continued to favor the moderates led by Frei, but rather the latter's lack of interest in leading the electoral campaign, as well as the candidate's influence in choosing for key positions persons who enjoyed his political confidence. Naturally, both conditions disappeared after the defeat of September 4. As a result, when the Christian Democrats chose new leadership in mid-December, 1970, the moderate majority was able to regain control of many important positions.

The new national leadership, led by Senator Narciso Irureta, resulted from a compromise between the two sectors, but it immediately attempted to differentiate the party from the objectives sought by the *Unidad Popular*. Irureta clearly indicated this disposition by heading a congressional investigation of those responsible for copper policy. (This investigation alleged certain illegalities in marketing; they were never proven.) However, to complete the picture of the Christian Democrats' political disposition in early 1971, I must add that they also desired to differentiate themselves from the efforts of the right and avoid serving their tactical designs. Still, the need for support in the 1971 municipal elections led the party leadership to refuse all collaboration with President Allende, except for congressional support of the constitutional reform concerning nationalization of copper. Curiously, although they hoped for important electoral benefits from this strategy, it did not bear fruit. The Irureta leadership had to confront a new drop in the party's electoral support.

FORMATION OF AN ANTI-SOCIALIST STATE BLOC

The National party, the congressional actor in the anti-socialist strategy of the combined Chilean right, began immediately to implement its offensive against the government of President Allende. Under the leadership of the "nationalist" and "integrist" sector, the party's objective was to besiege the government intensively through planned, coordinated political operations that would shake the coherence and efficacy of the political model of 1925 to its very roots. In doing so the right took advantage of the *Unidad Popular*'s lack of perception with regard to the functioning of key mechanisms in the political system. Its leaders realized that they possessed advantages derived from their superior knowledge of the morphology and operation of state institutions. This placed Allende's proposals for social change and the President himself in vulnerable positions.

During this period the Chilean right cleverly increased tension on the most sensitive and fragile points in Chilean institutions. Its purposes were clear. On the one hand, the opposition sought to change the nature of the regime so as to annul the President's strategic advantages and alter his position as the central political actor in the system. Once the political system no longer functioned coherently and Allende's ability to rule was weakened, they planned a multiple offensive to achieve his overthrow. During this second phase activities would be directed convergently toward the military, economic, and international arenas, as well as that of social organizations; for the moment, however, the strategy assigned a prior and preparatory character to actions directly affecting the political system.

The first phase was tactically characterized by a considerable autonomy in the actions taken in different arenas and by quiet efforts to rebuild the internal unity of the Chilean bourgeoisie, in both its political and its entrepreneurial organizations. At the same time the right sought an expanded alliance with the middle sectors which shared its fears of socialism and its essential goals. Although in the second phase the goal would be to provoke a *coup*, the right was very careful not to make this explicit. This first phase of counterrevolutionary activity extended from the end of 1970, when the leadership of the political right recovered from its initial paralysis following the Allende triumph, to mid-1972, when, having consolidated its unity, it was ready to undertake "greater operations." The most important of these would be the owners' strike of October, 1972, and the congressional election campaign of March, 1973. In the latter the opposition hoped to obtain the two thirds of the Senate necessary to remove the President constitutionally.

In their attempts to use the political system for their own purposes, the counterrevolutionary leaders selected three basic institutional mechanisms: constitutional censures; alteration of the normal legislative hierarchy (by making common bills constitutional reforms); and distortion of the legislative veto in the final state of lawmaking.

It is important to examine in detail these political and institutional offensives of the counterrevolution in order to understand their internal logic and the relationship among them.

Intensive Use of Constitutional Censure

The institution of constitutional censure in Chile is as old as the political system itself. It was included in the Constitution in

1833, borrowed directly from the 1787 Constitution of the United States. As is well known, the authors of the North American text included provisions for the political trial (impeachment) of the President in cases of serious crimes affecting the integrity, security, or honor of the nation. The mechanism was adopted from the British limited monarchy, in which Parliament, although not participating in the designation of cabinet ministers nor controlling the orientation of policy, had nevertheless achieved a degree of influence by asserting its right to try cabinet officers for serious infractions committed while fulfilling their duties.

Along with establishing presidential preeminence, the designers of the Chilean system adopted the institution of constitutional censure, making it applicable to the head of state and his closest advisors. In so doing, they pursued two clearly defined purposes. First, in accordance with liberal political theory, they reaffirmed the principle of checks and balances among the various branches of government. Second, from among the various forms of bourgeois-democracy, they chose to create a presidential system— that is, one essentially characterized by the absence of executive political responsibility to the congressional majority. The architects of the Chilean Constitution emphasized that it was not the role of the Chamber of Deputies or the Senate to judge the appropriateness of executive policies. Nor were they given the ability to annul specific government actions. Their role was limited to general political oversight and to examining specific crimes or abuses committed by the president, his ministers, or certain other high public officials.

In effect the Chilean system simply borrowed the basic North American conception of impeachment as a special penal responsibility of constitutional order. It had nothing to do with those forms of votes of confidence or censure that are common in bourgeois democracies of a parliamentary nature. It was naturally intended that censure be used only in exceptional cases, and until the *Unidad Popular* government this held true. Only once during the twentieth century was censure attempted against a President of Chile (against Carlos Ibáñez, unsuccessfully in 1956). Chilean history also showed that the censure of ministers was similarly infrequent, always under very special circumstances and following the legal requirements. The crisis of the political system more typically involved presidential powers, taking the form of attempts by Congress to reduce the prerogatives of the head of state.

The Constitution of 1925, however, was drafted with the opposite intent. The counterrevolution of 1891 had created a pseudo-parliamentary regime similar to what is now called "a system of assembly"—that is, one in which a congressional majority, though not subject to any responsibility nor obliged to govern, nevertheless unrestrictedly controls and censures a subordinate government. The 1925 Constitution was designed to repair this pseudo-parliamentary system by restoring certain political institutions that stabilized the balance of power, among them constitutional censure. In effect, this is what occurred.

A similar desire to defend presidential prerogatives inspired the constitutional amendments of 1943 and 1970, the most important modifications of the 1925 Charter. Briefly, these reserved for presidential initiative all matters relating to public and private sector income, government spending, and the social security system. Thus the amendments attempted to guarantee that the President would direct economic and social planning. In both cases the area in which Congress could initiate legislation was reduced. Thus it formally lost institutional power. In practice, however, the multiparty system and the real distribution of forces in Chilean politics ensured that Congress lost very little of its power to obstruct.

The battle facing President Allende confirmed another historical tendency of Chilean politics: in 1970, as in 1891 and 1924, attempts to disorganize the political system formed part of the strategy of those who opposed governments favoring change. When the leaders of the National party initiated their plan to effect multiple constitutional censures, they correctly anticipated that, even if unsuccessful, these would cause great difficulties for the government. If the petitions were successful, the various ministries would be denied stable leadership, and the government's efforts would be disorganized. The President would lose the aid of his best technical and political advisors and those who enjoyed his greatest confidence. The time-consuming parliamentary procedure of censure would leave ministries without leadership for prolonged periods, with the result that the implementation of economic and social policies would lose consistency. The achievement of proposed actions would be delayed.

I insist that simply initiating these accusations was sufficient to provoke many of these effects. In practice, the conditions created by these operations permitted the opposition to intensify its attacks on a new front. Here it is important to note the deteriorating image of effective authority that accompanied this political battle. Nevertheless, as important as these side effects may seem, they were secondary to the principal aim pursued by the right. In its use of constitutional censure, the opposition essentially sought to create a conflict among the branches of government that would lead, as its intensity increased, to the collapse of Chilean political institutions. They sought to create a structural schism in the state that would change its nature by paralyzing its ability to act. Curiously, the left explicitly refused to dismember the existing state. While Allende defended the stability and coherence of a bourgeois-democratic structure which he had not helped to create and which did not correspond to his ideas, his adversaries on the right, who had created that state, now sought to dismantle and paralyze it. The explanation for their attitude is simple: They wanted to eliminate any effective political organization capable of advancing social change.

Initially their designs encountered considerable difficulties. It was not enough for the National party, or the institutionalized right in general, to know clearly what they wanted to achieve. Their minority position (they had received only 20 percent of the popular vote and controlled a similar congressional bloc) obliged them to lower their sights to goals that could be shared by the combined opposition. Only in this way could they control a majority in both houses of Congress. Such control was prerequisite to building a broad anti-government force ready to challenge the plans of the *Unidad Popular.*

There were numerous difficulties. The confrontation between the National party and the Christian Democrats during the 1970 campaign had been bitter, reaching its greatest intensity in April with the assassination of a Christian Democratic leader, Hernán Mery, by a leader of the National party. Mery, an executive of the Agrarian Reform Corporation, was shot as a result of the expropriation of a *latifundio.* The campaign resentments placed a major stumbling block in the path of anti-socialist unity. The response of the National party leadership was to persist in its designs, maintain the intensity of its attacks against the President, and attempt new maneuvers to exert pressure on both the base and leader of the PEC.

For the right, 1971 was a year of barren efforts and a patient search for opposition unity. Three attempts to censure different ministers of state failed. The first was in February against the Minister of Justice, Lisandro Cruz Ponce, and the second in April against the Minister of Labor, José Oyarce. In both cases the Christian Democratic leadership abstained, instructing its representatives not to participate in the congressional vote. Thus the petitions were rejected during their preliminary phase in the Chamber of Deputies. In September, the National party announced its intent to censure Economics Minister Pedro Vus-kovic, the principal author of the Allende government's economic policy and the program to create and expand the Social Property Sector of the economy. Once again the national Christian Democratic leaders decided to abstain, although by now they were cooperating with the right in other areas.

Why did the PDC decide not to support a petition that, if successful, would have removed from the government one of Allende's most important collaborators? In part, the party clearly wanted to indicate that, within the opposition, it held the initiative and would not simply echo the activities of other groups. On the other hand, it needed to reinforce internal unity, threatened by the recent schism of the Christian left. To avoid pretexts for other progressive groups to withdraw, it did not want to appear to block programs very similar to those it had proposed during the presidential campaign. These considerations delayed for many months the formation of a united opposition front and implementation of anti-socialist plans.

The efforts of the National party to approach the Christian Democrats finally began to bear fruit at the close of 1971. On December 24, a group of ten Christian Democratic deputies brought a motion to censure the Interior Minister, José Toha González. To understand that decision, however, it is first necessary to summarize briefly the political situation at the time.

President Allende had gained power in November, 1970, under unfavorable conditions. Separate elections were held in Chile for each of several different positions of authority. This was justified by the need for periodic indication of public opinion. In practice it served to control the President by offering a response to his basic measures and programs. The duration of the mandates of different officials was such that every other President enjoyed the renewal of Congress only four months after taking office, when his support would be not only most solid but also enlarged. Given the tripolarity of Chilean politics, this was the only institutional opportunity for coordinating the political orientations of the executive and legislative branches. It was limited, however, by the fact that the Senate renewed only half of its fifty members.

This possibility, which helped Presidents Ibáñez in 1953 and Frei in 1965, was not available to Allende. In contrast, in April, 1971, he had to face national municipal elections which, though the results had no decisive value, involved all the disputes and confrontations typical of any electoral battle.

The right wing of the Christian Democratic party, whose long-run design to combat Allende involved the formation of a *de facto* civil-military front wherein they would speak for independent armed forces before the President, hoped to take advantage of the elections. They felt that a good show of strength would gain them undisputed hegemony in the opposition. For this, however, they had to eliminate the political and psychological ties that had linked much of their support to the left since the presidential campaign. For this reason they gave an aggressive, anti-Communist tone to the party's campaign. A daughter of ex-president Frei headed the list for Santiago, and along the length of Chile many old collaborators of the former President were candidates. As a result, although the Christian Democratic victory was precarious, the leadership succeeded in making the campaign an experience that unified opposition sentiments in the party's base.

The left made its greatest show of strength in the April, 1971, elections, obtaining 50.15 per cent of the vote. In terms of real political power, however, it obtained nothing. The mayors and councilmen of the 275 municipalities had no bearing on the march of the country. Nevertheless, the left's strong showing made their most determined adversaries aware that it was not impossible for Allende and the *Unidad Popular* to gain an absolute majority, which might make feasible their intended modification of the state by constitutional means. As a result, the opposition decided to intensify its efforts and speed up its plans to block fulfillment of the Allende government's program.

With the elections barely decided, the right began a new offensive to isolate and disorganize the forces of the left. An event of great importance facilitated their plans. At the beginning of June, Pérez Zujovic, a Minister of the Interior under Frei and one of the most important right-wing leaders of the Christian Democratic party, was assassinated by a commando group of the ultra-left *Vanguardia Organizada del Pueblo*. Not until much later was it learned that the intelligence services of the United States had played an important role in the perfectly executed operation. The assassination naturally provoked a wave of indignation, creating another psychological barrier between activists of the left and the Christian Democrats. Radomiro Tomić, the Christian Democratic presidential candidate in 1970, recently declared that this episode marked the "point of no return" in the widening gap between the two forces.

The immediate consequence was that the formal leadership of the Chamber of Deputies, until then controlled by the *Unidad Popular*, was censured. National and Christian Democratic deputies voting as a bloc elected new leadership composed entirely of Christian Democrats. The incipient alliance showed itself again, only one month later, in a special by-election for a Chamber seat representing the province of Valparaíso, the second most important in Chile. The right used the election to provoke another confrontation between two clearly divided blocs, and the government candidate was defeated by the representative of a united opposition, a Christian Democrat.

In the following months there was a simultaneous hyper-politicization of Chilean society and polarization of political actors. Characteristically, the motor forces behind these twin phenomena were the political parties. Practically all social organizations in Chile—unions, neighborhood councils, mothers' centers, student federations, professional bodies—became active centers of confrontation. Elections for leadership of these groups were defined in directly political terms—for or against the government. Although Christian Democracy enjoyed the greatest support, the National party maneuvered successfully to obtain leaders sympathetic to its aims.

In November the battle between the government and the opposition was increased by the presence of a new polemical element: the visit of Cuban Prime Minister Fidel Castro. Castro spent almost a month in Chile, traveling to the principal industrial, mining, and agricultural centers, meeting with workers, and offering suggestions that, while perhaps not constituting direct interference in domestic politics, at least involved an important labor of political pedagogy. His activities stimulated a counteroffensive by the *Unidad Popular*'s adversaries, once again led by the extreme right, which culminated in the now famous "march of the empty pots" on December 1, the eve of Castro's departure.

The women's march, backed by strong, right-wing shock groups, gave rise to numerous disturbances and forced the government, through the Minister of the Interior, to declare an emergency zone in the province of Santiago. This declaration, along with the accusation that the police had not given appropriate protection to the demonstrators, led to the preparation and presentation of a motion to censure Minister Toha. On this occasion, however, the National party showed that it had learned its lesson and did not insist on sponsoring the accusation, ceding the initiative entirely to the Christian Democrats. The motion opened the door for the right to pursue its tactical aim of an escalating series of political trials.

The charges against Toha were based on the principles enumerated in the Constitution: infraction of provisions in the basic

Charter, violating the law, failing to enforce the law, and endangering national security. However, the congressional debate turned into a political trial of the entire government and its program, in which all activities of the Allende administration during its fifteen months in power were questioned.

Joan E. Garcés, a principal legal advisor of the Minister of the Interior, has described the trial in the following terms:

> First, it was based on the charges of limiting public liberties, particularly those of expression and assembly, refusal to maintain public order, government support for organized political violence, and negligence in situations which could lead to military intervention, all gravely prejudicial to the security of the nation.
>
> Second, to preserve the integrity of and respect for the Constitution, the National Congress assumed its greatest powers and invoked that document to bring the most serious charges under its responsibility against a representative of the executive.
>
> Third, these exceedingly grave charges were made against the highest government official following the president—the Minister of the Interior—who was to be accused, judged, and removed from his position by the Congress. The transcript of his trial would subsequently be passed to the ordinary tribunals so that these might mete out the punishment indicated for the crimes committed and ascertain the civil responsibility due for the damages and prejudices caused to private individuals by the state.[8]

Toha's trial by the Chamber of Deputies and his removal by the Senate in January, 1972, marked the dividing line in its institutional arena between two basic periods. Until then the opposition had permitted the political system to function normally within the limits set by Chile's ongoing institutional crisis. The President had confronted an aggressive opposition exercising its political prerogatives to the maximum but accepting constitutional norms as the framework for its conduct. In traditional terms, the opposition refused to approve all of the executive's major proposals and energetically reviewed each and every activity of the President's closest collaborators. In contrast, after January, 1972, a unified opposition with combined leadership, rather than exercising the faculties of control provided by the political system, sought openly to destroy that system and the state. Its activities were directed toward the use of institutions, mechanisms, and government responsibilities to provoke a general collapse, in turn eliminating any possibility of implementing the President's program to transform society.

For the achievement of these goals, the use of constitutional censure was central. From the moment Toha's censure was approved, the opposition began to make new accusations, successively more removed from the letter and spirit of the 1925 Constitution. The opposition's parliamentary leaders realized that a slight modification of the original meaning of censure could convert it into a formidable weapon of political control, one denied them under the presidential system. Thus the opposition deputies and senators worked to convert the Chilean political system into a *de facto* "parliamentary" one. Ministers, administrators, and governors were brought to trial, not on the charges enumerated in the Constitution, but on grounds of political responsibility. To present a motion for censure, it became sufficient cause for the opposition to disagree with any decision or program implemented by government officials, even along lines determined by the President himself. The number of accusations in 1972 was six times the historical average, and in the first eight months of 1973 even this rate was surpassed. President Allende's collaborators found themselves choosing between being removed from office for correctly effecting the President's directives or being remiss in their constitutional duty of obedience to the head of state. In all cases the former attitude predominated, which goes far to explain the quantity of political trials.

What occurred in Chile in 1972 and 1973 represents theoretically something considerably more extreme than the "dual loyalty" consecrated in parliamentary regimes of the "Orleanist" variety. What was demanded of the ministers and closest advisors of the President was that they yield their right to lead the Chilean state in the areas of economy, society, and public order. At the same time they were asked to abandon their loyalty to a government program committed to the people—the source, in the last analysis, of their legitimacy.

Institutionally, President Allende sought to counter the constant use of censure to remove his ministers by assigning the deposed leaders to other government positions. Immediately after the Senate removed Toha as interior minister, Allende named him Minister of Defense, having requested and obtained from the Constitutional Tribunal recognition of this prerogative. However, this "ministerial castling" (to borrow a chess term) hardly corrected the excesses of the Congress. The complexity and specialization of tasks in the contemporary state quickly showed that such transfers could not be frequent, even though politically they reaffirmed presidential prerogatives. The operating efficiency of the government was noticeably affected. Moreover, as the number of accusations began to affect a high percentage of Allende's closest aides, the value and efficacy of his response were further diminished.

Alteration of the Hierarchy of Legal Norms as a Tool of Institutional Obstruction

The second tactic of the Chilean right in its confrontation with the *Unidad Popular* was modification of the constitutional criteria for the formation of new laws. To put the problem in perspective, it is useful to recapitulate the most significant characteristics of this segment of the Chilean system. In the 1925 Constitution, the process by which laws were passed followed the classical Kelsenian pyramid, according to which laws were arranged in the following hierarchy of importance: constitutional provisions, congressional legislation, and delegated laws (known in Chile as "decrees with the force of law"). In the Constitution, however, there were certain latent problems stemming from specific procedural peculiarities, particularly the period during which laws could be considered. Both houses of Congress were normally permitted to be in session for only a relatively brief period—between May 21 and September 18 each year. This was known as the "ordinary legislature." During this session, bills presented by senators and deputies could be discussed with no limitations save the prohibition of acting in the economic and social areas reserved to the President and in the few areas assigned obligatorily to a specific chamber. (Thus, new tax bills could be initiated only in the Chamber of Deputies; an amnesty bill could originate only in the Senate.) During the remainder of the year the legislature could meet only in "extraordinary session," normally summoned by the President. Moreover, the Congress was restricted in these sessions to debating only those bills listed by the head of state in his summoning proclamation.

Nevertheless, for reasons that are difficult to explain, the harmony of this legislative system was broken in the Chilean Constitution. Essentially, all bills designed to modify the basic Charter were excluded from the above limitations and could be initiated and debated by Congress at any time during the year. In this way the system presented a fissure that, if adequately exploited, could produce damaging results in periods of conflict. Restrictions on legislative initiative could be avoided simply by converting all legal bills into projects to amend the Constitution. The possibilities were obvious. The continuity of legislative sniping at President Allende was assured, turning these frictions into an incessant battle. Restrictions with respect to the areas and materials normally reserved for presidential initiative were avoided. Moreover, this activity strengthened the image of the political system's total disorganization. The multiplicity of constitutional reforms under debate undermined the very structure of the basic charter. Finally, systematic use of this tactic gave the opposition a chance to develop what amounted to a counter policy, presenting cultural, political, social, and economic bills in conflict with the most important policies of the *Unidad Popular.*

These possibilities were first perceived by Christian Democratic congressmen at the end of the ordinary session of 1971; later, use of the tactic became widespread. At the time of the *coup d'état* there were almost thirty different constitutional reform bills under debate, varying from one establishing full legal equality for women to one incorporating under secretaries of state into the list of those who could be censured. There were two proposals, however, of central importance in sharpening the conflict between President Allende and the Congress. These were the so-called Hamilton-Fuentealba reforms, introducing restrictions on the formation of the Social Property Sector of the economy, and a proposal by Senator Rafael Moreno to restrict the reach of agrarian reform by prohibiting certain reforms of public domain over expropriated lands. Both reforms affected strategic areas of the Chilean economy, and their application would have made achievement of the Allende program's principal goals impossible. The passage of both was completed considerably before September 11, 1973.

The initiative in this area was completely the responsibility of the Christian Democratic party, of which the authors of these bills were distinguished spokesmen. Senator Renán Fuentealba, at various times the party's national president, was linked to the "democratic" current in the PDC, while Senators Juan Hamilton and Rafael Moreno belonged to the "moderate" faction. The latter two were distinguished by the aggressiveness of their attacks on the Allende government, and both participated in activities that encouraged its overthrow.

The political conflict stimulated by these bills reached a surprising intensity; its description forms part of the following analysis.

The Dispute Concerning Legislative Vetoes and the Prerogatives of President Allende as a Colegislative Power

The third facet of the institutional conflict emerged in the process of passing the Hamilton-Fuentealba constitutional reform and revealed another fissure in the functioning of the Chilean political system. Basically, the problem concerned the role of the President as a unilateral colegislative actor within the total legislative process. The importance of the matter explains why Allende, despite innumerable pressures, maintained his position stubbornly up to the very moment of the *coup*.

Although the problem itself was very complex, it can be explained quite briefly and succinctly. The Chilean Constitution gave the head of state the right to disapprove of any proposed law or constitutional reform sanctioned by the National Congress. This faculty could be exercised over the entire text or over specific provisions (item veto). The President also had the right to propose new terms to replace or complement those already approved, and both houses of Congress were obligated to vote on these. The text of the Constitution distinguished between suppressive, additive, and substitutive vetoes, according to the nature and purpose of the proposal, and each was subject to a different congressional procedure. In general, for a new provision (whether substitutive or additive) to be approved, both legislative bodies had to concur. In the case of suppressive vetoes, the Chamber and Senate could override these if two thirds of their members voted to restore the vetoed provision, thus asserting their will over that of the President.

This was an additional indication of the theoretically dominant position of the head of state in the Chilean political system. The institutional conflict between Allende and the opposition majority in Congress involved the fact that the norms regulating presidential vetoes of constitutional reforms were somewhat different from those applied to simple legislation. Moreover, the text defining these special norms had been modified in the constitutional reforms of early 1970.

With parliamentary approval of the Hamilton-Fuentealba reform bill, in early 1972, began the most serious institutional conflict in the history of the Constitution of 1925. The battle over the resolution of the presidential veto involved all the branches of government in Chile: the President, the two houses of the National Congress, the Supreme Court of Justice, the Constitutional Tribunal, and the *Contraloría General* of the Republic. Only the Constitutional Tribunal maintained its neutrality; from the beginning of the conflict the others assumed a definite, coordinated opposition to the government of the *Unidad Popular*.

In October, 1971, Hamilton and Fuentealba presented their amendment to regulate the Social Property Sector, actually in quest of a "counter reform." The Allende government was then endeavoring to carry forward by all available legal means the formation of a dominant social sector in the Chilean economy. The reform would have limited this drastically by making the legal process itself exceedingly complex. For the *Unidad Popular* the means of transferring a firm to public control were flexible. In many cases ownership was acquired by purchase of a majority of the stock in a specific enterprise (as occurred, for example, in textiles, durable consumer goods, and other areas). The legal right for the government to act was based on a decree law of 1932. In most cases advances in fulfilling the program of the left were achieved with the active participation and support of the workers in the affected firms.

It was this tide that the Hamilton-Fuentealba bill sought to stem constitutionally. It derogated the 1932 decree, obligating the President to obtain a special law for each transfer of a firm from the private to the public sector by demanding that the various forms of property in the different industrial sectors be clearly indicated. It is worth noting that the proposal contained not only provisions of a constitutional sort but also detailed articles more typical of ordinary legislation.

The congressional opposition assigned highest priority to the reform, passing it quickly through committees and acting as a solid bloc—a fact that prevented clarifying its exact nature. In this manner, after only a few months, Congress readied the bill for the President. Allende, making use of his constitutional powers, proceeded to veto a number of its specific articles.

With the vetoes the institutional conflict was joined. The opposition leaders in Congress argued that, to restore the original text vetoes by the head of state, they were not legally obligated to obtain the two thirds vote of the members of each chamber—demanded generically for all legislation, of which constitutional reforms were obviously one kind. A simple majority would suffice. This, of course, was the only quorum they could raise.

The opposition opportunistically perceived that the prevalence of this thesis might modify the legislative process so as to produce both important procedural and important substantive consequences. Essentially, this left the road open for the members of the opposition to demolish any future presidential prerogative. They also realized correctly that this point affected one of the President's fundamental attributes and hence was one on which he could not yield. But to make sure the conflict was irresolvable, it was first necessary to block any institutional channel capable of resolving it. This is why the entire congressional opposition, in an open letter to the President insisting on the correctness of its own interpretation of the Constitution, rejected in advance the Constitutional Tribunal's competence to rule in the disagreement.[9]

It is necessary to insist on the essential positions of both sides. While the President upheld a thesis designed to resolve the conflict, the opposition advanced criteria to place that conflict beyond reach of possible solutions. For President Allende, the meaning of the Chilean constitution was clear: the Constitutional Tribunal had been created by constitutional amendment in 1970 precisely to avoid any impasse between the various branches of government. Hence it was competent to rule on the matter. The opposition, once more led by the National party, sought to enlist the participation and support of the remaining branches of government, which, at this point, were closing ranks behind the counter-revolution: the Supreme Court and the *Contraloría General*. The latter was an autonomous organ whose principal function was to rule in advance on the legality of executive decrees and resolutions, and the opposition argued that this was the body competent to judge the norms for processing legislation.

The anti-socialist block had by now achieved a high degree of coordination and efficacy and attacked the government on all fronts. When the President formally appealed to the Constitutional Tribunal, the opposition strongly pressured the members of that organ to declare their lack of competence and to refuse to accept the matter. In July, 1973, when the political conflict seemed to have reached a point of no salvation, the Constitutional Tribunal declared that it would not rule on the petition sent by the minority, *Unidad Popular* sector of Congress. The *Contraloría* then refused to approve the decree sent by the President, and the opposition majority in Congress declared that Salvador Allende had either to accept the legal provisions imposed upon him or place himself beyond the limits of the law.

These various activities in the institutional arena, all perfectly coordinated, fed upon one another reciprocally. Their result was a gradual destruction of the state, noticeable long before the *coup* of September, 1973, and a factor justifying that *coup*. A clear indication of this process was the fracture of government institutions into two antagonistic and irreducible blocs. Another was the complete dismantling of the presidential system established in the Constitution of 1925. It was replaced, in effect, by a pseudo-parliamentary system which had as its sole purpose the obstruction of government action but which did not assume the responsibilities of political leadership. A third was the paralysis of the legislative process, as President Allende found it impossible to obtain approval for new laws. With this, another theoretical assumption of the Chilean road to socialism was eliminated, for Allende had argued during the campaign that his government would be based on the approval of legislation consistent with a society in transition to socialism.

Thus the censure of Minister Tohá in January, 1972, initiated a tendency toward institutional chaos. It was further accentuated after the congressional elections of March, 1973, in which the *Unidad Popular* obtained 43.4 per cent of the vote and in the Senate won ten of the twenty-five seats in dispute. This eliminated any last opposition hope for impeaching President Allende himself. From this point on censures and other activities in the institutional arena were pushed to sanction a particular conduct or simply to accentuate the political collapse. The opposition in general, but particularly the leadership of the National party, which was the group working most tenaciously for Allende's overthrow, defined the institutional attack as groundwork for a *coup*. Institutional offensives were intensified on all fronts. When conditions for the military intervention finally prevailed, the opposition again turned to the political system they were about to demolish. Using it for the last time, they fabricated a justification for the *coup*.

In the second fortnight of August they decided that conditions were ready. They had left the constitutional faction of the army without leadership by driving from its ranks the Commander in Chief, General Carlos Prats, and two of his most loyal collaborators, Generals Sepúlveda and Pickering. Intense social agitation and street demonstrations were daily occurrences against which the police intervened less and less forcefully. The government's most bitter adversaries, led by organizations of truck drivers and merchants and by professional associations, had declared a second general strike of indefinite duration (as in October, 1972), demanding the government's overthrow. The disorganization of production and distribution had multiplied scarcities of essential products and fostered black markets, all of which began to erode, or at least shake, the government's support.

On August 22, opposition congressmen called a special session of the Chamber of Deputies. According to the 1925 Constitution this body had only two directly political responsibilities: first, to present motions of constitutional censure; second, "to review the acts of the government." For the latter the Constitution specified both form and procedure, establishing that review would be accomplished through documents sent to the appropriate ministers, indicating the specific points of contention to which they had to respond.

Deputies traditionally had used these requests to satisfy the demands of their electoral clientele or to establish political paternity over initiatives of local interest. (A review of the acts of the Chamber of Deputies would show that these petitions usually consisted of requests to finance public works, build monuments to local personalities, or transfer specific bureaucrats.) Over time congressional practice had given collective expression to these documents, calling them "projects of agreement." Groups of deputies presented them in special sessions called to deal with specific problems. This did not alter, however, the basic nature of an instrument that was simply a means of parliamentary communication containing an opinion and request for information or action from some governmental official. It lacked all coercive force and had no legal weight whatsoever.

But at this point it was clear that the opposition sought not a resolution of unimpeachable legal weight but simply one that could be used for political ends. The session requested by the Christian Democratic and National deputies began on the morning of August 22 and, after day-long debate, ended with the approval of a project of agreement explicitly declaring the activities of the President illegal. As later became known, the text was written by a Minister of Justice in the Alessandri administration, Enrique Ortúzar, who now serves the military *junta* as president of its Commission on Constitutional Reform.

In the debate, the *Unidad Popular* defended the prerogatives of the constitutional government and the appropriateness of its actions in permitting the widest possible exercise of political liberties. The opposition presented the argument—later amply reiterated by the *junta*—that the Allende government was "legitimate in its origins" but had become "illegitimate in its exercise" because of various illegal acts and abuses of power (not clearly listed). President Allende fully realized the seriousness of the meeting, but he hoped until the end that the Christian Democratic deputies opposed to a *coup d'état* would rebel when confronted with the text. (Among these were Bernardo Leighton, Mariano Ruiz Esquide, and Claudio Huepe.) This did not occur; at the moment of voting, there were no defections from the opposition camp. (Congressmen of the democratic faction of the PDC later explained that Senator Patricio Aylwin had promised them at a closed meeting to issue a statement specifying that the agreement had no seditious intent. Obviously, Aylwin never made any such declaration.)[10]

Thus, some weeks before the *coup*, every one of the institutional objectives set by the right to prepare the way for insurrection had been accomplished: 1) the nature of the political system had been distorted, eliminating the viability of an advance toward socialism by means of a reform of the legal system; 2) an open and unsolvable conflict had been promoted between an isolated President and the other branches of government, all controlled by the adversaries of socialism, who argued that President Allende's exercise of authority was no longer legitimate; and 3) the government's activities had been completely obstructed through reduction of and refusal to recognize its prerogatives. This third step, creating a problem of efficiency, was designed to reduce the government's base of support, as well as its support within the armed forces. This in turn reduced the government's ability to defend itself. Thus the opposition's institutional attacks accomplished their goal of creating an environment favorable to the *coup*. When there remained nothing to be done in the institutional arena, the political system provided one last service by offering a legal pretext for the military action against a constitutional government.

THE ROLE OF MASS ORGANIZATIONS IN THE POLITICAL CONFLICT

Until now I have limited myself to describing the confrontation between the *Unidad Popular* government and the opposition in the institutional arena. My analysis would be incomplete, however, if I did not examine as well, if only briefly, the dimensions of the social battle outside the institutions of government. This, of course, introduces the entire problem of people's power.

As late as 1970, the most dynamic and significant social forces of our time, with the broad network of institutions created since the mining proletariat of the North had formed its first class organizations at the beginning of the century, were not really included in the Chilean political system. The Chilean working class, composed basically of industrial and mine workers, had formed over the years three unified organizations, all explicitly committed to building a workers' society: the Labor Federation of Chile (*Federación Obrera de Chile*), formed in 1909 with a conservative orientation but converted by Luis Emilio Recabarren in 1917 into an instrument of agitation and struggle: the Chilean Workers' Confederation (*Confederación de Trabajadores de Chile*), organized in 1936 on the eve of the Popular Front's victory amidst street battles against the National Socialist Youth; and the United Workers Central (*Central Unica de Trabajadores*), created in 1953, which had played a distinguished role in preparing the political climate for Allende's victory and would be similarly important during his government.

To these was added, in the 1960s, the peasant movement. For years union organization in the countryside was proscribed, but it was finally legalized in 1967—simultaneous with the initiation of the agrarian reform. In a few years three national peasant confederations were created: *Ranquil*, Peasant Triumph (*Triunfo Campesino*), and Liberty (*Libertad*). Together they included 320,000 organized peasants and small owners.

The popular movement also included a variety of organizations that had emerged in the working-class settlements of Santiago and other large cities. Ever since the mid-50s, the struggle for a place to live and build a home had become an instrument of mass mobilization. Although activities in these settlements did not always pursue the goals of social transformation, they did give rise to a number of organizations of great significance: neighborhood councils, mothers' centers, youth centers, and cooperatives. Finally, in the heat of confrontation and battle during the Allende government, still newer forms of organization emerged: councils for supply and pricing, industrial belts, and the workers' communal commandos. All of these organizations contributed to the government's defense during the October Strike of 1972. Indeed, in that power struggle the mass organizations multiplied and were strengthened.

Obviously, these mass organizations as a whole had interests opposed to the traditional forms of organization and economic functioning of the Chilean state. They were excluded, moreover, from the decision-making structures that governed the functioning of that state. Certainly they were an essential reserve of support for a process of change, and their value increased once the possibilities for compromise vanished and the political system was paralyzed. To use their potential force effectively, however, it was first necessary to recognize their two most important characteristics: first, these mass organizations as a whole were ready to support anti-capitalist policies clearly directed toward socialism; and second, their value lay in that they did not form part of the state structure. They could be used from outside the state to resolve a conflict that could not be resolved within state institutions and to support President Allende's policies in open opposition to the counterrevolutionary strategy.

The great debate during the last year of the Allende government on the question of people's power unfortunately did not recognize these traits that today seem obvious. In this respect, the left incurred a double error. Some wanted to assign mass mobilization a role antagonistic to the two forces fighting in the institutional arena. These denied that the Allende government was in any way revolutionary, accusing it instead of being reformist. They sought to build a kind of autonomous power structure outside the government. Others, in contrast, could not conceive of any autonomy for mass organization nor of the rich opportunities such organization offered. Instead, they tried to make the mass movement supportive of and totally dependent upon the government. With this, the dynamism it derived from its popular base— not from the institutions of a state in crisis—was lamentably lost.

In this fashion the *Unidad Popular,* linking its fate to the Chilean political system without recognizing the advanced degree of decomposition in that system's power structure or the immense obstructive capacity that the rules of the game provided to its adversaries, proved incapable of using the political power of mass organizations to confront the strategy and tactics of the counterrevolution. It is difficult to make predictions based on events that did not occur, but we believe that had the "Chilean road to socialism" included a "legitimate defense" against its enemies' attempts to destabilize the system—which would not in any way have contradicted the original design of using the legal system to transform the nature of the Chilean state—the result of confrontation might have been different.

NOTES

1. On the process by which the national state was formed in Chile and later modified, see Julio Heise, *150 Años de Evolución Institutional en Chile* (Santiago: Editorial Jurídica de Chile, 1961), Fernando Campos Harriet, *Historia Constitucional de Chile* (Santiago: Editorial Jurídica de Chile, 1963), and Federico G. Gil, *El Sistema Político Chileno* (Santiago: Editorial Jurídica de Chile, 1962).

2. The tendency toward executive domination is particularly clear in the reforms of 1943 and 1970, which reserved for the President an ever larger area of legislative initiative. The purpose was clearly to guarantee him leadership in economic and social affairs and to place him in a position to direct national planning.

3. This had occurred in the last four administrations prior to the military *junta* (the governments of Ibáñez [1952–1958], Alessandri [1958–1964],

Frei [1964–1970], and Allende [1970–1973]). The only President who obtained a congressional majority in his favor was Alessandri, who, during a brief period between 1961 and the beginning of 1964, enjoyed the support of the so-called Democratic Front, an alliance of the Liberal, Conservative, and Radical parties. Yet even in this case the heterogeneity of the alliance prevented coherent political action. It simply transferred the process of negotiations and political compromise to within the government.

4. The flexibility and pragmatism of the Radical leadership is easily shown by recalling that the party allied itself with the Socialist and Communist parties in 1938 and the Communist and Liberal parties in 1946, while in 1961 it participated in the Democratic Front with the Democratic and Liberal parties.

5. The *"castillista"* theses were named after their author, the Christian Democrat ideologue Jaime Castillo Velasco, a neo-Thomist and follower of Jacque Maritain. Castillo argued that the party could reach power independently by attacking both right and left, breaking their unities and gaining support from their bases. Thus alliances would be unnecessary.

The "our own road" policy was advocated principally by Senator Patricio Aylwin, at various times the national president of the party. Aylwin, markedly conservative and anti-Communist, attacked the argument that the only force capable of presenting a new alternative for noncapitalist development and the transformation of Chilean society was "a people's social and political union." By this was meant an alliance between the Christian Democrats and the workers' parties—the Socialist and Communist. In a National *Junta* at the beginning of May, 1969, "our own road" won by a narrow margin (238 votes to 219). With this victory the possibility of an agreement with the left was eliminated. This prepared the way for two later schisms, leading to the formation of the *Movimiento de Acción Popular Unitaria* (MAPU) and the Christian Left (IC).

6. This centrifugal tendency affected both the Radical and Christian Democratic parties. In spite of their differences, both had to respond to the basic conflict of interests in Chilean society, and neither could avoid fragmentation and divisions that benefited those who maintained either a socialist position or a dependent capitalist one.

7. This neofascist group was so called because its nucleus was formed around the magazine *Estanquero*. It included *"integristas"* and "hispanists" and, in general, all partisans of an authoritarian and corporatist government with military participation. A number of the most prominent civilian counsellors of the military *junta* led by Augusto Pinochet emerged from this group.

In 1963, the *"estanquerista"* sector became the Movement of National Action, which in 1966 fused with the Liberal and Conservative parties to form the National party. The Liberals and Conservatives, embodying the old leadership of Chilean society, had entered into frank decline as a result of social change. In the congressional elections of 1965 they had elected only nine of 147 deputies and no senators. This is why the National Action leaders, representing the smallest group in the new party, controlled its leadership from the start. From this position they were able to implement their tactics without restriction.

8. In *El Estado y los Problemas Tácticos en el Gobierno de Allende* (Madrid: Editorial Siglo XXI, 1974), pp. 60–61.

9. The Constitutional Tribunal, created in 1970 but not established until September, 1971, had five members, all of whom were distinguished lawyers. The justification for its creation was precisely that of avoiding irresolvable conflicts in the legislative process. For this reason, the opposition's argument that article 78 Bis of the Constitution did not speak expressly of "constitutional reforms" was not only technically inconsistent but also clearly demonstrative that, at that point, the opposition wanted to sharpen the conflict and provoke the collapse of political institutions.

10. After the *coup,* Radomiro Tomić, at a meeting of the *Junta Nacional* on November 7, 1973, clarified the party's responsibility in the operation. ("El PDC Antes Después del 11 de Septiembre," published in the magazine of the *Universidad Nacional Autónoma de Mexico,* July, 1974). Tomić described two points of internal party conflict before the *coup:* a) the nature of the principal threat menacing Chilean democracy, and b) the kind of policies the Christian Democrats should adopt toward the Allende government and the *Unidad Popular.* He stated that although the leadership elected in May, 1973, considered the danger of a dictatorship of the proletariat to be the principal threat, there were clear differences of opinion on substantive questions.

Then self-critically evaluating his party's responsibility "in the destruction of the Chilean constitutional system," he referred to three definitive acts:

—having approved, in Congress, the press, and party bases, the truckers' strike that paralyzed daily the transport of more than one million tons of cargo, "in spite of its being, in the light of Christian morality, an absolutely illegal and profoundly immoral strike";

—having initiated the declaration in the Chamber of Deputies of "the illegality of the government's acts, abundantly cited since by the military *junta* and the 'White Book' as the immediate justification for its pronouncement on September 11, directed at overthrowing the government";

—having requested the military cabinet of August 9 and then, after initially visiting military ministers Montero and Ruiz, publicly reneging on its earlier commitment and provoking the fall of the cabinet.

The Political Problems of Transition: From the Assumption of Political Power to Revolutionary Power

HUGO ZEMELMAN

STRATEGIC DECISION OR CONTEXTUAL IMPOSITION?

The failure of the Chilean experience can help us to analyze problems that in general are not sufficiently emphasized in analyses of successful revolutions. In particular, we are thinking of the choice of options, presented at particular moments in the evolution of a historical process, that decisively influences its subsequent course. A detailed study of the analyses made by Lenin between February and October, 1917, provides us with a great lesson of the complexity implicit in any contextual interpretation of historical development. They are, moreover, an example of enormous lucidity in the relationship between tactics and strategy. In the Chilean case, there were numerous momentary contexts in which the government did not act, or did not have the political will to act, as the circumstances demanded. For this reason I intend to explore in the present essay some of the questions that underlie the peaceful or political road to socialism.

For example, was deepening the revolutionary nature of the process (by creating the social sector of the economy, broadening the agrarian reform, nationalizing the banks, etc.) compatible with a multiclass alliance? Did not its deepening, as well as its consolidation, demand that the monopolistic and pro-imperialist faction of the bourgeoisie be isolated? And did not this isolation, in turn, demand the formation of a broad political alliance? Was a strategy aimed at breaking up the ideological hegemony of the dominant bourgeoisie incompatible with a combative mobilization of the

274

workers, peasants, and radicalized middle sectors? Did a military policy of the people's forces demand, above all else, unified and integral political leadership? Why were the April, 1971, elections, when the combination of leftist forces obtained an absolute majority of the vote, not used to create a pressure group capable of forcing a realignment of social forces?

Why was the nationalization of the copper mines in July, 1971, not transformed into a catalyst of public opinion behind an advance in the modification of institutions? At that time, the Christian Democrats had adopted a defensive attitude, and a united bourgeois front had not yet been reestablished. Why, when the Christian Democrats presented their bill on the social property sector, was the dispute not carried to the masses, so that well-organized pressure could be brought to bear on a still weak and insecure Congress? Why, after the failure of the truckers' strike in October, 1972, when the political capacity of the united workers had been demonstrated, was it impossible to follow a strategy designed to isolate and liquidate the dominant faction of the bourgeoisie? Why was it not possible to mount a counteroffensive of the people's forces against the constant manufacture of events by the bourgeoisie, primarily through their control of the mass media? Why did the real force of the people not make itself felt continuously, instead of only in crisis situations, such as in October, 1972, or in sporadic street mobilizations? Why did the masses never become an organic force pushing for the transformation of political structures? Why did concrete policies evolve so differently from ideological prognoses? Why was there so much talk and so little effective action?

The answers to questions such as these would enable us to elucidate some of the great issues that underlie the peaceful road to socialism. Here I limit myself to the one that seems most fundamental. In essence, I want to examine the ability of a class or classes to advance in the materialization of historical transformations via the successive options presented by history (that is, by taking advantage of the favorable elements appearing in the evolving context of a historical process). I am also interested in those factors that so limit classes as to force them to undergo political metamorphosis, separating their class organizations from their strategic objectives. If historical processes are made by classes acting in particular circumstances, which are in turn the product of prior class struggle, there should be an evaluation of the capacity of a class to create situations that transcend the limitations of local circumstances and are consistent with their historical aims.

The capacity of any class to create these new situations will depend on whether the particular circumstances of a given moment are the product of its own strategy or the unexpected results of the actions of other classes. Hence, we begin by asking ourselves whether the Chilean (or peaceful, or political) road to socialism was a strategic decision. (The "historic compromise" of the Italian Communist party, for example, is such a decision. The Italian strategy for conquering power rests on a decision first to conquer civil society, which then determines the moment for assuming power, the nature of that power, and the forms of its exercise.) Or was the Chilean road imposed by a specific historical context, the result of circumstances (in the Chilean case, of an electoral nature) with unforeseen political and ideological consequences?

One can argue in response that for forty years the left (represented by the Socialist and Communist parties) had fought to gain power within the institutions of the bourgeois regime. Thus its triumph in the presidential election of September, 1970, was the natural culmination of a long process of "conquering" civil society (represented by the organization of workers' and peasant unions, including those of the salaried middle sectors, or the political parties themselves, which experienced uninterrupted electoral growth, expressed in terms of influence over public opinion, control of the municipalities, electoral circumscriptions, and a significant block in Congress). All this is undebatable, but it does not mean that, with the progressive penetration of bourgeois institutions, there was political leadership adequate to define and pursue a strategy of gaining power consistent with the increasing vulnerability of the bourgeoisie to the influence of the proletariat and its allies. In effect, the penetration of the bourgeois structure of domination was less the result of a deliberate strategy for conquering power than of the efforts of the bourgeoisie to expand its own social base.

The above explains why the increased strength enjoyed by the left did not have the integrated character necessary to transform each bourgeois retreat into a real advance of the proletariat and its allies. The penetration of civil society was not the result of a political act rooted in a global strategy to take over the institutions of the dominant political order. It was the result, rather, of concessions by the bourgeoisie itself, which thus disguised its true character. For this reason I affirm that the left's fight within democracy was not an option chosen from among others less viable but rather was a condition imposed by the bourgeoisie in order to maintain its domination intact. This circumstance led the people's forces to interpret their victory in the presidential election of September, 1970, as the result of a nonexistent strategy (nonexistent, at least, in any integrated political sense) and to assume that the same balance of forces would continue to exist. This led to the tacit conclusion that if the left came to exercise "democratic" power, the bourgeoisie, in opposition, would also continue to be a democratic force. The nature of the conflict between classes would remain substantially the same; only the level of conflict would vary.

I cannot maintain that this was the dominant interpretation among the parties of the Marxist left. There are no explicit declarations to corroborate such an affirmation. It can be shown only in the objective behavior of the leadership following the election, above and beyond different ideological nuances. In reality, had there been a prior strategy for taking over civil society, it would inevitably have transformed the pre-electoral phase into the principal determinant of the phase that began immediately after September. However, the lack of any prior planned strategy is revealed precisely by the absence of any link between the two phases. This is illustrated by the fact that the 1970 presidential election, a specific context provoked by a division of the bourgeoisie, was later described theoretically as the initiation of a new strategy that escaped the limitations imposed by all earlier political evolution. This description did not take into account the lack of any real conquest of civil society or a truly integrated structure of political leadership.

Thus the question of whether the Chilean road to socialism constituted a strategic decision or was imposed by a specific context can be answered in the following manner. Insofar as the electoral outcome, with all its political, economic, and ideological implications, was not foreseen, it was a contextual imposition. At the same time it was a strategy, constructed theoretically on the basis of a certain limited control over civil society, although it did not implement tactical measures consistent with that premise. In other words, the strategy was the formalization of the left's experience within a liberal democratic system of bourgeois domination, but it did not possess a vision of the fundamental changes that would be provoked by the bourgeoisie's loss of hegemony, nor of the difficulties inherent in the attempt to impose a new and legitimate system of domination.

The Chilean or peaceful road to socialism appeared at a moment in the class struggle after a shift in the correlation of political forces, but this change in itself indicated no more than the possibility of deep social transformations. In no way could it have prefigured a strict model to be applied at a predetermined rhythm. To arrive at a more precise definition, it would first have been necessary to transform the forces that characterize the context of September, 1970. What does this mean? One can argue that we face a vicious circle, if we maintain (with reason) that social forces mature only to the extent that a project of transformation is actually undertaken, though it is the maturity of those social forces—their organization, solidarity, and political capacity—that predetermines the nature of a concrete historical program.

If we limit the problem to establishing a direct relation between historical programs and social forces, there is apparently no solution. The correct formulation, and the beginnings of a solution, can only be found by examining the forms of the political expression of classes. These forms are the structures responsible for driving forward class development and in the long run reflect the historical demands of these classes. They establish the rhythm of the revolutionary process, decide among options, and adjust tactical moves to strategic needs. In this sense, because the different political parties embodied different interpretations of the working-class program, the Chilean road opened up a gamut of conflicting possibilities. For this reason, the resolution of the integral problem of class was prerequisite to any definition of the model of transformations and their rhythm.

In what did the problem consist? For years the classes struggling in Chile had expressed themselves within a system that permitted and even encouraged numerous forms of class representation. The bourgeoisie, interested in broadening the social base of its domination, perceived in the multiplicity of workers' organizations a mechanism for opening up new alliances. But, at the moment of the electoral triumph, these historical forms had their own influence. The same class scheme—parties—was maintained when a drastic redefinition was necessary. Without this, the social force represented by the *Unidad Popular* government could not be transformed into an equivalent political force. On the contrary, the political forms imposed themselves upon the social base, resulting in fragmentation, weakness, ideological confusion, and a lack of strategic perspective. Reacting to this political fact became a prerequisite for measuring the reach of the evolving revolutionary program, its potential, limitations, and historic relevance. To do so without attending to the real correlation of forces was no more than a purely ideological and subjective exercise, because the correlation of forces is measured according to the mediation between an integrated social force and its effective political weight. It follows, therefore, that the first tactical objective of the revolutionary project should have been to create a political structure that, from a position of formal power, could assemble a strategy for conquering civil society, and not the reverse; that is, the political structure should have been a function of the revolutionary program—a program that was not and could not be defined.

This presented an organizational problem that is, in some ways, the inverse of the problem of the political party. The political party is always created in relation to potentially possible tasks. However, when what is at issue is the margin for utilizing an institutionalized power structure to realize the potential advance within a context defined by the possession of formal power, then what is demanded is not the creation of a party but rather the transformation of those which already exist. It is precisely this potential that, according to the capacity of the political structure, must be translated into reality. Given the parameters of the project, all that is lacking is the definition of the viable options.

The parameters are determined by the existing institutional structures at the initial moment of the revolutionary process; the viable options are determined by the existing party structures, since the different parties are only embryonic forms or parts of a collective will. The electoral context (of September) made it necessary for this will to express itself in a new political structure, transcending the partial character of the individual, existing political structures. Whether a new structure emerges as a renewed expression of collective will or the old structures dividing and fragmenting that will are maintained represent two alternatives for the evolution of the process.

The need for the political parties to undertake their own transformation instead of preserving their old structures is one of the basic problems in the initiation and evolution of the Chilean revolution. It touches directly on the responsibilities of those who have assumed the duty of promoting change. If one accepts the task of leading a historical program (of the workers in this case), one must, above all, accept the demands that program presents, even if these include one's own disappearance. This argument may be laden with psychological rationalization and good intentions, but granted that this is so, the basic problem remains. Any revolutionary program passes first through a stage of diverse interpretations that must give way to a second stage of uniformity, in which one interpretation predominates over the rest. Where this does not occur, the persistence of the various interpretations becomes an obstacle to the future progress of the project.

Movement from the first stage to the second may not occur in two instances: one, when different programs coexist (for example, one of the working class and another of the small bourgeoisie); another, when diverse interpretations of the same historical program are sufficiently contradictory to make their simultaneous application impossible. Both situations lead to basic difficulties. In the first, if two projects coexist, we must consider the Chilean road to socialism in relation to the nature of the historical program of change it embodied. In the second, we must explain the disparity between two representations of the same historical project. Is there a class program as such? Or are programs the product of the political organizations representing classes? How is it possible that one class can have various political representations? Is it the case, perhaps, that over time political representatives tend to become independent of a class program and impose their own vision? Then what explains this separation between representation and class? Do the forms of representation that emerge in the heat of certain transitory contexts prolong a particular vision in their bureaucratic structure, beyond the limits of its historical relevance? Or, thinking in terms of a social dialectic, are political parties characterized by a lack of "self-movement"? Do they not then run the risk of being left without content or importance? This is indeed the case, but only in part. A party can be a "dead document" if it relates to classes without their own historical program, but it can also be an "anachronistic document" if its ties are limited to an interpretation of the history of a class (and of its own political history) that is bound to be a specific transitory context.

In effect, if the evolution of a class is not reflected in the party's evolution, a disjuncture may result in which the party remains at a past moment in the development of the class (if by moment we understand a specific possibility—still potential—for future evolution). An example of what we are describing can be found in the anti-Stalinist representations of the working class, which attempt to indicate a clearly defined direction for the development of that class (but one that is probably ever less viable). Another example can be found in the insurrectional representations based on the idea of foci. The same can be said of the democratic forms of representation, in that they constitute forms of struggle but not conceptions of an eventual transformation of capitalism.

Both "anti-Stalinism" and the idea of "foci" are specific moments in the history of the working class. They can generate *ad hoc* political structures, but in essence they are temporary and contextual. If prolonged beyond the specific context that gave them birth, they become anachronistic forms of political representation. Chile reveals examples of these anachronisms that were overcome only superficially. Their political content was very strong and explains, to an important degree, why various interpretations of the "same" historical program could coexist.

SYSTEM CRISIS, IDEOLOGY, AND PRAGMATISM

The *Unidad Popular* experience represents the culmination of the crisis of the liberal democratic system, in that the contradictions generated by the economic structure could no longer be resolved within the established institutional rules. The system of domination by delegation, and with it the bourgeois political class itself, entered into crisis. Thus the military *coup* of September 11, 1973, represented not only the defeat of the people's movement but also the collapse of the traditional form of bourgeois domination. A new form was inaugurated, replacing the old political class with a new authoritarian administrative caste residing in the military. Unlike the previous elite, this new caste is able to maintain the unity of the different factions of the bourgeoisie, countering the effects of the social polarization during the last twenty years. In this sense, the repressive policies of the military *junta* have also fulfilled a function.

The *Unidad Popular* thus marked the end of liberal domination. It was the last opportunity for the bourgeois political class to participate in the exercise of power, albeit precariously, given its weakness relative to the weight of the masses. The bourgeoisie's politics of alliance had created the bases for its repression, to the extent that a considerable proportion of its social support gravitated toward the people's parties (a shift not only of political allegiance but also of an entire ideological and cultural superstructure, with consequences which we will examine below). In the course of this process, the dominant faction of the bourgeoisie (that is, the monopolist, pro-imperialist faction) was rapidly alienated from the political sectors most inclined to favor alliances (a phenomenon clearly observable throughout the Christian Democratic government). Under the *Unidad Popular* government, as a result, alliance politics implied the isolation of the dominant faction, culminating a process begun within the bourgeoisie itself but also seeking to avoid forcing other bourgeois sectors for ideological reasons to support that faction. This was clearly the disjuncture: isolation of the dominant faction (which was moving toward a repressive, anti-liberal form of domination) or reconstruction of bourgeois ideological unity, absent during the years of liberal-democratic domination.

Under the liberal-democratic regime, traditional supporters of the bourgeois political class transferred their allegiance to the people's parties, contributing to the disorientation of the leadership after September. These forces, particularly the middle sectors, had historically participated in alliances alternatively antagonistic to and supporting the dominant bourgeoisie. This ambiguous political character had also penetrated the people's parties, which to a lesser extent formed alliances between the working class and the middle sectors. We can cite the example of the Socialist party, formed by workers and peasants as well as ideologically radicalized *petits bourgeois*. From its origins the party represented a heterogeneous social group allying industrial workers with *petits bourgeois,* thus facilitating the development of different ideological orientations. As these rarely had to confront concrete organizational problems, they coexisted more or less peacefully throughout the party's history. Nevertheless, this coexistence took its toll: the sterility and inability of the Socialists to articulate the political problems that emerge at each stage of the revolutionary battle.

This divorce between ideological definition and political action in the leadership of its internal factions reflects a typically *petit bourgeois* phenomenon—the lack of concern for the broad implications of theoretical differences. Consequently, I feel certain that the ideological struggle within the Socialist party reflects its political ambiguity, necessitated by its nature as an alliance among social forces. Symptomatic of this nature is the fact that the party never, except on a general ideological level, addressed the concrete tasks of revolution. Its program always enumerated broad objectives, capable of sheltering diverse tactical aims—aims which were incompatible if the organizational consequences of each ideological and political position were rigorously considered.

The party's history explains much of the above. Until September, 1970, the requisites of the liberal-democratic system emphasized the political-ideological function: daily political tasks required an electoral organization more than an organization of cadres. The completion of electoral tasks (such as winning zones of influence, co-opting leaders, etc.) allowed the various tendencies to coexist without taking decisive stands. Strategic contradictions were resolved by tactical pragmatism, imposed by the predominant forms of struggle in a liberal-bourgeois democracy. Consequently, theoretical confrontations arising from ideological discrepancies were always resolved according to pragmatic criteria. In this manner the various tendencies found unity in commitment to an electoral pressure group; but it caused a divorce between political line and ideological strategy and between ideological strategy and tactical moves. It channeled debate away from any integrated plan, any serious effort to forge a real collective will. When, after 1970, the institutional framework was radically transformed, the political struggle demanded more efficient party operation, clearer criteria for membership, greater congruency between strategic and tactical objectives, and the effective reciprocal development of political and ideological analyses. These, however, did not occur.

Following September, the rigid adherence to the old political pattern became an obstacle to taking advantage of the crisis in the system of domination. The problem was to utilize the available margin for maneuver without precipitating a frontal attack on the system or succumbing to its limitations and mystifications. Here is a central aspect of the problem: the political crisis following the presidential elections permitted an effort to restructure state power, but it simultaneously required maintaining the illusion that the old system would continue in force. This was difficult in the extreme, and it was necessary to move with great care. A violent break could serve to rebuild the dominant bourgeois alliance—in effect, what occurred. The possibility of widening the internal divisions in the bourgeoisie was frustrated when numerous portions of the middle sectors (as well as the masses), instead of committing themselves to the revolution, moved toward an ideological alliance with the bourgeoisie.

The crisis of the democratic system of domination suddenly took concrete form when the left was able to develop (or begin to develop) its revolutionary program by a "nonrevolutionary road." This violated the doctrinaire predictions of most of the parties, none of whom had ever believed the left could triumph. This situation obliged the parties to revise their ideological formulations, which, during the election, had temporarily been laid aside. Never before had the parties of the left confronted the exercise of power from a position of social and political dominance. (The Popular Front did not really attempt to follow a revolutionary trajectory.) It had always been possible to interpret the program in a certain utopian light, but no longer. Nor could they continue to interpret real opportunities according to the doctrinaire prerequisites of the program (or rather, the various programs offered by the left). What was needed was a programmatic analysis taking into account the real possibilities offered by the electoral triumph. It was necessary to define a coherent and consistent plan, capable of being applied in the future, to create new forms of legitimation. Unfortunately, the very nature of the parties militated against this.

Clientelistic by tradition and revolutionary by ideological orientation, party conduct was characterized by ambiguity. With a certain fluidity, the parties shifted between maintaining their status as electoral pressure groups and accelerating a process of profound and irreversible change—running directly counter to their clientelistic nature. This circumstance caused the parties themselves to act as brakes on the process they proposed, debilitating the cohesion of the masses and fortifying the bourgeoisie. Finally, it was the reason why the parties could not understand the true dimensions of the circumstances propitious for initiating a revolutionary political process.

In reality, to transcend the electoral perspective, it was necessary to understand clearly the role traditional forms of legitimation would play in consolidating political power. It was also necessary to abandon or drastically revise the traditional ideological formulas and to develop a critical, theoretical evaluation of the concrete conditions needed for a peaceful transition to socialism. This implied defining the correct tactics for a gradual but inexorable imposition of new institutional organizations and legitimation. It also implied defining the process of fostering and articulating ideological alliances and resolving the relation between institutional political power and social power—that is, the power emerging from the force of the working class and its allies, once their bonds were broken. The question of the bureaucracy, with its considerable weight in Chilean social institutions, likewise demanded attention. Last in this indicative enumeration, the issue of security factors in the definition of international policy, and how these affected the revolutionary and domestic policies of the *Unidad Popular* government, would have to be addressed.

One of the theoretical questions illuminated by the *Unidad Popular* experience concerns the capacity of a political force to take advantage of specific concrete conditions, without losing its ideological identity and, at the same time, without forcing the process to assume forms historically impossible. Did the *Unidad Popular* do everything possible to take advantage of the conditions offered by a peaceful transition to socialism? We can respond by examining the great strategic tasks that should have been completed: 1) the measures (initially of a legal nature) designed to increase the institutional power of the coalition of people's parties; 2) the measures (more specifically political) oriented to changing the form of legitimation, fundamentally by dividing the bourgeoisie through the development and consolidation of "people's power"; and 3) the preparation for breaking the rules of the Chilean institutional game in case an impasse emerged that endangered not only the advance but also the consolidation of the popular share of institutional power. We should study, in the light of these tasks, how the left, given its structure and traditions, could and did correctly interpret and take advantage of the conditions for a peaceful transition of socialism. What was the nature of these conditions in the particular Chilean situation?

The basic conditions indispensable for a peaceful transition to socialism were all present in the case of Chile. These included an electoral majority, state control over a sector of the economy, and a certain capacity for decision making in the state's bureaucratic apparatus. However, we should pause for a moment to examine the nature of these conditions and how they were used by the people's parties.

Although the *Unidad Popular*'s electoral support increased between September, 1970 (when it obtained 36 per cent of the vote), and March, 1973 (when it received 44 per cent), this passive support was not transformed into an integrated front uniting all active and combative social forces. One reason for this was the traditional character of the parties. Unable to shed their electoral, parliamentary orientation, they subordinated the global, strategic interests of the movement to their own ideological objectives. As a result, mass support was fragmented into zones of influence which, despite constituting political control of the masses, impeded their transformation into an active force able to surpass the party structures themselves. To become a real force, the electoral majority required political organization; more accurately, the requirement of a majority could only be expressed through an organization. When the parties divided that majority into zones of influence (furthering their own importance as pressure groups), it ceased to be a condition facilitating a peaceful transition to socialism.

Simultaneously, the government advanced in the formation of a social sector in the economy, with which it intended to create the basis for effective people's power. The social sector, however, was caught between two contradictory circumstances—both inherent in the transition through which the economy was passing. On the one hand, the social sector was to be the embryo of workers' power; yet, on the other, its growth began under conditions in which bourgeois ideology still predominated, embodied in the market economy through which values proper to a capitalist economy (particularly consumerism) were transmitted. The leadership succumbed to the temptation of populist demagoguery as the easiest way to mobilize the masses, thus transmitting *petit bourgeois* values (payment in kind, fringe benefits, privileges, speculation, etc.) to broad sectors of workers. The inability of the leadership to forge a rational, coordinated policy with clear ideological objectives inevitably sharpened these negative effects.

At the same time, the leadership was quite inflexible with regard to the forms of property it was creating. This was particularly significant in agriculture. There was no effort to have the workers assume responsibilities concordant with their political development. In this manner, the substantive base for people's power was not complemented with policies contributing to the emancipation of workers from their *petit bourgeois* bonds and confinement as small pressure groups, isolated in their factories, without a vision of the entire process. Not until early 1973 did the leaders attempt to overcome this fragmentation by creating the so-called industrial belts. However, these too were definitively frustrated by political disunity, as revealed, for example, in the long and futile polemic between the United Workers' Central and the emergent industrial belts, resulting in demobilization and political confusion.

In examining the conditions for a peaceful transition, we find that they were not transformed from mere historical circumstances into a political will capable of advance within the limits imposed by electoral conditions and political organization. This political will was most dramatically absent in the decisive area of control over state bureaucracy. It is true that, to further construction of the Social Property Sector, the government did take advantage of contradictions in the existing legal system (the so-called legal "opportunities") and formed, in addition, mass organizations to alleviate problems of supply (the Supply and Price *Juntas*). However, neither measure formed part of a global institutional strategy, responding rather to short-term economic strategy.

In referring to global strategy, we are thinking of the conquest of civil society, whose most important political result would be the isolation of the dominant faction of the bourgeoisie. The conquest of civil society suggests that to destroy the dominant class, it is not sufficient to destroy its economic power alone. The Chilean experience shows that a strategy thus limited leads to erroneous policies and wasted opportunities. When political power is captured by a people's coalition, the class struggle shifts into the arena of political institutions, where the conflict is definitively decided when the ideological means of reproduction of the dominant class are left intact. There was, however, no strategic conception for using existing institutional mechanisms to impel the repressive apparatus through a period of transformation during which the revolutionary process could advance and create its own forms of domination. In other words, there was no perspective linking institutional political power and the new forms of legitimation. This demanded that the state pursue policies aimed at destroying the bourgeois ideological hegemony by creating an alliance that would isolate its dominant faction.

The collapse of the bourgeois class does not imply its disappearance, for it can be reconstructed politically through alliances with groups, sectors, or factions whose behavior is determined more by ideological factors than by location in the productive process. This was the case for sectors in the bureaucracy, the military, and the independent middle class. It follows that a strategy to conquer civil society assumed the creation of a contradiction between the monopolist, pro-imperialist bourgeoisie and the political system. This accords with the position that, for the proletariat, democracy is in all circumstances a political necessity, while for the capitalist bourgeoisie, it is under certain circumstances only a political inevitability. It was necessary to overcome the fear of the middle groups, who felt themselves dragged along by the proletariat. This fear was manipulated by the bourgeoisie to block an alliance antagonistic to its interests, while at the same time the people's parties did very little to counter it through the available mechanisms.

The absence of a global institutional strategy to deal with the problem of the state can be illustrated by the *Unidad Popular*'s handling of the questions of the duality of powers and definitive confrontation with the bourgeoisie. The left was never able to define a policy that could resolve the question of the transfer of decisions from traditional institutions to the newly emerging forms of power. The problem was basically whether that transfer was facilitated, or indeed only made possible, by consolidating institutional power. Transfer through a rupture would create such contradictions between the two powers that both would be weakened. This contradiction undoubtedly favored the bourgeoisie, for it implied a break in the unity of political leadership, which, rather than focusing on alternative roads for reaching strategic objectives, split over whether the "Chilean" road was reformist or revolutionary.

A revolutionary process consists of realizing the possibilities within a society at specific moments. If the advance of the Chilean process depended on the unity of the people's movement, the creation of new forms of domination adjusted to changes in the correlation of forces produced by economic policy, and the decomposition of the bourgeoisie, then the transfer of decision making could not be effected by creating conflict between the two forms of power (in effect, a conflict between the two strategies of the people's movement itself). Regardless of whether the bourgeoisie were defeated or not (because of a military defeat of the popular forces), in both situations it had to be isolated—a difficult achievement when the dominant class has not totally lost its hegemony and still controls a good part of civil society. If the bourgeoisie were not isolated, then the popular forces themselves would begin from an isolated situation, increasing the probabilities of a military triumph. I think, therefore, that the conquest of civil society, even if insufficient to guarantee power, at least serves to create the best conditions for the workers and their allies to approach the confrontation. It follows that the speed of change should be coordinated with the ability to form new structures of power. These would reflect, consolidate, and advance the new configuration of forces.

I deduce from the above that the Chilean process evolved on two levels that were not adequately coordinated. While progress was made in weakening the economic and financial power of the banking, industrial, and agrarian bourgeoisie, there was no parallel advance in integrating tactical and strategic political leadership. Thus there emerged a conflict between increasing demands by the mobilized base and the political possibilities for meeting these. In this respect, serious errors in interpreting the correlation of forces were committed. A false problem was articulated and never resolved: Was the pace of transformation to be dictated by the spontaneous movement of the base, ever more conscious and radical, or by an integrated political leadership able to channel and orient the pressures originating from the base?

We are thus obliged to ask this question: Is the correlation of forces determined by the physical magnitude of mobilized forces or by the effectiveness of their political expression? It was unlikely that the theoretical errors would be committed, but in its practical analysis the leadership allowed itself to be misled into identifying a simple expression of power in the streets with combat ability. The correlations were almost always analyzed from a perspective that favored the popular forces (electoral mobilization, street mobilization, the key importance of the working class in the national economy, the pusillanimity or passivity of the middle sectors, and the minority character of the monopolist and pro-imperialist faction of the bourgeoisie). It was never, or very seldom, realized from the point of view of the requirements of confrontation, perhaps because this contingency was never seriously analyzed, although the conviction that it was inevitable was widespread.

It was also necessary to consider the impact of the lack of party coordination on the formation of a military front, the lack of a homogeneous military policy, the disproportion in the logistical resources of the people *vis-à-vis* the armed forces, the behavior of the latter as an institutional group and as a class, the efficacy of repression, the active complicity of the lesser bourgeoisie, the legitimacy of the *coup* after the bourgeoisie reconstructed its ideological alliance, etc. The pressures from the base, without prior integration of the political leadership, caused each segment of leadership to compete for control over the mass organizations then being created. Thus, between the base and the political superstructure, a complex reciprocal relationship emerged.

Because social polarization was not accompanied by modification of the political structure, the leadership began to be surpassed by the expanding energy of the masses. Given the partisan fragmentation produced by the pursuit of bureaucratic and ideological interests, a disjuncture was produced between the political structure and the imperatives revealed by the course of events. All this was embodied in a single, fundamental fact: an increasing lack of direction.

CAUSES OF THE FAILURE

I will summarize my comments by briefly reviewing the most significant causes influencing the failure of the Chilean experience. I am conscious that this simple enumeration provides only a basis for more complete inquiries concerning the specific influence of each individual cause.

Problems of Political Leadership

The lack of internal cohesion in the leadership of the government impeded the formation of long-term strategy as well as opportune implementation of tactical measures. We note the inability to rectify economic policy, even when such action was urgent;

the lack of any clear agrarian reform policy; the delay in deciding whether to call a plebiscite, without posing real alternatives; the indecision over removing those generals implicated in anti-government activities; the disagreement over military policy, etc. The lack of cohesive leadership was also shown in its inability to take advantage of public administration to develop an effective system of planning. (The *Unidad Popular* government was a government that did not plan.) It also failed to utilize skilled political and technical personnel in specific roles, nor was it preoccupied with forming such personnel.

Finally, and particularly, the loss of any sense of vertical authority opened the gates to indiscipline, disguised as ideological discrepancies. The loss of political authority (primarily because power was not articulated) generated a power vacuum. Because the leadership found it impossible to adopt a policy of mass mobilization transcending the limits of electoral mobilization—thus to create conditions enabling the transfer of decision-making power—this vacuum grew more profound. Moreover, the parties themselves were not interested in change, for in this manner they avoided the necessary integral rectifications to which we have referred. How, then, could one speak of people's power?

Limitations of the Liberal Democratic System

The implementation of structural change, within the liberal political system, rapidly led to a situation in which the mechanisms for arbitrating and reconciling opposing interests were called into question. As a result, the system's basis of legitimacy broke down. First the monopolist, pro-imperialist, and latifundist factions, then the bourgeoisie as an ever more compact force, began pursuing a strategy to make political power illegitimate by destroying the traditional consensus. In this way a regrouping of the dominant class was precipitated, along with the isolation of the people's forces. It is in relation to this situation that the problem of Christian Democracy acquired its greatest significance. It was felt that deepening the social crisis at the Christian Democratic base would suffice to break its political control over workers and peasants. Perhaps in the long run this would have occurred, but it assumed, first, that an alliance providing sufficient time for conditions to mature existed and, second, that social polarization would break down partisan control. In precipitating the process without accepting an alliance, the opposite result was produced:

the Christian Democratic bases were radicalized not according to their objective, material interests but in conformity with their ideological and partisan commitment. Thus the policy that should have been followed—at first—was less to divide the PDC than to strengthen the faction that favored alliances, such as that which made possible the Christian Democratic vote in Congress for Salvador Allende. The division, before the *Unidad Popular* could destroy the ideological alliance of the bourgeoisie, contributed to a definition of forces imposed by the conditions of that alliance. Specifically, it permitted the expansion of anti-Communist sentiments in the Christian Democratic popular base and, with this, the beginning of a growing and overwhelming fascist wave.

The Incongruence between the Economic and Political Objectives of Government Policy

Economic policy overlooked the fact that, during a transition stage, the laws of capitalism would continue to function. Thus the expropriation of industries and farms and the intervention in many others did not neutralize the bourgeoisie's economic influence, which it continued to wield through the monetary system and commercialization, transferring great resources to speculation. In this fashion the bourgeoisie not only distorted the government's economic plans but also influenced the feelings of vast sectors seeking to satisfy their aspirations and, in a given moment, their basic necessities. Scarcities became a political problem because the government could not change the orientation of numerous social groups, pursuing its policies of "purchasing their adhesion." In this respect, the populist income redistribution had enormous impact, since it unleashed consumer expectations that were impossible to satisfy. These income distribution policies (which increased demand) were accompanied by the transfer of the industrial and agricultural productive apparatus to the workers (reducing the ability to supply goods) in circumstances with no homogeneous political leadership or sufficiently mature control over the economic and institutional system.

The Disarticulation of the State Institutional System

The lack of an alliance policy blocked the construction of a political front that would keep the class polarization from penetrating the institutional structure of the state, provoking a conflict among its different branches (the Executive, the Congress, and the Judiciary). As a result, the revolutionary forces lost even more of their capacity to control the rest of the institutional apparatus. This situation was created as much by the activities of the people's parties as by the bourgeoisie's strategy of tightening the institutional noose around the government's neck. The popular movement, unable to adjust its tactics to real conditions, provoked a questioning of the entire political system at a time when it lacked the force to impose any alternative organization.

International Factors

The Chilean experience demonstrated that, in the seventies, the anti-imperialist struggle had acquired a more specific character than that of a simple battle against the material interests of the metropolis. The worldwide *status quo* is being disrupted by the strengthening of the socialist bloc, the proliferation of national liberation movements, and the increasingly patent crisis of a bourgeoisie that seeks to maintain its domination through liberal structures or populist alliances. As this occurs, a concern with continental and global security begins to predominate in the center's evaluation of the dangers of national revolutions. It is security in its geopolitical sense, rather than the defense of specific enterprises, that serves as a guide for action. And insofar as it is the enterprises that guide, it is to guarantee as much the security of the metropolis as its investments.

Chile, whether because of the Allende doctrine of discounting excessive profits and thus not compensating foreign firms or because the success of its project would radiate a disintegrating influence throughout the continent, was inexorably condemned to become a preferred target. Nevertheless, no international factor is sufficient to explain the failure. If it were, it would condemn in advance, by virtue of a reactionary fatalism, any attempt at national liberation. What is questioned are those projects that are maintained strictly within national limits. Perhaps one of the lessons left by the Chilean tragedy is that this barrier must be overcome. To understand this lesson in all its richness, we must dedicate ourselves to analyzing the content of this internationalized political struggle, conditioned by *détente* between the United States and the Soviet Union, the domination of transnational enterprises in the world economy, and, finally, the role of a new political class played by the armed forces.

In our historical environment of convulsion, it becomes necessary to rethink old themes, shake off shrouded concepts, and penetrate more profoundly into that reality which escapes us. We should not fear to throw out our myths, discover falsehoods or partial truths, hunt down doctrinaire simplicities, or destroy idolatry. We must reencounter the solid elements with which to undertake the construction of the road that will lead us to the future—a future that will not arrive unless we are capable of conquering it. For this reason, as painful as it may sound, the labor of theoretical criticism is today fundamental.

Commentaries

The Viability and Failure of the Chilean Road to Socialism

JORGE TAPIA VALDES

In 1972 President Salvador Allende and General Lanusse, then President of Argentina, met in the Argentine city of Salta. During the reception ceremony at the airport, General Lanusse mistakenly took his place to the left of President Allende, when according to protocol he should have stood on the latter's right. Upon noting his error as they were reviewing the troops, Lanusse said to President Allende, "Mr. President, excuse me. I am on your left." Allende, breaking the somewhat cool and tense atmosphere that appeared to surround the reception, replied immediately, "Mr. President, be careful! To my left lies chaos."

The anecdote reveals both Allende's personality and his clear historical and political perceptions of the left and the possibilities of the Chilean road to socialism. Allende reiterated his ideas explicitly, and at times dramatically, in many important meetings of the higher leadership of the *Unidad Popular* (UP). The activities of his government, he believed, could only be conceived within the framework of the existing constitutional order, using the powers derived from that order to the maximum. It was important that the government obtain the greater political and social support necessary for it to expand its power base, but the electoral system would be maintained without qualification. The phrase that Allende often used to emphasize the strength of his convictions was, "In 1976 there will be elections, and we should win. But if we do not, I will hand over the reins of power to whoever is elected president."

This position of the leader of the Chilean people's forces does much to clarify the theme that concerns us here. In this analysis I will first discuss the "viability" of the Chilean road to socialism

297

and then the inevitability or avoidability of its failure. Finally, as examples of important events in the political evolution of the period, I will refer to two concrete cases, which I will describe more as a protagonist than as an analyst. These are the educational reform project known as the National Unified School (ENU) and the negotiations with the Christian Democrats during June and July, 1972.

THE VIABILITY OF THE CHILEAN ROAD TO SOCIALISM

In earlier presentations the essential viability of the program of the Allende government has been recognized. This viability was inherent in the historical nature of the program, insofar as it resulted not from laborious, abstract, and idealistic theorizing but from the maturation of the objective conditions of its existence, both nationally and internationally. The country's sociopolitical development and the strengthening of the principles of nonintervention, peaceful coexistence, and negation of ideological frontiers, in Latin America and the world, constituted real guarantees for the program's implementation.

If we accept this point of view, it becomes more necessary than ever to analyze the elements and evolution of the program that, three years after its initiation, made it appear destined to fail. This presupposes an attempt to define the Chilean road to socialism; that is, to specify its goals and tactics.

The Chilean experiment consisted basically of a transitional economic, social, and political model. It was designed to prepare the way for later socialist and democratic development. But that development required the creation of the objective conditions for the existence of a popular majority capable of expressing its will freely and consciously. The Chilean experiment was, by definition, a dynamic experience. It was capable of creating conditions for rapid social and political change and a more democratic democracy, demystifying those principles and forms of liberal political democracy that only serve to maintain capitalist domination. At the same time it sought to conserve and perfect the authentic values of a democratic order, such as the people's sovereignty, individual and social rights, the periodic election of governors, and the principles of legality and official responsibility.

It is important to keep in mind that the socialist goal of the program was never defined as Marxist-Leninist. This was historically and politically impossible. To be more exact: the goal was never a Marxist-Leninist regime, because if it had been, the Chilean road to socialism would never have existed. This was the understanding of the majority of the participants in the *Unidad Popular*. At the same time, as a political combination, the *Unidad Popular* was the most that Chilean reality permitted: a federation of socialist parties historically committed to democratic institutions in applying a developmental model of socialist inspiration. The revolutionary character of the process did not lie in the rapidity or radical nature of proposed changes. The concrete economic and social goals of the *Unidad Popular*'s program were, in truth, modest: to expand the already existing social sector of the economy by nationalizing monopolistic and strategic enterprises, to nationalize the banking system, to recover the natural resources of the country and put an end to imperialist exploitation and dependency, to produce a real distribution of income, and to democratize political and economic decision making through a substantial increase in popular participation.

The planned structural changes were never designed to, nor could they, create a socialist economy. Undoubtedly their purpose was to liberate man from the economy and place it at his service, but above all to liberate him from the system and its inherent poverty. It was hoped that the support of other social sectors could be won, forming the political majority necessary to democratically transform a semi-capitalist, dependent and underdeveloped country into a nation with a truly popular base—socialist, independent, and rapidly developing. Those who believe that this was mere reformism have never understood its tremendous revolutionary potential. The novelty and importance of the process lay not in its economic goals—which in the long run depended on the consolidation of new, non-capitalist socioeconomic structures—but in the road chosen.

Expressed in other words, *the goal of the Chilean road was specifically the kind of road chosen, not the type of socialism to which it might lead.* This new tactical proposal was made possible by the tremendously rich potential derived from two sources: the political democracy that had matured in Chile during the preceding forty years, and the socialist ideas of a left that, insofar as it had been able to emerge and develop within liberal democratic institutions, had learned to trust and preserve that democracy. This was the great historical conjuncture in the search for a more humane road to socialist humanism and what is truly significant and valuable for free men everywhere.

We cannot conclude this definition of the historical program of the *Unidad Popular* without alluding to the base of power that supported its electoral triumph and should have supported its realization: the alliance of the working class and the middle sectors. The entire project was inconceivable at any stage without this alliance. Such alliances had existed in Chilean politics ever since the general parliamentary election of 1917, but with one significant difference. Until 1970 it was the middle sectors that requested and obtained the support of the working class. In 1970 the distinction was that the working class, as the principal political actor, sought and obtained the support of the middle sectors. But in 1970 it was still indispensable to protect the assumptions that made the alliance possible, as a *sine qua non* for the viability of the political project. Lamentably, it was the attack on these assumptions that most sharply affected the implementation of the *Unidad Popular*'s program, as I shall explain below.

Given this definition of the Chilean road to socialism, we may consider some of the basic circumstances that obstructed its realization.

In my opinion, the *Unidad Popular* government did not know how to confront three crucial problems characteristic of this sort of revolutionary process. These can be summarized as follows: a) the complex and rapid response of the Chilean sociopolitical system to the stimuli derived from the *Unidad Popular* policies; b) the consolidation and expansion of the social bases of political power; and c) the nature and potential of state institutions and the law in Chile.

1. First, the *Unidad Popular* government was incapable of adapting its policies and manner of exercising its powers to the conditions of rapid and interdependent socioeconomic change produced by Allende's victory. Behavior tainted by "me-first" and certain doctrinaire, anachronistic attitudes made it difficult to give lasting, objective attention to the collection of information and the analysis of the changing conditions of the political and social struggle.

The people's victory alone created such chaos and such a sensation of annihilation on the Chilean right that it obviously decided, as would later be proven, to abandon the battleground of institutions and carry the social conflict toward direct confrontation. The trend was accentuated when the first measures to form the social sector were put into practice. Economic policy, like the measures leading to mass mobilization and participation, began not only to displace the traditional forms of power within the system but also to relocate these and suggest new tactics. The government did not adequately foresee these effects, nor were they considered in later planning. Indeed, the administration proceeded as if the entire institutional democratic system and its implicit values continued to function in the traditional manner.

Despite its advances during the last forty years, socialism, in the broad sense of the word, still faces a number of great, unfulfilled tasks. Among these are the elaboration of the nature of transitional economy, the discovery of the true mechanisms of the ideological superstructure, and the knowledge of the real role and importance of the middle classes. In the Chilean case, this lack of theoretical development weighed heavily. Because of its unique characteristics, Chile required very careful management of each of these aspects, minimizing improvisation and conducting policy as a true science. The Chilean road to socialism required a "general command post" to centralize all the information concerning the different operational sectors, to measure the impact of each factor on every other factor and on the aggregate as well as vice versa, and to introduce corrective actions and foresee behavioral changes accurately enough to maintain the functioning of the system. This, of course, necessitated a prior comprehension that the conditions permitting the *Unidad Popular*'s victory derived from a very sophisticated superstructure, capable of subverting all endeavors beyond the acceptable and working powerfully through new channels and forces. Because the weight of this factor was underestimated, the *Unidad Popular* in essence permitted the bull to enter the china shop. The ideology of the system, which had permitted victory, was damaged to such an extent that it became an important factor in the defeat.

2. Second, for basically the same reason, the government did not know how to maintain the minimal objective conditions necessary to conserve and increase its power among the middle classes.

It was predictable that domestic and foreign opposition would try to break the class alliance supporting the *Unidad Popular*'s program by doing everything possible to win over the middle sectors. To this end it orchestrated an incredible press, radio, and television campaign against the government, emphasized the scarcity of basic necessities, utilized the truckers' strike, unleashed waves of terrorism, and carried disorder to the streets. In synthesis, the opposition unleashed a devastating psychological war. A major portion of the middle sectors were convinced that total chaos reigned, along with maximum insecurity for both person and property.

The impact of the government's own economic policies added to the pressures generated by the right. There are many valid justifications for these policies at the beginning of the Allende government, but there is none, save absurd obstinacy, for maintaining them without even the most elementary adjustments to the reality and requirements generated by the process. The massive, violent redistribution of income and the lack of any definition of the economic sectors far longer than was rationally necessary struck not against the right, the great enterprises, or foreign capital, but exclusively against the middle sectors.

While economic policies during the government's first eighteen months injured the economic interests of the middle sectors, the extreme left—outside of the *Unidad Popular*—and certain sectors of the Socialist party took it upon themselves to threaten their ideological security. Although we may disagree with the values, ideas, principles, and motives of the middle sectors, it is obvious that the need for an alliance with them demanded that we not attack their ideology systematically and directly. No political pretext except a blind, futile, and anti-historical voluntarism could justify such tactics.

The legitimate takeover of a factory by its workers, because of subhuman working conditions, poor salaries, or management activities to sabotage the economy, was adequate reason for government intervention in that enterprise. However, the indiscriminate seizure of dozens of factories, most of scant economic significance, only succeeded in creating problems for the administration while frightening the thirty thousand small and medium-sized entrepreneurs. A similar argument holds for the agricultural sector. At the same time, the political activism of "shock groups"—not terrorists, for the Chilean left never really practiced terror—and the abuse of *economicismo* (see note, p. 227) as a means of mobilization never created greater class consciousness. They did, however, contribute to disorganizing production and decreasing productivity. What is more important, such actions alienated the skilled sectors, which resented the breakdown of hierarchy based on qualification and leftist "suspicions" of technocrats and professionals.

I cannot omit in this summary the attacks on government institutions, including the executive branch—attacks that were usually intemperate, emotional, and politically irrational. While it is true that the middle sectors had also criticized the inadequacy of Chilean political structures, they had never ceased to consider these institutions a prerequisite and guarantee of democratic government. But simultaneous attacks on these institutions by the right, which accused them of being unable to halt "communism," and the extreme left, which called them mere instruments of repression in the hands of the bourgeoisie, convinced the middle sectors that they had lost all value and utility.

Finally, when the *Unidad Popular* proposed a global educational reform, in spite of repeated internal warnings against it, it supplied a final weapon to the right for mobilizing the middle sectors in its favor. The technical content of the reform never came to be known; such was the blind passion of the attacks against it. The right called the measure (which was no more than a reform) a basic attack on cultural independence and freedom of thought, ideals so dear to the middle sectors because they are the essence of their individual superiority.

For the *Unidad Popular* government, it was overwhelmingly important to obtain support from the middle sectors beyond the ranks of its partisan followers. For this reason it was imperative to demonstrate, based on the nature of the program, that the Chilean road to socialism belonged to and equally favored all workers, including those who, though possessing some capital, were still dependent upon and controlled by capitalists as such—in other words, all those who relied essentially on their own work to prosper. In practice, the *Unidad Popular* was unable to convince the middle sectors that the government not only did not exclude them but in fact needed them, and that the procedure and goals of the program represented a commitment to their interests and values. As a result, an important portion of the middle sectors, initially inclined to support the government—one need only remember the April, 1971, election where the *Unidad Popular* obtained more than 50 per cent of the vote—became an instrument of the opposition. What is more important, this sector became "undemocratized"; that is, it fought not to resolve the social conflict within the traditional democratic framework but to radicalize it in order to provoke the overthrow of the government.

3. Finally, the *Unidad Popular* government never knew how to exercise the political, legal, and institutional power it gained in September, 1970.[1]

Forty years of democratic and orderly presidential succession, following a hundred years of rigid oligarchic authoritarianism, had inculcated in the mind of the average Chilean an involuntary respect for order, social tranquility, and the exercise of authority. In few other countries was it esteemed so correct and natural that a government should govern—that is, that it should effectively exercise its discretionary powers. The *Unidad Popular* government was unable to face this fact, much less use it advantageously, and appeared uncertain in adopting, implementing, and enforcing decisions.

Allende's own democratic convictions and the nature of his political support led him to share his decision-making powers with the leadership of the *Unidad Popular*. The latter, however, lacking internal unity, was incapable of elaborating decisions or making policy. Moreover, the adoption of this mode of decision making diminished the importance of the cabinet. Cabinet meetings during the Allende administration were very infrequent and generally served not to plan or coordinate respective policies but rather to search for joint remedies to the grave problems of contradictions among administrative units and opposition acts of sabotage. The government, in a permanent morass, was perceived by the public as lacking competence or skill in elaborating and carrying out its plans or, worse yet, as deliberately creating uncertainty and chaos in the areas those plans were to affect.

At the same time, the legitimate goal of not emulating the repressive character of previous governments gave a free hand to subversion, both from the extreme left and particularly from the extreme right and its paramilitary organizations. Undoubtedly the problem of using the state's police power to maintain order was misunderstood. It was not a matter of choosing between the physical integrity and liberty of the workers, on the one hand, and the maintenance of social order for its own sake, on the other. The judicious use of the available means for guaranteeing public order would have halted the development of subversive forces at their inception and avoided the disorder of *"espontaneísmo" directed* by the extreme left.

The appropriate use of authority could have and should have also avoided the problems created by sectarianism (political patronage) in public administration and the social sector of the economy. The purpose of sectarianism was less selfish proselytism than calculated improvements of position within the *Unidad Popular* coalition. In any case, it lessened the advantages of controlling an extensive administrative structure, with appreciable resources and wide powers, within a largely interventionist and socializing state. Instead of serving a central and unified command with a clear policy, public administration was divided into sectors, each responding, often against all reason, to the demands of the most audacious groups or those with the most powerful political patrons.

Certain extreme-left groups wanted to destroy the liberal

bourgeois state and its administrative apparatus, but apart from these few extremists, the idea was never suggested by any responsible actor. In any case, it was entirely antithetical to the goal of implementing the program through existing institutions. Some did argue superficially that any state not based directly on the dictatorship of the proletariat is essentially an instrument of bourgeoise domination, but for reasons which are unnecessary to present in detail here, this point of view was unacceptable to the Chilean experiment. The only center of power controlled by the people's forces was precisely the part of the state it would have been necessary to destroy.

Nevertheless, these attitudes created a kind of prejudice within the *Unidad Popular* against full use of the administrative powers of the state. As a result, a sense of authority was absent, encouraging those who pretended to create power through chaos. The arguments for building "people's power" were invalid from the start and lacked any coherent, unified form or plan. In fact, people's power was neither an alternative nor a complement to government activity, although it did increase the sensation that authority either could not or would not act. It was not an initiative that President Allende desired or with which he agreed. Allende was always of the opinion that the power of the people was that which he represented and that workers' organizations should support government policies, not arrogate power to themselves or implement policies different from the official ones.

On the other hand, as a result of the 1970 constitutional reform, the traditional role of Congress in resolving sociopolitical conflict was diminished to a minimum, and for the same reason, the importance of political parties was reduced. The executive branch was the only remaining effective arena for conciliation and compromise. In effect, the 1970 constitutional reform and the revolutionary nature of the Chilean road to socialism had de-institutionalized social conflict, eliminating the system of checks and balances formed by the political parties and legislative chambers, which until then had acted to mediate among the different interests and powers. Of course, one could not ask a socialist government that, in the midst of class conflict, it play the role of an arbiter "above contingent and partial interests." That would have contradicted the popular character of its base and goals. But the fact that the Constitution had made the President virtually omnipotent, capable of giving and denying, encouraging and discouraging, permitting and prohibiting, governing with or without the people, should have been confronted in some manner.

The reform gave the President room for maneuver. It gave him powers that virtually allowed him to control the Congress as a legislative and constituent body. Had these powers been exercised opportunely and according to defined plans, they would have permitted the executive to establish the rhythm and form of social conflict. It would have been possible to profit from the dynamics of the conflict, instead of being controlled by them. A mobilized and conscious mass may not accept paternalism, but it is unrealistic to pretend that it does not accept or require authority. This situation was falsely presented by some members of the *Unidad Popular* as a dialectical contradiction. As the government was then incapable of creating an alternative form of power, the result. was something even worse than the abuse of power—the disuse of it.

At this point we should remind the reader that the strong criticism, or self-criticism, above is based on a prior belief that the Chilean road to socialism was essentially viable.

The tremendous accumulation of tactical and strategic errors summarized above—without detail and ignoring others—was neither the inevitable result of the nature of the Chilean process nor sufficient to determine its collapse. If the appropriate measures had been opportunely adopted, the opposition seeking an extra-constitutional outcome would not have had so many advantages and would have been obliged to change the timing and form of its tactics. Furthermore, one must remember that, in spite of the errors, a slow but persistent development of class consciousness was observable. This was evidenced by the March, 1973, election. Among the *Unidad Popular* parties, recognition of the need to consolidate the important structural changes already implemented and seek compromise with all mass political and social forces was finally, if tardily, gaining ground. This and other facts to be presented below make it possible to suggest ways in which the collapse of the Allende government might have been avoided.

THE AVOIDABILITY OF THE FAILURE
OF THE CHILEAN ROAD TO SOCIALISM

For some biased observers of the Chilean experience, its collapse was the price paid for confronting a process of class struggle within the framework of a liberal democracy. Today it is increasingly evident that, despite the accentuated polarization and wide-

spread social conflict in Chile, that error did not have the characteristics nor the definitive causal importance in Allende's overthrow that many wish to attribute to it. Just as important, and
perhaps more so, was the fact that the Chilean experience confronted from the first the grim decision of the United States executive, the Pentagon, and the immense North American companies
not to permit a socialist government to succeed in Chile. One can
no longer ignore the tremendous impact of this decision on the
fate of the Chilean experience. Whatever policies had been
adopted by the *Unidad Popular,* the effort to undermine the government would have occurred just the same.

The *coup d'état* of September, 1973, was a careful work of
political and social engineering. Taking advantage of even trivial
characteristics of Chilean society, the errors committed by the
Unidad Popular, and all the forces unleashed by the dialectic of
the process, it provoked a collective psychological panic, and it
did so by trumpeting imaginary danger and insecurity and the
arrival of a totalitarian government.[2] Each trait of Chilean middle-
class psychology was skillfully manipulated during the entire period. Its consumption habits and appreciation for a certain life-
style were used by manipulating scarcities of essential goods and
propagating rumors affecting its sense of status. Other targets were
the middle sectors' appreciation of the right of privacy, of owning
a home and even an automobile, their respect for the notion of
legality in government and administrative acts, for the intangibil-
ity and authority of the courts, for the principle of an impartial
government, for order and social tranquility, for the strong use of
authority, etc. Even though all signs indicated the contrary, the
middle sectors became convinced that freedom of the press and
opinion, of teaching, and of personal movement, and many other
freedoms as well, were threatened. It is unnecessary to add that,
except for the valuable if unconscious aid provided by groups of
the extreme left (passing over the opposition infiltration of these
groups), none of these campaigns was based on verifiable facts.

Perhaps the most characteristic trait of the Chilean middle
class is the high value it places on education and the status derived
from it. The middle class looks with anguish on the possibility of a
dictatorship of the proletariat, not because it is a dictatorship, but
because it is proletarian. Taking advantage of this attitude, those
who engineered the *coup* fostered the horror of "proletarianiza-
tion" and the "hegemony of the uneducated and ignorant."

To this brief summary of the skillful and cynical manipulation
of the ideological values and attitudes of the middle sectors

should be added, of course, the use of direct action, especially the terrorism of the extreme right.

Although I maintain that this "subversive engineering" utilized the class struggle to provoke a *coup d'état,* that struggle did not produce the *coup.* Undoubtedly some sectors of the national bourgeoisie were motivated by an intransigent defense of their interests, but their motivation was also manipulated by foreign actors on whom they were dependent. These foreign interests sought to make the national bourgeoisie the instrument of a global hegemonic policy based on premises far more complex than the simple class struggle. The class struggle was only the detonator of a charge exploded by the Chilean military—the explosive material was imported from abroad. Paradoxically, the most orthodox theoreticians of the class struggle have not understood that, in spite of its historical and sociological potential, it can also become a simple means or instrument when the forces that manipulate it have the capability and strategy to convert an entire country into a simple laboratory.

From this point of view, it seems clear that the failure of the *Unidad Popular* government could have been avoided—that is, that it was viable not only in theory but also in practice—if two conditions had been present: a) if the North American government had decided not to intervene or b) if, even given that intervention, the *Unidad Popular* had avoided or corrected its tactical errors, especially those affecting the middle sectors, and if it had had realistic, unified, centralized, and more authoritative strategic leadership.

Nevertheless, in focusing on this problem, we should keep in mind that once an experience like the Chilean road to socialism is under way, it is not socialism that fails to follow a peaceful and legal road but rather democracy that fails as a system of government. The socialist goals rapidly push the right toward fascism, making it an enemy of democratic institutions. Thus is produced the paradox of a socialism that loyally tries to fit the democratic mold, while those who call themselves the defenders of democracy radically change the form of their opposition, according less value to constitutional institutions and resorting to direct and violent action. Capitalism does not want more or less humane roads to socialism, because it rejects all roads. This has long been clear but appears even more so after the Chilean experience. As long as it is led by the bourgeoisie—from the courts, the armed forces, or through economic control—a democracy will never be sufficiently democratic to permit a free and orderly transition to socialism.

For the same reason, all peaceful, electoral, and institutional roads to socialism are, above all, peaceful roads to democracy. It is first necessary to democratize democracy. It must be given an effectively popular mass base consolidating a class alliance, confront the bourgeoisie, and eradicate anti-progressive and anti-democratic attitudes within the armed forces. That, precisely, was Allende's basic project—what the "infantilism of the left" could not understand and what the domestic right and North American imperialism could not permit. The *coup d'état* of September, 1973, took place in order to prevent this political project from being implemented. The enormous pyre on which the alienated Chilean military incinerated democracy is the most categorical proof of the viability of the Chilean road to socialism.

TWO CASE STUDIES OF POLITICS DURING THE ALLENDE ADMINISTRATION

Negotiation of an Agreement with Christian Democracy, June and July, 1972

As a result of agreements adopted at the so-called *El Arrayán* meetings, President Allende and most of the parties in the *Unidad Popular* sought to negotiate a broad agreement with the Christian Democrats after early 1972. Together with facilitating laws and policies essential to the program, an agreement might have halted the increasing alienation of the middle sectors and restored their confidence and security through the establishment of clear economic "rules of the game." The first effort to reach such an agreement had ended badly, amidst reciprocal accusations by the government and the Christian Democratic party and the withdrawal from the government coalition of a dissident movement from the Radical party known as the Party of the Radical Left (PIR).

After restructuring the cabinet in April, 1972, President Allende personally asked me, as Minister of Justice, to seek a renewal of conversations with the Christian Democrats. These conversations were to focus on the form and content of a proposed constitutional reform concerning the definition of the economic sectors. The reform represented a double threat to the executive: first, it would deny the President economic and administrative powers that he had until then enjoyed; and second, it was a pretext for the majority opposition in Congress to advance a new and dubious interpretation of the vote necessary to override an executive veto of a constitutional amendment. Its passage would have signified recognizing the power of a simple congressional majority to approve a constitutional reform more easily than a common law, thus giving the Congress extremely wide powers as a policymaker.

President Allende specified only three essential requirements for an agreement: 1) the administrative powers given him by existing legislation had to be maintained; 2) which large monopolistic or strategic firms should immediately become part of the social sector of the economy would be specified; and 3) he would not accept the opposition's new interpretation of the procedures for reforming the Constitution.

Through personal contacts, the conversations were reinitiated in a reserved but diligent fashion in May, 1972. They progressed and became official, although preserving their limited nature, thanks to the favorable disposition of the left-wing faction then leading the PDC and the firm position of President Allende and the Communist and Radical parties. The Socialist party maintained its opposition to the negotiations until mid-June, at which time it declared that, despite believing it highly unlikely that the negotiations would bear fruit, the party would not present any further obstacles to their taking place. Meanwhile, in spite of pressures within the *Unidad Popular* to respect the Christian Democrats' natural request that decisions or attitudes tending to make the negotiations more difficult not be adopted, certain political and administrative sectors in the government and groups on the extreme left undertook actions whose aim, and foreseeable effect, was to make any agreement fail. This problem was discussed at the highest level of the government, which kept these negative pressures to a minimum.

In the second half of June, after most of the basic problems had been resolved, the conversations were publicly made official. Over the next fifteen days there were further advances on each of the major points remaining in contention. A broad series of agreements covered almost all the problems likely to create serious political, legal, or social conflicts. The most important of these dealt concretely with the following areas:

1. The transfer of about eighty large monopolistic or strategic enterprises, both national and foreign, to the social and mixed sectors of the economy. In each case the sector was specified. The agreement also established rules for indemnifying the owners;

2. The need for a general or specific law governing future transfers of enterprises from the private sector to the social or mixed sectors;

3. Regulation of the executive's powers to intervene temporarily in private enterprises;

4. Rules for the participation of workers in the administration of mixed enterprises, particularly banks. Various enterprises of this kind would be primarily administered by the workers;

5. Creation of workers' enterprises;

6. Creation of a judicial organ to resolve disputes over discriminatory policies toward firms not pertaining to the social sector; and

7. The allocation of a substantial portion of public resources used for publicity to those newspapers, radio, and television channels that were not state property.

Implementation of this agreement was greatly complicated by the nature and number of the matters covered. It required that the President present a number of bills to Congress and that he withdraw various vetoes of the opposition's constitutional reforms. It also required a sophisticated system for voting on the reform in each of the two Chambers. These points, elaborated by common agreement, were ratified by the President and respective ministers and were being prepared for submission to Congress at an opportune moment.

It is true that the agreement did not deal with all these matters in detail, for it was physically impossible to do so. Moreover, a number of points had to be left for more careful elaboration during parliamentary debate. Given the problems covered, however, it is far more significant that an agreement was actually achieved. Regrettably, despite the efforts of those then leading the Christian Democratic party, the opposition of that party's right wing, along with senators from the remaining opposition parties and the extreme right, blocked final ratification of the agreement.

It should be clearly understood that the failure of the negotiations did not result from insufficient flexibility on the part of the government of President Allende. Within the preestablished limits, everything the Christian Democrats presented as essential was accepted. The failure of the negotiations was caused, in fact, by the lack of any agreement to reinstitutionalize the political and social conflict. The opposition chose to continue the fight by means that were increasingly removed from democratic procedures.

The Proposal of an Educational Reform: The National Unified School (ENU)

During the administration's first two years there were no serious problems for the government in education. True, the opposition did all it could to create difficulties, principally by using student organizations to provoke strikes and disorders, but it was unable to convey a general feeling of trouble in the sector. Meanwhile, government educational policy was very cautious, limited to preserving texts and programs inherited from the previous administration. Relations with private education were excellent, and state economic aid to private high schools was actually expanded beyond the traditional levels. Under the auspices of the highest ecclesiastical authorities, and in collaboration with representatives of Catholic schools, the possibility of creating a semiautonomous body responsible for the administration and growth of private education was being studied.

At the same time, however, the Ministry of Education was preoccupied with studying reforms it felt necessary in Chilean education. The Frei administration had attempted some changes, but the system had continued to grow in an unintegrated and unplanned fashion, with serious imbalances. The number of classrooms and professors was insufficient to meet the enormous demand for education, particularly in secondary schools and universities. Moreover, educators had long been aware of the need to reform secondary education, to give it a unified and integrated character capable of preparing the student either for higher studies or for the labor market, if he or she was unable or did not want to continue higher studies. In spite of this ideal, however, the system was discriminatory and scarcely useful to the students. The low standards of secondary technical education placed graduates of technical high schools in a disadvantageous position for continuing higher studies. On the other hand, if the students of academic high schools were unable to enter the university, they were not prepared to go directly to work.

There were other problems as well: preschool education, adult education, and education for workers and the elderly were all seriously inadequate. In addition, the system was characterized by typically obsolete teaching in which the educational phenomenon was divorced from reality and the school from society.

To confront these problems the Ministry of Education prepared a reform based on the most modern educational techniques. It evolved through studies and agreements with the respective professional organizations and was to be implemented following discussion and approval by the pertinent bodies.

In September, 1972, the technical divisions of the Ministry of Education approved the project along general lines and, to move quickly toward implementation, requested the Superintendency of Education to elaborate the appropriate report. This was written in November, at which time I was made the new Minister of Education. When I was shown the text, I objected to the lack of concrete detail, the phrasing, and, above all, the suggested timing for implementing the reform. Therefore I returned it for further study. The technical and political divisions of the Ministry then began a long and heated debate over the convenience of accelerating or delaying public discussion and application of the reform. The Radical party and I considered the form and timing of the project a tactical political error that would permit the opposition to distort the reform's purpose and campaign vigorously against the government. In contrast, the representatives of the Socialist and Communist parties—proceeding in this case without consulting their Central Committees—opined that "the revolution had to be carried to education in order to take the initiative against the enemy." This serious disagreement was submitted to the President, who requested a solution that, while solving the grave problems in the educational system, would not provide the opposition with a new and advantageous battleground. For this purpose, I then proposed that the effective date of the reform be postponed, that adequate time be allowed for discussion by the relevant organizations, and that the text of the technical report be modified. All these proposals were accepted.

For a broad and integrated educational reform such as this one to succeed, it was indispensable that, not only should specifically political factors be considered, but sufficient time be available to divulge and diffuse its ideas, prepare the appropriate curricular and program changes, elaborate new texts, and find adequate sources of financing. Similarly, the educational philosophy underlying the reform and the specific policies of its application had to be discussed and approved. In January, 1973, very little of this had been adequately prepared. As a result, it was obvious that in June, the date chosen for initiating the reform, various aspects of the project would be left hanging. In practice this meant postponing the reform until March, 1974. I was convinced that, at least from an educational and technical viewpoint, the reform should not be implemented before it had been duly studied, discussed, and approved in its entirety.

Nor had its political aspect improved significantly. In spite of my earlier remarks, the final report presented by the Superintendency of Education continued to employ unnecessarily partisan language, which obscured the reforms' true motives and goals. Moreover, although it should have been distributed to the entire educational sector in early February, distribution was inexplicably delayed until mid-March. As a result, the topic was presented for discussion in a way doubly advantageous to the opposition, even though it had virtually lost the general parliamentary election of March and the new school year had already begun. Lacking new arguments to maintain its strong attack against the government, the opposition was gratuitously handed a new theme that permitted it to mobilize, on favorable terms, wide sectors of the middle classes, the Catholic Church, and the armed forces.

Powerful and visible problems demanded reform, and valuable technical ideas were put forward for implementation, but these were virtually ignored in the passionate national debate which erupted. Very few people who protested against the project had any idea of its true content. The entire debate focused on the supposed aims of the government: to proletarianize education and convert it into an arm of Marxist-Leninist indoctrination. No empirical reason or proof, however powerful or obvious, could demonstrate that this was not the case.

It must be recognized that the most serious aspect was not the ensuing national debate, which was favorable politically to the opposition. Rather, though it had been foreseen and warned against, the contradictions and differences within the coalition permitted a very powerful weapon to be handed to the opposition. And this was only one of many cases that can be cited.

One consequence of this problem, so unnecessarily and extemporaneously caused by the *Unidad Popular* itself, was the reaction it produced within the armed forces. In April, 1973, at a meeting with the entire high command, I made a lengthy speech explaining the bases and purposes of the reform. It was like speaking to a stone wall. When the opportunity for questions and observations arose, it became clear that the meeting had been arranged to demonstrate to the government the unhappiness of the armed forces, not with the reform, but with the government's entire range of policies. The commentaries were all markedly political (in Chilean terms) and used the same arguments put forth by the press and by opposition politicians. Moreover, the military officers present repeatedly raised questions or doubts that I had clarified in his speech. I was finally led to remark that, given the administration's reasons for an educational reform such as the one proposed, and after constantly reiterating that its goals had nothing to do with those denounced by the opposition, the entire problem boiled down to "having confidence in the executive." Various voices were heard to reply, "That is the problem, Mr. Minister, having confidence."

These incidents were reported to the President. No decision on the matter was adopted.

NOTES

1. To analyze accurately the influence of legal-institutional structures and the political system on the implementation of the Chilean road to socialism, one must keep in mind that the European arguments for a peaceful transition to socialism through a democratic conquest of power all assume the existence of a parliamentary system, while what existed in Chile was a strong presidential regime. Electoral victory in a European system means winning a majority in Parliament and thereby gaining control of the executive—in sum, the totality of political power. Electoral victory in Chile, where there is a more rigid separation of powers, gives control of one or the other branch, but never both simultaneously. As yet, no one has studied in depth the political impact of the constitutional reform of January, 1970, which noticeably increased the powers of the President at the cost of the Congress.

2. It is interesting to note the information on the role of the military in Chile contained in the *Area Handbook for Chile,* prepared for use by North American military personnel assigned to that country. According to this publication, a 1965 survey revealed that 98 per cent of the lower class, 89 per cent of the lower-middle class, and 71 per cent of the middle and upper classes were of the opinion that the armed forces were necessary to "forestall possible violations of the Constitution on the part of the government." The book then expresses the opinion that "public opinion has accepted the military as a safeguard against arbitrary actions by the authorities and *as an alternative to ineffective civilian governments"* (Thomas E. Weill *et al., Area Handbook for Chile,* p. 450). This "very particular" opinion contrasts with the results of polls conducted only weeks before the *coup d'état,* which showed that in spite of strong opposition to the government, more than 70 per cent of the respondents opposed military intervention.

Errors of the Unidad Popular and a Critique of the Christian Democrats

JULIO SILVA SOLAR

ERRORS OF LEADERSHIP

Certainly the Chilean process faced powerful internal and external enemies, willing to do everything possible to destroy it. This is beyond debate. Yet it would be a mistake to believe that these enemies were all-powerful and capable of obtaining whatever they wished with no additional help. This would be to assume a fatalistic position. I think these enemies are not all-powerful, they can be defeated, their success can be prevented, the conditions they need for victory can be avoided. In a word, I do not believe the *Unidad Popular* was condemned to fail, even though it was a new and very complex experiment. The causes for its failure, moreover, should not be sought in its enemies. These did only what they had to do as enemies—although this does not deny the moral and legal responsibility for which they should be judged. Their activities could have been foreseen and countered. Their success was not inevitable. The causes of the failure lie in the errors of the *Unidad Popular*. This is the assumption from which I begin.

In this essay I will try to indicate the most important of these errors, from which many others were derived.

The first error was the failure of political leadership. We have already spoken of the two lines or orientations found within the *Unidad Popular*. This problem of a double line was never resolved. There was never any determined or coherent choice. This lack of definition had an impact on leadership and the unity of command, and in the end leadership as such no longer existed. The people were left paralyzed and confused. Because of this double line the parties, as a governing alliance, were unable to

316

reach agreements on an articulated, homogenous, leadership structure. Only President Allende, by assuming personal leadership, could have filled the vacuum, and he did not do so. Without a clear, coherent, and single line, it was impossible to direct the extremely difficult situation the government was forced to confront. One or the other of the two lines could have been adopted and pursued in depth, but this was not done because it would have produced the rupture of the *Unidad Popular* and, as a result, weakened the government. Yet by not choosing, President Allende allowed the two lines to continue to coexist, mutually annulling and blocking one another. This took form in an absence of leadership and initiative along either of the two lines. The President tried always to conciliate, but the differences were irreducible. With neither rudder nor compass, it was impossible to sail those seas. Unified direction was the first condition for arriving anywhere.

Because concrete historical examples are lacking, there is little theoretical elaboration of the course followed by the *Unidad Popular*. Until Chile, all socialist revolutions had followed other roads, and the majority of the theoretical elaborations of Marxist-Leninism reflected those experiences. Even the hallowed notions of the "peaceful" and "violent" roads did not really clarify matters. The Chilean road was an institutional one, and although the institutional road includes and assimilates the peaceful, it does not dismiss possible resort to arms or even civil war to fight sedition. Normally, however, the peaceful road is considered to be that in which there is neither war nor armed confrontation, even though the masses may be armed or have armed support. In Chile the institutional road was one in which the mass movement was not armed. Its access to the government occurred without the use of arms. Armed might was controlled by the armed forces of the state, pre-established and professional, owing obedience to constitutional authority (obviously neither revolutionary nor socialist authority, but the authority of representatives of the middle sectors under the influence of the bourgeoisie and the Pentagon).

Thus, in Chile the institutional road was peaceful not simply in the sense of an absence of war or armed confrontation, but in the sense that the people had no arms and that their advance, even their access to government, occurred without arms. On the subtle nature of such a road very little has been written. Reference to existing revolutionary experience and theory suggests rather that the road be denied. We should prepare to leave or detour from it. In Chile socialism derived from democratic development, but the theoretical writings describe a socialism that did not derive from democracy. Our experience showed that this vacuum and maladjustment of theory had important consequences.

The institutional road evolves naturally within a structure governed by the Constitution and by law. However broad, solid, and flexible that structure may be, its resistance has a limit. When this limit is surpassed, the structure either explodes or collapses. Moreover, this structure always takes the form of a state based on class. Therefore it is necessary to weigh the forces in combat, the advances, the retreats, and the intensity of the conflicts, and this should all be done with careful and dispassionate analysis. Only thus can we establish what can and what cannot be done within a particular structure during any given period.

The institutional road, simply because it does not have its own military force available, requires a very broad political front based on consensus. We are not referring simply to 51 per cent of the vote but to a far broader alliance of forces. The *Unidad Popular* was not aware of this need for a front far larger than the UP itself and was even less aware of how to form it. In September, 1972, the *Unidad Popular* had received only 36 per cent of the vote.

This explains why the *Unidad Popular* did not have a sufficiently elaborated, clear, and systematic policy toward Christian Democracy. What it had instead was various policies. Any negotiations or dialogue with the Christian Democrats was met with suspicion by the Socialist leadership, which saw in it a sellout or reformist conciliation. Yet it depended definitively on the behavior of the Christian Democrats whether the right would be isolated or, conversely, the *Unidad Popular*. Within the coalition there was very little clarity on this matter.

Nor was there a policy aimed at dividing the PDC; there simply was no policy toward that party. What there were, were differences of opinion with respect to the relations or attitudes that the UP ought to hold toward the Christian Democrats. However, these really reflected no more than the greater or lesser hostility that the latter awakened with the coalition. Relations were abandoned to follow the course of events, and what developed with greatest force was confrontation.

The internal conflicts over the problem of a broad front and the policies to be implemented also paralyzed activities affecting relations with the armed forces. In October, 1972, the head of the army, General Prats, became Interior Minister and publicly identified himself with the fundamental programs of the *Unidad Popu-*

lar. At that moment the clarity of the ideas advanced by the people's government could have permitted committing a sector of the military led by Prats to support the activities of the government. Obviously Prats and the constitutionalist faction of the military did not favor establishing the dictatorship of the proletariat or advancing beyond the program in the area of socialization. Nevertheless, their presence was considered a reformist impediment by that faction of the *Unidad Popular* that wanted to advance further. As there was no definition or clarity in this respect, practically no action was undertaken.

It thus seems that a broad front that includes the middle sectors cannot be Marxist (unless one speaks of a forced imposition), cannot use Marxist-Leninist language and categories, and cannot propose socialism and power for workers. None of these seems compatible with the desire to form a broad front. It is necessary to establish limits and advance by stages, according to successively articulated programs, and this must be done with the greatest coherence. The limits on a program can be made clear only by scientific political and social analysis, elaborated with method, equilibrium, and objectivity.

The *Unidad Popular* felt that a government implementing revolutionary and socialist measures would be supported by an unstoppable mass mobilization. What it did not foresee was a fascist mass reaction, which in the end was what predominated. The people's forces did grow (in September, 1970, the UP received 36 per cent of the vote; in April, 1971, 50 per cent; and in March, 1973, 44 per cent), but fascism was able to unite everyone else in a single combative block to oppose the *Unidad Popular.* This united alliance included most of the middle sectors (truck drivers, merchants, doctors, professionals, small and medium businessmen, employees, important numbers of secondary students, and, to a lesser degree, university students) and even a portion of the popular masses (women, certain workers' groups in copper, etc.).

Under the fascist baton the opposition held great public demonstrations against the *Unidad Popular* government. The advance toward socialism necessarily generates a fascist reaction, and under specific conditions this can acquire great strength and dynamism—particularly when socialist advances surpass the real (but not potential) force that objectively supports them.

Political leadership thus failed in two ways. It did not resolve within the coalition and the government the problem of the double line, and at the same time it did not elaborate sufficiently the institutional road that in practice was followed. With respect to the noninstitutional or armed road, it was an option that, in my judgment, offered scant possibilities. Some did struggle to prepare and lead the confrontation between classes to the terrain of force, of clashes, and eventually, of armed conflict; but in any test of armed might the correlation of forces would have been even more negative and the destruction of the people's movement perhaps even greater.

In a democratic system, in contrast to an authoritarian one, it is tremendously difficult to establish social discipline, to place limits on the excessive economic demands of the labor movement, or to adjust expectations to economic reality. In Chile the initial need to reactivate the economy led to a policy of salary adjustments and fixed prices (which increased purchasing power and the power to consume), increased state spending, and other measures of a similar sort. These produced at first a climate of well-being and relaxation, but excessive demands and expenditures soon overtaxed the possibilities for relatively ordered management of the economy and created grave problems: scarcities, inflation, disequilibria, and general economic deterioration. The net result was to facilitate the activities of those who, from both inside and outside Chile's borders, applied a careful plan to sabotage the country's economy. To meet this challenge what was necessary was a level of discipline, of authority, of work, and of sacrifice that the *Unidad Popular* government was far from achieving.

It goes without saying that there were serious errors in economic policy, but there were also errors in the sense and exercise of authority: a certain anarchistic optimism attributing to the masses an ability to adopt and administer decisions and to resolve problems by themselves; an inability to perceive the divisive, negative, and selfish tendencies that also existed in the hearts of the people; a certain reluctance to use the very character of the state, that is, its capacity for command and coercion—to the extent of refusing to use any other means than persuasion. The government announced that it would abstain from repressive measures. In a way it was almost like renouncing the function of the state itself. Of course the majority of mankind and society as such are still not able to organize themselves and function under such circumstances. The result was increasing disorder and anarchy and the loss and breakdown of authority. As is known by all, these finally created the environment that made necessary an authoritarian regression.

From my point of view, the principal errors of the *Unidad Popular* can be presented as if responding to separate problems.

Yet they are intimately interrelated and could be reduced to a single nucleus or central root. In any case, what seems most clear at the moment is that they can be summarized in the following manner:

1. Errors in political leadership, particularly in not having resolved the problem of the double line or orientation;

2. Errors or inadequacies in the elaboration of the institutional road being followed by the *Unidad Popular;*

3. Errors in the management of the economy;

4. Errors in the conception and exercise of state authority and its functions.

THE BOURGEOIS CHARACTER OF CHRISTIAN DEMOCRACY

Tomić's presentation lacks a spirit of self-criticism. But even accepting his analysis, we can reconsider the real course of the process. In effect, his entire analysis (which focused particularly on the first epoch of relations between Christian Democracy and the *Unidad Popular,* at the beginning of the Allende government) leads to the conclusion that it was the *Unidad Popular,* through its errors and its sectarianism, that pushed the Christian Democrats into the arms of the right; then came the fascist reaction and finally the *coup.* I can, in general, admit that this conclusion is valid. But it then becomes necessary for me to deny the other assumption on which Tomić bases his presentation—that is, that the PDC is a party with a "consciousness of the left," committed to the historical task of "substituting capitalism," and profoundly linked to the people in the struggle to construct a new socialist society.

I think this is a false image of Christian Democracy. It is unreal, utopian, and mythological. If the PDC were really a party with the characteristics attributed to it, I do not see how—whatever errors the *Unidad Popular* might commit—it could be pushed to the right, to the *coup* and fascism. Nor do I see how it could adopt such rapid opposition to a government of the left, a government that within democracy and the law was, precisely, replacing capitalism and opening the way to a new society. In spite of all the process's deficiencies, the attitude of the Christian Democrats is inconceivable if Christian Democracy is what Tomić claims it is. That attitude is only conceivable, it can only be explained, if moving beyond mere appearances, we get to the true substance of the

PDC: to wit, that it is a party of the bourgeoisie, representing the progressive sectors of that class and receiving strong support from the middle sectors and the masses (peasants, urban squatters, and workers). However, these middle and mass sectors are under the influence of the bourgeoisie. Their consciousness is still dominated by the consciousness and ideology of the bourgeoisie, and they still have not acquired independence.

Naturally there are conflicts and contradictions within the Christian Democratic party. (There have even been divisions.) But what predominates is the bourgeois character of the party, expressed essentially in the profound link between the party and capitalism as a system and as the power of the bourgeoisie. The Christian Democratic struggle for power occurs within the bourgeoisie, against its traditional or fascist factions. Its struggle against capitalism is against some forms of capitalism and tends to introduce reforms and to give some limited participation in the system to the people. Naturally it favors a democratic capitalism—one that is not fascist—with parties, a parliament, unions, and freedoms. But as soon as socialism and workers' power threaten the system and the power of the bourgeoisie as such, Christian Democracy resists with all its strength and closes ranks with the entire bourgeoisie, even at the price of an unconstitutional military *coup* and fascism.

It is because the PDC is a bourgeois party, with all the characteristics just indicated, that it acted as it did during the *Unidad Popular* government. This does not preclude, of course, the government's errors with respect to Christian Democracy. But the consistency and seriousness of these errors arose precisely from not having taken into account this profoundly bourgeois character of the PDC. Not only was this fact repudiated verbally, but its lessons were not drawn in practice. Nor did the government foresee the isolation, or rather the new alignment or correlation, of forces unfavorable to the *Unidad Popular* that would result from the PDC's bourgeois character.

The above is sufficient to understand the behavior of the Christian Democratic party. I will describe its principal lines in a schematic fashion, however, in order to illustrate what I have been arguing.

From the government the *Unidad Popular* unleashed a rapid and intense process of socialization: expropriations, seizures of factories and land, a rapid agrarian reform, nationalization of copper without paying the foreign companies, rapid formation of a broad and important Social Property Sector to which were passed the banks, large distributive firms, and a good number of industries, and so on. To this we must add that the central and provincial governments of the country were controlled by the workers' parties, the Socialists and Communists. The truth is that the bourgeoisie as a whole felt itself profoundly attacked and threatened by the simple existence of the government. Very soon the bourgeoisie, relatively democratic in its traditional way of life, saw itself transformed into a fascist bourgeoisie, reacting spontaneously in a fascist manner, revealing a profound and instinctive class consciousness capable of being expressed with enormous power. (One of its first manifestations was the so-called March of the Empty Pots, led by women at the end of 1971.) Thus the bourgeoisie was available for the political strategy and ideological plans of the small fascist groups (fascist both in action and thought) that were active in certain sectors: in the large business associations, the armed forces, *El Mercurio*, the Catholic University, and the National party, and in explicitly fascist groups such as *Patria y Libertad* (Fatherland and Liberty) and others.

This violent fascist reaction was thus the bourgeoisie's response to the expropriations and the socialist offensive carried forward by the *Unidad Popular*. The process itself created the conditions for the bourgeoisie and the great majority of the middle sectors to fascism. In this way we can explain how small fascist groups finally took over the leadership of the bourgeoisie and the middle sectors, leading the opposition to Allende and then the orientation that the *coup* and the military government immediately adopted. The PDC itself was swept along by the fascist strategy to a political alliance with the right and an irrational emulation of the "hardness" and "raving" against the constitutional government.

Why could not the PDC avoid being carried to these extremes? Why could not even the leadership of Fuentealba and Leighton avoid it? Because of what we have said, because the body and the base of the party were captured by the strategy and spirit of fascism. It is in the PDC that we find the doctors, engineers, lawyers, and businessmen who tenaciously and furiously promoted the strike and the overthrow of Allende. The lucid minority of Christian Democratic leaders that did not favor the *coup* but a reasonable political solution were every day more isolated within the party. The fascist reaction that involved the Christian Democrats was, consequently, a social phenomenon, a phenomenon of the masses, generated also by a social process of intense class confrontation. While personal responsibilities should not be denied, one cannot refuse to recognize that conflicting social currents acquired an implacable dynamism of their own which suffocated any individual dissidence. Any analysis of the situation must begin with the movement of social forces.

In the April, 1971, municipal elections, the PDC campaigned under the slogan, "Chilean, you are not alone." Naturally, it was directed to those Chileans who were disconsolate because of the people's advance. To these, Christian Democracy gave courage and offered itself as a shield. Nevertheless, the *Unidad Popular* obtained 50 per cent of the vote, increasing its share from 36 per cent in the September, 1970, presidential election. As a result, the political division into three blocs which had characterized the presidential election (Alessandri-right; Tomić-PDC; Allende-UP) collapsed. In all future elections there would be only two blocs; a new alliance of forces was produced, a new correlation. From the moment of the municipal elections until the fall of Allende the PDC would always move in alliance with the right. The growth of the *Unidad Popular* to 50 per cent made the Christian Democrats see that it was impossible to defeat the government in any election without such an alliance.

In August, 1971, Jaime Castillo, a widely respected ideologue of Christian Democracy, wrote (*Qué Pasa,* no. 40) that the government and political experience of the *Unidad Popular* were evolving in accordance with a model that aimed for "the total and anti-democratic assumption of political power, in order to install a system in which a new bureaucratic class exercises its dictatorship in the name of an impersonal and frightened people." On other occasions it was said that the government sought to repeat the totalitarian-Stalinist model. The PDC—with limited exceptions—did not see the "Chilean road" as the entire world saw it. It did not see the danger of a fascist dictatorship. Its entire effort was directed against the danger of a Communist dictatorship.

Nor did this occur by chance. In this world it is common to see what one wants to see and not what one does not want to. At that moment the Christian Democrats were only interested in defending themselves against the "Communist" danger. The Christian Democratic-National Party Alliance, led by Jarpa's fascist group, was objectively guided by the principle of the Allende government's illegitimacy, by resistance and civil disobedience, and by the need to put an end to Allende "with two-thirds or without two-thirds." (This was an allusion to the electoral campaign of March, 1973, in which the electorate was asked to give the PDC-NP opposition the two thirds of the Senate necessary to overthrow Allende legally.) The conditions for the military *coup* were built upon this alliance, and its final expression was the declaration of the Chamber of Deputies, approved by the opposition majority (PDC-NP), that the military later invoked as one of the bases for the *coup.*

Already in August, 1972, five opposition parties, among them the National party and the PDC, stated in a joint declaration, "In Chile there no longer exists true democracy." At that time Fuentealba was president of the PDC. In the same epoch Aylwin, together with other senators on the right, spoke of the "illegitimate exercise" of the Allende government. In October, 1972, the Christian Democrats openly supported the national strike led by the truck owners.

In mid-1971 the so-called Hamilton-Fuentealba constitutional reform bill was submitted for the purpose of creating an insuperable conflict. Along with blocking the formation of the "social sector" it sought to revoke the presidential nature of the Chilean Constitution, converting it instead to a parliamentary system. With this proposal the will and prerogatives of the President would be subordinated to the opposition majority in Congress, a majority that would become able to make or break the legislative and constitutional system of the country while the President stood by helplessly. Naturally, Allende had to resist this twisted and opportunistic interpretation of the Constitution, presented in obviously bad faith, but in doing so he opened himself to charges of not respecting what Congress had legislated.

In the end, the Christian Democrats supported the great truckers' and professionals' strike of August, 1973; they impugned the incorporation of the military leaders into the cabinet; and they refused to support any feasible political alternative. Immediately following the *coup* the PDC leadership excused it, calling it necessary and unavoidable.

In summary, the strong antagonism between the *Unidad Popular* and the Christian Democrats was not due simply to sectarianism, prejudice, error, or the poor management of the relations between the two. Nor was it caused by the *Unidad Popular*'s primordial desire to divide the PDC or the latter's hope of becoming an "alternative" to the *Unidad Popular,* supported by the right as in 1964. In our judgment, the antagonism has more profound roots, and these can even explain the proliferation of errors or sectarianisms as well as the exaggerated importance they acquired. These roots can be found in the very nature of the social model that one or the other parties professes. Christian Democracy resists the rupture of capitalism and the substitution of the power of the bourgeoisie for the power of the workers. During the Frei government the Christian Democrats also resisted a similar attempt, known as the "non-capitalist road to development" (even though it was considerably more moderate than that of the *Unidad Popular*). In that case there were not problems of sectarianism or others of a similar nature, since the initiative emerged within the Christian Democratic party and even obtained its official approval. Nevertheless, the bourgeois forces, led by Frei himself, were quickly mobilized. Calling the program "Marxist," they attacked it with fury and in the end were able to turn the party itself against it.

The bourgeoisie is a very powerful force, and it is an error of the left to underestimate its power. An important portion of the middle sectors and even the masses (small and medium entrepreneurs, professionals, employees, certain groups of workers) are under the bourgeoisie's ideological and psychological influence. In it they find a model for their aspirations and life-style. The bourgeois communications media, powerful and efficient, have been able to provoke in these groups a hatred and violent fear of socialism, which they imagine is a kind of ant hill where they will be "proletarianized" to the level of the impoverished. Christian Democracy very quickly discovered that a good part of its social base and its electorate (the middle sectors and the masses) was under this influence, while the most powerful faction of its leadership (so-called *freísmo*) participated only in the bourgeoisie's high command. Under such conditions the party was won from within to an alliance with the right, and it was swept along in that alliance to the worst extremes. That is, it was available to follow a strategy imported by the fascists.

If anything can be concluded from all the above, it is that the transition to socialism encounters obstacles and resistance far greater than what is obvious at first glance. It is fundamental that an objective analysis not be misguided by our desires or some vague wish fulfillment. The Christian Democratic party always spoke of wanting to replace capitalism, but it showed in deeds during the two governments (Frei and Allende) that it really sought no such end. Christian Democracy was not only unprepared to replace capitalism; it resisted that substitution with immense, spontaneous energy and a willingness to pay a high price (even sacrificing principles that it had always defended with conviction, such as constitutional democracy). This analysis is important, because it permits us to measure accurately the forces in combat, know to what point we can successfully advance, and elaborate programs appropriate to reality. Christian Democracy, for example, can support an anti-oligarchic program (agrarian reform) but not a socialist agriculture; it can favor the nationalization of copper (at least after Tomić was nominated in 1970) but not a social sector of the magnitude envisioned by the *Unidad Popular*. Christian Democracy was not prepared for a front or alliance with the Communist party, because it is still profoundly anti-Communist. It is, therefore, not available for the social and political unity of the people, nor even for an anti-fascist front, together with the Marxist-Leninist forces.

Its anti-communism is not gratuitous. It reflects, fundamentally, a refusal to see the destruction of its way of life—that is, the western civilization in whose economy, in whose democracy, and in whose culture the bourgeoisie has power and functions. It is, of course, also a refusal to see incorporated into a broader and more general culture values that they fear to lose: individual freedom, critical spirit, pluralism, etc.

I have sought to view this subject with realism, to avoid disguising reality to suit our pleasure, because we must plan our future activities beginning with reality as it is, and not with fiction.

The PDC during the Allende Years and Some Comments on the Origin of the Christian Democratic Left Wing

RADOMIRO TOMIC

My purpose here is to complete my exposition and correct any impression I may have left that the Christian Democratic party has no reason to blame itself for the Chilean institutional disaster or that all the responsibility belongs to others.

Of course that is not the case. The PDC was an important political force, with a significant influence in Congress among interest groups, workers', peasant, youth, and student groups, and in the media. Because of what it was, and because of what it did and did not do, the party must carry a heavy burden of responsibility for the destruction of the constitutional regime in Chile. Christian Democracy was neither the major cause nor the only one, however.

Before responding as precisely as possible to Julio Silva's question about how I evaluate the role of the PDC during the three Allende years, there are two points that must be clarified in order to avoid oversimplification that confuses and misleads. First, in the Christian Democratic party as in all Chilean political parties, and just as in the vineyard of our Lord, "there is a bit of everything." There are idealists and opportunists, persons motivated by profound convictions and by ambitions, passions, and interests, persons with good judgment and bad, some with a sense of history—a few—and many with no greater perspective than the next election. Consequently it is useless to use *individual cases* to demonstrate that the Christian Democratic party was this or that, or that it acted in this fashion or another.

The second point is that the same argument is valid with

respect to the "lines" or dominant positions within Christian Democracy. For ten years at least, from 1963 to 1973, two great factions, tendencies, or orientations were clearly discernible. One was directly committed to denouncing the capitalist system and sought an agreement with the Marxist and secular left. The other preferred the "modernization" of Chilean social structures, tried to express principally the interests of the middle class and win its confidence, and proclaimed its "historical mission" that of being an alternative to Marxism.

Christian Democracy is not the voice of a single class but multiclass—as are all the Chilean parties, including the Communist. It is not monolithic in either its composition or its positions, and it prefers not to be, convinced that in Chile to be monolithic is not a strength but a weakness. To be so would contradict a pluralist and tolerant national reality and, moreover, could only be imposed by the arbitrary actions of the leadership.

For this reason it makes no sense to pick specific attitudes or declarations of certain spokesmen or groups within the party to prove that Christian Democracy did not desire an agreement with the left or acted in collusion with the right, or vice versa. The Christian Democratic party is one in which leadership is selected by the democratic rule of the majority. The decisive factor is the position of the internal majority.

It is customary to add, "But they had influence." Of course they had some degree of influence. Everyone has—some more, some less. Invariably, however, the decisive influence within Christian Democracy has been exercised by the majority which emerged from an internal process of definition and leadership selection. When Gumucio was president of the party, the dominant influence was the left wing, just as it was throughout my presidential candidacy and under the successive party presidencies of Benjamín Prado, Narciso Irureta, and Renán Fuentealba. "Dominant" of course is not the same as "exclusive." The other faction also elected a number of members to the National Council, to the different National Departments, etc. The reverse was the case when the left wing was a minority, as during the presidencies of Patricio Aylwin and Jaime Castillo.

One should not see this internal battle as combat with knife in hand. Most of the Christian Democratic base, and many of those who occupied leadership positions, supported one or the other faction or tendency, but this did not imply a commitment *per secula*.

For this reason, in developing a policy toward the Christian

Democrats, just as toward the Radicals or the Socialists, the decisive factor for the Allende government and the *Unidad Popular* should have been to have asked which faction was the majority and what were and had been its basic political positions.

To reply specifically to Julio Silva's question about the role of Christian Democracy and the Allende government, I think three stages are clearly visible: 1) a period in which there was a clear desire to support the government; 2) one in which the party adopted an expectant attitude; and 3) one of direct confrontation "by any means."

ONLY AN AGREEMENT BETWEEN THE PDC AND THE UP CAN GIVE GOVERNMENT TO CHILE: AUGUST, 1969, TO JULY, 1971

By March, 1969, the "Revolution in Liberty" had exhausted its ability to guide government or to serve as an instrument of mobilization by the PDC. The specifically Christian Democratic vote had dropped from 43 per cent in March, 1965, to 36 per cent in April, 1967, and to 29 per cent in March, 1969. The right was resurging more powerfully and haughtily than ever as a result of the essential contradiction between the Christian Democratic government's "economic" and "social development" programs, and the Marxist parties were consolidating and broadening their support in all areas of national life.

After 1966 the internal confrontation between the two Christian Democratic factions sharpened as their forces became more or less equal in weight. By narrow margins one and then the other succeeded in the leadership of the party. In 1969 the approaching presidential election forced a clarification of the internal situation, and the left won an overwhelming majority for its position of "Political and Social Unity of the People." The Tomić candidacy was proclaimed by unanimity, and two official declarations, "Fundamental Political Statement" and "The Programmatic Bases for a Second Christian Democratic Government," called unambiguously for the replacement of capitalism and, to accomplish this, an agreement between the Christian Democratic and Marxist parties.

The response of the Marxist parties and then, after it was organized, of the *Unidad Popular* was equally clear. We will have "nothing to do with the Christian Democrats, and with Tomić, not even go to Mass."

Their attitude was unchanged following Allende's election by

Congress, although it was the Christian Democratic decision to vote for Allende (decided by a two-thirds vote in the National *Junta*) that determined that Allende and not Alessandri would be the next President of Chile.

From October, 1970, to July, 1971, four Christian Democratic initiatives for an agreement of profound national political consequence were rejected by the *Unidad Popular* or the government:

—October, 1970: The PDC proposed that the two blocs designate jointly a common Christian-Democratic candidate (Bosco Parra, Gabriel Valdés, or someone else) to occupy the Senate seat vacated by Allende. The reply was, "Impossible!"

—December, 1970: The recently elected National Directorate, presided over by Senator Irureta, officially visited Allende to express its desire to help him govern.

—April, 1971: Irureta proposed to the highest officials of the government, "Let us elect jointly all the mayors of Chile, because between the *Unidad Popular* and Christian Democracy, we have won more than 80 per cent of all municipal councilmen." One week later Minister Tohá informed Irureta, "We have decided that it is better not to continue negotiations."

—June, 1971: The UP rejected an offer to elect jointly Luis Badilla, national president of the Christian Democratic Youth, as deputy from Valparaíso, to replace another Christian Democrat who had died. The *Unidad Popular* preferred a virulent electoral confrontation, which it lost yet hailed as a victory because it had obliged the Christian Democratic candidate to accept the vote of the right.

For two years the Christian Democrats followed a policy of convergence, but constant rejection of the idea of "People's Unity" exhausted the viability of that position, both outside and within the PDC.

The Valparaíso by-election, in which the *Unidad Popular* forced Christian Democracy to stand with the right, provoked a second division in the PDC—this time of the Christian left and nine deputies—and represented the "point of no return."

WE ARE A REVOLUTIONARY PARTY CONFRONTING A REVOLUTIONARY GOVERNMENT: FUENTEALBA-LEIGHTON, 1972 TO MAY, 1973

The second period of relations between Christian Democracy and the government was defined by Renán Fuentealba, the new national president: "We are a revolutionary party confronting a revolutionary government"—neither systematic support nor systematic opposition.

Nevertheless, during this period two important situations once again produced confrontations between the government and Christian Democracy: the constitutional reform to create the Social Property Sector and the abusive reinterpretation of the existing electoral law that permitted united party lists, thus violating an express prohibition. In both cases—in my opinion—the *Unidad Popular* was directly responsible for negative developments.

Creation of a Social Property Sector was also a plank in the Christian Democratic presidential program, and the Christian Democrats and the President agreed to submit jointly to Congress, at an opportune moment, a bill with that objective. Pressure by parties and groups in the *Unidad Popular,* however, made it difficult for the President to fulfill his commitment. Instead of appealing to Congress to fix by common agreement the rules for the Social Property Sector, the government preferred to act on its own, using administrative procedures and "legal opportunities" to nationalize the private commercial banks and "to intervene" by expropriating businesses, etc. After fruitless requests, each more strongly phrased, that the government meet its commitment of nine months before, Senator Fuentealba himself presented a constitutional reform bill to the Senate. It would establish the rules guiding creation of the social sector. Only when the government was faced with this accomplished fact did it offer to negotiate an agreement. After two weeks in which there was substantial advance, new difficulties arose that led the PDC to set a final date for agreeing on a common text. If no agreement could be reached, the Christian Democratic bill would be submitted for vote. When the deadline had passed, there was an exchange of letters between the Minister of Justice, who represented the government, and Senator Fuentealba, each blaming the other for the impasse.

Still worse was the *Unidad Popular's* conduct with respect to unified electoral blocs. Many are disconcerted by the fact that the Christian Democratic party, led by Fuentealba and Leighton in the 1973 parliamentary elections, joined with the National party in the so-called "Democratic Confederation" or CODE. One must realize, however, that the Christian Democrats, and particularly Fuentealba, did everything possible to prevent violation of the electoral law that expressly prohibited single lists of candidates from different parties. It was a deputy of the *Unidad Popular,* together with a leader of the Alessandri campaign—both enjoying the support of their respective organizations—who requested and obtained from the Election Review Court a decision reinterpreting the electoral law. The court (on which the majority were representatives of the right, including ex-congressmen of the National party) authorized the parties to form "federations" that supposedly would replace these parties. It stated also that these "federations" could legally present single lists of candidates, made up of representatives of the parties in the "federation."

This gross violation of a law that had obliged each party to stand alone before the electorate was made possible only by collusion between the *Unidad Popular* and the National party. Christian Democracy requested in vain that the Election Court reconsider its illegal decision and later that the Supreme Court reverse it. The Supreme Court, however, refused to rule, arguing that "The Election Review Court was an *ad hoc* tribunal not subject to its jurisdiction."

If one keeps in mind that Chile is ruled by proportional representation that mathematically favors "federated" parties and hurts those that stand alone, one will realize it is not an abuse of words to claim that CODE was imposed upon the Christian Democratic party by the *Unidad Popular.*

It was absurd to assume that just because the *Unidad Popular* would prefer for the Christian Democrats to stand alone—thus losing a number of deputies and senators—the latter would sacrifice themselves resignedly. The real world does not work like that, and much less so the political world. The PDC stated clearly that CODE was purely an electoral agreement that would be dissolved following the elections.

Thus the deterioration in relations between the *Unidad Popular* and the Christian Democrats continued under the leadership of Renán Fuentealba and Bernardo Leighton, in spite of their sincere desire to prevent an open break. It is hardly necessary to add that both Leighton and Fuentealba have been expelled from Chile by the military *junta.*

THE MARXISTS ONLY UNDERSTAND THE LANGUAGE OF FORCE: WE MUST HIT THEM WITH OUR HATCHETS AND OUR CLUBS! MAY TO SEPTEMBER, 1973

The third stage, what we might call "the fight to the death," crystalized shortly after the March, 1973, congressional elections. The *Unidad Popular's* 44 per cent share of the vote, increasing its parliamentary bloc by two senators and eight deputies, definitively eliminated any possibility of removing Allende constitutionally. The opposition entered a period of increasing frenzy, as did ever larger portions of the Christian Democratic base. The internal divisions became increasingly inflexible. For the sector led by Aylwin as candidate for the presidency of the party, "the imminence of a Marxist-Leninist dictatorship" was the menace that had to be confronted. For the left, which proposed reelecting Fuentealba and Leighton, the political weight of the Christian Democrats in Congress and the labor unions and among youth, peasants, etc., was so enormous that such a stance "would paralyze the functioning of the state and destroy Chilean democracy in a matter of months rather than years."

In May, 1973, the National *Junta* elected a leadership presided over by Aylwin by 53 per cent of the vote.

Aylwin had argued unambiguously before the public and the leadership his opinion that Christian Democracy "would combat the Marxist government by all possible means, because the Marxists only understand the language of force." The slogan he advanced was "We won't let them get away with anything."

Yet, in spite of all the above, during the first months of the Aylwin presidency, the PDC still refused to form a "common front" with the National party. A number of the motions for censure introduced by the right did not receive PDC backing and had to be abandoned. On the occasion of the abortive *coup d'état* on June 29, 1973, Aylwin even telephoned Allende to express his support.

But the dynamics of their respective positions rapidly turned the UP-PDC confrontation ever more virulent. The Christian Democrats began to promote—or at least to participate actively in—all the great interest-group and labor union movements and public demonstrations attacking the government. The distinction between "just" and "unjust" strikes and between "legal" and "illegal" ones disappeared. Under the slogan "We must give it to the Marxists with our hatchets and our clubs," the party supported the copper workers' strikes that demanded a double salary adjustment and the shamefully illegal seven-week stoppage of fifty thousand trucks. It also gave explicit backing to the anti-union and anti-worker operations of military units, disguised by the term "arms control."

The dialogue requested by the Episcopate produced a brief truce—less than a week. The combat was renewed with equal fury, however, and crowned with the declaration of the Chamber of Deputies "making illegal the acts of the Allende government."

On the first day after the *coup d'état,* the Christian Democratic leadership remained silent. However, on the twelfth Aylwin and two others issued in the name of the National Council, which had not yet had time to meet, a declaration that, in sum, justified Allende's overthrow by the military. Two days later sixteen high-level Christian Democratic leaders countered with a statement repudiating the *coup* and paying homage to the memory of Allende. I would like to add, as an illustration, that Aylwin, at the end of September, 1973, in a long speech that was printed but not circulated, expressed reservations about the "repressive character and quite reactionary politics" of the recently installed dictatorship.

The passage of time has accentuated the disillusionment of that Christian Democratic sector that judged the *coup d'état* "indispensable and patriotic." The dreadful consequences for the workers of a "capitalism backed by machine guns," the imprisonment and torture of not a few Christian Democratic union leaders, the deportation of Leighton, Fuentealba, Huepe, and other high-level spokesmen have all caused disagreements with the military *junta* and have modified without any doubt the internal correlation of forces in Christian Democracy . . . or in whatever remains of that party after a year and a half of "obligatory recess."

FRUSTRATIONS OF THE CHRISTIAN DEMOCRATIC LEFT

References have been made to the apparent inconsistency between a Christian Democracy that in 1970 adheres to a program of struggle against capitalism and then does not support a *Unidad Popular* government that applies a similar program. Worse, it accepts and adopts in 1973 the position of its mortal enemy of three years earlier, the National party, which through its president, Senator Jarpa, espouses "the unity of the opposition." Why did the Christian Democrats act with such apparent lack of principle and "accept an alliance with the National party"? Those who ask that question should add immediately, " . . . instead of allying themselves with the government and the *Unidad Popular!*" If they had any knowledge of the persistence with which the Christian Democrats proposed and sought, from August, 1969, until June, 1971, "the unity of the people," they would know that the second part of the question "Why didn't they prefer an agreement with the left?" has a regrettable answer. And that answer is, "Because the *Unidad Popular* and the government rejected for two consecutive years the

Christian Democratic position favoring the unity of the people"
and all the Christian Democratic efforts to reach agreement.

"Nature hates a vacuum" was the explanation our ancestors
gave for certain physical phenomena. The nature of politics, even
more! Today we know, for example, that early in the government
the Socialist party, at its Congress of La Serena in January, 1971,
rejected out of hand any agreement with the PDC, adopting instead a strategy of "separating the leadership from the rank and
file and dividing the Christian Democrats." The blind and narrow
sectarianism at the base of the *Unidad Popular,* in opposing the
Christian Democrats among peasants, workers, students, and modest officials of the public administration, destroyed any possibility
for agreement among leadership and the base. Thus it paved the
road for Senor Jarpa's call for "the unity of the opposition." What
did they want to accomplish in a country charged with tension like
Chile? In a country with parties that respond to very concrete
realities, with men of skin and bones who inevitably react against
those who attack them? After all, it is many centuries since Lafon-
taine ended his famous fable with the couplet:

> That animal is so evil
> That when attacked, he defends himself . . .

I have already explained how and why the CODE was born
when spokesmen of the *Unidad Popular* and the right conspired
with the Election Review Court. I will give one more example to
reply to those who may be thinking that "whatever may have been
the errors of the *Unidad Popular* in the first two years, it tried to
approach the Christian Democrats in 1973." Even then it did not!
In May, 1973, the Christian Democrats were to elect new leadership. I have already explained the sharpness of the confrontation
between the two factions: that which proposed the name of
Aylwin "to fight against the Marxist government by every means,"
and that which sought the reelection of Fuentealba and Leighton
precisely to impede the "unity of the opposition against the Marxist government." It was obvious that the chance for the Fuente-
alba-Leighton slate to win depended to a great extent on its capacity to be heard by the government and exercise some influence. In
the second half of April, when only two weeks remained before
the meeting of the National *Junta* of the PDC and all the parties
and public opinion in general were focusing their attention on
which of the two positions would win control of the largest Chilean political party (40 per cent of the Senate and Chamber, two
thirds of the peasants, one third of the CUT), the official news-

paper of the Socialist party, *Ultima Hora,* property of three cabinet ministers, published an insane full-page editorial attacking the Christian Democrats. It alluded by name to Fuentealba in the following terms, which I will be excused for repeating literally, "Fuentealba is a whore, and we ask the whores of Santiago to pardon us for comparing them to him." And then it added, "Fuentealba is the pimp of Chilean politics. . . ."

The aggression of that newspaper and its owners was so monstrous and insolent under those circumstances in Chilean politics that I sent a letter of protest, convinced they would attempt some explanation. They replied to my letter with a brief, disrespectful article and reprinted a second time the same full-page editorial, beginning, "At the request of our readers, we reprint our editorial of two days ago: Fuentealba is . . . , etc." In this way the official voice of the Socialist party "collaborated" in May, 1973, in defining the internal battle in Christian Democracy and its attitude to the government.

What could lie behind this schizophrenic attitude? The "temptation of death"? It is impossible to say.

Although we are to analyze "the causes of failure," perhaps a few more words are justified on a factor that is fundamental for building the future, even more than for explaining the past. I refer to the gradual emergence in the world, and particularly in Latin America and Chile, of a left-wing current of Christian inspiration that is not Marxist-Leninist. Its numbers are every day more numerous, and its political, economic, and social positions in favor of socialist structures, in direct confrontation with capitalism, every day more articulate.

It is difficult to imagine another phenomenon more important for the future of socialism on the continent. The citation is from Ché Guevara: "When the Christians make the revolution theirs, it will be irresistible in Latin America."

Yet in spite of this radicalization every day in the thought and conduct of greater numbers of Christians who are committed to socialism *as a function* of Christian values, it is a phenomenon that continues to escape the attention of the Marxist left. Or else it is interpreted in a mocking fashion, or on other occasions used not for what it contains that is creative or authentic but simply as an inconsistent caprice to be exploited in favor of the positions and interests of the Marxist parties as such.

As I believe that for many decades—as long as the superpowers prefer to avoid nuclear confrontation—in Chile the "step to socialism" will still inevitably depend on an agreement of great transcendency between the socialism of Christian inspiration and that of Marxist origins, I think I am justified in presenting a brief outline of the origin of the Chilean PDC and its left wing, of such great influence on the political and social thought of our continent.

When in 1935 those of us who were the original founders and leaders of the Catholic Youth Action decided to become active in politics, we did so within the Conservative party. This was inevitable in the decade of the 30s, when the symbiosis Catholic-in-religion-Conservative-in-politics was still not discredited.

In 1938, however, this umbilical cord was broken, and the National Falange organized. The movement during the decade of the 40s from right to center and the cooperation with the Radical party were notorious. Already in 1946 a left wing had emerged, espousing the idea of a "proletarian democracy" and gathered around its principal spokesman, Bernardo Leighton. In 1947, reacting to the National Falange's public opinions on the Chilean labor movement, to its relations with the Soviet Union and its repudiation of the Franco dictatorship, the archbishop of Santiago publicly condemned the party, stating that "it did not merit the trust of the Church."

In the early 1960s, Julio Silva, Jacques Chonchol, and others began to define an anti-capitalist stance ideologically. In 1950 I was elected Senator for the North against a candidate of the Radical government. In that election I was supported by the Communist and Socialist parties. Victory in all the Chilean university federations also gave life to and expanded the increasingly anti-capitalist, anti-imperialist, and anti-fascist orientation of the Christian Democratic party, founded in 1957. However, parallel to and as a result of the above, another sector began to take embryonic shape within Christian Democracy. It espoused a thesis that a few years later would come to be known as "our own road" and that rejected any possibility of important convergences between Christian and Marxist viewpoints. After 1963 the debate ceased to be purely ideological and began to affect concrete activities directly. The thesis of "the political and social unity of the people" was born. Seven years later, in the 1970 presidential campaign, it would be developed fully. But from 1963 on, it confronted systematically the idea of "our own road."

The supporters of "our own road" argued that ideologically Christian Democracy is equidistant from both capitalism and Marxism. Without discounting the possibility of coincident positions on concrete matters or even collaboration with either the right or the left on specific political questions, the party—they argued—should strengthen its capacity to give its own integral response to all of Chile's problems. And, they announced, their intention was to do just that. Pressed by the reality that the struggle to win the consciousness of workers, youth, and peasants confronted Christian Democracy with the Marxist parties and not with the right, which lacked any presence among those sectors of the Chilean population, the most prominent political figures of this faction formulated the position that the "historical mission of Christian Democracy is the fight against communism." From this position to a generalized agreement with the right—which certainly would use no other terms to define its own historical mission—was but a short step.

In contrast, we who favored the "unity of the people" argued from 1963 on that all the evils we denounce in Chilean society, and that moved us to form a new party, *are the work of capitalism and not socialism*—poverty, underdevelopment, the unjust distribution of wealth and opportunity, national frustration, external dependence, and massive alienation of the people. Therefore, in the reality of Chilean history, the fight for a new society is above all the fight against capitalism. To seek "the historical justification of Christian Democracy in the fight against communism and Marxism" only consolidates and perpetuates capitalist domination by dividing and neutralizing its enemies. From a slightly different perspective, it is a political reality in Chile that the Marxist forces represent one third of the national electorate, two thirds of the industrial and urban organized workers, and a significant portion of university students, youth, professionals, and technocrats. They also have considerable influence through the communications media. Given the profound nature of the country's problems and its limited capital resources and international influence, agreement between the two great representatives of the masses, the Christian left and the Marxist and secular left, is indispensable to mobilize the creative force of the united people. This does not mean that we must seek an ideological union; to do so would be impossible for both.

During the six years of the Frei government—from 1964 to 1970—the confrontation between the two tendencies was continual, tenacious, and of varied fortune. In 1966 the National Congress of the PDC approved a "Report on the Non-Capitalist Road to Development," in spite of desperate resistance by spokesmen for the government and the "official" faction. In 1967, 1968, and 1969 the struggle between the two sectors—"official" and "rebel"—became increasingly sharp, so much so that a third faction emerged, calling

itself *"terceristas."* The relative balance of force among these gave
rise to dramatic encounters in the struggle for control of the National Directorate and the different National Departments. In 1970
the proximity of the presidential election precipitated an internal
confrontation in which concrete circumstances permitted the left
wing to win majority control over the power structure of the party
and, above all, over its bases. This control later became decisive.
The proposed program of the government and the presidential campaign consolidated for two years—in spite of the profoundly disturbing desertion by the MAPU at a decisive moment in the internal battle—support for the thesis of "unity of the people"—that is,
for the search by the Christian Democratic leadership for an agreement of historical transcendence with the Chilean Marxist and
secular left.

It is this complex, profound, and rich process that escapes
almost completely the perception of the *Unidad Popular*.

Of the many causes that underlie the tragic failure of the
"Chilean road to socialism," this was the greatest, and of all the
lessons to be learned, it is the most important for the future.

PART THREE

Effects of the Military Coup:
Its Repercussions Abroad
and the Emergence
of the Authoritarian State

Lessons of the Chilean Coup in Europe: The Case of Portugal

PHILIPPE C. SCHMITTER

The violent overthrow of the Allende regime was, on one level, a mere regional event, belonging to a general class of phenomena both current and common in Latin America. Granted its brutality and ruthlessness was virtually unparalleled by regional standards, conceded that the crudeness and thoroughness of ensuing military rule has been extraordinary, again by comparison with other *régimes d'exception* in contemporary Latin America; nevertheless, the Chilean *coup* of September, 1973, could be identified, classified, quantified, and analyzed merely as the fourteenth instance of a seizure of power by the armed forces in Latin America since 1963.

On another level, the violent transformation of the *vía chilena* into a *callejón sin salida* was a lesson of worldwide importance and impact. Given the exceptional attention and hope which focused on this experiment in a peaceful, electorally initiated, and legislatively guided transition to socialism, politicians, activists, and ordinary citizens in a wide variety and number of countries have been vicariously affected by its demise—often without their knowing it. Through a complex and unintelligible process, information from the Chilean experience has been gathered and weighed; differences and similarities with other national and regional contexts have been debated and evaluated; finally, conclusions and maxims have been drawn with respect to the classic praxeological dilemma of "What is to be done?" These "lessons" from Chile—for we shall see that this massive exercise in international analogizing and intersocietal learning has by no means produced singular or unanimous results—have become part of the world's collective revolutionary experience at a moment of great uncertainty and crisis.

343

However confused its message, it will not be simply and conveniently forgotten. (Whether "history" will function, as Debray suggests, to remove its multiple cosmetic appearances is much less likely.)

Paradoxically, while the empirical *case* of Chile has been firmly anchored and enumerated within its regional—i.e., Latin American—context, the exemplary "lesson" of Chile has had its greatest impact elsewhere—i.e., in Western Europe. Rhetoric and scholarly fashion to the contrary notwithstanding, Latin Americans tended to recognize the "exceptionalness" of Chile and its political system. Europeans, inversely, suddenly discovered a striking family resemblance in this far-removed fragment of its civilization. It is as if, inverting Marx, for the first time a later developing, more peripheral part of the capitalist system and European culture offered to show to the earlier developed, most central units of that system and culture the face of their own future. Previous examples of such historic "lessons" had been largely, if not exclusively, European: the collapse of Weimar, the civil war in Spain, the appeasement of Munich, the takeover of Czechoslovakia, the violent end to the Spring of Prague, the "events of May" in Paris, and so forth. Only these larger, more salient, more consequential, more advanced units seemed capable of the sort of experimentation, innovation, elevated expectations, and high drama which combine to produce precedents for international political *praxis*, maxims of what should be avoided or what would be tolerated in a given world situation. For the first time, a small, remote, economically dependent, and relatively unknown country was offering lessons to Europe about her possible future.

Although, as we shall see, it may be doubtful whether the lessons have been learned, no one can say that Europeans, especially those on the political left, have not pondered them carefully and protractedly. Virtually from the moment the Allende regime was overthrown, they began to emit a massive volume of statements, position papers, analyses, and "agonizing reappraisals" based on their evaluation of what had gone wrong (or not gone right) in Chile from 1970 to 1973 and how these conclusions should affect their future tactics and strategy. Unable as we are to sift through and analyze the entire mass of this material, we will summarize briefly a portion of it which has general relevance for Western Europe and then concentrate our attention on the current case whose "lesson" may be displacing that of Chile in the eyes of many Europeans—namely, that of Portugal.

THE IMPACT OF CHILE ON EUROPE

European attention to the Chilean experiment in a peaceful (Communists generally prefer the expression "nonviolent") transition to socialism through a broad coalition of popular unity long antedated the overthrow of Allende, of course. Representatives of virtually all currents of the European left saw an important analogy between their dilemma and the events in Chile well before the 1970 elections gave Salvador Allende a modest (36.3 per cent) plurality and congressionally certified access to the presidency. On the one hand, Chile had a relatively secularized, structurally differentiated, ethnically homogeneous population with a level of capitalist development and type of class structure not far removed from those of Southern Europe. On the other hand, it had a history of continuous legislative and electoral processes (despite an initially more restricted electorate due to the disenfranchisement of illiterates), freedom of the press and association, executive accountability, civilian rule, and, most of all, a party system which virtually replicated the ideological range, class cleavage and support, degree of organization, and voting patterns of several Western European polities. In particular, the Chilean left (Communists and Socialists in particular) faced a dilemma identical to that of their comrades in France and Italy: they constituted a substantial and entrenched proportion of the nation's electorate and organized working-class movement, which was having great difficulty in breaking out of its subcultural, ecological, and class-bounded ghetto. Previous experiences with Popular Fronts in the 1930s and, to a lesser extent, the success of the West German SPD in becoming a majority party after renouncing an exclusivist class base pointed to the potential success of broad coalitions of "progressive and democratic forces" in perforating the ceiling placed on their electoral strength by Cold War pressures, calculations, and fears. Khrushchev's endorsement of a plurality of paths to socialism at the XXth CPSU Party Congress in 1956 served to remove whatever "unconditionalist" objections might have existed to impede the participation of national Communist parties in such alliances.

Chile, by virtue of its past experimentation with popular fronts, its relatively high degree of party organization and articulation on the left, its more or less equilibrated relations of force between Communists and Socialists, and the disarray created within its party system by the rapid rise to power and subsequent fragmentation of the Christian Democrats, became a prototype for this experiment in "nonviolent" transition to socialism. This status was dutifully underscored by the attention lavished upon it by European intellectuals and by innumerable laudatory references to the *Unidad Popular* and *Gobierno Popular* by leaders of European Socialist and Communist parties. At this point, differences between Chilean and European social structure, economic development, international position, and party and interest representation systems were underemphasized if mentioned at all.

Nowhere did this prototype seem to fit more naturally than with Italy. From a certain crude ecological similarity in levels of capitalist development, urbanization, literacy, and so forth, to a marked political, cultural resemblance in a common, negotiative *(trasformista)* style of policy accommodation, to a striking matchup in the ideological identity of the principal partisan actors, the two countries could be thought to mirror one another. While the "French Connection" was for longer-term cultural and intellectual reasons more visible in terms of visiting scholars, books, articles, etc., the lessons of Chile were probably more carefully scrutinized and would have their greatest analogistic impact upon the Italian Communist party (PCI).

The PCI with its traditional independence and intellectuality within international Communist circles had, in fact, been the first national, non-ruling Communist party to speak of "frontism" and "polycentrism." Aleady in the 1920s, Togliatti had been denounced as a right opportunist by Stalin for his espousal of united front tactics against Fascism and his suggestion that a "post-Fascist democratic transitional stage" would be required in which the PCI would collaborate in a broad, majoritarian alliance for the reconstruction of Italy. He even implied that the transition to eventual socialism might be accomplished through democratic-parliamentary means without the uncontested hegemony of the Communist party or the dictatorship of the proletariat.

Togliatti's prophetic heresy does not seem to have been forgotten. When in 1956 Moscow in effect gave the green light, the PCI (under Togliatti's direction until 1964) immediately seized the opportunity and proclaimed a distinctive "Italian path to socialism" which initially involved participation in power at the local level within the structures of bourgeois democracy and the advocacy of broad welfare and regulatory reforms through parliamentary alliances. This line of theory-*cum-praxis* was pushed even further by Togliatti's successors, Luigi Longo (1964–1972) and Enrico Berlinguer (1972–   ). The latter in his famous report to the XIIIth Party Congress in 1972 proclaimed the need for a *compromesso storico:* a lasting political alliance of Communist, Socialist, and Catholic forces, each of which would retain its organizational autonomy and continue to compete with the others in various electoral and syndical arenas "through a constant confrontation of programs and ideas which doesn't presume to eliminate the differences which exist." The PCI would not, in short, insist on its hegemony within this broad coalition, and the transition to socialism would not necessarily entail fusion or elimination of competing perspectives. Rather, the eventual hegemony of the working class would emerge from convergences and agreements among its multiple representations. *"Unitá nella diversitá"* became a predominant slogan of the PCI; *"pluralismo"* was stressed not as a temporary expedient, a ploy to attract votes, but as a desirable end in itself.

This Italian line, of course, went far beyond the "frontist" tactic endorsed by the CPSU and practiced in postwar Eastern Europe. It also, incidentally, surpassed that proclaimed by the Chilean Communist party (PCCh). The latter, while it insisted on unanimity and equality within the ranks of the *Unidad Popular* (UP)— and went to rather considerable and often debilitating efforts to ensure them in practice—remained suspiciously silent or ambiguous on the nature of political relationships which would prevail once the transition to socialism was over. Despite repeated assurances to its Socialist partners (but not to other "tactical opponents") that their identity and autonomy would be respected and that cooperation between them was "unlimited in time," the PCCh did not speak with the same relish about pluralism and competition in an eventual new socialist order as did their Italian comrades.

What is particularly important to recognize in this context is that the experience in Chile and the lessons drawn from it fell into the middle of a major ideological dispute between Eastern and Western European Communist parties, or more specifically between the CPSU and the PCI, over the role which such parties should play in the present stage of capitalist development and bourgeois democratic political domination. "One senses in the . . . divergence regarding the nature of Chilean developments under *Unidad Popular* a significance transcending the fate of that distant Latin American nation of but ten million people and impinging directly on the relationship between the two giants of European communism, East and West: Soviet and Italian spokesmen utilized the Chilean events to buttress and clarify their preferences regarding revolutionary strategy in the capitalist world."[1]

The *golpe* in Chile could hardly have been better timed to produce a maximum impact upon the European left, at least in its two major centers: Italy and France. In the former, ideological dissension over socialist pluralism and *opposizione diversa* had deepened as had the crisis of Italian politics in the fall of 1973. The PCI directorate found itself harassed, not only internationally by the Soviets and their Eastern European spokesmen, but also from within its own ranks by militants pressing the party to take greater advantage of the evident disarray and weakness in the dominant Christian Democratic (DC) party and to refuse to "manage the crisis" of Italian capitalism by supporting ameliorative right-centrist reforms, often at the expense of mass and working-class interests. In the latter, in such case, the overthrow of Allende fell right in the middle of an electoral campaign in which the Socialists and Communists were running allied with the aim of capturing the presidency and using it in a "nonviolent," parliamentary manner to institute the major reforms of their Common Program. Although the French Communist Party (PCF) had by no means taken such an original and experimental ideological stance as the PCI, their "frontist" tactics were clearly called into question by the Chilean events. In addition, the sheer fact of their occurrence came as a sort of "divine surprise" to their opponents and threatened to affect the outcome of the elections themselves.

Going through but a small proportion of the immense commentary provoked at the moment of the *golpe* and periodically thereafter, one cannot help but be struck by one obvious and overwhelming observation: the capacity of virtually every organization of the European left to interpret the "lesson of Chile" in such a way as to reinforce the tactical or strategic line it had previously decided upon. To this impressive example of cognitive dissonance on a grand scale, there were practically no exceptions. Regardless of the enormous diversity in their previous positions with respect to the appropriate *praxis* to follow in order to achieve a transition to socialism, all managed to find something in the Chilean experience which reinforced their position. The *coup* against Allende "miraculously" proved the veracity and historical necessity of everyone's prior analysis.

To the *gauchistes* in France or in Italy, of course, the Chilean case demonstrated unequivocally the "romantic and idealistic" nature of electoral routes to power for the left, the absurdity of relying on bourgeois legality, the myth of the existence of apolitical or benevolently neutral armed forces, the danger of an insignificant mobilization of the masses, and, of course, the imperative need to create an armed popular militia. From this "we told you so" perspective the lesson was clear: organize small, dedicated, elite formations prepared to ignore the niceties of bourgeois justice and to move to armed attack when necessary; seek to penetrate and proselytize autonomous popular organizations, all work places, and, where possible, military units; maintain the ideological purity of the revolutionary party and refuse all compromise and alliance with electoralist and opportunist factions—in short, continue to do what they were already attempting to do, but with an added sense of urgency and conviction.

If the groups and *groupuscules* to the left of the Communists and Socialists found it possible to draw their lesson from Chile without much delay or further analysis, interpretation by the latter demanded more reflection and posed weightier problems, especially where they had to be made in the midst of an electoral campaign.

Perhaps the French Socialists had the most difficult time bending the Chilean events to fit their needs and perceptions. After all, Mitterand had proclaimed the *Unidad Popular* "a model of its type" in 1971, had met personally with Allende, and was the leading figure in an obviously analogous French experience. Initially and immediately upon hearing of the *coup*, he blamed the Chilean right for its intransigent defense of privilege and the "invisible blockade" of imperialist forces. He ended with a question: "Does this mean that when the people decide to defend its interests, violence and rioting will always come from the right?"[2] Several days later, Mitterand and with him most European socialists had found a satisfactory interpretation: they rediscovered the fact that Chile was a Latin American, not a European, country. Given its reliance on a single export commodity, its imbalance in agricultural and industrial production, its absence of trained administrative talent, its lack of multiple and sophisticated policy instruments, "it would be absurd to compare an underdeveloped country and a developed country. Our socialism will be a socialism of abundance."[3] In effect, the Chilean catastrophe was explained away as the joint product of scarcity, which placed greater demands for sacrifice on the middle class and afforded a smaller surplus for redistribution, and dependence, which permitted a single external power to exercise such leverage on domestic elites and the internal economy. *Ergo,* there was no need to revise the basic frontist strategy of the union of the left in France or elsewhere in Europe. By clear implication, "it couldn't happen here."

The French Communists were in a somewhat more comfortable interpretative position. After all, their comrades in Chile had consistently and concertedly followed a policy virtually identical to theirs, unlike the Chilean Socialists, who had opposed an alliance with the Christian Democrats and pushed for measures considerably more radical than their French comrades. In a press conference held barely a week before the *coup,* a member of the PCF Secretariat had already candidly spoken of "certain errors in the policy of *Unidad Popular"*: insufficient attention to productivity; excessive occupations of nonessential factories by workers; a salary policy which ignored the interests of engineers and technicians; tolerance of irresponsible adventurism on the part of *gauchistes*—all of which was leading to an alienation of middle strata and a growing isolation of the working class.[4] In short, the roots of Allende's downfall lay in the coalition's unwillingness or inability to follow the advice and policies of the PCCh. According to this interpretation, the PCCh line (and by inference that of the PCF) was absolutely correct and *Unidad Popular* "was on the way to success"—if only it could consolidate its accomplishments, preserve legality, and "get through the winter."[5] Imperialist maneuvers and blockades, sabotage by reactionary groups, a slanderous press, and the adventurist activities of ultra-left groups—basically conjunctural factors—intervened to bring about the regime's downfall. The sheer fact of its occurrence, however, was no reason for radically revising the PCF's strategy—least of all in the midst of an electoral campaign. In the longer term, however, one can imagine that such an interpretation would lead eventually to second thoughts about dependence upon a "bourgeois" legality which tolerates open opposition by dedicated class enemies and open incitement by ultra-left fellow travelers; on a certain *naïveté* which ignores the problem of the class allegiance of armed forces in capitalist societies and on a conception of equality within the Union of the Left which permits less disciplined and dedicated allies to engage in opportunistic and demagogic adventures on their own. While there is no evidence that the hardening of relationships with the PS and the renewed independent aggressiveness of the PCF which have occurred since the fall of 1974 had anything to do with the lessons drawn from Chile one year earlier, the logic of such a change in strategy is contained within them.

If the analyses of the French left seem somewhat superficial, more interested in explaining away than explaining, such is not the case with the Italian Communists. For one thing, the PCI had been making a serious and concerted intellectual effort to understand events in Chile long before the *golpe.* They tended to regard

Chile as "a capitalistically mature society"—hence similar in structure to Italy—and to define its *Gobierno Popular* as already having entered the transition to socialism—contrary to the Soviets, who argued that this could be accomplished only under the uncontested hegemony of the Communist party. Their publications *Rinascita* and *Critica Marxista* evinced a deep interest and respect for the experimental nature of the *vía chilena* and portrayed it as "unexplored and exceptional, as all revolutions have been and will be, compared to the schemes and the manuals of scholasticism."[6] In essence, the PCI clearly saw in Chile both a prototype for their own brand of pluralism and a useful example in their more or less continuous ideological struggle with Moscow.

The September *coup* naturally forced the PCI to rethink and redefine its position and strategy within Italian politics. Its rather weak and dispersed critics on the extreme left immediately arrived at the conclusion that "Chile puts an end to the romanticism and electoral idealism of the left, especially in Italy."[7] Its rather more powerful opponents on the right readily agreed with that assessment—for different motives, of course.

The PCI responded initially by attributing major responsibility for the *coup* to the right wing of the Chilean Christian Democratic party, which in alliance with reactionary groups, it argued, had polarized political forces and impeded the UP from forging an effective alliance of the working class, the peasantry, and middle sectors.[8] While another essay warned against "false analogies" and reminded readers of the profound difference between Chile and Italy in historical background, geostrategic location, social and economic structure, and nature of political conflict[9] and still another placed greater emphasis on the role of dependence and foreign manipulation, what is striking is the continued effort on the part of the PCI not to explain away the Chilean case by reclassifying it or by "exceptualizing" it. More than any other element in the European left, the Italian Communists have analyzed the lesson of Chile primarily (but not exclusively) in terms of generic categories of class structure, relations between political groups, and national goals and aspirations. Their descriptions of the three years of UP rule go into rather considerable detail concerning differences between alliance partners, "economicist" distortions, resistances to specific policy measures, declines in production and productivity, efforts to co-opt or control the military, the role of the middle classes and marginal groups, the loss of political initiative and authority by the government, the appropriation of naturalist and patriotic symbols by the opposition, and so forth. The inferences drawn from this complex data base are neither monocausal nor simplistic. One senses here an honest effort to seize the meaning of a multitude of objective material, tactical, political, and subjective ideological factors simultaneously—as if the knowledge acquired was to be used not to berate enemies or to protect the party from its critics but as the basis for answering crucial questions of *praxis*.

These answers were astonishingly quick in coming. In three successive articles in *Rinascita* (Sept. 28, Oct. 5, and Oct. 12, 1973), Enrico Berlinguer, the PCI's secretary general, took advantage of the debate over Chile to come out with a set of major theses designed to guide the political strategy of the party in the future. Given the rapidity of their appearance and the fact that they reinforce and extend positions already articulated, one may question whether the Chilean *débâcle* was really responsible for their elaboration or content; nevertheless, they do represent the most interesting effort to date on the part of the European left to cope with the failure of the *vía chilena*.

What is immediately apparent (and historically not very difficult to understand) is Berlinguer's preoccupation with Fascism and/or the resurgence of a dominant, exclusively right-wing alliance. Chile clearly reinforced that danger, already evident in Italy in the form of a revival of a neo-Fascist party (MSI), various right-wing terrorist groups, and rumors of impending *coups d'état*. While elsewhere the PCI may have been a bit more explicitly articulate about the transformations in Italian society which it wishes to promote, here the accent is upon what it wishes to avoid and what is historically necessary in order for Italy not to slip into political chaos and economic ruin.

The first strategic observation illustrated by the case of *Unidad Popular* is that a mere minimal winning electoral or congressional majority "would be insufficient to guarantee the survival and policy success of a government which would be the expression of that 51 per cent of the votes."[10] Hence the need to build the widest possible voluntaristic base in the social structure in order to avoid a 50/50 polarization between working and middle classes. Thrust aside is the Leninist formula of the revolutionary minority which seizes power and makes itself into the majority by using revolutionary controls as well as the strategy of the purely expediential "frontist" alliance of interests which seeks a minimal winning majority. The social structures, especially due to the growing importance of middle strata, and the productive systems of modern capitalist society no longer favor revolutionary strategies based on frontal encounters between revolutionary and reactionary forces. The Allende regime may not have intended such a polarized confrontation, but it did lead to such an outcome. Berlinguer doesn't spell it out, but such a clash under the delicate, interdependent conditions of modern society could produce the mutual exhaustion or destruction of both warring classes and their replacement by a relatively autonomous authoritarian state.

The alleged fact that "there can be no profound democratic transformation of society unless it is the production of a revolution supported by the great majority of the population" means that the issue of alliances becomes crucial, and in the specific historical conditions of Italy this means a *compromesso storico* incorporating all the major organized political groups—the Communists, the Socialists, and the Christian Democrats, with a particular emphasis on the Communist-Christian Democratic alliance. In short, Berlinguer's response is that, as far as Italy is concerned, the UP experience did not go far enough and should have included the DCCh. Moreover, the *compromesso* must have some, if not all, of the properties of Gramsci's *blocco storico,*—i.e. must be based on a real programmatic compromise, an organic link in the economic system, and coherent internal decisional structure, and not on the sort of parity and unanimity principle and policy confusion which characterized the UP. In the words of a PCI spokesman: "You don't produce a majority with scattered chips (*tucioli sparsi*). Scattered chips—we have seen what they have done in Chile."[11]

So far these theses of Berlinguer have only succeeded in provoking widespread debate. Smaller intermediary parties have resented being left out of the calculus; the Socialists fear being squeezed between the two giant partners; the Christian Democrats, or better their leader, Fanfani, has come out flatly against the idea. Regardless of whether this ambitious and highly unorthodox effort to bring a natural Communist party out of its ghetto into full governmental participation in a major capitalist country succeeds, it has certainly been the most interesting and encouraging rebound of the otherwise dismal and depressing aftermath of the violent overturn of Allende.

Ironically, the PCI's current strategy, itself the product at least in part of lessons learned from a previous historical experience, is now being threatened again by lessons just being generated by yet another precedent shaking experiment—that of Portugal. Let us turn very briefly to that country's astonishing liberation from authoritarian rule and rapid transformation into a "socializing" society to see how, if at all, it may be affected by the lessons of Chile.

THE IMPACT OF CHILE UPON PORTUGAL

When they occurred (September, 1973), there was no country in Europe upon which the events in Chile were less likely to have an impact than Portugal. Far from being on the brink of a possible shift in electoral alliances and/or gaining access to governing responsibility, the partisan left in Portugal was in jail, in exile, or on the defensive, suffering a wave of renewed repression following upon the modest and abortive liberalization of the earlier Caetano period. The prospect for a "peaceful transition to bourgeois liberalism" seemed far higher on the agenda than any "peaceful transition to proletarian socialism," and neither seemed at all imminent.

Immediately after the *coup* of April 25, 1974, by junior military officers, the "lesson" of Chile made its appearance. The Portuguese Communist party (PCP) was the first to warn of the danger of "another Chile," by which was meant a right-wing countercoup. The praxeological conclusions it initially drew from this lesson seem to have been: 1) Do not move too fast; 2) Do not alienate the *petite bourgeoisie;* 3) Avoid any premature "frontism" with other parties of the left. The highwater mark of such a "Chilean complex" came at the party Congress in October, 1974, when its platform dropped the phrase "dictatorship of the proletariat" and stressed moderation in virtually all policy issues—complete with reassuring phrases about property and international obligations.

By the time these positions were publicly uttered, the *praxis* of the PCP had already been radically altered. While the Communists continued to wave the spectre of Chile where useful, they seemed to have discovered that, at least as far as they were concerned, Cuba offered a more appropriate analogy. The probable "enemy" lay not on the extreme right, and its likely instrument was not the armed forces. Quite the contrary. It lay on the left, in the danger that, as in Cuba, a rigid and orthodox Communist party would be bypassed and displaced by a more revolutionary, *petit bourgeois* elite, itself in control of the armed forces and the state apparatus. Seeking to avoid the fate of Blas Roca and other "historic" leaders of the Cuban Communist party, they "glued themselves" to the initiatives and efforts of the Armed Forces Movement (MFA). Offering their "social power," i.e., their control over the organized working class and their ability to turn out acclamatory masses in Lisbon at critical moments, the Communists were able to move very rapidly in their efforts to penetrate the civilian and military agencies of the state and to dominate the mass media.

Ironically, their "Cuban complex" led them into a dead end.

Their very success in obtaining control over local administration, the trade union movement, and the media of Lisbon, and their close association with Vasco Gonçalves, Prime Minister in the ruling civil-military government, made them highly visible agents and isolated targets—scapegoats for policies they often had neither initiated nor supported. To their left, *groupuscules* and radical factions organized workers at the factory level bypassing the imposed unity of the trade unions and fomented the creation of soldier-sailor councils within military units, thereby undermining the military command structure upon which they were relying. On their right, the Socialists (PSP) and Popular Democrats (PPD) rallied an increasingly alienated *petite bourgeoisie* and independent peasantry. International reaction, which the PCP seems to have thought it could manipulate *à la cubana*, became stronger and more menacing.

If the PCP seems (erroneously, in retrospect) to have fastened on the lesson of Cuba, the Socialists seem to have been more potentially affected by that of Chile. Their most persistent theme has been that a distinctive, nonviolent, and democratic Portuguese road to socialism can only be realized if Portugal can somehow avoid the catastrophe that befell Chile. Needless to say, the *groupuscles* of the far left have continuously reminded the PSP of this fact—with the clear implication that Chile has proven that such a peaceful transition is impossible. Not so, say the Socialists. Portugal differs from Chile in several important aspects: 1) the PSP itself is a larger, more moderate, "catch-all" party than the Chilean Socialist party and, therefore, doesn't have to attempt continuously to outbid its Communist coalition partners; 2) the country's European location and the relative absence within it of a large and relatively intact "dependent bourgeoisie" makes it more difficult to subvert from outside; 3) the PSP's intimate contacts with ruling European social democrats and labor parties lessens the danger of subversion from that quarter and isolates the United States in whatever effort it might undertake; 4) and, most importantly, the armed forces in Portugal are a highly politicized, direct protagonist in the revolutionary process—not a force outside and above it.

Ironically, the Socialists seem to be implying that something like the *Unidad Popular* coalition might be expected to work much more successfully in Portugal than in Chile, but they have done little or nothing to establish it. At the time of the elections, neither the PSP nor the PCP seriously discussed a common list, joint program, or binding alliance. Since then, in the constituent Assembly, in the formation of various cabinets, in trade union elections, as well as in the streets, the two have manifested only their mutual hostility. On several occasions, the PSP has come close to forging an implacable anti-Communist alliance with all the elements further to its right (and even some on the far left). Such a bloc, irrespective of its majoritarian electoral support, would not only be incapable of dominating Portuguese political life (unless accompanied by military dictatorship and physical suppression of the "social power" of the PCP) but would almost certainly mean an end to the socialist nature of the revolution. To this, the PSP, in the person of its leader, Mario Soares, protests that it has not reneged and will never renege on its commitment to socialism and laments that Portugal's Communist party is not closer in ideology and leadership to those in neighboring Spain and Italy, making it more *koalitionsfähig*.

So the political lesson of Chile for Portugal has been "suspended"—suspended until the potential coalition partners become more symmetric in size and resources and more respectful of each other's terrains and intentions, and until the former ruling groups (largely in exile) and their potential external allies become better organized and more coherent in their counterrevolutionary threat. One suspects that it may take several tests of strength, shifts in partisan allegiance, disaggregation and reaggregation of the Armed Forces Movement, and the common perception of a clear and present external danger before such a "historical bloc" becomes firmly cemented, if it ever does, in Portugal. After all, in Chile the social basis for such a political outcome took several generations and continuous iterations of the electoral process to establish.

However, the economic and social lessons of the Chilean case are being experienced (if not learned) much more quickly. Transitions to socialized ownership and production in the current period generate immediate expectations about remuneration and consumption and strong demands for power and control over units of production and local governance. This potent and spontaneous set of demands from below creates great uncertainties with regard to production, accumulation, and investment, not only on the part of former privileged propertied classes but also within the now ruling coalition. These place an enormous burden on the government budget and the nation's balance of payments—a burden which in the best of circumstances can only be managed when total economic resources are expanding, the ruling bloc united and coherent in its objectives, and the administrative-technical apparatus of the state competent and consequent in its actions. Where these conditions are not met, the disarray within the state apparatus combines with the deliberate efforts of previously dominant elites and their external allies to create monetary, fiscal, and economic chaos—alienating in the short run domestic classes which would contribute in the longer run to a more orderly transition to socialism and discrediting the experience in the eyes of foreign observers.

This contradiction between the need for concerted calculation and control in the political realm and the likelihood of explosive voluntarism and spontaneity in economic and social domains is the real lesson of Chile for Portugal. Unfortunately that previous experience shows primarily "what is to be avoided" and not at all clearly "what is to be done."

CONCLUSION

The transformation of the pacific *vía chilena* into a murderous *callejón sin salida* has not blocked or even impeded the likelihood of a nonviolent, electorally monitored transition to socialism in Western Europe. The experience produced not a single, obvious lesson which influenced political calculations on the left in some consistent and predictable manner. Rather, its praxeological legacy has been differentially absorbed by the varied elements of the contemporary European left, each interpreting the *coup* and its aftermath in such a way as to reinforce previously elaborated strategies for seizing or participating in political power.

Those who advocated a *vía armada* have been reconfirmed in their beliefs and have dug deeper into their conspiratorial, subcultural ghetto. Those who advocated a peaceful, electoral path to power have reacted by extending their coalitional embrace to reach far beyond "mere" 51 per cent majority. Both seem to be reevaluating their assumptions about the "neutrality" or "permissiveness" of the state apparatus and armed forces and to be paying more attention to demands for changes in "immediate" instances of authority at the level of productive units and local or regional governance.

To a certain extent, the lessons of Chile have been displaced by those, yet to come, of Portugal. Chile calls us to the sobering reflection that all attempts to install socialism in this century by nonviolent means have led either to the eventual establishment of a party dictatorship, laying the basis for domination by a new bureaucratic class, or to a military dictatorship, preparing the way for a restoration of the previous order. Portugal reminds us that hopes for "liberty, fraternity, and equality" are eternal and capable of assuming a great variety of expressions and focus—including (so far) peaceful and tolerant ones.

NOTES

1. Joan Bartu Urbau, "Socialist Pluralism in Soviet and Italian Communist Perspective: The Chilean Catalyst," *Orbis*, #18, 2(Summer, 1974), p. 486. My interpretation of this internal Communist debate on these problems has been strongly influenced by this excellent article.

2. *Le Monde* (September 13, 1973).

3. *Le Monde* (September 17, 1973); also *L'Express* (September 17–23, 1973).

4. *Le Monde* (September 2–3, 1973).

5. *Le Monde* (September 14, 1973).

6. Renato Sandri, "La Sfida che Abbiamo Reccolto: A Colloquio con Luis Corvalán," *Rinascita* (April 30, 1971), p. 7.

7. *L'Espresso* (October 28, 1973).

8. For an example see, Georgio Napolitano, "Pericolo di Destra e Svolta Democratica Considerazioni Sulla Crisi Italiana dopo il 'Golpe' Cileno," *Critica Marxista* (September–October, 1973), p. 13.

9. See especially Renato Sandri, "Cile: Analisi di un'Esperienza e di una Sconfitta," *Critica Marxista* (September–October, 1973), pp. 15–40.

10. *Le Monde* (November 8, 1973).

11. Mino Manicelli, "Falce Martello e Scudo," *L'Espresso* (October 28, 1973), p. 10.

Elements for a Critical Analysis
of the Present Cultural System

P. BULE *

The present essay is divided into three parts. The first describes the essential traits and contents of the dominant system of values. The second analyzes the mechanisms by which these values are reproduced and diffused: that is, the educational system—primary, secondary, and university—and the system of informal education, particularly the mass communications media. The third part analyzes the significance and consequences of the dominant ideological program.

THE IDEOLOGY OF THE REGIME

Here we attempt a general outline of the basic ideological and cultural values that underlie the regime and that serve to legitimate the system of domination it has imposed. We then analyze more deeply the ideological and political program of the military *junta* by focusing on five key elements: its ideology of community and "national unity"; its concept of democracy; nationalism; its concept of development; and depoliticization.

The Scheme of Ideological and Cultural Values

It is not possible to delineate precisely the system of ideological and cultural values that reigns today in Chile, for it is difficult

* A pseudonym used by a group of social scientists presently residing in Chile. This collective effort is one of nine presented for the use of the participants in the seminar.

359

to speak of any one clear, dominant ideology. What one finds is a system of authoritarian domination that acquires and concentrates political power in the state while passing economic power to private hands. The official ideology has various sources and currents, and these give its ideological and cultural program an incoherent character. At the same time, it presents a mixture of abstract values that, without forming a homogeneous ideology, still serve to conceal, legitimate, and perpetrate its domination.

We believe that the ideological values of the regime can best be seen by looking at three general areas—the economic system; political and social thought; and military thought.

A summary analysis of the present economic model permits us to discern the principles on which it is based. These basic principles generate specific values, the acceptance of which is a *sine qua non* for the model to function. It seems to us that there are five basic principles underlying the economic model. 1) *The economic system is based on inequality.* It follows that values are introduced that make hierarchical social stratification acceptable, not only so that each person will accept his social position, but also so that he will accept as just the situation of those persons who occupy inferior positions. 2) *It is based on competition.* For this reason the individualistic values of achievement and success are emphasized. 3) *It is based on exploitation.* Therefore, values are diffused that make passive acceptance of this exploitation possible. 4) *It is based on individual property.* For this reason values are diffused that make property a maximum social interest; i.e., property becomes "sacred." 5) *It is based on efficiency.* Substantive criteria (value and content) are replaced by a merely formal one (the adequacy of means to ends, in which the latter are not discussed).

The regime's political and social thought seems to have a fundamentally Spanish basis. Its principal elements are the following: 1) *A Thomistic conception of the "common good."* It is never made clear just who defines this "common good," although in practice, of course, it is obvious. 2) *An authoritarian conception of power and rule.* An authoritarian model of the family is transferred to the plane of social relations. 3) *Traditionalism* in contrast to ideas of transformation and change. History is frozen. That which already exists is valued *per se,* while modern technocratic advances are incorporated (i.e., a modernizing traditionalism). 4) *Depoliticization.* The political expression of opposing interests, alternative models, and conflict is suppressed. 5) *The formation of an anti-democratic consciousness.* Democracy is "contaminated";

it is dangerous; it corrupts and weakens the unity of national interests. 6) *The formation of a corporative consciousness.* Although there is still no process specifically directed toward this end, a conception nevertheless predominates of a hierarchical society whose unique interests are expressed corporatively. The corporative system thus appears as a system of social control. 7) *Anti-Marxism.* The regime is characterized by denial of the "class struggle," opposition to the conception of a socialist society, social Manichaeism, and a worldwide anti-Communist messianism.

The regime's military thinking meshes directly with its political and social thought. Yet military theory has other sources, such as the German conceptions of geopolitics, the Western and Cold War ideology of the Pentagon, and, as one aspect of the latter, the Brazilian corollary of "ideological frontiers." Linked to its geopolitical concept is the idea that Chile's destiny is that of a "great nation," destined to play the historical role of a "power" but frustrated by "demagoguery and petty politics." Such a nationalistic concept compels the regime to oppose the expression of conflicting social interests and politicization. The nation is conceived as being organized to fulfill its historical destiny, and the army is the model of organization for all society (authority, command, etc.). In the regime's idea of "national security," following the lead of the Pentagon, political dissidence is considered "enemy infiltration."

Some Elements of the Political and Ideological Program

Every political and ideological program rests upon a material base, a model of growth and economic development which it serves to legitimate. An authoritarian program finds its material base in a process of economic growth and capital accumulation that is achieved through repression. In modern societies, unlike the dictatorships of old, authoritarianism appears as the response of capital to the workers' struggle to enjoy the fruits (material, spiritual, and political) of their labors.

Our intent here is not to examine the economic model of the military *junta*, i.e., the material base of its authoritarian political and ideological program. Rather we attempt to probe more deeply into some of the present regime's values and ideological principles. We analyze these as elements of an ideological program that seeks to conceal and legitimate a repressive process of economic growth.

When the military *junta* exalts the idea of "national unity," it is not issuing a call to dialogue or solidarity. On the contrary, "national unity" is no more than the watchword of a particular group that—*pers pro toto*—imposes its own interests, prohibiting all opposition. Thus the military *junta* proclaims higher and permanent truths and values that are above political debate. "*Chilenidad*" is the fundamental principle that defines society as a community. It is the "essence" of the nation. Therefore it cannot be subject to debate or personal interpretations. It is a dogmatic truth that allows only unconditional allegiance. The "crusade" mentality of the present regime, the fanaticism of those who believe they hold the absolute truth, logically follows.

The military regime is based upon an "ideology of community," built on values postulated as common, undebatable, and unalterable. From this, two clear notions that inspire the conduct of the government are derived. First is the distinction of friends from enemies. This simple dichotomy permits an easy identification of those who believe in the predetermined values and who therefore are members of the community (patriots) and those who are excluded because they do not accept these values (extremists). This serves not only to divide the "good guys" from the "bad guys" within Chile but also as a method of universal classification. The regime holds a Manichaean vision of the world in which "good guys" struggle against the powerful forces of evil; international policies are dictated by the knowledge of who Chile's friends are (determined by their votes in the United Nations). The community must defend itself as much against external enemies as internal ones, both of whom plot against the nation (the conspiracy theory). Since truth itself is at stake, there can only be a fight to the death between friend and enemy. There is no room for negotiation or compromise; pluralism signifies weakness. Thus the military *junta* considers itself "at war"—whether or not there is any actual armed resistance.

Second, the regime maintains that there is an identity between governors and governed. This is, of course, no more than the other side of the same coin. The representation of competing social interests is replaced by the mystifying unity of the "national will." The armed forces appropriate for themselves the "general will," pretending that it is the "will of all." The conflict of interests is camouflaged behind a supposed "general interest" that is dictated *ex cathedra*. Thus the ideology of community hides the irresponsible power of a minority. Similarly, the opaqueness of the political decision-making process creates the illusion of a will free from particular interests.

Beginning with its ideology of community, one can come to understand what the military *junta* means by "democracy." On December 3, 1974, *El Mercurio* summarized the point succinctly when it advanced an argument contrasting the democracy of medieval Spanish jurisdictions with the "contaminated democracy" of today:

> The modern democratic order—as it has been experienced in the United States, Europe, and, of course, Chile—is in essence subject to electoral majorities. The vote of these changes governments, defines political orientations, and, paradoxically, even permits democratic suffrage to contribute to edifying the negation of democracy. General Pinochet seems to use the concept of democracy in the broad sense it has in hispanic tradition, as it was manifested in the oldest medieval Spanish jurisdictions. Thus he affirms that power is subject to law, to the inviolability of the person and to respect for freedom. But he certainly does not allude to liberal democracy, for he also affirms that the new institutional order must prevent our fatherland from returning "not only to Marxism but also to petty politics and the demagoguery of political parties."

However, the military *junta* did not perceive that its concept that "power is subject to law," expressed in a government that rules through decrees, is very different from the concept of medieval Spain. In Chile law is limited to establishing *formal* rules that do not touch upon the *material content* of the exercise of power. To the extent that "higher and permanent truths and values" are admitted but kept from public discussion, the government alone fixes their content. Specifically, it is the armed forces (in consultation with economic forces and interest groups) that define what is "national," "Chilean," etc. The "common good" does not emerge from a consensus of the citizenry but from decrees published in the official newspaper. Such a concept of democracy hides within it its own *de facto* negation: the systematic criminalization of all disagreement with official opinion.

This concept of democracy shows its authoritarian roots once more when the military *junta* refers to what it calls the "crisis of Western democracy." If such a crisis exists, it is due to the lack of greater citizen participation in real life situations which are extremely complex and which require increasing political, economic, and cultural education to be understood. Authoritarianism is not an integral solution to this crisis, as is suggested by the military *junta*.

Through the reactionary notion of the *junta*, not only does democracy cease to be a political method for regulating contradictions, but—more seriously—a style of life that Chilean society, through the course of its history, had acquired as a cultural patrimony is destroyed. What is occurring today is an acritical importation of foreign (i.e., medieval) ideas, contrary to the pattern of social coexistence long established in Chile.

Chile could be proud of being one of the few countries in which freedom was a living value; all citizens—and the government as the first servant of the state—respected the opinions and activities of the rest. Today, under the slogan of "national unity," an official opinion that is obligatory for all is codified *de facto* (by force). It walks on well-known soil, although demagogic prudence dictates that it not be made explicit: the old notion of private property. Those who share in the unrestricted defense of *established* private property are members of the community. Those who seek to modify its distribution or to socialize *access* to it are enemies. As in the days when suffrage was restricted to those possessing property, we have returned to distinguishing two classes of citizens. Real freedom is in fact restricted to private owners (the privatization of economic power); the remainder have only to work and obey. The proposal for a new Constitution is quite explicit in indicating who are the "evil Chileans" who should be expelled from the community. Here the ideology of community serves also to support a campaign of pacification that installs a "social peace" based on repression, the peace of the cemeteries.

The fundamental value professed by the military *junta* is nationalism. Insofar as *nationalism* expresses the historical and cultural unity of a nation, it requires concrete expression. It exists in reference to something. Although the military *junta* has been relatively sparing in making explicit its own points of reference, official documents permit us to indicate two—history and power.

Nationalism, as it refers to Chilean history, principally seems to exalt the figure of Diego Portales. But what does this retrospective reference imply? The exaltation of Portales is not so much to pay homage to a celebrated statesman, for to admire the genius of Portales is to recognize his works *in his time*. The invocation of Portales today is ahistoric. It is the exaltation of a *legal dictatorship* as a permanent model, as the quintessence of the Chilean soul for all time. Thus it serves to discredit later eras and to legitimate the present regime. Nationalism functions as a conservative ideology that justifies the restoration of the "benevolent dictatorship," but it does so from a historical perspective that is not applicable under present conditions.

Paradoxically, this nationalism based on history actually breaks the continuity of history. The exaltation of the Portalian creation is ahistoric in that it implies condemning political parties, and political parties have been the essence of Chilean political life for the last century. Chile had a relatively homogeneous historical conscience; no person or period was "expelled" from its history, ignored, or discredited. Different opinions of O'Higgins or Carrera, the Popular Front, or the Law for the Defense of Democracy did not obstruct the evolution of a consciousness of Chilean history as a process of increasing democratization. Today we live the collapse of this historical consciousness, an anathema in the name of the "good old days" (the "weight of the night")—in short, we live a *cultural counterrevolution.*

The other reference point for the regime's nationalism is power, a geopolitical concept that invokes the destiny of Chile as a great nation. But to what grandeur does this nationalism refer? It refers simply to power as an instrument of foreign policy, that is, to the power of the Chilean state *vis-à-vis* other states. The power of the state is not used to further the well-being of Chilean society but rather the opposite: the development of the country is oriented by the needs of a "great power" foreign policy. This geopolitical vision finds its ultimate logic in the survival of the national state. It is a policy inspired by criteria free from all valuation; the state becomes an end in itself. Nationalism is no more than power for the sake of power. It is chauvinism disguised as *realpolitik.*

What must be questioned about this nationalism is not its geopolitical orientation but the absence in it of any true national *interest*. The "realistic and pragmatic" policies of the military *junta* demonstrate the inability of the groups which govern Chile to formulate and implement programs around which to unify Chilean society. In this sense we are governed today—beneath a façade of order and unity—by patchwork policies that only muliply and perpetuate the structural crisis of the country.

The notion of *development* proclaimed by the military *junta* also serves as a means of legitimation. Two central ideas appear tied to the government's vision of economic development: a changing mentality and efficiency.

Particularly in its speeches to youth, the government emphasizes the importance of a *changing mentality* as a spiritual renovation. Here too, however, what is desired is a restoration rather than a renovation. The government wants nothing new, and it emphatically rejects the idea of the "new man." Independent of whatever political connotations the concept may have acquired, the "new man" represents a fundamental desire in Western-Christian culture: the perfecting of man. Yet the government's policy of a "changing mentality" essentially denies this possibility. Influenced by middle-class social-psychological assumptions (the Chilean is lazy, etc.), it seeks to restore old Chilean virtues. However, to preach the value of work and discipline while at the same time denying that man can be perfected leads to a kind of moralism; that is, to moral rules divorced from practice. The idea of a "changing mentality" is determined by an abstract morality. In turn it serves (in its connection with school texts, etc.) as a psychological mechanism of individual adaptation to existing structures. The "changing mentality" thus signifies renouncing rebellion against injustice and resigning oneself to the *status quo*.

Along with this concept of a changing mentality, the government elevates efficiency as a guiding principle for development. It refers, however, only to a formal criterion (that of relating means to ends) unrelated to the material content of decisions. Thus the exaltation of efficiency serves to hide existing relations of domination. In other words, the merely formal character of efficiency camouflages the relationships of exploitation that are its material base. This is demonstrated by the way the military *junta* deals with "extreme poverty." It adopts a typically technocratic approach in which formal indices of misery ignore the conditions from which that misery arises.

Along with the above two ideas, the concept of "social development" is constantly juxtaposed to the idea of development. Here, too, there is a mechanical transposition of what once were called "the social aspects of development." In the military *junta*'s program "social development" plays the role of a palliative and hides economic exploitation.

All the above facets of the government's ideological program coalesce in what is simultaneously an agent of cohesion, an ideological principle, and a tactical byword: depoliticization. The ideas of a community of sacrosanct values, indeterminate nationalism, and a technocratic notion of progress all require and produce the absence of discussion and political criticism. Truth, general interest, and the common good are all revealed, and the citizen should express his *adherence* through interest groups or other official organizations. He cannot express an opinion, or doubt, or differ. His participation as a citizen is replaced by his collaboration as a producer (professional). The first objective of depoliticization is the destruction of democracy, not only as a form of political organization (parties) but also, and more importantly, as a style of life and a system of values (freedom). Depoliticization is a tactic of social "disciplining," designed to create a new kind of society—the authoritarian society—in which all is subject to the law of the expansion of capital. Depoliticization thus implies camouflaging the structural violence of underdeveloped capitalist society by transforming *political* problems into *technical* questions. To seek administrative solutions to political problems is to deny the citizen all responsibility and to transform society into a mass that supports bureaucratic rule (both public and entrepreneurial). In depoliticization the false nineteenth-century myth of infinite socioeconomic progress is revived in technocratic form. In this sense, the authoritarian regime is the political expression of technocracy, and both authoritarianism and technocracy are based on the formalization of reality. They deny the transcendence of social structures, that is, the ability of institutions, by negating the existing oppressive reality, to engender from within a more just society.

THE MECHANISMS FOR TRANSMITTING VALUES: FORMAL AND INFORMAL EDUCATION

This portion of our work explores the principal means by which official dominant values are transmitted. We have limited ourselves to two which seem most significant. Moreover, these lend themselves most easily to a relatively rapid analysis not requiring complex methods of investigation. Thus, on the one hand, we concentrate on formal, systematic education, distinguishing two aspects: primary and secondary education, and university education. On the other, we consider mechanisms of unsystematic education and informal or latent socialization. We emphasize particularly the values transmitted by the mass media.

Formal Education

1. Primary and Secondary Education

The educational reforms implemented between 1965 and 1970 fundamentally involved extensive quantitative expansion, modification of the educational structure by prolonging primary school to eight years, and some technical changes modernizing pedagogy. The educational policy of the Christian Democratic administration aimed at creating equal educational opportunities for all and at linking the educational system with the needs of national economic and social development. During the *Unidad Popular* administration the process of quantitative expansion was continued, for similar reasons, and a series of basic educational transformations was proposed. As a result of existing political circumstances, however, these were never put into practice. A central goal of the *Unidad Popular*'s educational policy was to democratize education by increasing participation in decision making by all interested sectors: staff, students, parents, workers, slum dwellers, etc.

The educational policies of the two administrations were inspired by different ideologies. Nevertheless, it is possible to note some important common elements: a) in both, educational opportunities were extended by policies expanding matriculation and attendance to the most needy sectors; b) development of programs, technical and professional education, and other measures linked education to socioeconomic development and change; and c) students and professors both enjoyed a greater role in decision making.

All these modifications in the Chilean educational process between 1965 and 1973 indicate trends that it is important to keep in mind in evaluating the significance of the present situation.

To analyze the basic orientation of the government's educational policy, we use two sources: official documents, which define the direction of policy explicitly, and the measures already applied, from which certain trends emerge. In official documents the government presents the fundamental lines of the ideological change it desires to introduce. It emphasizes nationalism, apolitical attitudes, and the elimination of Marxist thought. The following quotations show this clearly.

Education should be animated by a common spirit, identified with national values, the Christian cultural tradition, and the historical purposes of the Chilean nation.[1]

Education will not accept the participation of professors who teach national or foreign doctrines, such as Marxism, that attack the essentially free and democratic spirit of Chilean institutions. Nor will the infiltration of political doctrines or of any party be accepted in public or private education.

Therefore we propose a profoundly humanistic and apolitical education, in which the use and development of scientific and technological advances is subordinate to the well-being of man and in which man becomes the expert, responsible for building the common good. The nation needs men capable of creating, upon the base of the patrimony inherited from our ancestors, a superior order, in which respect for the individuality and inviolability of each person will reign.[2]

If, on the other hand, we analyze educational measures adopted since September 11, 1973, the tremendous reduction in the possibility for participation by professors, students, parents, and other sectors of the community immediately becomes obvious. In direct contrast to a democratic model, authoritarian leadership styles that assign a passive role to students and professors have emerged at all levels. This has been demonstrated in a series of concrete measures.

There has also been scant reference to the relationship between education and socioeconomic development. As we have seen, in the last ten years an education at the service of development and social change has been strongly emphasized. Under the *junta*, however, references to abstract values such as the nation, fatherland, authority, humanism, and others predominate. In effect, these tend to alienate the child or youth from his reality.

The total number of students matriculated decreased between 1973 and 1974 from 2,847,955 to 2,844,720, a drop of 0.1 per cent. From 1964 to 1970 the average annual growth rate was 6.2 per cent; between 1970 and 1973 it was 5.6 per cent. Since 1960 total matriculation had never even remained constant, much less declined. In 1974 matriculation in primary education decreased by 0.5 per cent and in secondary education by 0.6 per cent. The data show a drastic reversal of the trends of the last ten years, implying a reduction in the overall level of education, which is no longer able to absorb even the vegetative growth in the population.

The study programs used through September, 1973, were created by the Educational Reform Act and were not modified during the *Unidad Popular* administration. The military *junta* was immediately preoccupied with changing these and was unwilling to wait even for the end of the 1973 school year. The motivation for acting with such speed was that, in the judgment of the educational authorities, there were in the existing programs "conscientizing" elements ideologically opposed to official positions. Given that these programs had been elaborated during the Christian Democratic administration of Eduardo Frei, their content was not Marxist. What the *junta* objected to was simply that they referred to contemporary social problems and thus constituted a danger to the ideological control the *junta* sought to exercise.

Since it was impossible to elaborate new programs at once, the government chose to exercise a more negative criteria by eliminating certain specifically indicated topics. The Education Minister indicated that "all themes with conscientizing purposes should be eliminated and replaced by others that give youth a better knowledge of the history and geography of Chile."[3] These changes were concentrated in the social sciences and philosophy, topics classified as "divisive."

The precise rules for social science teachers were enumerated in a Office of Secondary Educational memorandum, published in *El Mercurio*. It listed "some divisive topics it is convenient to replace."[4]

In 1974 new and different programs were introduced in General Primary Education and Humanist and Scientific Secondary Education. These have a transitory nature, and it is assumed they will be rewritten for the coming years. Nevertheless, no efforts in this direction have been made public.

The programs applied during 1974 present two essentially different characteristics from earlier ones. First, they contain a well-defined nationalistic and individualist ideology that systematically avoids topics relating to national socioeconomic reality. Second, the new programs are far more rigid.

The Superintendency of Education elaborated an official document, "General Considerations on the Application of Transition Programs," that was distributed to all schools as a guide for the development of the new programs. The document indicates that the social sciences suffered the most substantial modifications because they "are the subject that suffered perhaps the greatest pressure to serve the ends of totalitarian conscientization." The fundamental modifications are as follows:

a) Give new importance and feeling to the teaching of the History of the Fatherland. Within that history, place emphasis less on the simple chronological enumeration of events and more on the heroic achievements and labor of the pioneers of our nationality. Also emphasize the economic, cultural, social, and artistic planes and the effective action of the armed forces in national history.

b) Eliminate those topics that lend themselves to hateful and sterile discussion or that refer to subjective evaluations of ideas, events, or personages of doubtful transcendency.

c) Note the value of labor as the tool of human progress and of true satisfaction for man. The History and Geography of Chile, now a unified discipline included within the required studies, should be given privileged treatment, whatever place it is given in the development of the curriculum. The professor of social sciences and Chilean history should become the major dynamic element in the school or high school, embodying national values, both of a civilian nature and those corresponding to the armed forces.

New units are added in both primary and secondary education. The following are worthy of mention: in fifth year primary, "Men and Events in Chile during the Last Century"; sixth year, "Men and Events in Chile following the War of the Pacific"; third and fourth years of secondary, "Genesis and Consolidation of our Nationality." In the fourth year of secondary education, the unit on political science is eliminated. On the other hand, in courses one to four of primary education, six complementary units are added, each of which is to be taught for three days, that is, for twelve teaching hours. These units are the following and should be included on the dates indicated.

—"The Symbols of the Fatherland: Flag, Shield, and National Anthem" (last week in March)
—"The Naval Glories of Chile" (week of May 21)
—"The Heroes of Concepción" (week of 9 and 10 July)
—"O'Higgins Week" (week of August 20)
—"Fatherland Week" (week of September 18)
—"Forgers of Our Nationality" (week of October 20)

Finally, it is worth noting that the "Project for Courses on National Security," though not put into practice, has the importance of being the result of instructions from the Governing *Junta* to the Ministers of Education and Defense. This project contemplates activities at the primary, secondary, and university levels.

This background is sufficient to demonstrate how the new study programs constitute an efficient tool for cultivating the values of the nationalist ideology.

Textbooks were changed with the same speed as study programs. Certain texts were immediately classified as "conscientizing," and their destruction was ordered.[5] As a result, along the length of Chile great quantities of didactic material were burned. At the same time, the Office of Secondary Education ordered school principals to withdraw from circulation a number of books published by the National Publishing House *Quimantú*. In the province of Antofagasta, nine mathematics and Spanish texts previously used in primary schools were censored because they contained, according to official declarations, "the seeds of Marxist conscientization."

Following these hurried measures, the Superintendency of Education paused to analyze in detail the variety of texts produced by the free regime that existed until September, 1973. On this basis, a list of texts rejected or to be revised was published. The rejected texts included seven in the social sciences, one in

Spanish, and two in French. Those to be revised included seven in the social sciences, four in Spanish, and one in French.

The new Rules for Evaluation and Promotion mark a change of some significance. These establish more strict regulations to replace the system of automatic promotion based on student responsibility. This stricter control over scholarly achievement is reflected in the introduction of global tests, very similar in nature to the old exams. Thus, the tendency is to return to a system of selective evaluation, which is isolated from the educational process itself. Beginning with the educational reform, such isolated evaluation was gradually being overcome.

Characteristic of the present organization of schooling is the return to authoritarian discipline. On the one hand, in all official documents there is repeated emphasis of teaching the concepts of authority and hierarchy. On the other, all organizations channeling student participation in school life are eliminated or weakened. The ideal student—one can deduce from official documents—is one who obeys all given orders and dedicates himself exclusively to studies. Disproportionate value is placed as well on the personal appearance of the student, and there are numerous memoranda which refer to the use of uniforms, the length of hair or hemlines, prohibitions on the use of makeup, various kinds of shoes, etc.

For the purpose of promoting values such as fatherland and nation, certain para-academic activities were ordered in addition to the above program. These were of three kinds:

1. Weekly patriotic acts. The Ministry of Education ordered (via Permanent Ministerial Order No. 1, 1973—repeated this year) that "all teaching establishments, both public and private, begin their labors each week with civic acts of homage to the flag, which will be raised in a place of honor. These acts will point out some individual, event, or circumstance that will exalt patriotic sentiment and develop in the students a pride in being Chilean."

This nationalistic tendency was reinforced in the same order by prohibitions on acts of homage to other nations: "Foreign symbols and portraits or effigies of personages or foreign rulers should not be exhibited in public places. This includes hallways, classrooms, dining halls or patios. Special permission must be obtained from the Intendency of Governation to celebrate any non-Chilean anniversary, for example, in the case where the establishment carries the name of a foreign country, the independence day of that country."

2. Para-academic activity weeks. For similar ends, two para-academic weeks were planned: the first from May 15 to 21, the second from September 11 to 17. The common objective of both is to commemorate the respective historical events and emphasize patriotic values. Different activities are planned, including parades, civic acts, literary contests, expositions, etc.[6]

Taking advantage of their proximity, the September week of para-academic activities not only celebrates national independence day but also the anniversary of September 11. Thus the government openly contradicts its proclaimed apoliticism. In effect, the document cited indicates that the following should be emphasized and given equal value: September 11 (commemorating the first Anniversary of National Reconstruction), September 18 (the 164th Anniversary of the first Government *Junta*), and September 19 (the Day of the Glories of the Army).

3. *Repression and military control.* Immediately after assuming power the military *junta* initiated activities designed to control education, beginning with an attempt to eliminate or intimidate all personnel who were not followers of the government. In the first weeks three measures were adopted:

a) *Cancellation of teaching contracts.* This did not occur to a significant extent, for it would have resulted in a scarcity of professors and consequently impeded the entire educational process. Nevertheless, there are cases such as that of the province of Valdivia where forty-four professors were expelled. Many others were detained.

b) *Provisional contracts.* By Decree no. 6, the *junta* placed all professors, as well as all other public employees, on provisional status. All rights acquired through tenure competitions were eliminated. This meant that professors suddenly found themselves at the mercy of any ruling by their respective superiors.

c) *Replacement of school principals.* The great majority of principals who had been followers of the *Unidad Popular* or who did not enjoy the absolute confidence of the executive were replaced. This occurred most frequently in secondary schools.

At the same time, after September, 1973, direct and strict military control was established over teaching. A military delegate was named in each educational sector to visit the schools in that sector periodically, meet with the faculty, and threaten them with drastic measures if they did not faithfully follow the dispositions of the *junta*. In August, 1974, this military control was further institutionalized in an unusual memorandum from the Commander of Military Institutes to all local educational authorities in greater Santiago. It established a dual system of leadership over education. On the one hand, the Ministry of Education directs administrative and technical or pedagogical aspects; on the other, the Commander of Military Institutes is responsible for ideology, discipline, and security. Obviously, there may be conflicts between the two. It is not absolutely clear how this memorandum has been put into practice, but its simple issuance has great significance, for a school principal cannot ignore it without running grave personal risk.

The memorandum establishes an organization by areas or sectors, each led by school directors or regiment officers. That is, each area or sector of Santiago finds itself under the supervision of a military authority, with wide powers. Among the powers emphasized are the ability to adopt disciplinary measures, to summon the director and professors to the Military Unit, to visit the school at any moment, to attend and suspend meetings of teachers, parents' centers, etc.

The school principal, in accordance with the memorandum, has two different channels available for solving problems that occur in his establishment. Problems which are totally pedagogical or administrative he should appeal to the respective educational authority. Security problems or problems of teaching divisive ideas he should direct to the corresponding military authority.[7]

All these elements clearly form the climate of terror the government seeks to impose on students and teaching staff in all educational establishments. In this manner it seeks to guarantee its strict ideological control over education.

The *junta*'s educational policy recognizes private education and guarantees it a position similar to that it has enjoyed with minor variations during recent years. Under this policy, subsidies to free private education have been maintained. Nevertheless, private establishments are subjected to the same strict control as state institutions, and the intervention of military authorities, established by the Circular of the Command of Military Institutes, is equally valid for private schools. Since the autonomy of direction in these establishments is thus eliminated, the "private" nature of this kind of teaching is reduced to a pure legalism. Moreover, all restrictive measures relating to student and teacher participation are also applied to private education. In cases in which government authorities viewed official organization to be in greatest danger, the government went even further and ordered direct intervention.[8]

Considering the high level of development that high-school Student Centers had achieved, the military *junta* decided in October, 1973, to declare these organizations in recess.[9] The discontent this measure provoked among students was noted by General Gustavo Leigh, who expressed in a speech delivered to high-school students, "On you lies the responsibility for creating and promoting new forms of youth participation that will reflect the New Chile that is being reborn. The present recess of the high-school Student Centers should not be seen as a restrictive measure, but as a challenge to replace styles of youth participation that have been surpassed by the Movement of September 11 with new and imaginative forms. These will place youth in the vanguard of the new institutions that today are emerging."[10]

However, the new regulations concerning Student Centers, expressed in Decree no. 741 of July 25, 1974, neither emerged from the creativity of the youth nor established new participatory forms. In effect, the decree reduces to a minimum the area for student participation and establishes a controlled and dependent form of student organization. The functions assigned to the students centers are basically contributing to the development and formation of personality; channeling cultural, social, and sporting interests; and promoting greater dedication to school labors. The decree also states that "Student Centers should dedicate themselves exclusively to fulfilling their own ends and objectives. They cannot intervene in political or religious activities, in technical or pedagogical matters, or in the administration and academic organizations of the establishment." Thus students in secondary education are denied an organization where they can freely express their desires and interests or struggle to realize these.

In regard to teacher participation, the Military Government suppressed the Unified Education Workers Union (*Sindicato Unico de Trabajadores de la Educación*, SUTE), the organization that embodied the Chilean teachers' labor movement, and created the College of Teachers as an alternative. Although this reflected a long-standing aspiration of a sector of teachers, the way in which it was put into practice did not correspond to their desires. The College of Professors, as a professional organization, should have been formed by the professors themselves and expressed their interests. In contrast, it was imposed by decree, and its first officers will be named by the Ministry of Education and will remain in their posts until the month of April three years after they are designated. Since the College of Professors has not begun operations, for the moment its true dimensions are unknown. At the same time, with the suppression of SUTE, non-teaching workers in education, such as para-teachers, aides, and administrators, have been left with no form of representation.

In recent years Parents' Centers had also become active participants in educational development, and the tendency was to create a school community projecting the school toward the family and local neighborhood. The Parents' Centers still continue to exist, but their ability to meet, the topics they may consider, and their liberty to develop new initiatives have been curtailed. The Parents' Center today is expected to collaborate with the school, from outside, but without participating in decisions concerning school activities. The Command of Military Institutes states that military authorities in charge of educational sectors can "attend, without prior notice, meetings of Parents' Centers, and may suspend these if they do not comply in form and essence with the rules established for such meetings."[11]

Finally, we note two examples of attempts to exercise ideological control over children and youth through education and institutions outside the school. A study document of the Ministers' Social Council, presided over by General Leigh, proposed the creation of Community Centers for children in an irregular situation (calculated by the government to number some 650,000). The study saw such centers as a way to "displace the class struggle, replacing it by the opposite concept of Social Integration." The "primordial" basis for these centers is stated as follows: "There exists a primordial coexistence that can be considered as an element of social integration. Toward these centers can be channeled all the active human and voluntary capacity for supporting the government. Through these can be channeled the activities of Mothers' Centers, the Secretariat of Women, the Secretariat of Youth, the Women's Voluntary Association, the Committees of Social Development of the municipalities, and all those persons who wish to participate in the social development of the country. Any person able to do so will feel directly linked to the government and can offer his quota of solidarity to the community."

Similarly, the Permanent Seminary Corporation (*Corporación Seminario Permanente*, SEMPER), with official approval of the Interior Ministry and its National Emergency Office, organized in February, 1975, a Youth Jamboree in the province of Osorno, for "96 children, from periphery populations and squatter colonies in the province of Santiago, whose ages vary between 12 and 15 years." Its purpose was "to offer the youth specific values and concepts that will permit them to enrich their personalities and reorient, positively, the negative traits of their daily existence."

CONCLUSIONS

We have now indicated and analyzed the principal characteristic of the *junta*'s educational activities affecting the formation of a new role for education. This analysis permits us to conclude that the different measures adopted have been directed in two directions, that is, toward a change in ideology and values, and toward the negation of participation. Ideological change is faithfully reflected in the modification of study programs, suppression of texts, and promotion of patriotic values. Restriction on participation is pursued in measures such as control from above of Student Centers, the College of Professors, Parents' Centers, and through reinforcing the so-called principle of authority. To guarantee the new orientation of education and the subservience of the educational base, a vast system of repression has been created that operates through direct military control over educational establishments and the adoption of severe punitive measures against any deviation from the official line.

2. Values and Ideology in the University

An analysis of the situation of the universities within the context of the values and the ideological and cultural program dominant in Chile today reveals a number of distinct traits. In effect, it is far more difficult to change the content of messages transmitted by university education than to change secondary and primary education and the mass media. Hence, in the universities such change is less clearly evident. In other words, a drastic and massive change in the programs of university education is not possible, although, as we will note below, some innovations can be introduced. The new values, ideology, and program can best be perceived in the university structure, in the principles ruling academic activities and teaching, in the norms orienting the relations among actors within the university, and in those regulating interactions between the university and the remaining institutions in the country.

THE VALUES OF THE REFORMED UNIVERSITY

The principles and values forming the Military Government's university program cannot be understood except in comparison with those characterizing the Chilean university system between 1967 and 1973, i.e., those commonly labeled "the University Reform." This was recognized explicitly by the Ministry of Education in its arguments for the military *junta*'s intervention in the universities and its nomination of delegate-rectors. Today's policies essentially seek a reversal of the principles and values that characterized the Reform.

The principles and values for the university sanctified by the Reform and put into practice between 1967 and 1973 are an expression of the general social process in Chile. They reflect the culmination of the modernizing and democratizing trends evolving since the 1920s, whose most significant trait was the continual sociocultural and political rise of the "middle sectors." To this was added in the period from 1970 to 1973 the eruption of the "popular classes." The university of the Reform is an expression of this process. It becomes, to a relatively large degree, a university of the masses. The middle-sector presence is preponderant, and one begins to see the emerging presence of the popular sectors as well. Its principles and values, therefore, reflect the characteristics of the system and the political process in the country. Five seem essential to us:

Democratization. We understand the term to mean the trend toward unrestricted access to the universities by the middle sectors, the limited adoption of programs for workers, the conversion of the university into a vocational market, and the adoption within it of a democratic decision-making model with participation by all sectors. The phenomenon of the growing sociocultural and political participation is thus also expressed in the university.

Pedagogical and structural modernization. A consequence of opening universities to the masses, modernization occurs in the replacement of faculties with departments and the renovation of pedagogical methods of increasing curriculum flexibility. The latent purpose of this structural modernization, though not always implemented, is on the one hand to place value on scientific work and to create an institutional arena for its development and, on the other, to break down the model of education based on training professionals.

Intellectual and ideological pluralism. A reflection of the political pluralism of the country, this characteristic in the university takes the form of a multiplicity of academic units. Its latent purpose is to convert the university into a cultural and intellectual forum that will manifest the mix of ideas and orientations existing in Chile and in the modern cultural world.

Autonomy. Autonomy takes form in the legal and financial basis for the university, but its latent purpose is to recognize the value of intellectual work and preserve cultural and scientific freedom.

Linkage between the university and the rest of the country. On the one hand, this is understood as coordination of academic investigations with the activities of those sectors of society involved in development and change. On the other, it is the formation within the university of its own social force, embodied in the student movement.

Any evaluation of the university Reform involves a double judgment, one negative and critical, the other positive. The negative judgment notes the restricted character of the Reform's fundamental purpose, that is, a democratization or modernization of the university that is tied to a social and cultural program identified almost exclusively with the "middle sectors" and their particular interests. Thus, it is necessarily exclusive. In contrast, the positive judgment sees in this modernization a dynamic which is more powerful than the dikes containing the power and institutions of the universities. It implies recognition of the universal right to higher education. As a consequence, it obliges a radical revision and reformulation of the function of the university and the construction of a new foundation for the institution.

PRINCIPLES AND VALUES OF THE UNIVERSITY RESTORATION

The Military Government today seeks a reversal of the principles of the Reform. In speaking of eliminating the negative aspects of the mass university, it hides its intent to eliminate the dynamic recreation of that university. The university is frozen in a professionalizing model, subordinate to the program of economic and political domination. The confrontation between political reality since September 11, 1973, and the principles of the Reform permits us to discern the cultural role assigned to the university today. The principles directing this cultural function are projected as the ideals for society as a whole.

The basic measures adopted that affect democratization, both internal and external, are the following reversions to elitism and an authoritarian model: In 1974, a 10 per cent decrease in university vacancies in comparison with the previous year and suppression of a significant number of courses of study; elimination of massive special programs for workers; proposals that the university be self-financing; elimination of the internal democratic system and a sanctification of "unipersonal delegated power."

There are two arguments for these measures. On the one

hand, the explosive increase in matriculation during the last years is criticized; claims are that it has led to mediocre teaching and that the increase in national spending has become insupportable. On the other, the existing democratic model is criticized because it is excessively politicized and because multiple opinions impede the unity of decision or command, unity that is an essential support of the present regime at all levels of social life.

Two central values directing university life can be discerned underlying this criticism of democratization. One is elitism, counterpoised to the mass university and the universal right to higher education; the other is authoritarianism, counterpoised to the pluralism of intellectual life. As if to ameliorate the former, the government notes that selectivity in the university does not discriminate socially or economically, because funds are dedicated for loans and scholarships for needy students. This is no more than a demagogic and rhetorical claim. Implementation of a massive system of loans and scholarships is absolutely impossible in the near future. Because of the negative redistribution of income, vast sectors live under extremely difficult economic conditions. They cannot assume the expense of a university education for their children.

The principle of authority has not eliminated political conflict within the university but only changed its character. What occurs now is simply a struggle for power and influence, a struggle without programs or content. Moreover, it has been reduced to a struggle between two sectors; the third has been eliminated.

The fundamental changes in the structural and pedagogic transformations of the reform are the following reversions to a "professional" model, to student passivity, and to a "pragmatication" of scientific and cultural work:

—An authoritarian structure challenges the academic life of the departments, which are reduced to purely bureaucratic structures. In the Catholic University, the old faculties have been restored.

—Flexible curricula, based on the idea that the student "creates his own course of study," and pedagogical methods in which the objective of teaching is to "learn to learn," give way to a new rigidity in curricula dedicated exclusively to professional formation. Materials, orientations, and methods of work that stimulate critical capacity are eliminated.

—Scientific work is no longer valued for itself. Rather, the usefulness of investigation is measured in terms of its ability to satisfy demands generated by private enterprise and the state.

—Scientific accumulation of knowledge has been affected by

the exodus of scientists from the universities. The exodus of professionals since September, 1973, is different from that of earlier years. As is indicated in official reports, now the basic sciences are also affected. We need not even mention what is happening in the social sciences, which have disappeared as a separate entity in many schools.[12]

All this suggests values in which the university ceases to be an intellectual center and becomes once again an efficient factory for producing professionals. This conception of the university is reinforced by a vision of the student which is authoritarian, paternalistic, and competitive. Programs are offered to the student in a closed package. They lack answers for his intellectual curiosity, and his attitude toward them must be fundamentally passive. The student is supposed to prepare himself through his studies to be a professional success and, outside of his studies, to entertain himself, particularly in sports. (Note the interview in *El Mercurio* with the Delegated Rector of the University of Chile.) The intellectual curiosity of the student toward contemporary thought, such as existentialism, Marxism, or Christian personalism, is seen as an expression of an extremism that must be eliminated. (See the same interview.)

To eliminate the ideological pluralism of the university of the Reform, the military government adopted, among others, the following policies:

—Massive elimination of professors and investigators whose academic work and intellectual orientation were sympathetic to the political programs of the left. The pretext is that the government is extirpating Marxism.

—Elimination of courses, materials, and orientations that, within the curriculum, placed professional training in a critical intellectual context. Publication and the principal lines of investigation in Chilean history and social structure have been prohibited.

—Creation of a rigorous climate of self-censorship that eliminates controversial topics from teaching and investigation.

In this manner, the "professional" nature of university education was reinforced, as was a vision of a society without conflict over value or direction. Social problems are no more than technical problems that adequate scientific and technical preparation will permit resolving. This was expressed by one of the delegate-rectors in the following terms: "In the Law School what has always been taught is law and not a vision of society." Intellectual thought, understood as a critical attitude toward the problems of society, is suspect and inappropriate for "the formation of the student." It is synonymous with politicization in the university. By eliminating confrontation among values, the university sanctifies anti-intellectualism and ideological intolerance. The tendency toward dogmatism is inevitable. Both scientific work and education are conceived purely as processes of adaptation to the existing sociocultural and political structures. It is in this, more than in the physical process of eliminating professors, that the seriousness of the above measures and the liquidation of pluralism resides.

The suppression of university autonomy is reflected in the following measures:

—University authorities are named by the military *junta*. In turn they have been given the power to name lesser officials within the university.

—A major current of contemporary thought has been drastically eliminated.

—Financial autonomy has been restricted. Formally it is temporarily maintained until 1976, but it has suffered serious limitations.

—Obligatory university-level courses on national security have been created. Professors for these are named by the Ministry of Defense.[13]

The elimination of university autonomy is a direct consequence of the three elements analyzed above: the authoritarian model of government, the suspicion of intellectual labor, and the utilitarian and pragmatic concepts of science and education. Underlying the attempts to limit legal autonomy are the authoritarian values and ideological principles of totalitarianism. Underlying the elimination of a proper arena for scientific labor are technocratic values. Underlying the restrictions on financial autonomy are the liberal values of the marketplace and competition. Only those programs are maintained for which there is demand, whether by the state or by private enterprise. By this we mean a demand both for the "product" of education—the professional—and for investigation.

A university "serving change" and functioning as birthplace of social movements is replaced on the one hand by an efficient university serving the established order and on the other by student passivism and individualism. The measures adopted in this respect in one way or another have already been indicated. They aim toward creating a "professional" formation of social elites, forging a role for investigation that efficiently serves the demands of the state and private enterprise, and eliminating totally, except in the Catholic University, student organizations that might serve as a base for social movements. These are replaced by controlled associations of students, dedicated exclusively to recreation and, in some cases, to "student welfare."

These measures hold as supreme values the formal efficiency of the university, that is, its ability to adapt to the existing economic and sociocultural order. Consequently, they deny any critical role the university might have as a social conscience. They also encourage the values of passivity and individualism among students. The only permitted activities are professional studies, recreation, and, at times, paternalistic social work.

AN EVALUATION OF THE OVERALL UNIVERSITY POLICY

The principal points in the military *junta*'s university policy seem to be five: massive purification that eliminates academic personnel and students; incorporation of the university into the strategy of "national security"; order, discipline, and cleansing (emphasized in all public statements by the designated rectors as the most important achievement of the new authorities); regionalization directed toward forming regional divisions of the universities; and self-financing. It is easy to appreciate that the total effect of these policies is restrictive and repressive. This is most evident in the first three, which are precisely the principal purposes of military intervention in the universities and those on which most advance has been made. The last two appear directed over a long term toward university programs with greater content. Nevertheless, these five points have been characterized by indefiniteness, ambiguity, and lack of viability. Thus the initiatives and measures that form the *junta*'s university policy, because of their contradictions, have not all been fully materialized.

The policy seems to be derived from three sources. First is the attempt to submit the universities to a system of political, bureaucratic, administrative, and financial decision making that is characterized by absolute vertical command. At the same time the universities are included in a system of national security. Second is the need for ideological control in the universities, an expression of the overall intolerance of the political system. The third source is the need to strengthen the power of those political groups within the universities that have supported the military authorities. These three sources for the university policy are insuperably at odds with any authentic academic life or with the development of the universities' cultural role. Neither the submission to a system of external military-political decision making, nor ideological control and intolerance, nor the existence of conflicts among groups that can be resolved only by force and the support of military power are compatible with the development of scientific and intellectual labor.

CONCLUSIONS

The significance and consequences of the various values and principles that reign in the university today can be summarized as follows:

—The university has ceased to be a center for intellectual discussion and is no longer the place where society systematically elaborates alternative social programs based on scientific and technical knowledge.

—The moral climate of the universities has been reduced. The individualistic struggle to maintain one's employment and power position has lost all reference to curricula with ideological and cultural content. It has become exclusively a fight for the survival of privileges and for the sympathy of the enshrined military power.

—Although in isolated, minor areas serious scientific work survives, in general it has tended to disappear. Its ability to introduce new criteria into the sociocultural life of the country has been subordinated to the decisions of the political power (the state) and the economic power (free enterprise).

—The young find their opportunities for education reduced, a vacuum in their intellectual and spiritual formation, and an absence of channels for expression. This leaves them no alternative but competition for individual economic success and escapism or fanatical devotion to the dominant power. This reality has demanded a revitalization of the para-academic institutions for cultural formation that played an important role before the University Reform.

—Given its position and its unique functions in the life of the country, the university thus appears to prefigure a society in which the principles that guide intellectual and spiritual life are authority, discipline, anti-intellectualism, and intolerance. The general principle that underlies this new society is efficiency at the service of the goals and hallowed institutions of the dominant power.

Informal Education

Under the rubric of informal education we must consider both the so-called mass media (the press, radio, cinema, and television) and "agents of socialization" (the family, work groups, religious congregations, neighborhoods, etc.). Unfortunately, there is little information available on groups that act as socializing agents, and we can note only some general trends. Nevertheless, we believe these have considerable importance for an evaluation of the educational problem. For the mass media the situation is radically different. Their very character puts us in constant contact with them, and hence it is far easier to analyze their impact carefully.

1. Structural Conditions

Above all, we must keep in mind that the state today controls all the mass media, whether directly or through censorship or self-censorship. Under such conditions the problem of truth and information is radically transformed. Since there are no longer various sources of information from which to choose, one can only evaluate the apparent probability that information is true. Events, or one version of them, are presented as true long before one can confirm their veracity. Whether or not the people believe a particular account, it will be very difficult to discover the truth.

This monopolistic control of information is successful precisely because of the pluralistic nature of the mass media in the past. Previously, the individual believed the truth he himself discovered from the versions offered to him, the most dependable criterion being that consensus he might find among the differing media. Now uniformity of information inevitably creates consensus in every case. The reader finds it difficult to deny the truth of information repeated in the same form everywhere.

A problem that must preoccupy those who are concerned with education as a whole is individual isolation and atomization. It touches directly on the existence of groups that act as socializing agents, imparting knowledge, guides for conduct, and values. Here the activities of the state seek to eliminate social groups based on kinship, cooperation in work, neighborhood, religion, etc. The most likely goal is to form enormous mass organizations that will increase individual insecurity while permitting more easy manipulation.

Thus union and student organizations have been modified and secretariats of youth, women, and interest groups created. Discrepancies in the heart of religious organizations are encouraged. At the same time the ideology of the internal enemy—the negation of the opponent's condition as a citizen, a member of the nation, and almost as a human being—has deepened the crisis of the family. In many cases relatives have become irreconcilable enemies. Similarly, those called upon to denounce their neighbors or instill terror impede the normal evolution of neighborhood or friendship groups. We are not engaging in whimsy when we affirm a tendency toward individual isolation, an atomization of society into island-men. When all functions previously performed by these socializing groups are acquired by the state, individuals become open to domination without counterweight.

2. *The Content of Messages Transmitted*

What first draws attention in any perusal of the mass media today is the generalized search for what is essentially non-information. Political, social, labor, and economic news—relating to the most important problems of the population—has practically disappeared. It is present only on those occasions when it can be manipulated to support the activities of the government. The recent public debate over economic policy, or that between merchants and industrialists, does not disprove our conclusion, for it dealt with limited differences concerning how best to achieve official objectives.

In the few surviving newspapers, cinema newsreels, radio, and television, it is easy to confirm this profound lack of news. It almost seems that political or social events more important than the commemoration of some regiment or the presentation of some trophy or decoration no longer occur. Information has been replaced with the exaltation of public morbidity. The masses are given stories on crimes, orgies, sexual degradation, delicate intimacies, etc.

By exalting instinct and "base passions," this regression to morbidity seeks not only to replace news concerning social and political problems but also to lower the human condition to a level of animal irrationality. In turn, this reinforces and justifies a system based on the complete absence of human feeling. Although it is true that morbidity was always present in the Chilean press, today for two reasons it has acquired a unique new character. On the one hand, it is present in the midst of non-information and the "absence of significant problems"; on the other, it appears associated, as we will see, with a perception of the political enemies of the regime.

In this same spirit of non-information, it is possible to discern another significant characteristic. The basis of news becomes the constant and massive reiteration of trivial "daily events." These are not concerned with the problems faced daily by the population but rather with those activities most removed from such problems—for example, ways to occupy leisure time. Thus, greater attention is devoted to sporting events, spring parties, the election of beauty queens, commercial exhibits, popular singers, etc. In turn, this allows the media to emphasize "social normalcy, tranquility, and order"—necessary prerequisites for the development of these healthy activities.

Finally, there has been an enormous diffusion of products whose sole purpose is to entertain: soap operas, light cinema, magazines in newspapers, etc. The attempt is to distract, to withdraw the individual from a preoccupation with personal and social problems and to place him in an unreal world in which he is satisfied with carefully calculated psychological rewards.

Order, tranquility, and security are particularly relevant in the messages transmitted through the mass media. The idea itself is quite simple. Through constant repetition an effort is made to emphasize the contrast between yesterday's chaos and the order of today. The presence of the armed forces leading the state is a guarantee of this internal order. Internal order is reflected in the tranquility with which all the varied activities of life take place. The combination of order and tranquility provides security, and security has always been an appreciated value. Hence its reiterated emphasis also helps legitimate the new order. Nevertheless, the concept acquires a new and distinct meaning under present circumstances. Security has always been one of the basic supports of a state of law, but only as long as it has been expressed through and based upon juridical norms. Today's security results from an acceptance of arbitrary rule. "Order" is no more than armed force, and a person is "tranquil" insofar as he accepts the prescriptions of those with power. He cannot appeal decisions, nor are there any longer general rules to which power must also submit.

The ideology of competition versus solidarity is transmitted in government propaganda—through news releases, editorials, and the like—but it is also assimilated and conveyed in the commercial publicity of private enterprise. A liberalism more than Manchesterism has given rebirth to ideas and precepts of individual battle and competition. Only the best rise to the top; hence, those on the top are naturally the best. All human element has been eliminated from this extreme liberalism, a fact which has two important implications. First, it, too, legitimates privilege, while simultaneously transforming the frustration of those who did not "make it" into self-incrimination—if we did not, it was because of our own incapabilities or weaknesses. Second, the exacerbation of the "self" in confrontation with "others" reinforces the idea of struggle, a struggle in which a preoccupation with others—solidarity—would be a mistake and a weakness in the competitive race. The idea of struggle in all areas of life generates a warlike attitude that, at the level of politics, justifies both the destruction of the internal enemy and the need for external war.

In the cohesive message of the media there is a clear effort to define the political opponent as an "enemy," for repression becomes legitimate when the action or thought of opposition to the system is transformed into a "criminal act." Normal everyday activities become crimes, and even social gatherings are seen as criminal; the enemy is waiting in ambush (political meetings). What is prohibited or permitted has imprecise limits, subject to constant redefinition by those in power, who constantly keep in mind confrontation with and annihilation of the enemy. To justify this kind of activity the dehumanization of the opponent is crucial. The perverse "extremist," whose political acts are impregnated with criminal content—robbery, licentious living, drug trafficking, etc.—is no longer just "one of us with another idea of politics." He becomes another species, the incarnation of evil. A dichotomy is produced between the citizen, who is identified with honor, and the enemy, who is unworthy of the rights of citizenship.

In spite of constant reference to the order and normality of the present, the possibility and actual exercise of repression is constantly emphasized. Troop parades, massive arrests, prisoner transfers, concentration camps, deaths in confrontations, and the like occupy a privileged placed in the mass media. There are also hidden and open threats that the repressive apparatus will be drastically applied against anyone who does not appear to support the regime. Even the most minimal acts can justify repression, for, as we noted, they have been made criminal.

The emphasis on omnipresent repression and terror has an additional effect. Those who receive the message, for self-protection, must project these same pressures toward their peers. What occurs in the heart of the family is particularly dramatic. Parents must carefully watch what they say to their children (a form of self-censorship) so that the latter will not mistakenly utter dangerous ideas in public. Simultaneously, and for the same purpose, a warlike ideal is exalted to one's children, also as a way to "protect" the family group. This repressive climate functions at the level of both the family and the work group, and suspicion and fear prevail even in casual relations with third parties.

The idea of conspiracy is a classical characteristic of authoritarian systems. In Chile today propaganda and informal education in general distort historical reality by creating the idea that a group conspiracy is the single cause explaining the course of history. The "Communist conspiracy" plays the same role here that the "Jewish conspiracy" did in Germany. A realistic interpretation of the most varied events is twisted to fit the same comparative scheme. From the drug traffic to agreements in the United Nations, passing through poverty, forest fires, delinquency, price rises, production difficulties, external or religious criticism, etc., all are attributed to conspiratorial maneuvers by international communism. Reality is falsified; it is distorted by an ultra-simplification. At the same time, this distortion seeks to channel all the frustrations and resentments provoked by present difficulties toward an "enemy" who is the cause of all problems. His annihilation becomes absolutely necessary. Even the most passive begin to wish that he disappear—although mentally they block any understanding of what the disappearance of this enemy would really mean. Thus, the repression and terror against the "guilty ones" is justified, while, by definition, those who receive punishment are guilty.

The theory of conspiracy can lead to organizing the civilian population in an aggressive effort to "clean out" the enemy. Yet even when this does not occur, it is sufficient justification for the "hard liners" to celebrate each punishment inflicted upon that "enemy," while the mildest refuse to understand what is going on, deny its existence, or justify it by saying "there must be some reason"—*"por algo será."*

CONCLUSIONS

We have presented a general overview of the value system that dominates today in Chile and the way this system is reproduced and diffused. At this point a methodological observation is in order. Any schematic analysis such as this tends to give a consistency and coherence to values that, in practice, they do not always have. For a critical understanding of the logic underlying an ideological problem, this relative simplification is indispensable. However, one must keep in mind that in reality the complexity of social life is far greater.

We can now reply to three questions concerning the significance of the ideological program and value system we have described. The first refers to its specific and definitive character. It is not sufficient, in our judgment, to define such a system in terms of a character that hides and legitimates authoritarian politics or that distorts the use of traditional institutions. It is insufficient, therefore, to conclude that it requires no more than a "correction" that will limit the exaggerated use of power. Such a conception recognizes that the present system, in which all political power is passed to the state and all economic power to private interests, is distant from a totalitarian model. It preserves characteristics more typical of an authoritarian regime—one that the ideological and cultural system is called upon to legitimate and reproduce. In our judgment, this vision is only partially accurate. If it is true that the political model is somewhat ambiguous and preserves some traits that are not totalitarian, the system of values and ideological and cultural program are in their essence strictly totalitarian. What is sought is control over every kind of social and personal expression. The purpose is not simply to legitimate a system of authority. Rather it is to create structural conditions that will permit imposing on all persons and groups a type of behavior in which "dissidence" has no place. Totalitarian values can tolerate no expression or idea that differs from their own. On the one hand, such ideas are suppressed violently. On the other, the system seeks to generate behavior leading to an acritical acceptance of its own ideas. As the circumstances warrant, a great variety of resources can be applied to these tasks. This is the case, for example, in the institutionalization of routine obedience. Step by step, the ability to reject an order is broken, until obedience to any order, without discussion, becomes a matter of course. It is in this sense that the relevance of orders affecting cleanliness, personal appearance, hair length, and the like is clear.

In addition to certain political requisites, the viability of a totalitarian ideology depends on two conditions. First, those who hold other ideas must be physically repressed or, at a minimum, their opinions must be negated by some means that degrades their importance. Other ideas are not policies but "playing politics"; other ethical schemes are but "corruption and immorality." Similarly, the personal identity of the opponent must be degraded also. The politician is an ambitious person without scruples, the Marxist a common delinquent, and the delinquent a subhuman being. Second, a "totalitarian behavior," rejecting everything that is not officially accepted, accepting no diversity and denying humanity to those who are different, must be created. This requires abstract, ahistoric values, values that generate a mannequin mentality of a dogmatic nature. When emotions are exacerbated through the use of symbols, this mentality acquires irrational and even fanatical characteristics.

Behavior that denies the possibility of rational choice and distorts the essence of the social being (that is, the ability to accept others) becomes individually, socially, and politically pathological. A totalitarian ideology is necessarily born of pathological circumstances. But for such an ideology to be permanently projected from a position of power requires that these pathological conditions be maintained. Only in this way can the manipulation of the individual, an essential element in the totalitarian concept, be made viable.

Two clarifications are necessary. First, the ideological program we have considered is a principle that is independent of the good or bad motives of those who impose it. It cannot be dismissed as an arbitrary imputation without basis in the consciousness or will of its originators. Second, although there is no coherent totalitarian ideology and value system, and although there are internal inconsistencies (for example, the need to create "political apathy" while simultaneously generating expressive social support for the government, or the latent contradictory ideological visions), these do not detract from the nature of the system or from its tendencies and dangers. On the contrary, they explain its constant resort to repression. What they indicate, negatively, is the absence, in spite of all the efforts, of certain necessary requisites for the definitive creation of a totalitarian system. Thus, there is no single, monopolistic party nor, in its absence, the militarization of civil society. Positively, they indicate the presence of resistance, both within the population and in relevant spiritual and cultural social institutions.

The second question asks what role or function the ideological and cultural value system plays in relation to society as a whole and to particular social sectors. We start with an image of the two worlds existing in Chile today. One is formed by all those who suffer economic misery and political repression as well as those who, because of their contact with the first, understand what this implies. The other is formed by all those who, in "good conscience," think there is absolute normality and order in Chile. For this second world, economic misery and political repression are an inevitable evil, and selective blindness a necessary response to international communism. They cannot understand the true conditions under which the first world of Chileans live, for to do so would be unacceptable and intolerable. It would signify the collapse of the social-psychological world and entail questioning their own identities. The major social function of the ideological and cultural program we have analyzed is to maintain the barrier between these two worlds, reinforcing the "good conscience" of the second and justifying the world of lies in which they live. Any knowledge and understanding of reality is blocked through an appeal to abstract and absolute values and a Manichaean vision of the world.

One can examine the social significance of the dominant value system from yet another perspective. We cannot deny the existence today of an economic crisis. Nor can we deny the political crisis. Nevertheless, unless these are lived as daily crises, neither can give rise to massive resistance movements such as those that existed in various sectors of the population during the last regime. Today the sector that personally feels these daily crises is the principal object of physical repression. The creative element of public opinion (that is, the middle classes) has a series of social-psychological mechanisms that keep it from internalizing the social crisis on an individual basis. Thus the middle sectors can avoid by ideological sublimation confronting the crises of daily life until they reach certain physical limits. Another of the functions of the value system and the means by which it is reproduced and diffused is to block any global and general internalization of the economic and political crisis, to bring into action psychological evasive mechanisms, and to project guilt upon enemies via abstract values, fear of the past, and naive confidence in a great future.

From a third perspective, the ideological system serves as a substitute for a political model that does not provide mechanisms for expression and participation. The growing weakness of the military regime's political support forces the government to reinforce the legitimating role of the value system. To this end, the symbols and means of communication of educational institutions and the control over all forms of social organization are manipulated. Ideological and cultural domination is thus a reflection of the political weakness of the regime and a mechanism for replacing political support. Its end is to legitimate existing power, and its basis is a massive internalization by the population of the idea that there is "institutional normality." The idea is inculcated that social problems disappeared with Marxism and "playing politics." The future only depends on efficiency, order, and discipline.

To whom is an ideological and cultural program such as that

we have described principally directed? We believe it is aimed particularly at that vast conglomerate of individuals and groups known as the middle classes. By their nature and the particular characteristics they assume in Chile, they are particularly sensitive to ideological mechanisms. These operate upon them with relative independence from their economic base. Against the masses in contrast, repression and police methods acquire preponderance over ideological and cultural instruments. Among the working classes control is achieved by keeping individuals at minimum levels of physical subsistence and by physical repression. Terror plays the manipulative role *par excellence.* Propaganda is complementary to and reinforces terror but is not essential. For the middle sectors, where ideological control plays the principal role, propaganda is the key mechanism and terror is complementary.

The means by which ideology is manipulated are easily comprehended. However, we must remember the attitude of the middle classes prior to 1973, an attitude that to a great extent made possible the ascent of the current governing group. First, the middle classes anticipated great social restiveness and loss of security for the immediate future. They felt menaced by possibilities previously unimagined. Individual and collective insecurity was increased in a situation of growing abnormality. Second, they felt endangered by the aggressive advance of other social groups. Not only did the middle sectors perceive a threat to their economic situation; they also failed to comprehend a process which they felt threatened their very survival. Third, as a result of the first two fears, they came to reject politics in its traditional sense. Normal political activities were seen as impossible or ineffective. They lost faith in their ability to participate in decision making. They came to encourage the intervention of extra-political forces, a fact which contributed to increasing their sense of abnormality and insecurity. Today these feelings and activities (in part a cause of the present conditions) are manipulated. Their causal link with the governing group is broken, and they are diverted toward the prior enemy, who is present but hidden. This manipulation is a condition for the power that was thus generated to maintain itself. It is for this reason that the great mass of the middle classes becomes the principal target of the dominant ideological and cultural program.

Finally, the viability of an ideological and cultural program such as that described demands a parallel process of individual atomization. All social organizations that are not controlled by those with political power must disappear. Each individual must be isolated from all others. Even free interpersonal communication appears threatened. Thus the individual's acritical receptivity to official values will be increased. In turn, this will facilitate his incorporation into the massive organizations controlled by the state.

We are left with one last question. What meaning and consequences can a value system such as the one described have for society? Three consequences seem most relevant to us. First, there is likely to be a general reduction in the collective moral level. A number of elements tend to degrade the moral climate of a society and corrupt its members: the conscious or unconscious acceptance of massive repression and violent acts produced by men as something inevitable and a lesser evil; a Manichaean vision of society and the world; intolerance toward other visions of man and society and toward those who hold such visions; refusal to accept reality under the pretext that it is no more than an invention of the enemy; efficiency and competition as the maximum motives of social life; servile attitudes toward armed force and an acritical acceptance of official truth. In a cultural process such as this, all of society, including its highest and most respectable institutions, is degraded and reduced in moral quality.

Second is the problem of the formation of a new generation. A youth who sees educational possibilities restricted by the imposition of a restrictive and elitist model at all levels of education; whose intellectual formation is directed toward individual economic success, does not respond to its intellectual curiosity, and is imparted through authoritarian mechanisms; and that has no way to express itself or participate in the political life of its country, runs a grave risk of falling into an escapism manifested by a massive increase in drug addiction and alcoholism or the acceptance of imported styles and stereotypes. According to the official press, this is what is happening in Chile today. The opposite danger is the fanaticizing of youth in the service of organizations controlled by the state. Both phenomena can occur simultaneously in different social strata—as in effect it is beginning to occur.

Third, as a result of all this, a value and cultural system such as that we have described prepares and teaches the population only one kind of political order and socioeconomic scheme. Unlike a pluralistic or open value system, one that permits the population to accept freely diverse social programs and political alternatives, in Chile today mental barriers are erected to block the implementation of any future alternative policies. The present system of values, and the ways it is communicated, creates conditions designed exclusively to maintain and reproduce authoritarianism.

NOTES

1. Clauses from Decree 1.892 of November, 1973, which created a commission to evaluate educational reform.

2. "La Educación en las Líneas Generales de Acción del Gobierno," *El Mercurio* (June 15, 1974), p. 33. We should also cite the words of the President of the *junta* on the occasion of the anniversary of the General Secretariat of Youth: "One of the most fundamental vehicles of this moral resurgence is education. It logically follows that the present government has decided to replace totally the Marxist 'conscientization' of youth with a nationalist formation of free men and women." *El Mercurio* (October 20, 1974).

3. *El Mercurio* (October 1, 1973), p. 21.

4. "Second year of secondary education. In the IV unit the following are divisive: The Human Profile of Latin America, Title II, the Characteristics of the Social Structure. In Title III, the contents of No. 3, Social Reforms, particularly the examples that are not taken from Chile.

Third Year of Humanist Secondary Education: the Section on inflation should consider it as a worldwide phenomenon, and the concepts and examples should be at a general level.

Fourth Year of Humanist Secondary Education. Second Unit. Contemporary World History. The Industrial Revolution should be considered, as indicated by its title, in its aspects of scientific and technical change, eliminating the theories and conflicts that lend themselves to social and political discussions which have already been sufficiently publicized. In the [section on] Political Revolution it is not convenient to consider point III, 'The Forces of the West and the Triumph of European Civilization in the World,' and point IV, 'The Crisis of the West and the end of European Hegemony.'

Political Science. The Second Section: 'The Doctrines and new Political Forms' has already been too much publicized; it should not be considered. The Third Section. The Political Institutions of Chile. It is convenient to emphasize that our institutions have not died; some are in recess, and the events through which we have lived had the final objective of their preservation; documentation is very precise on this point and can easily be found. Considerable professionalism and even-handedness is necessary to focus on these problems. If the theme is not considered in this fashion, it is preferable not to consider it, or to replace it with the following instructions by the Minister.

In the section dealing with the 'Problems of Today's World,' although the theme is divisive, its development depends on the skill and ethics of the professor." *El Mercurio*, October 18, 1973.

5. The Director of Primary and Normal Education stated on September 25, 1973, "Conscienticizing texts are being withdrawn from circulation in the high schools in order to be burned. We cannot permit the student's

mind to be poisoned with texts that lead to nothing." The Offices of Primary, Secondary, and Professional Education hurried to instruct school principals that "they should withdraw all texts and didactic material that in one way or another contain materials tending to conscienticize the student in different ideologies." *El Mercurio* (September 25, 1973, and October 1, 1973).

6. The general objectives of the September week are particularly illustrative. They are formulated in the following fashion:

"Revive in the student one of the most noble sentiments of mankind: love for the fatherland.

"Recognize, place value on, and enrich the basic principles that form our nationality, such as, 'a love for the history and cultural tradition that unites us.'

"Strengthen national unity as a goal for the integral development of the country. This begins with the interaction between school and community, at both a local and regional level.

"Place value on nature in Chile as a basic element in the future development of the country.

"Stimulate the creativity and dynamic participation of the student. Begin with geographic and cultural reality as a way to help him identify responsibly with Chile and its future.

"Emphasize the positive activity of our Army in the historical development of Chile."

Superintendency of Education, "Documento normativo de orientación general para la segunda semana de Actividades Para-academicas." September 11–17, 1974.

7. It is worth transcribing those materials the headmaster must submit for consideration by the Commander of Military Institutes.

"Confirmed denunciations of professors, aides, or administrative personnel under his direct command who in their classes or activities do any of the following:

—Comment on current politics.

—Propagate evil-intentioned rumors concerning the activities of the government or extremist groups.

—Propagate jokes or stories relating to the activities of the *Junta* or its members.

—Distort patriotic concepts or values.

—Distort the ideas contained in study texts, giving them whimsical or partial interpretations.

—Do not fulfill work hours or programs.

—Propose or hold meetings, within or outside of the school, without the corresponding authorization of the Military Authority.

—Do not rapidly and effectively fulfill regulations emanating from the Ministry of Education or from the Military Authority, particularly those relating to the exaltation of patriotic values.

—Propose ideas pressuring directors or presidents of organizations such as Student Centers, Parents' Centers, or Teachers' Centers, or any other organization authorized by the Ministry, to introduce a system of voting to elect its component members, according to partisan purposes now irradicated.

—Any other deed that indicates a clear intent to interrupt, make difficult, block, distort, dislocate, or undermine discipline or to alter the normal development of educational activity by students at any level.

Confirmed denunciations of students or parents who, in their activities inside the school or in Parents' Centers, promote or carry out any of
the above mentioned activities."

They add, in addition, that "all omissions or lack of decisiveness in
relation to the activities summarized above and any delay in bringing
account to the Military Authorities will be the exclusive responsibility of
the headmaster." It is also interesting to note that the circular emphasizes
the authority of the director of the school, giving him power to suspend
both students and teachers.

8. A most typical case is that of the *Colegio Saint George,* in which a
number of priests and professors were expelled and a military interventor
was named to take charge of the school. In response, the Congregation of
the Holy Cross, owners of the high school, ordered all the priests to
resign. The school's future is still in doubt. These measures applied to the
Colegio Saint George indicate that all private establishments have to be
on the alert, for any deviation from official policies can give rise to similar
measures.

9. The Minister of Education, Admiral Hugo Castro, declared at that
time that the "measure was adopted so that the students could better take
advantage of their time by dedicating themselves exclusively to their
classes for the remainder of the present year." *El Mercurio* (October 7,
1973), p. 37.

10. *El Mercurio* (December 21, 1973), p. 37.

11. An invitation to attend a meeting of the Parents' Center of the private
high school of Santa Rita illustrates how extensively these are controlled.
It was extended "by order of the Commander of Military Institutes, General of Brigade, don Nilo Floody Buxter," and ends with the following
exact phrase, "Non-fulfillment of the present summons will be more than
sufficient cause to proceed with your immediate detention."

12. A report of the Faculty of Physical Sciences and Mathematics finds
that the exodus has increased since 1973 from four to six per month. The
Subcommission on Basic Sciences of the Council of Rectors in June of
this year noted that of the 228 investigators who have left the country
since 1971, 165 left after Sept. 1973. From a qualitative point of view, this
exodus has left various areas of importance in the sciences without any
personnel.

13. In Memorandum no. 127–2 of 1974, the Minister of Education (an
admiral in active service) proposed to the Minister of Defense (an army
general in active service) a program of studies on National Security, to be
established in all schools in Chile. In the university, the program consists
of two cycles, one theoretical and the other practical. The first consists of
an obligatory course, "National Security and National Defense," whose
objective is "to form a consciousness in future professionals of the multiple
threats to the life of the State." In the section "Threats to the integrity of
the State," the program includes three points: "subversion," "political de-
viations," and "others." The practical cycle consists of "attendance at a

National Security garrison, installation, or unit for a minimal period of three months. . . . To fulfill the program of Defense at this level, the Council of Rectors and the representatives of the Ministry of Defense that you designate will undertake studies to put this course into practice, contracting professors, etc."

The program was elaborated by a committee on which the universities were not represented. There were delegates from the "Ministry of Education, the Army, the Navy, the Air Force, the Police, and the Heads of Staff of National Defense."

In September, 1974, the Minister of Defense, General Bonilla, and Rector Swett of the Catholic University signed an agreement by which their respective institutions promised to implement a pilot project on the courses of Security and National Defense. This is now being done and is based in the Faculty of Engineering Sciences.

Chile, 1973/Spain, 1936: Similarities and Differences in the Breakdown of Democracy*

HENRY A. LANDSBERGER
JUAN J. LINZ

INTRODUCTION

Drawing parallels between Chile and other parts of the world of more self-evident historical importance far antedates any retrospective analysis of the 1973 *coup*. Indeed, Chile's exceptionally stable parliamentary system, and her general bourgeois political civility, had caused many people (including Chileans themselves) to look upon her citizens as "the English of South America," especially since an influential British "colony" did indeed live there, and since the Chilean Navy, at least until the end of World War II had patterned itself after the British, up to and including its uniforms. The Prussian influence on the army—up to and including

---

* This contribution, both insofar as much of its general conceptualization and specifically insofar as events in Spain are concerned, relies considerably on two essays by Juan Linz, "Crisis, Breakdown and Reequilibration of Competitive Democracies" and "From Great Hopes to Civil War: The Breakdown of Democracy in Spain." These have been published in volumes edited jointly by Juan Linz and Alfred Stepan (eds.), *The Breakdown of Democratic Regimes*. From Linz's extensive bibliographies, only Gerald Brenan's *The Spanish Labyrinth* (Cambridge: Cambridge University Press, 1950) and Hugh Thomas' *The Spanish Civil War* (New York: Harper and Row, 1963) are occasionally cited in this chapter, as being among the most systematic, balanced, and, at least for English readers, the most accessible accounts of the antecedents of the Spanish Civil War. Both Chile and Spain have produced an enormous literature. But to keep the style of this chapter congruent with that of the remainder of the book, it seemed inappropriate to weigh it down with frequent citations, especially since the events on which we base our interpretations are relatively well-known and, in themselves, noncontroversial.

the shape of the steel helmet, martial music, and goose step—had also been noted, but generally with a more cautious pride and a less relaxed smile. Chile's unquestioned efficiency had always been tempered with more humor than one associates with Prussia. More positively, the highly developed social conscience of a significant sector of the Catholic Church (clerical but, above all, lay) had spurred *La Unión* of Valparaíso to call Chile "the Belgium of South America" as early as 1910. (Belgium had been among the leading European countries in which, in the late nineteenth century, progressive Catholicism had attempted to vie for working-class allegiance against the obvious success of various streams of socialist thought.)

But as social tensions mounted from the early 1960s onward (the failure, in 1961, of President Alessandri's price stabilization program is, at least in retrospect, as good a marker as any for the rising curve of tension) the historical parallels became more specific, and more poignant. Not only did the right, from 1964 onwards, use the argument that Chile *might* in the immediate future go the way of Cuba, but ex-President Frei *was actually seen* as "the Kerensky of Chile"—again, by the right, which accused him of a mismanaged, chaotic reformism and a dangerous tolerance of left-wing violence. In the eyes of the right, he had opened the door to Chile's equivalent of Bolshevism—i.e., the *Unidad Popular.* President Azaña had been accused by the Spanish right, throughout 1936, of being Spain's Kerensky.

The parallel with the Russian revolution seems to have been taken up during cocktail banter in a mostly tongue-in-cheek fashion (i.e., in a manner of pretended seriousness only in order to ridicule it) by those sophisticated intellectuals and professionals in the *Unidad Popular* who were knowledgeable about world history. But as it became clearer that the *vía chilena* might well have a tragic end (and to many, this possibility was apparent at least by the beginning of 1973), local actors began to be cast in the ominous roles of figures from the Republican Spain of the 1930s rather than in the more optimistic ones of Russia at the time of the revolution. Senator Carlos Altamirano, the guiding spirit of the left wing of the Socialist party, who had been compared to Lenin, was now recast as Francisco Largo Caballero, one of the two leaders of the Spanish Socialists (*Partido Socialista Obrero Español*, PSOE), who, in contrast with the more moderate Indalecio Prieto, had the PSOE veer to an ever more polarized, extreme position, fundamentally uninterested in compromises which might have helped to preserve Spain's republican institutional framework.

The parallel between these two tragedies, those of Chile and Spain, is indeed a saddeningly enlightening one. It clarifies further—though never totally—the forces at work in each; and it clarifies also, at a more abstract level, what can and what cannot be expected from historical parallels, and how they can be fruitfully used.

The fruitful use of parallels does not, of course, consist in highlighting only what is similar in two situations, let alone doing so at the relatively trivial level of finding names which can be substituted for each other. It consists also of drawing attention to (1) elements which really have no parallel whatever (regional nationalism, so important in Spain, played no part in Chile); and (2) factors which were present in very different degrees, or which may have had an impact in one setting that was actually the reverse of the impact in the other. Thus, the Chilean Catholic Church or, more accurately, the predominant strongly progressive stream within it, played and was almost unanimously perceived as playing a conciliatory, moderating role in Chile—very different from the role of the Church in Spain.

Even at the level of actors, the more fruitful approach is not that of finding specific individuals who can be completely matched with each other. Rather, we should think in terms of the roles that actors played, their functions, and the relationships between them, in the complex process which characterizes the breakdown of democracy. It is not particularly fruitful to pursue the question of whether or not Eduardo Frei can be equated with Manuel Azaña (since both had been cast in the role of "Kerensky") or with Alejandro Lerroux, the leader of the Spanish Radical party whose drift to the right was among the factors making the left uninterested in seeking a compromise with his party, its closest neighbor on the right.

What is important is to understand that the fateful process of polarization and the disappearance of the center is often embodied and symbolized by movements in the position of certain key individuals and of consequent changes in the relations between these individuals. As ex-President Frei moved, or at least was perceived as moving (and that is what counted), to the right, and as Dr. Allende's ultimate commitment to defend the Constitution against threats from the extreme left was beginning to be questioned (again, rightly or wrongly), relations between the two, which had once been good, deteriorated. And that process is, in principle, paralleled by the mutual perception of each other's position by Lerroux and Azaña respectively and the resulting fateful deterioration in their relationship and, of course, in the relationship between their parties. Others who attempt, as individuals, to mediate and stay in some kind of middle ground suffer a relative erosion of support and consequently do not even figure as major individual actors on the scene in the last stages of the disintegrative process. Prieto, the Socialist, was in that position in Spain, and so were several distinguished Christian Democrats in Chile.

Process, function, and role, often more meaningfully studied at the level of parties, organizations, and institutions rather than at the level of individuals and certainly not in terms of specific names and formal characteristics: these are what matter. In some situations, Indalecio Prieto's role was played by Radomiro Tomić, in others, Prieto was, of course, equivalent to Dr. Allende, the evidently more conciliatory Socialist in relation to Senator Altamirano, who was indeed rather obviously Chile's Largo Caballero. We shall find, altogether, that similarities are stronger at the level of processes, and of subtle ones at that, than at the more superficial level of names or even formal issues. For that reason, we shall first emphasize, although already with certain *caveats*, certain differences between the Spanish and Chilean situations, before going on to those similarities in structure and process which we believe to be much more significant.

MAJOR DIFFERENCES

The long-term historical context in which the breakdown of Chilean democracy occurred was, in at least three major respects, very different from that which we customarily associate with such disintegration in Latin America and in Europe, and especially in Spain. Chile had had an almost unbroken record of constitutional governments for over 130 years; during that period, newly emerging classes had been admitted into the political system with comparative smoothness and speed; and the entire process had been characterized by exceptionally little violence. These three characteristics are interrelated: the absence of violence and the (relative) continuity in constitutional civilian government were presumably the positive consequences of the system's flexibility in admitting new "power contenders" relatively soon after they emerged.

Above all, formal constitutional democracy in Chile had evolved smoothly with but minor interruptions from 1830 onwards. The brief civil war of 1891, which did have overtones of social class confrontation and certainly of the influence of foreign capitalism, and the military interregnum from 1924 to 1931 were, however, not traumatic enought to leave lasting divisions behind, although the suicide of President Balmaceda in 1891 is said to have been very frequently in Dr. Allende's mind. From 1920 onwards the system had given access, however slowly, to ever larger proportions and to ever more diverse sections of the Chilean population. Indeed, the dramatically accelerated mobilization and inclusion in the political process of different groups from 1965 onward was one of the factors often adduced as being involved in the breakdown, albeit in complex and indirect ways. But however that may be, and we shall analyze the point further, Chile was not at all a country in which constitutional democracy had been but weakly and recently established, as could be said of Peru and Brazil in the 1960s, of the Weimar Republic and Austria in the 1930s, and, above all, of Spain. After all, the Second Republic had been institutionalized in Spain a mere five years before the revolt of the army in July, 1936.

Admittedly, one can overdraw the peacefulness and stability of Chilean democracy. That democratic stability of the Chilean system was, after all, briefly interrupted both in 1891 and between 1924 and 1931. But the military-inspired regimes of 1924–1931 were not severely repressive but, on the contrary, were partly responsible for the establishment of various progressive social measures and for the admission of certain social classes to the political system. There is indeed something of a parallel in this respect with the friendly policy, at exactly this same time, of Primo de Rivera toward the Socialist party in Spain and especially toward its trade union wing, the *Unión General de Trabajadores.*

But despite these progressive tendencies, the 1924–1931 period in Chile needs to be noted as a break in its democratic tradition. It foreshadows the proscription and severe repression of the Communist party and of Communist trade union leaders between 1948 and 1957, while Socialists were tolerated or even encouraged, because Communists were considered to be a revolutionary threat much as the Anarchists and their trade union federation (CNT) had been considered to be by Primo de Rivera in the period 1923–1931 while he was flirting with Socialists. In Chile, the proscription was the act of a centrist Radical party drifting to the right, much as the Spanish Radical party had done before it. The act of repression was not repeated in the late 1960s by the then successor of the Radical party in the center of Chilean politics, the Christian Democratic party, which might have copied it in relation to the revolutionary successor of the Communist party, the *Movimiento de Izquierda Revolucionaria* (MIR). Indeed, the Christian Democrats were much criticized by the right for not proceeding vigorously. It was the MIR itself which went underground in 1969.

At a more substantive level than that of the merely formal, the Chilean system was also not quite as open to the admission of the "lower classes" as might appear. The peasantry was not, *de facto*, free to vote until certain changes in the electoral laws were made in the late 1950s and mid 1960s. It did not become a politically important factor until the latter date and even then more as a mass following of various ideological currents and elites than as an independent actor. And both the peasantry and other "marginal groups" (the urban underemployed, especially recent migrants from rural areas) were underprivileged in the substantive economic and social benefits they received from the political system in the form of housing, health care, income maintenance, and so forth. Nor did they have organizations available to them which could articulate their demands vigorously. Very significantly, however, there were no indications prior to this time—i.e., prior to the mid-1960s—that these groups had reached a level of consciousness and psychological mobilization which might have left them deeply embittered against the system because of their relative exclusion from it. Exactly why such passive acceptance of underprivilege should have prevailed is very difficult to explain. Was it that the management of the Chilean social and economic system by its oligarchic elites, supplemented by the middle class, never was objectively as totally selfish, and on occasion corrupt and brutal, as was that of Spain? Or was it a matter of difference in national temperament and tradition—factors which Brenan so much employs to explain both the far more selfish policies (or absence of policies) of the Spanish elites in the first place and the much more violent reaction of the Spanish masses to it?

But whatever the explanation, all the evidence, from studies emanating from the left as well as others, shows that while these underprivileged groups were, of course, intensely desirous to improve their standards of living, both material and spiritual, and wanted to change those parts of the system which it might be necessary to change to improve their lot, they were not fundamentally alienated from the system and certainly did not wish to overthrow it by violence.

Another characteristic distinguishing the two countries, as we have mentioned, is the far lower level of actual violence in Chil-

ean history. Of course, the history of no country is free from
bloodshed. The massacre of nitrate miners and their families in
the north of Chile in 1907 is proof of this, as is the less well known
confrontation in the outskirts of Santiago as late as 1957 between
the army and a heterogeneous group of persons who were essentially protesting the severe deflationary measures on which the
government of the time had embarked (on American advice!). We
will have more to say about the increasing rhythm of violence in
Chile in the years more immediately preceding the army *coup* of
1973. But none of this can even remotely compare to the level of
violence which had been characteristic of Spain from the end of
the Napoleonic period onward, i.e., from the beginning of the
attempt to make it democratic.

In the period between the Bourbon restoration of 1875 and
the establishment of the Second Republic in 1931, violence was
endemic in Spain at a level which Chile did not approximate by
any stretch of the imagination, except in the massacre in Iquique.
Three prime ministers were assassinated between 1897 and 1921,
and so were church dignitaries and army officers—and, of course,
countless workers and peasants. In 1909, during the *semana
trágica,* there were over two hundred deaths, and later, in Catalonia between January, 1919, and December, 1923, there were hundreds of assassinations. Police torture in the 1890s provoked public outcry in Paris and London—a gloomy parallel to Chile today
which reminds us that such behavior is far less unusual than we
would like to think.

This violence was symptomatic of a situation which, insofar as
the mobilization of masses and their admission to the political
system was concerned, thus differed considerably from that of
Chile. Various "mass" groups (especially the very heterogeneous
peasantry) were much more class-conscious and more ready to act
in unison than was the case in Chile. Spain's peasantry, partly
under Anarchist guidance, had reached a higher level of organization in the first decade of the twentieth century than the Chilean
peasantry would reach until the early 1970s. And Spain's industrial working class was perhaps twenty years ahead of the Chilean
if the widespread strikes during the first part of the century, and
especially from 1910 onward, are taken as an indication.

The incorporation into Spain's post-restoration political system of the urban working classes, but above all of various rural
masses, encountered much greater resistance than it did in Chile
and was accompanied by much more violence. Various factors
contributed to this. There was the fierce rivalry between socialists

and syndicalists and there were the peculiarities of the situation in
Barcelona, where class conflicts were related in complex ways to
the issue of regionalism as posed by the Catalan bourgeoisie. Social tensions were also aggravated in Spain by colonial conflicts,
especially the Moroccan War and the fiscal crisis of the state.
None of these had any parallels in Chile. Hence in 1923, before a
democratic evolution with some degree of institutional continuity
was possible, the restoration regime essentially collapsed. When
the system of *caciquismo* disintegrated during the elections of
1923, some of the leaders of the traditional dynastic parties
wanted to deal with the growing discontent of the lower classes
and with the protest of sectors of the middle classes. But the system could not cope. The proclamation of the Republic in 1931,
and the rapid and extensive mobilization which accompanied it at
this rather inopportune historical moment, contrasts sharply with
the slower and more continuous evolution of the Chilean political
system.

In sum, Chile had urban and rural masses which were, admittedly, far from ideally incorporated into what appeared to be, on
the surface, a pure democracy. But the degree of their resentment
seemed to be far from intense, when viewed from an international
comparative perspective. When the masses did begin to stir—e.g.,
participate in land invasions and factory takeovers in the late
1960s and early 1970s—the interpretation even by their antagonists was likely to be that they had been misled by outside agita-
tors rather than that they constituted an independently acting,
self-confident revolutionary mass. In Spain, on the other hand, the
degree to which mass organizations were allowed to exist or, better, insisted on existing was historically much greater than in
Chile. And their antagonists were much more likely to recognize
that over and beyond the agitation of counter-elites, these groups
were acting independently on the basis of aims they themselves
had formulated. But for all their activism, the results they obtained
were meager, and partly for this reason, these masses were much
more intensely alienated from all political systems, including the
Second Republic.

The posture of the traditional right in each country was comparable to that of their respective lefts and relatively dissimilar
from each other. The Spanish Church and Catholics in general
(especially after the anticlerical outbreaks in the first year of the
Second Republic) never accepted fully an institutional system
they associated with policies fundamentally hostile to themselves.
And the same could be said of large land owners and, indeed, of

many middle peasants. The Second Republic was born in an atmosphere of anticlericalism and a general, if vague, left tenor with a specific threat to those who owned land. The affected groups, not unnaturally, equated the republican system with its specific early policies and, as a consequence, had as many reservations about the former (democratic republicanism as a system) as about the latter.

The omnious symbolic equivalent in Chile of merging the basic elements of the Constitution with a policy of a specific government came precisely at the beginning of the UP regime. Newly elected President Allende, in one of those many moments when the more radical strand of this thought dominated, declared defiantly that, unlike other Presidents, he was "not the President of all Chileans"—a phrase with which the right would haunt him from then on. It was the exact Chilean equivalent of the cry of the Spanish left after the establishment of the Republic in 1931: "The Republic [exists only] for republicans." To this, hostile landowners would later reply, as they evicted thousands of peasants in the final years of the Republic, "Let them eat Republic." Did Dr. Allende give a different meaning to the statement from the way it was interpreted? Did the right purposely give the statement a meaning it did not have, as an excuse to justify its own behavior? Chilean politics, like Spanish politics before, was to consist of these kinds of dangerous ambiguities, of partly real and partly pretended threats and perceptions of threat. And it was these aspects of the disintegrating process, not only much of the objective political structure, which the two countries had in common.

Let us, however, draw one important conclusion from the difference between a Chile which, until at least 1965, appeared to most if not all observers a constitutionally highly stable, democratic, and nonviolent society and its Spanish opposite. Quite simply, the case of Chile indicates tragically that the danger of breakdown is not confined to countries that have self-evidently and obviously always been unstable. The Chilean case indicates that stability, nonviolence, and both formal and (a good deal of) real democracy in the past do not guarantee their continuation even in the most immediate historic future.

SIMILARITIES IN STRUCTURE

The most apparent similarity between Chile and the Second Republic is to be found in the posture of the various political parties that composed the ideological spectrum in each country and, further, in the moving and shifting of their positions as polarization increased.

Governments and Parties

Let us note at the outset that the two changes in political orientation which the Republican governments underwent in Spain in the period of 1931–1936 were very similar to those which Chilean governments manifested in the period 1964–1973.

Just as the fall of the Spanish monarchy in 1931 brought forth a progressive but definitely not revolutionary regime beneath which an immense amount of militant mobilization got under way, so too did the election of President Frei in Chile in 1964, which ended the conservative regime of Jorge Alessandri. And just as in Spain, a reorientation in policy—i.e., a shift toward the right—marked the period 1933–1935 when the Left-Republicans under Manuel Azaña were replaced by the Right-Republicans under Alejandro Lerroux and Ricardo Samper (the so-called *bienio-negro*), so did President Frei's government see itself obliged to slow down the speed with which it attempted to change the structure of the economy and the degree to which it wished to remove controls from the continuing process of mass mobilization, stimulated in part by the extreme left. It is from most points of view quite inappropriate to compare the bloodily repressed revolutionary mass uprisings of October, 1934, in Catalonia, Madrid, and Asturias, with their many thousands of dead, with the confrontation in Puerto Montt between *carabineros* and squatters, resulting in a casualty list of nine. Nevertheless, their significance was similar in one important respect. The draconic official reaction to these popular uprisings, especially in the case of the revolutionary outbreak in Asturias, resulted in the permanent alienation of the extreme left and in a leftward shift of other political sectors. This, together with the not totally unjustifiable anxiety of the more privileged and conservative sectors, produced from 1934 onwards a polarization which finally carried with it a failure to support constitutional democratic institutions based on tolerance and compromise.

The conservative reaction of the second stage (much less pronounced in Chile than in Spain and much less bloody, as we have already noted) was followed in both countries by a third stage which represented a swing to the left far more extreme than that represented by the first. The Popular Front elected in Spain in

February, 1936, and especially the forces supporting it from outside the government, was obviously well to the left of the Azaña governments of the 1931–1933 Constituent *Cortes*. And similarly the *Unidad Popular* elected in 1970 was obviously to the left of Frei's first stage.

In both countries, but more in Chile than in Spain, the enthusiasms generated in the victors by the triumph of a Marxist coalition and the debacle of the center obscured to some extent the fact that the right was regathering strength after a period in which its imminent death had been widely prophesied. In Spain, the polarization between the Popular Front and the forces of the right was much greater. The Spanish Popular Front obtained almost 50 per cent of the vote (whereas the Chilean UP obtained only 36.3 per cent) and, with it, 60 per cent of the seats in Parliament—an absolute majority which the Chilean left never achieved. The Spanish center practically disappeared, above all in the *Cortes,* especially with the disintegration of the Radical party, which saw the number of its deputies reduced from one hundred to four. On the other hand the candidates of the Spanish right (CEDA, *Renovación y Tradicionalistas*) obtained 31 per cent of the vote. In Chile, Christian Democrats (centrist) and the right represented by the *Partido Nacional* divided the vote much more evenly: 27 per cent and 34 per cent respectively in the 1970 election. In Spain the center was not only much weaker in terms of electoral support but was much more divided as compared with the relative unity of the Christian Democrats. The *Unidad Popular,* on the other hand, began its term in office with a level of popular support far below that achieved by the *Frente Popular* in Spain—yet with a program far more explicitly radical than that of Spain.

We shall return later to the ominous fact that Chile ended in the same kind of tragedy as did Spain despite the fact that its center, while it may have been weaker than in 1964, was immeasurably stronger than Spain's ever was, and that its right was far weaker than Spain's and so, indeed, was its left. Hence compromise without a breach in the institutional structure should have been possible. Yet it did not occur. Instead, the government, and the political system as a whole, lost control of events in much the same way as in Spain. Relative to its *own* history, Chile was admittedly in a much more anarchic state in 1973 than Spain was relative to *its* history. But in relation to Spain, the Chilean situation was peacefulness itself. Yet the army rose up against the government in both cases. The speed with which it succeeded in Chile, as compared with three years of civil war in Spain, was due to the fact that the left was indeed not as strong as it was in Spain. It did not have the backing of as mobilized a proletariat as in Spain, the means, nor the long tradition and the ethos, of actual physical combat. In Spain on the other hand it was the bourgeoisie which was divided, which showed itself split even in its armed forces.

Chile and Spain were similar in the fact that neither extreme of the political spectrum—and especially the right extreme—was especially strong. Hence, while the left extreme—and much, much more than just the left extreme—lost in the *denouement,* yet in neither country did the right extreme win in the form in which it had hoped to do so. On the civilian right, neither the *Falange* in Spain nor *Patria y Libertad* in Chile could conceivably have destroyed the existing institutional framework by itself. And its destruction benefited the extreme right less than it had hoped. Pablo Rodríguez was soon at odds with the Chilean *junta;* the Spanish *Falange* was soon shunted aside by Franco.

The military—and not the civilian—right was the crucial element in each country in the final *denouement.* And in neither country did it act as the simple extension and servant of the civilian right, even though, *de facto,* it acted substantially in its interest.

In both countries, certain elements of the civilian right had, of course, made attempts to have the military act directly on its behalf. Not only were public demands made for military intervention, but there were private contacts. Yet it is indicative of the much greater prestige and the greater force of constitutional norms of behavior in Chile as compared with Spain that no group in Chile with the exception of the extreme right, *Patria y Libertad,* had admitted to behind-the-scenes contact with the military prior to the *coup,* even with the defense that it was done to save the Constitution. In Spain, on the other hand, there was never anything beyond an immediate tactically useful attempt to hide the role of José Calvo Sotelo as intermediary between the military and the monarchists, nor the negotiations between general Emilio Mola and the Carlists represented by Manuel Fal Conde. The chief role of the extreme right (*Falange* and *Patria y Libertad,* respectively) was ultimately limited to aggravating the climate of violence and chaos which the extreme left (Anarchists and Socialists in Spain, MIR and Left-Socialists in Chile) were in any case vigorously fostering as part of their own policy.

The somewhat more substantial right in each country—the crucial CEDA (*Confederación Española de Derechas Autónomas*) in Spain, to which we will return later, and the *Partido Nacional* (PN) in Chile—played a different role from the extreme right. They served at least partly to legitimate the intervention of the military. Since they represented very substantial forces and blocks of opinion and were so clearly in favor of military intervention "to save the country," they could serve a legitimating function which the really extreme right could not do, since it had neither a base that was numerically large nor one that was weighty and reputable.

On the left, the extremist movements in both countries were much larger than their respective extreme rights and much more important in the evolution of events. Even so, they were not in themselves powerful enough in either country to overturn the institutional order. Anarco-Syndicalism in Spain, organizationally manifested through the CNT (*Confederación Nacional del Trabajo*) and the secret FAI (*Federación Anarquista Ibérica*) which guided the CNT, was very similar to the MIR in Chile and the organizations which the MIR in turn controlled: the FTR (*Frente de Trabajadores Revolucionarios*), the MCR (*Movimiento de Campesinos Revolucionarios*), and the MPR (*Movimiento de Pobladores Revolucionarios*). Both the Anarchists and the MIR (the former more so than the latter) were followed by substantial numbers of workers and, especially, peasants, so that they could and did organize for, and in fact in part obtained, major political objectives. These were not only significant in themselves but even more important in the reactions they called forth.

As in Spain, the Chilean extreme left was not only larger than the extreme right, but it was also on the scene first, well before the extreme right. The MIR was founded in the mid-1960s; *Patria y Libertad* not until 1971. In Spain, fascist groups which were ultimately to coalesce with Jose Antonio Primo de Rivera's *Falange Española* (founded in 1933) were not established until 1931, while the FAI was founded in 1927 and Anarchism itself goes back to the late nineteenth century and earlier. The ideology of the Chilean MIR did in fact have an anarchistic flavor, in the sense of strongly stressing anti-statism, anti-centralism, and hostility toward bureaucracy, whether socialist or otherwise. It emphasized grass-roots control and spontaneity in industrial and agricultural organizations, both as fighting entities and as productive units. And in both countries, the Communist party (a latecomer in Spain but an old-timer in Chile) was among the bitterest enemies of the extreme left, for ideological reasons among others, as well as tactical prudence.

In both countries, the extreme left pursued explicitly the policy of ignoring, with scorn, the political Constitution in the narrow sense and of attempting to undermine in a broader sense both the fact and the concept of what it conceived of as bourgeois law and order. These groups were explicitly left-revolutionary in ideology and in action. But their significance lay not so much in the force of their deeds and ideas as in the reactions to them of others and in the problems they posed for others.

In both countries, the center and moderate right reacted with genuine outrage and fear against offenses to values which they held dear—the Republic (or the Constitution, in the case of Chile) and law and order. At the more extreme end of the spectrum, the right used the extreme left more as an excuse for its own counter-constitutional activities. Indeed, in both countries there were suspicions that the right fomented supposedly left-wing violence or used it as a false screen to hide behind. In Chile, unclarified aspects of the assassination of the moderate right-wing Christian Democrat Pérez Zujovic raised the possibility that the right, not the left, was responsible, at least in part. And vice versa: aspects of the assassination of General Schneider in October, 1970, raised the possibility that the extreme left, and not only the extreme right, was to some degree involved. At the time, however, when appearances made it seem an act of the left, the assassination of Pérez Zujovic was compared with the murder of the much more extreme Calvo Sotelo by Socialists and Left-Republican police in Madrid in 1936. So conscious was Chile of the parallel with Spain.

In any case, the evident power of the extreme left and its willingness to use its power in violent and unconstitutional ways served to harden attitudes on the right from the center onwards. To the left, its own extremists represented two quite different problems. The moderates—the Communists in Chile and the followers of Prieto and some Republicans (Maura, Sanchez Román) in Spain—were aware of the dangers of alienating the bourgeoisie and providing the more extreme right with excuses to foment a *coup.* Hence they considered the extremists and their activities as highly dangerous, the more so since the moderate left was itself often attacked by the extreme left. In Chile as in Spain, the resulting encounters between left extremists and left moderates resulted in deaths.

To the Socialists of both countries, the problem posed by the extreme left was different. Indeed, the problems faced by the Socialists and their reactions to these problems were in both countries so crucial to the evolving tragedy that they deserve rather fuller treatment.

Salvador de Madariaga, the distinguished Spanish writer, has stated that the division of the Socialist party made civil war inevitable. The same can be said of the Chilean *Partido Socialista.* Both parties had been essentially reformist. Through their occasional association with centrist governments (in the Chilean Radical governments of the 1940s; in Azaña's Left-Republicans in the period of the Constituent *Cortes,* 1931–1933) the Socialists had been softened and somewhat corrupted by the taste of bureaucratic privileges. Both had been able to demonstrate their capacity to govern responsibly. But both parties suddenly moved to the ideological left, or at least crucial segments of the party did so.

In Spain, the Socialists' move to the left came after the experience of the first *"bienio"* (1931–1933) because of their growing doubts that profound institutional changes, especially in the countryside, could be effected in alliance with a bourgeois left which had shown its lack of enthusiasm for such change. Socialists also felt increasing discomfort at being a part of a government which attempted to control by force the extreme left (Anarchists) as well as the extreme right, killing workers and peasants in doing so. They also suffered from the organizational fear of losing their own followers to the extreme left. Nor did the rise of fascism in Germany (and the equivocal reaction to it of Austrian Catholic rightists in bloodily repressing the Socialists there) add to the Socialists' confidence in an alliance with moderate forces in Spain.

In Chile, the situation was in part similar. The Left-Socialists always symbolized, within the *Unidad Popular,* the position of *"avanzar para consolidar"* (advance in order to be able to consolidate) as against the more cautious Communist line of *"consolidar para avanzar"* (consolidate in order to be able to advance). Whether in their support of land invasions, their objection to the Communists' plan to return to their owners factories which had been seized by workers without prior government approval, the pressure they brought on Salvador Allende to purge the armed forces of hostile officers, or their general revolutionary rhetoric, the Left-Socialists as embodied by Senator Carlos Altamirano were closer, and moved progressively ever closer, to the MIR than to their supposed partner in the coalition, the Communist party. And just as in Spain, where the Socialists suffered severe pangs of conscience for participating in a government ready to stifle with force the revolutionary stirrings of the masses, so did the shoot-out in mid-1972 between police and the MIR in *Lo Hermida,* a MIR-controlled shantytown, cause concern among Left-Socialists. (The shoot-out left one person dead, indicative of the relative levels of violence in the two countries.) And the Chilean Socialists' formal commitment to a generally revolutionary posture occurred, as in Spain, at a time of disillusionment with a reformist government, though in the Chilean case it was not a government in which the Socialists themselves had participated. At the party congress in Chillán in 1967, as the Christian Democratic government turned to the right, and after the killing of six persons at the copper mine of *El Salvador,* the Left-Socialists persuaded the party to adopt a platform declaring revolutionary violence both inevitable and legitimate.

However, in Chile and Spain, some aspects of the dynamic of the leftward move of the Socialists were quite different. In Chile, the Socialists' move represented more a continuation of their long-standing feud with the Communists and a desire to separate themselves from what they deemed to be—ever since the spontaneous success of the Cuban revolution and Moscow's subsequent disapproval of Castro's attempt to export it—a Communist party that was far too reformist and much too foreign dominated, centralized, and bureaucratized. The Chilean *Partido Socialista* was less motivated by *fear* of competition from the extreme left and more by the desire to *benefit* from what they sensed was a leftward shift in the mood of the lower classes beyond a point they thought would be tolerable to the Communist party.

In Spain there was no Communist party to the right with which to differ. There existed, rather, a successful Anarchist rival to the left. The sector of the PSOE dominated by Largo Caballero moved to the left for the same reason that it did so in Chile: because it thought (rightly or wrongly) that it sensed that an important part of the "proletariat" was moving in that direction. But since in Spain the extreme left was already occupied by an anarchist movement much more robust than the MIR ever was in Chile, the two inevitably were organizational rivals. Therefore, even though the program and actions of the Spanish PSOE became more and more similar to that of the Anarchists (as did that of the Left-Socialists in Chile to the MIR), their organizational relationships both between the parties and between the labor federations they sponsored (UGTVS, CNT) remained as ambivalent as ever: mutual support at some times and places but, more frequently, bitter hostility. Indeed, there were shooting affrays between the two groups even during the critical months preceding the military uprising in July, 1936.

In Chile, on the other hand, the Socialists' ideological shift to the left was also accompanied by closer organizational relations with the MIR. During the congressional elections of March, 1973,

Senator Altamirano's senatorial candidacy was officially supported by the MIR; a number of Socialists were also members of the MIR; and Senator Altamirano, together with MIR leaders, was reported to be involved in attempts to influence navy ratings against their officers.

The effect of the leftward shift of the Socialist parties of the two countries was similar and twofold, though the relative importance of the two effects differed as between Chile and Spain.

In both countries, the emergence of the party (or of an important sector of it) as explicitly disloyal to a bourgeois Constitution and in favor of revolution had the effect of mobilizing the opposition. This ranged from those of the left of center (the Communist party in Chile, which at times sought to restrain and combat the leftward drift) through more centrist groups, primarily the Christian Democrats in Chile (there were, *de facto,* no centrist groups of significance surviving to be mobilized in Spain toward the end of the Republic). And, of course, it mobilized the right of all shades. This effect was similar in the two countries and of great importance.

The second effect of the leftward drift of the Socialists into the column of those who would be explicitly disloyal to the existing institutional regime was that it made impossible any last-minute attempts to forge an alliance at the center, at least not without splintering the Marxist left. Just as the left consistently vetoed all of President Allende's (more or less vigorous) attempts to arrive at a compromise with the Christian Democrats, so did Francisco Largo Caballero and his followers in effect veto Indalecio Prieto's last-minute plan for a coalition government with the Left-Republicans. In his tour of Spain in the spring of 1936, Prieto was shouted down by many Socialist audiences, especially amongst the youth, much as President Allende was being increasingly repudiated by some groups within his own party.

The difference between Spain and Chile as regards this latter phenomenon (the impossibility of re-creating a center and left-of-center coalition) lies in the fact that the forces on either side of the center in Spain were so small that an agreement between them could not have meant very much even had it come about. The *Izquierda Republicana, Unión Republicana,* and other Spanish center-left groups and such parts of the Socialist party as might have gone along with Indalecio Prieto and Julián Besteiro were unable to form a coalition which might have implemented reforms that would have satisfied the claims of workers and peasants on the one hand and, on the other, the desire of the middle classes for some kind of stability.

There was a difference as between Chile and Spain on the right side of the center, or straddling the center. (Placement depends very much on the particular author's—and on the reader's—point of view!) There, in Chile, was its single largest party, the Christian Democratic party. In Spain, on the other hand, to the right of the center there were only various small parties such as the PNV, as well as a totally disorganized Radical party (comparable to Chile's Radical party in that sense). CEDA was well to the right, not just "right of center," and would have corresponded in Chile to the National party. This difference between Spain and Chile in the size and nature of their two center parties is a reflection of the much more basic fact that opinion in Chile was far more progressive and far less polarized than in Spain on many important issues, e.g., the need to restructure the economy and to redistribute power and privilege in general.

More specifically, the existence of a very large progressive Christian Democratic party signified that a change-oriented mood prevailed among a large sector of Catholic opinion, not only lay but also clerical. Unlike Spain, there was no recent history of Church support for a right-wing dictatorship (that of Miguel Primo de Rivera in Spain, 1923–1930). In Spain, too, the Archbishop of Toledo, Primate of Spain, had issued an extremely hostile pastoral against the Second Republic at the time of its establishment. In Chile, on the other hand, the bishops issued a series of very friendly and conciliatory pastorals both before and after the 1970 elections. And these were only some among many pastorals going back as long as thirty-two years earlier when, in 1938, the Archbishop of Santiago, José María Caro, Chile's primate and first cardinal, had called on Catholics to be loyal to the newly elected Popular Front government. He had done so despite his and everyone else's knowledge that his sister church in Spain was embattled to the death against a government of similar name and quite comparable composition. Not until March, 1973, was there in Chile any kind of formal difference between the Church and the government (over plans to introduce drastic changes in the educational system). The opposition of the hierarchy was then formulated in the most carefully measured terms, precisely in order not to carry the confrontation beyond the point at issue. But, of course, precisely because it did represent the first time that a policy difference of importance had become public, it was taken seriously by all concerned.

There is no doubt that Christian Democrats represented a wide range of views, including a right which might well have been incapable of tolerating a coalition with even the moderate

Marxist left, had that ever come about. But it contained also a numerically significant left, headed by persons of great personal stature and prestige. All parties the world over contain a range of opinion, as do the publics they represent. We see no evidence to justify characterizing the Christian Democrats in Chile as less cohesive and as more subject to centrifugal forces than any other party. Even the MIR, small and extreme though it was, was subject to schism. The group which assassinated Pérez Zujovic was said to have been one such dissident group. The Socialist party was subject to internal divisions *par excellence*. Even the Communist party suffered from those occasional defections to the left which have plagued it in all countries including Spain: witness the departures of Nin and Maurín in 1931, leading to the establishment of the POUM (*Partido Obrero de Unificación Marxista*) in 1936. By any realistic comparative standard, the Christian Democrats were a center which was weak neither numerically nor organizationally as compared with other Chilean parties or with parties, left or right, in other countries. Nor was it less willing or capable of compromising and negotiating than other parties, as it had done on many occasions during its six years in office.

The parties on the left which were closest to the Christian Democrats, namely the Communists and the center and right wing of the Socialists, were approximately equally flexible, provided one uses as the standard of judgment not what one wishes had happened but comparable situations in other countries such as Spain. There did not exist in Spain a center (neither center-left nor center-right) even approximately as sizeable and cohesive as the Chilean one. Nor was the motivation to compromise in Spain even remotely as strong as that indicated in Chile by the many efforts that were made by both sides from 1970 up to August, 1973, to arrive at an agreement, whether over possible electoral alliances or over the specific legislative or constitutional matters in dispute. The persons involved had had many years of experience with each other, and their relationships were excellent by any reasonable comparable standard. Hence personal factors, too, contributed as little to the debacle as is realistically conceivable.

Granted that this was a society which was moving *toward an aborted civil war,* the conditions for avoiding it could not have been better. Yet the breakdown was not avoided because, in the end, the level of personal trust was insufficient and adequate compromise could not be reached.

Was this due to the fact that the various mass publics supporting the political elites as they negotiated with each other would not have supported such a compromise? This could be reasonably maintained in the case of Spain. But even in the case of Spain, as insightful an observer as Brenan felt that this was not a point on which certainty is warranted. On the left at least, the highly reformist Socialist Julián Besteiro had received more votes in Madrid than Largo Caballero. And it was unclear what a ballot in the UGT (the Socialist labor federation) would have produced. In other words, there are indications that both at the level of leadership and at the level of its mass following, the drift of the Socialist party to the left might have been reversible. However, the area right of center had been almost deserted in Spain, and the followers of the CEDA were in no mood for compromises with the Socialists even if its leaders had been. Massive desertions to the more extreme right had occurred. The desertion of Gil Robles (himself no moderate) by the youth organization he had founded is an illustrative piece of evidence.

In comparison, the vote obtained by the moderate Christian Democrats in the elections of 1973 had risen from the low of just over 25 per cent in 1971 to 29 per cent in March, 1973, which was also above the 27 per cent obtained by its presidential candidate in 1970. Perhaps the recovery was due to the increasingly intransigent stand which the Christian Democrats had taken *vis-à-vis* the government. The recovery would have been aborted had the party begun to compromise with the left. But our point is not that of denying that a compromise with the *Unidad Popular* might have cost the Christian Democrats some support. Nor would we argue that the right and center Socialists might not have lost considerable support had they compromised. The argument, once again, is only that of showing that the situation in Chile looked much more hopeful than it did in Spain and as good as might be expected under the circumstances. And yet it was simply not good enough; in the end, personal trust was insufficient and adequate compromises could not be or at any rate were not reached.

Giovanni Sartori (using a methodology which we cannot detail here) has formulated an index which reflects the degree of polarization over time toward right and left extremism in different European democracies and Chile. The index for the Weimar Republic stood at 6.16; for Spain, it stood at 15.9, but for Chile (1945–1973), at only 3.11, and for Italy (1948–1972), at 1.85. These figures and other more detailed ones support our own more impressionistically derived conclusion that the possibilities that the final confrontation might have been avoided in Chile were much greater than in Spain.

We are left with the same ominous, puzzling conclusion at which we arrived at the end of the first section. The constellation of political forces in Spain and Chile had a good deal in common, especially insofar as the relative weakness of their extremes and the position of their Socialist parties just this side of the extreme were concerned. But insofar as the two countries differed—the much greater vigor, in Chile, of parties spanning the center and, by definition, the much smaller significance of the two extremes in Chile—the situation in Chile was much more propitious for avoiding a breakdown than it had been in Spain, just as Chile's stability, low level of violence, and generally democratic political evolution had been much more favorable than that of Spain had been. And yet, a breakdown was not avoided.

Issues

To what extent were the basic issues which polarized these two societies similar? To what extent were the issues sufficient to explain the breakdown in each country? (And these are two very different questions: the issues may be similar, and still, analyzing them, we may feel that they were not sufficient to have led to the abyss.)

There were, of course, two important issues which, as we mentioned at the beginning of this chapter, played a major role in Spain, one of which was altogether absent in Chile. There was, first, the issue of regional nationalism, which contributed to the fragmentation of various parties and especially lessened the possibility of establishing what might have been a coherent conservative focus. In this way, it contributed to the radicalization of a centralist authoritarian "right." Second, Spain continued to be plagued by intense controversy over clericalism and religion, whereas the Chilean Church exercised a calming influence.

Once again, therefore, the Chilean situation turns out to have been far less pointed toward confrontation than that of Spain. And yet the confrontation occurred.

The third major group of issues confronting Spain (and it is indeed a complex group of issues rather than a single one)—the conflict in its class and economic system, especially its agrarian system—is one which Chile shared, though there were differences. Though others will no doubt be less puzzled than we are, we may raise the question whether these conflicts, though partly common to both countries, were really sufficient to produce a final rift in either country. Precisely in what way would the conflict have produced a rift? In whose eyes?

One issue on which the parallel between Spain and Chile was close is that of land reform and of peasant activism more broadly. It was of key importance in both countries. The similarity existed not only at the most obvious level: the crude fact, or threat, of land reform alienated landlords from an institutional system which permitted the passage of legislation so obviously against their interest. The similarity existed also at more subtle but equally if not more important levels. In both countries the peasantry became impatient, and with more or less incitement and leadership from groups that had an interest in confrontation *per se,* it began a process of land invasions. This set off a similar psychological chain reaction in both countries: visions on the part not only of landowners, but also of the urban bourgeoisie, of anarchy and of total loss of control over law and order by the government, or even more hostile visions of government collusion in the subversion of law and order and of constitutional procedures.

A second subtle but critical similarity between the two countries in the area of land reform was that the combined effect of ill-considered formal legislation, an impatient lower peasantry, and the encouragement of elements at the extreme left of the ideological spectrum was to antagonize from the agrarian reform specifically, and therefore from the regime supporting it in general, substantial portions of the middle peasantry and even of certain groups of small peasants.

Instead of confining the threat of expropriation to the largest landowners, a mass of middle and even lower peasants were also threatened in various ways, thereby immensely broadening and popularizing the base of the opposition to the government. And, ironically, there were no compensating benefits for the reform program, since middle and lower peasants had little land to contribute to it.

In Chile, the attack, or threatened attack, on groups of peasants who had previously benefited from agrarian reform through membership in so-called *asentamientos* and were unwilling to share its benefits with the much larger groups who had not so benefited added their hostility toward the government to the opposition of the large landowners. As a result, a variety of paramilitary "White Guard" protective organizations sprang up in the Chilean countryside, especially in the South. These began to embrace not only landowners, as would be expected, but also smaller peasants and even peasants from *asentamientos,* which was much more worrisome to the government. The policy which the Communist party advocated both in Republican Spain and in Chile, of respecting the property of the peasant, fell, *de facto,* on deaf ears with harmful consequences for the government.

The question that arises is whether these "excesses," as they were termed in both countries by all, including Communists, were really the result of spontaneous uncontrollable mass pressure or whether they represented rather the putting into practice of revolutionary and utopian ideologies of certain radical political elites, the control of which would have been possible and whose actions were, therefore, in that sense not inevitable. At least, the consequences of these actions and their magnitude could have been controlled. Certainly much empirical evidence from studies undertaken in the Chilean countryside suggests that peasant demands for the expropriation of landlords (as distinct from demands for better wages and living and working conditions) had often to be externally stimulated. Certainly the demand for establishing a communal organization of farming was not widespread among peasants. What was at work was ideological commitment to this point on the part of their urban mentors. The excessive radicalization which so much endangered the system does not appear to have been a spontaneous mass phenomenon but one characterizing radical elites.

A somewhat similar case can be made if the question of the fundamental viability of the then-existing economic system is approached not from the more specific issue of some aspect of class conflict, such as land reform, but directly from that of the productivity and adaptability of the economic and social system itself.

In Chile especially, there was explicit agreement among political elites, extending at least as far right as the moderate left of the Christian Democrats, that the then-existing system was played out—had "had it"—*"ya no daba para más"*—and that some kind of major change was essential and even inevitable. Without, as authors, asserting the contrary, we can at least maintain that this evaluation of the objective situation is not fully self-evident, and, even more strongly, we can maintain that it may not have been felt as deeply by the masses as by some of their leaders. The average economic growth rate of Chile had not been lower, and certainly not dramatically lower, than that of many other societies at comparable stages, which later "developed" successfully. Nor was the distribution of the benefits of growth markedly more unjust. In absolute terms, the six years of Christian Democratic government had seen a remarkable increase in social benefits (housing, education, health) going to the neediest, especially in the countryside, as well as a considerable redistribution in income.

The rising external debt and the rising cost of servicing it, as well as the increasing foreign ownership of some of the most dynamic sectors of the Chilean economy, might have had a damaging effect on the rising curve of welfare *in the future*. That is a matter about which economists do and should debate. A broad spectrum of the leadership of the left and center were much concerned about these phenomena. But it had not yet produced, by the early 1970s, any absolute decline in Chile's well-being or in the well-being of the poorer segments of her population.

We do not wish to argue about the benevolent or malevolent impact of these structural phenomena. All we wish to do is point out that while their purported existence served to fire the ardor for change of some of the left elites, they could not, at this stage, have had such an effect on the masses. At most, various masses might have been disappointed, because their aspirations were higher than those of comparable publics in the past, and the structural constraints of world capitalism might have meant that their situation did not improve *as fast* as they had hoped. But there is no convincing evidence of exceptionally intense disappointment. And certainly there was no objective decline nor even a severe stagnation. In short, it is doubtful that in Chile pressure from the masses alone would have resulted in a confrontation.

In retrospect, after the breakdown of a regime, the societies which have suffered it appear always to have been subject to basic unsolvable problems. But when we look at societies in which there have been no such breakdowns, we often find, to our confusion, that many of them have been beset by problems equally as severe for an equally long time. It is not self-evident that Chile's structural problems in 1970 or 1973 were so much worse than they had been in her own past, or that a revolution or counterrevolution was inevitable, and certainly not that these problems were spontaneously felt to be worse. Nor is it easy to demonstrate that her problems were, or had been felt to be, so much worse than those of other countries in which a breakdown did not occur.

Once again, as in the case of land reform, the insistence that there was an unsolvable problem and an inevitable conflict, and the drive for extremely rapid change in the social-political and economic structure, both came more from the elites and their perceptions than from the masses, at least in Chile. As between Chile and Spain, what is *similar* are the ideological commitments of the various elites, especially those of the extreme left. The postures of the masses seem *different* as between Chile and Spain. The masses were much less radical in Chile than in Spain, though certainly even in Chile much more radical and mobilized than in the past.

Insofar as the outcomes in the two countries were similar, we are inclined to attribute it not to the similar levels of radicalism of the masses, for there was no such similarity, but to similar ideological commitments to change (in thought, rhetoric, and action) of the elites that were mobilizing the masses. That mobilization, though objectively far less in Chile than in Spain, represented a dramatic increase over the past, and this frightened the elites on the right. But in itself, and unlike Spain, we doubt that the level of mobilization would have been sufficient to produce a breakdown in Chile. Perhaps the breakdown occurred, or at least was given its final push, only by the elites which used mass mobilization, and partly stimulated it in the first place, sensing that the masses were ready for it.

In any case, we conclude this section with the thought that it was not so much the objective gravity of Chile's structural problems (which were probably less serious than the severe underdevelopment in Spain in the mid-1930s) but the interpretation of this situation by various elites (which Chile shared with Spain) that contributed critically to the common breakdown.

SIMILARITIES IN PROCESS

Among the most startling similarities between the Spain of the Second Republic and Chile from 1964 onward are certain critical processes which symbolically marked the path toward final confrontation. Such similarities are perhaps not surprising since the nature of the conflicts and the kinds of actors arrayed around these conflicts were very much alike.

In both countries, the left was either formally in office or close to it: in Spain from February 1936 onwards; in Chile between 1970 and 1973. In both countries, public support for the officeholders and their real power were far less than the occupancy of office seemed to indicate. Yet both governments were intent on making, or at least initiating, very substantial and irreversible institutional changes—changes which were explicitly designed to displace certain classes and institutions from the control they then exercised over power and wealth. About these aims there was no ambiguity or doubt, particularly in Chile.

The ambiguity arose—in Chile at least—over whether these changes would be instituted only if existing constitutional mechanisms permitted the left to do so legally, or whether the left regarded these mechanisms as themselves so much a part of an illegitimate institutional structure that they would feel no need to respect it. The right accused the left of taking the latter position. A part of the left, but a far smaller part than stood so accused, freely admitted that this was indeed its posture. Another part of the left vigorously and consistently denied it. A crucial middle part of the left was ambiguous in its position. This ambiguous posture was then utilized by the right, whether in good faith or otherwise, to picture the entire left as ready to disregard the Constitution. And disregard of the Constitution was, in turn, equated with the willingness to use violence; in other words, to resort to civil war. Once again, a part of the left admitted this freely. But the right extended the accusation well beyond that group to include not only those who seemed ambiguous in their stand, but those who denied any such intentions.

The right, of course, had its own ambivalence about constitutionality and violence. In both Spain and Chile (though much more massively in Spain) right extremists would have been ready to resist in unconstitutional and violent forms any fundamental alteration whatsoever in the institutional structure, even if only constitutional means had been used by the left and even if the left had eschewed violence. Indeed, in Spain, the right, too, was determined to change the institutional structure (albeit in a different direction) by either constitutional or unconstitutional means.

In both countries, the justification of the right for the use of force to resist institutional change would be, partly, that such changes even if legally executed by the left would be fundamentally contrary to some more basic values and principles: natural law, Christian-Catholic values, and the essential traditions of the nation. Another part of the right's justification for stopping unconstitutionally changes made constitutionally would be that such changes would in practice ruin the nation and result in chaos. "The nation" and its historical characteristics was the ultimate reference point of the right in the two countries. It is no accident that in both Spain and Chile (as in Germany) the very name of the right included in it the word *national: Partido Nacional* in Chile; the *Nacionalistas* in Spain. "The nation" was deemed to be a more basic value than a particular constitutional form of government.

And, just as in the case of the left, the center of the right was ambiguous as to when exactly it, too, might resort to unconstitutional means, including violence. The leader of what might be termed the center of the right in Spain, José María Gil Robles, head of the CEDA, never did unequivocably declare his loyalty to the Republic and its Constitution. This position was much more equivocal than that of the *Pardido Nacional* in Chile, at least until the latter part of 1972. These are, obviously, very subjective judgments. But it is certain that the right in Spain was at least as anti-constitutional as the left and as ready to employ violence. In this, it differed substantially from its equivalent in Chile. Whether because it benefited from it or for other reasons, the Chilean right, at least until the last few months of the UP regime, was not in principle opposed to the existing Constitution. Only the extreme left took that position and explicitly proclaimed it. In Spain, on the other hand, both extremes rejected the Republican Constitution in principle.

The readiness by one side to use violence is widely accepted as a justification for its opponents to do so. Hence every accusation by one side that the other seems to be preparing for a civil war is taken by the accused side as an indication that the accusers themselves are getting ready for a confrontation. And this in turn provides the accused with an excuse to prepare for violence, even if they are not already doing so. It is in this manner that escalation occurs, until a point is reached tragically similar to that in a Western movie but on a much larger scale. Each side fears and suspects that the other will pull the gun first. Hence each side feels that it has to get into a dominant position first and in decisive coercive control of the situation lest the other side do so. It is the mentality of the "preemptive first strike," in the nuclear thinking of the superpowers of today. At the very least, each side feels it has to organize for self-defense—which the other side, of course, fears may be not for defense but for attack, and therefore it, too, begins to arm.

Any incident which can be interpreted to indicate that one or the other side is arming itself is, therefore, of obvious delicacy in a situation of this kind. Ironically, but logically, it is the left which is more likely to get into trouble on this score. The left is generally unarmed at the outset of the process of polarization. Aristocrats, landowners, and property owners usually have firearms of some sort—whether to protect themselves, to hunt, or as a consequence of their having been in the armed forces or having relatives in the armed forces. Also, there is often the more or less firm and warranted assumption that in a showdown the army would protect and be on the side of the right, as it certainly was in both

Chile and Spain. For all these reasons, the right generally has no need to take formal steps to arm itself, at least in the early stages.

On the left, the situation is quite different. With the exception of miners, who may have access to crude explosives, there is no group which will have any large quantity of usable weapons. The left, therefore, feels under pressure to catch up. And precisely because workers and peasants are ordinarily unarmed, the attempt to arm them is a particularly frightening indicator that something very unusual may be about to happen. It upsets the customary, totally unbalanced balance of violence even if it does no more than make the balance objectively equal. And unless arsenals can be raided (which presumes a high level of organization) arms for the left must necessarily be bought abroad and therefore come from foreign sympathizers.

The clandestine import of arms with the help of highly placed politicians acquires very real but, above all, highly symbolic significance in such a context of suspicion. In both Spain and Chile, various incidents (real or imagined) which appeared to indicate that the left was importing arms sharpened the confrontation between the two tides. For example in Spain in mid-1934, the unloading of arms from the steamer *Turquesa*, in the presence of the Socialist leader Indalecio Prieto, became an incident which the right exploited from then on.

A very similar incident occurred in Chile. In March, 1972, thirty crates were unloaded from a Cuban airliner at an out-of-the-way corner of the Santiago airport. Upon personal orders of the Minister of the Interior, who overruled a customs official, they were transported directly to the home of the President without customs examination. In subsequent parliamentary debates, and in the press, the right asserted that the cases contained arms. The government denied this and asserted that they contained gifts for President Allende. It was a turning point for the Chilean right, which had visions of massive clandestine arming with the complicity of the government.

In both countries, the extreme right maintained foreign contacts. In Spain, we may recall the 1933–1934 agreements between the monarchists and fascist Italy and the fact that José Antonio received Italian financial support. Yet these contacts played practically no role in the initial rising of July, 1936. But foreign help was to make the critical difference between success and failure as the civil war wore on. In the case of Chile, the role of foreign mentor was of course played by the United States. In Spain, the rebel army established contact with Hitler through the Nazi party.

In Chile, the army maintained contact with the CIA. In both countries, the Foreign Ministries pursued one course while other channels facilitated foreign intervention.

The extent to which a government of the left is capable of (and, even more important to the right, is prepared to) control sporadic acts of violence and more massive breaches of the law originating from its own supporters or left extremists is another symbol to which the right pays a good deal of attention. Whether or not the government acts firmly to prevent acts of violence; whether or not the perpetrators of violence are prosecuted; whether or not amnesty is extended to those who have been convicted: all of these acts of omission or commission on the part of the government are scrutinized by the other side for symbolic indications of where the government really stands. The governments of both Spain and Chile were well aware that some degree of law and order had to be maintained. Hence there was some degree of what the revolutionary left then called "repression." We have already referred to the *Lo Hermida* incident in Chile in which the MIR was involved. It was symbolically equivalent to the many acts of "repression" undertaken by all Spanish governments of the Second Republic, including even the cabinet in power after the Popular Front victory in February, 1936. (We refer to the clash at Yeste in Estremadura, in which eighteen villagers and one Civil Guard were killed.)

But these acts, while alienating the extreme left, were insufficient to reassure the right. It was more upset by what it regarded as the leniency of the respective governments. This was symbolized for the right in Chile by the government's failure to prosecute leaders of the MIR when they appeared in public in 1971 at a time when arrest orders were out against them. Even more, it had been indicated by a general amnesty for political prisoners (including leaders of the MIR) proclaimed in the early months of Allende's presidency, in December, 1970. In Spain, the failure to prosecute some of the highest party leaders of the left in connection with the revolutionary outbreak of October, 1934, upset the right, as did, in 1936, Azaña's amnesty for all those involved in the uprising. Nevertheless, the left was alienated by the massive repression and the legal prosecutions which were staged after October, 1934, contrasting them with the gentle treatment given to those who had participated in the uprising headed up by General Sanjurjo in 1932. In both countries there had been a perceived failure to repress acts of violence. In both countries there was outrage on the part of the right over amnesty granted to extreme leftists, and it was utilized to question the government's legitimacy.

As the process of polarization progresses, and as the political authorities lose control over different branches of the governmental apparatus, the reaction of the judicial branch and the armed forces to events involving arms becomes more indicative of the absence of an agreed-upon policy and the absence of any kind of control than of any particular policy. In Chile, this became dramatically evident when the armed forces began with ever greater frequency to search for arms among workers and peasants. This was something which the government could not or, at least, did not stop for fear of alienating the armed forces. But these searches did not represent any determined governmental policy. The government in fact had no consistent policy on the issue, nor even did a single individual such as President Allende.

Assassinations, too, were common to Chile and to Spain, although in a ratio objectively so unequal as to make one hesitate to compare the two countries. But precisely because they were practically unheard of in Chile, the fact that they took place at all stirred public opinion much more than it might have done in other countries.

In the case of Spain, the uncounted number of such acts was climaxed by the assassination by Falangists of a leftist lieutenant, José Castillo, and finally by the assassination by the left of the leader of the monarchists, José Calvo Sotelo, an outright enemy of the Republic. In Chile, the assassination of the President's *aide-de-camp* (an act still unclarified) did not signal, as it did in Spain, that both sides were prepared to resort to murder against each other. For the opposition, it signified, rather, the breakdown of law and order. The fact that the victim was not clearly identified with either side, nor the assassins clearly known, highlighted the act as a symbol of anarchy.

It also signaled the increasing breach between the armed forces and the government. A member of the armed forces had been the victim—as the armed forces interpreted it—of the government's inability to control the situation. The armed forces insisted on appointing their own investigator. The friction which developed almost immediately between the civilian and the military group investigating the assassination also symbolized the increasing gap between the armed forces and the government.

There were other similarities between Spain and Chile in the matter of the relations between the armed forces and the government. The dilemma had to be faced in both countries whether or not the government, at the risk of precipitating a *coup*, should attempt to neutralize senior officers known to be unsympathetic to it. In Chile, President Allende was repeatedly urged to do so. But he did so no more than had previous Presidents, at least not until August, 1973, when he forced General César Ruiz Danyau, known to be very hostile to the *Unidad Popular,* to retire from his position as Chief of Staff of the Air Force because he had resigned his position as Minister of Transport. Whether justified or not (the entire situation was unprecedented) this *contretemps* resulted in the first independent act of protest against the government by a section of the armed forces (the flight of a fighter squadron from Santiago to the South) which went undisciplined by the military hierarchy: a significant omen.

In Spain, the Popular Front government acted more in line with what the more radical left was recommending in Chile. General Sanjurjo, who had staged a rising in 1932, in the very early years of the Second Republic, was in any case in exile in Lisbon. He may be compared to Chile's General Viaux Marambio, whose rising in 1969 (supposedly merely over salaries and insufficient budgetary support) similarly went for long without a sequel, and who was similarly exiled after rather mild treatment. More relevant to the crisis of 1936, Generals Franco and Goded were removed from their high position in the Ministry of War in the spring of 1936 and given commands in remote areas (the Canary Islands and the Balearics, respectively). But the Spanish government's somewhat more vigorous action was, obviously, no more effective than was the *Unidad Popular*'s failure to act. It will remain a matter of unending argument whether earlier attempts at intervention in the military hierarchy would have produced an earlier *coup* (as skeptics maintain) or a serious division in the armed forces and hence a civil war of uncertain outcome (which appears to be all that the advocates of intervention maintain and was certainly all that happened in Spain). It seems certain that in no country can a government of the left expect the solid support of the military in the face of growing polarization.

Several more parallels in the military realm might be noted: (1) as early as spring 1936, General Emilio Mola specified that the projected action would have to be "very violent" in order to crush the enemy as quickly as possible. This was, of course, the manner in which also the Chilean armed forces ultimately proceeded, to the surprise of most, but not all. (The action of the Spanish army was no surprise to anyone.) Was this ferocity due to the inherent tactical logic of the situation? Or was it due to pent-up emotional fury after a long wait? General Mola and other generals involved in the *coup* planned for action in April but had to postpone action several times, in part because some of their fellow generals were vacillating. The Chilean army, according to General Pinochet, began contingency planning as early as May, 1972. But the decision to overthrow the government may not have been a single one. The process may have been of a rapidly incremental nature and may not have begun until after the March, 1973, elections. After that critical point (essentially similar to the February, 1936, elections in Spain) senior officers were put under pressure by their own middle ranks, by elements of the civilian right, and by what they felt (with greater or less sincerity) to be attempts to establish a parallel people's militia. But in any case the fact is that two very different armies behaved in the same extremely harsh manner.

(2) In both countries, a plan for an uprising of the left was supposedly found after the military *coup*. In both countries, there are two very similar ambiguities about these plans. First: were they (Plan *Zeta* in Chile) forgeries or not? And second: even if they were not, were they serious plans, centrally agreed upon? Or were they dream-like creations produced by this group or that in the ever more feverish atmosphere into which these countries drifted?

(3) In both countries, there was a good deal more vacillation among officers and more mistrust within the armed forces than was apparent on the surface. Plans for the uprising which were being considered after February, 1936, had to be abandoned again and again for lack of agreement among commanding officers over the circumstances that would make military intervention appear justified, the extent of civilian support on which several officers wished to be able to count, and the political significance that the result should be given. Only at the beginning of June does it appear that General Mola had been able to coordinate all the different groups that were to rise on July 18.

In Chile, even as late as June 29, 1973, the army as a whole was not ready to support an attempted *coup* by the officers of the Second Armored Regiment. And there was considerable doubt in the navy in the days and even hours right before the *coup* as to whether the army would really go along: written self-incriminating statements were demanded as proof. The same kind of hesitation characterized many German officers in their relation to the plots to assassinate Hitler in July, 1944, and before.

Any military interference in public affairs still comes as a highly arbitrary and shocking surprise to many civilians living in bourgeois democracies. This is true of academics above all, perhaps in part because academics find themselves among the most definitively and abruptly displaced from power and the most severely assaulted when the military does take over. There is a great deal of indignant surprise that the military can be disloyal to an established constitutional order. There is revulsion against the use of naked and overwhelming force. But all these emotions, understandable though they are, may lead the civilian observer to overestimate the extent to which the armed forces are united in principle in their hostility toward democracy and toward policies with progressive content. They may also lead to an underestimation of the extent to which the military men are assailed by doubt and divisions before they act, and are propelled by a great variety of motives when they finally move with decisiveness.

Civilian observers may also overlook the extent to which the armed forces take steps to avoid intervention: for example, by communicating clearly what resolution of issues would avoid intervention. Thus the Chilean military appears to have expressed its concerns several times in the first months of 1973, but especially in April, 1973, shortly after leaving the cabinet. Since the explicit idea of a *coup*, or of unconstitutional action of any kind, was taboo in Chile, the military's concern was expressed as just that, not as a condition for avoiding a *coup*. In Spain, Franco's letter of June 23, 1936, warning Premier Casares Quiroga of restlessness in the military because of the ouster from their commands of several right-wing officers, may have been written more for the record than as a genuine attempt to avoid the imminent rising. Yet there is some real reason to doubt whether General Franco was as yet fully committed. In Chile, General Pinochet had appeared to many (including President Allende) to be a constitutionalist, and it is not yet finally certain that this was merely highly skilled dissimulation on his part.

The hesitancy and delay of the military meant that when it did act, many of those who had been doubtful earlier were convinced that action was necessary. The consequence of delay was, therefore, greater unity of action both within the armed forces and also among civilian political groups. No more than one fifth of the senior officers remained loyal to the government in Spain, while in Chile an unknown proportion did so, but probably not a greater one than in Spain. In Chile, by late August, 1973, the majority of the Christian Democrats were no longer vigorously opposed to a military *coup*, to put a controversial matter extremely conservatively. In Spain, the right, from Gil Robles' CEDA onwards (Gil Robles had hardly escaped assassination on the evening of July 12), was obviously united behind the idea of a *coup*, despite earlier reservations by various groups, including—for political reasons—even the *Falange*.

On the side of the governments, however, and this was again true of both Chile and Spain, there was a growing state of paralysis. The governments were paralyzed *vis-à-vis* the military conspirators themselves, whose plotting was toward the end an open secret. They were also paralyzed *vis-à-vis* their followers and quasi-allies. Ever more incapable of controlling their own side— indeed, ever less in charge of any policy, group, or events—these governments were obviously capable neither of rallying their own side nor, therefore, of putting up a united front against the threat of the military to stage a *coup*.

In Spain, this division of the left was very explicitly symbolized by the failure of the largest party constituting the Popular Front during the February, 1936, elections, the Socialists, ever to join the government (not to speak of the Anarchists). Hence the post-February cabinets consisted only of Left-Republicans and of regionalists, while depending for survival completely on the parliamentary support of Socialists, who were not represented in the cabinets. It was a vivid demonstration of what can happen when the left does organize itself explicitly into separate sectors consisting of constitutional and compromise-oriented groups on the one hand and, on the other, non-constitutional revolutionary sectors, as was so often recommended in Chile, by both extremists and moderates! As the time of the *coup* approached, neither President Azaña nor the (very ill) Prime Minister, Casares Quiroga, seemed capable of adopting any specific policy. The latter, when told on July 12, five days before the *coup*, that it was imminent, is reported to have said jocularly, "So there is to be a rising? Very well, I, for my part, shall take a lie-down." In the following days, however, his cabinet took more energetic steps than did the Chilean to neutralize the *coup* by arresting certain generals, having ships put to sea, and so forth.

In Chile, President Allende knew by Friday, September 7, 1973, that a *coup* was definitely planned for the middle of the next week. But the weekend passed in a series of inconclusive discussions, so that no specific steps were taken to defuse the situation. The decision to hold a plebiscite was taken, at last, by President Allende and a very small group of advisors and communicated to the military members of the cabinet on Monday, September 10. By that time, the commanders of the three branches of the armed forces clearly had no desire to change their plans.

Above all, in those last critical days, both governments faced with the probability of a *coup* had to decide whether to facilitate the arming of civilian groups likely to support the government. In Spain, on July 13, 1936, four days before the rising which was known to be imminent, even the moderate Socialist Prieto joined Largo Caballero and others in a request that arms be distributed. That request was refused at the time and only acceded to on July 18 and 19 after the army had risen. In Chile, the pressure on President Allende to arm the workers, which had become substantial after the abortive *coup* by Colonel Souper's Armored Regiment on June 29, was similarly resisted until September 11. Conscious of the fact that in Chile, unlike Spain, any attempt at armed resistance would be totally futile, President Allende in his penultimate broadcast at 9 a.m. on Tuesday, September 11, asked workers to stay peacefully at home.

The consequences of the *coup* in Chile are, of course, dreadful in terms of death and torture among the adherents of the *Unidad Popular*. How many lives were, nevertheless, saved by not resisting can perhaps be calculated—however distasteful such comparisons are—by noting the minimum of 400,000 violent deaths, on both sides, which it is estimated were suffered by Spain, in a population in the late 1930s only twice as large as that of Chile in 1973. The figures for Chile are not thought to be anywhere near half those for Spain. They may be in the region of 20,000, or 10 per cent of Spain's, once population differences are taken into account. However somber a result, it differs from those of a civil war, even a brief one.

But as the governments of both countries became more paralyzed, the two extremes, especially the left, became more daring, seemingly quite oblivious to the real balance of forces and to what the most likely outcome of the crisis would be. In both countries, a rising level of optimism and a general triumphant calling-to-arms—reminiscent, as Brenan notes, of the atmosphere of August, 1914—characterized both the extreme left and the extreme right. It was an optimism which even for the right would turn out to be no more than half justified. For the left, this optimism was a total disaster in both countries.

Thus, in both countries, weak, relatively moderate left governments became paralyzed internally as the *coup* approached. They also became delegitimized in the eyes of ever more numerous and certainly more vociferous sectors of the public. In Spain, in the eyes of many such publics, the Republican governments did not from their very beginning in 1931 have a great deal of inherent legitimacy. But whatever little they had was challenged by the bitter parliamentary debates through May, June, and July of 1936, which further crystalized what had been a strong, delegitimizing undercurrent all along.

In Chile, despite its long history of constitutionalism, the process of delegitimization was much more pronounced and apparent to those who were opposed to the government. For the right, the process very clearly began at the very moment when Salvador Allende became President. There was in itself nothing at all new and unsettling about the fact that the representative of a coalition who had obtained only 36 per cent of the vote assumed the presidency. After all, Jorge Alessandri had received only 31 per cent of the vote in 1958. What was perceived to be challengeable by the opposition was the attempt to completely reorient Chilean society on this very narrow basis of support. Previous major shifts in policy, none of which in any case even approximated what the *Unidad Popular* promised to do, had occurred only under Presidents who had been elected with substantial majorities. Both Pedro Aguirre Cerda, head of the Popular Front in 1938, and Eduardo Frei, head of the Christian Democrats in 1964, were seen as representing a considerable break with the past. But both candidates had obtained over 50 per cent of the vote, i.e., a clear majority. The opposition never forgot that the *Unidad Popular,* offering a much more drastic program, had obtained far less support.

There is neither space nor need to describe the rapid loss of legitimacy that the Chilean government suffered in the eyes of the opposition. A very surprising early honeymoon with various forces of the right followed the tense and hectic period between the elections of September, 1970, and Allende's final confirmation as President by Congress six weeks later. But by mid-1971, as the economic clouds gathered and the problems of land invasions and the takeover of industrial plants became acute, the honeymoon ended. Questions of constitutionality and legitimacy rapidly became acute and central. They reached a crescendo from May, 1973, onwards, when first the Supreme Court, then the Comptroller General, and finally the Chamber of Deputies all accused the government of acting systematically in an illegal and unconstitutional manner. Like the debates in the Spanish *Cortes* after April, 1936, the attitude of the legislature was (*de facto* and partly with intent) a call for the armed forces to intervene. Chile had arrived at a point similar to that reached in Spain in July, 1936.

CONCLUSION

This comparison between Spain and Chile has shown that the process which marked the breakdown of constitutional democratic government in these two countries was in part strikingly similar. There was much parallelism in the ever increasing mistrust and fear between right and left and in the incidents which caused as well as symbolized the escalating polarization of their positions, with their accompanying violence in both rhetoric and deed. Similar, too, were the specific ideologies and the kinds of actors involved, both at the level of individuals and at that of parties. In both countries the left was much more divided within itself than was the right; in both, abandonment of the constitutional road by a sector of the Socialist party may well be regarded as of determining importance, or at least as one of several critically important factors in bringing about the final *denouement.*

In both countries one can imagine a point of progression from a situation which most actors believed could be, would in fact be, and should be dealt with by nonviolent constitutional means to one in which most actors thought of stepping outside the Constitution, partly because they felt that their opponents were planning to do so. The approach of civil war is evidently a situation that lends itself to interpretation in terms of what sociologist Robert K. Merton has called a "self-fulfilling hypothesis." If enough groups believe that there may be a civil war, they will behave toward each other in a manner which assures that it will come about.

In both Spain and Chile, there had always existed political extremes on both the right and the left which had in principle rejected the nonviolent road to change and to resisting change. In Spain serious resistance had faced the liberal regimes of the nineteenth century and the process of democratization toward the end of that century and the beginning of the twentieth, even though the process had advanced. The latest resistance had been the dictatorship of 1923, and the Republic born with such hopes in 1931 survived for only five years. In view of such a history, the relevant question for Spain might well be: Why did the Second Republic last even as long as it did? Why was its fall not the usual *pronunciamiento* but the beginning of a civil war? New and unexpected about the civil war was only that the left and various masses which supported it, or constituted it, were for the first time in Spain's history strong enough to resist during three years the reimposition of the kind of nonrepresentative regime and social order that had been customary until 1931. Previously, the various middle-class, working-class, and peasant groups that constituted the Republican side had had to accept such regimes. They had been too weak and too disorganized to fight against them. In 1936 they were for the first time strong enough to resist.

In Chile, the fundamental question would more appropriately be the reverse one: How can one explain the breakdown of a system that had been sufficiently stable and flexible to survive for 140 years, enduring without continual violence or even an extraordinary amount of politically focused discontent?

In the context of this essay, devoted to a historical comparison, one answer in particular needs to be highlighted among the many which would have to be adduced to account for both the Chilean and the Spanish breakdown. While its importance relative to other causes may be difficult to weigh, it is certainly not negligible. It is a fact that the actors in Chile and Spain were themselves conscious of historical situations which were in some ways equivalent to their own. And, indeed, among these historical parallels in Chile, the Spanish Civil War was itself one, although not the most important.

By mid-1971, when the honeymoon period with the economic right was obviously at an end, and when the political center (the Christian Democrats) was moving toward an electoral alliance with the right in the form of the *Confederación Democrática* (CODE), both sides could and did draw on an ever larger number of pre-revolutionary, pre-civil war, or pre-*coup* situations in other countries, past and present, in order to analyze events in Chile. And, as unfortunately so often happens, each actor—whether individual, party, or ideological current—drew from each example the kind of conclusion needed and wanted to justify the position the actor had already decided to adopt.

In Spain, the contending parties, especially the Socialists, had been quite conscious of historical parallels from the inception of the Republic. These came in part from what might seem today the somewhat distant past but which were then still considered relevant. In Europe in the mid-1930s, the revolutions of 1789, 1848, and the Paris Commune of 1870 were not yet at all out of people's minds. But most of all, both the right and the left were living under the shadow of the Russian revolution of 1917 on the one hand and, on the other, under the shadow of many counterrevolutions or preemptive counterrevolutions and *coups* of the right which sought to justify themselves precisely on the basis of stemming the tide of bolshevism.

In Spain, therefore, it was above all the Russian October

Revolution of 1917 which appeared either as an ideal to imitate or a threat which had to be averted at all costs. Even more real and closer in time for the left was the defeat of its comrades in Italy, Portugal, Germany, and Austria. Above all, the brief but bloody civil war which consolidated the power of Engelbert Dollfuss, a Social Christian, in Austria in February, 1934, seemed to be a warning. It was not difficult to perceive Gil Robles as the Dollfuss of Spain, in the light of both his ideology and his career.

It would be a grave error to forget that Spanish democracy sought to establish itself at a time when all of Eastern Europe except Czechoslovakia was falling to right-wing authoritarian regimes, when the wave of fascism was at its highest point, and when the *Estado Novo* was establishing itself in Portugal. It is no surprise that the monarchist right in Spain obtained part of its inspiration from *Action Française,* that Catholics were formulating corporatist ideas difficult to distinguish from the experiences of fascist Italy, and that the desire to imitate fascism would become widespread among Spanish youth. In truth, the real surprise is how weak Spain's own brand of fascism really turned out to be. But in any case, a weak pluralist democracy did not seem like a strong bulwark against a left with revolutionary potential nor an adequate defense against an authoritarian and fascist right.

In Spain, both sides knew exactly what the future would hold for them if they lost in the process of escalation (as the right had done in Russia in 1917 and the left had done everywhere else). And each side felt that it had sufficient information on how to avoid failure, or sufficient examples of success, to make victory seem possible. This was more true for the right than for the left— as was to be the case in Chile also—but the left made up for the scarcity of examples from the past with the belief that historical trends would favor it in the future. And the future was here, now.

Chile, in the early 1970s, was probably even more conscious than had been Spain of the fate of revolutionary and counterrevolutionary attempts and preemptive *coups.* Just as the Russian revolution of 1917 was still, in the 1930s, a fascinating success for its admirers but one against which a whole decade of failures and reversals had to be balanced, so was the Cuban revolution of 1959 the brilliant post-World War II revolutionary success in Latin America. But it, too, was one against which a substantial number of more recent failures had to be weighed. The most dramatic reversal—the Latin American Germany of the 1960s, so to speak—was Brazil, where the military had taken over to forestall, so its supporters claimed, both chaos and a left dictatorship.

Armed revolts by the left had failed in Peru, Bolivia, and Venezuela in the early 1960s, soon after the Cuban revolution, just as they had in several European countries immediately after World War I i.e., after the Russian revolution.

And most other Latin American countries had also drifted to the right, at least in the sense of not permitting free political competition from the left. The military had taken over in Argentina in 1966. Uruguay was drifting to the right and under increasing military influence as the threat from the *Tupamaros* rose. The Peruvian military, after first crushing various attempts at establishing rural guerilla foci, had taken over the government in 1968 as much to forestall uncontrolled mass mobilization by the left as to oust an old oligarchy on the right from the socioeconomic structure—something the civilian government had been unable to do. And in August, 1971, Bolivia's dramatic and explicit flirtation with populist policies was abruptly ended with the ouster of General Juan Torres. This compressed counterrevolution occurred shortly after a people's assembly with the flavor of an alternative-style government and a call for arming workers had met in Cochabamba—much as such an assembly was to meet a few months later in Concepción under MIR and Socialist auspices, provoking a great deal of anxiety among the right and deep concern in the Communist party of Chile.

As in Spain relative to the Russian revolution of 1917, so the Chilean right was deeply aware of—and deeply frightened by—the success of an earlier left revolution, the Cuban. But it interpreted the long series of later right-wing military *coups* as representing the obvious solution if the threat of a left revolution were to become real in Chile, as it appeared to do in the eyes of the right. And the extreme left, while once again conscious that statistically the tendency of the immediate past and of the present might be against it, was not in the least deterred. At some point, historical inevitability was sure to make past statistical probabilities change.

That moment had not arrived. Chile, with a left almost as divided as it had been in Spain, and a center and right ultimately more powerful and more united than the left (just as in Spain), turned out to be as disastrous for the left as Spain had been in the 1930s. Conscious, on the basis of historical examples, of the kind of ultimate threat represented by the radical left, and more aware even than Spain of the details of the process which might lead in that direction, Chile needed to depart only modestly and for a relatively brief period from her nonviolent and overtly placid historical ways to arouse her middle and upper classes to the kind of fear to which the armed forces ultimately responded.

Commentaries

An Alternative Strategy for the Exercise of National Power: Italian Communism and the Historic Compromise

ALAN J. STERN

INTRODUCTION

These are years of precarious stability in Italian politics. Following the parliamentary elections of June, 1976, there was no longer any doubt that in order to govern the nation with any degree of effectiveness the Christian Democrats (DC), who have dominated Italian political life since the end of World War II would have to cooperate with the Communist party (PCI). For in the 1976 election the PCI made significant advances, bringing their share of the poll to 34.1 per cent in comparison to the 39 per cent for the DC, whose proportion of the vote was virtually unchanged since the 1972 election. With these results the PCI continued its record of growth in each parliamentary poll in the postwar period.

The electoral gains came in the wake of a 1974 national referendum decision in favor of limited divorce, making clear the willingness of the voting population to reject the directives of the Church. All this took place within the context of continuing disarray in the Italian economy and in the massive bureaucracy that is supposed to regulate it. These conditions make closer ties between leaders of the Christian Democrats and Communists essential. The two Andreotti governments that have followed the 1976 election and subsequent events, including the murder of Aldo Moro, survived because of various forms of PCI support.

This partially explicit and partly tacit cooperation between Christian Democrats and Communists appear to foreshadow the vindication of long-term PCI political choices. These choices, which have led to emphasis on a historic compromise (*compromesso storico*), are based on a system of broad social alliances and an insistence on gaining an accommodation with major Catholic forces. This perspective distinguishes the PCI from many other Marxist parties that operate within the frameworks of democratic societies. The French Communists, for example, until recently worked for ties only with other left-wing forces and preferred to court predominantly working-class support. When considering strategy, the Chilean Socialists led by Allende resembled the French Communists more than their Italian counterparts. Commitment to the *compromesso storico*, to working with the forces of organized Catholicism, expresses the deep belief of the Italian Communist party that their best chance to attain and retain a share of national decision-making power lies in partnership in a broad coalition spanning the political spectrum, rather than in domination of a narrow majority government drawing only upon the political forces of the left. The Italian Communists have spent much effort in analyzing and absorbing the lessons of the debacle of the Allende government in Chile. PCI secretary Enrico Berlinguer warns that "it would be dangerous to forget the tragic lesson of Chile," which, he argues, depended on too narrow a political base, thereby polarizing the nation and nourishing the conditions for its own demise.[1]

But reliance upon participation in a coalition of broad political scope is not a recent lesson coming from Latin American observation. The roots of the strategies embodied in the phrase "historic compromise" predate by decades the Allende years. For the PCI, the failure of the Chilean left-wing government only reinforced the sense of urgency the leaders give their emphasis on a broad societal presence. In the brief comments that follow, I hope to touch upon the historical underpining of the *compromesso storico*, to note the means by which it has been steadily pursued, and then finally to discuss some of the complexities the PCI or any similar party committed to fundamental societal change may encounter if it succeeds in attaining a share of national power through alliance and partnership strategies.

HISTORY

The Italian Communist party has always had respect for the strength of the forces of the Italian right, which essentially revolves about the forces of organized Catholicism. For example, a major source of the difference between the Italian and French Communists was the former's understanding of the potential hegemonic power of the Church on political life until after World War I. Drawing on his analysis of Italian conditions, Antonio Gramsci, the brilliant theoretician of the PCI, in several places broached the notion of alliances with portions of the Catholic world.[2]

Research conducted by the present writer in two small communities in the heart of the Catholic subculture in northeastern Italy revealed the extraordinary ingenuity of the local clergy as it countered the threat of left-wing politicization before the birth of an organized sacral party, the *Partito Popolare*. On the one hand, an undated version of Christian social ethics was widely dispersed, together with a strengthening of traditional welfare organizations. More importantly, the Church was able to deliver concrete benefits to the majority of the population, who were small farmers. Credit unions and agricultural cooperatives were established and helped tie the northeastern populace to the Church and its conservative politics. It was during this period that the Catholic Church proved that it could transfer its special legitimacy in many areas so that a political movement linked to the Church was endowed with a special sense of appropriateness for the local culture and for those who perceived themselves as loyal Catholics.[3]

In a certain sense the early coherence and strength of the Italian Catholic forces benefited the PCI in giving its impetus to develop a method of coexisting with such strong opponents. This historical respect for the right was buttressed by the unsettling experience of Fascism. The Italian Communists saw large numbers of working-class people and peasants who had once supported Marxist programs march enthusiastically to Mussolini's tunes. Thus chastened, as few similar Marxist parties were, the Italian Communists, led once again by the theoretical guidance of Gramsci, aimed to establish the party's presence in sectors of society other than the lower strata, so as to guard as much as possible against another desertion toward Fascism.[4]

The PCI had few reasons to believe that a largely working-class party, whether alone or with a few left-wing allies, could come to national power. Early possible experiences with reversals and strong opponents taught the PCI caution and foreshadowed the later development of the *compromesso storico*. Parties with less hazardous formative years may have been lulled into too easy belief in the acceptability of their appeals.

THE ARTICULATION OF THE PCI STRATEGY

From its earliest years, the Italian party stimulated by Gramsci has been a magnet for intellectuals dissatisfied with social and political conditions. Indeed, it became fashionable in certain intellectual circles to be a PCI member. This migration of intellectuals is certainly not unique to the PCI, but what may distinguish it from other left-wing parties of similar ideology—again the PCF provides a suitable contrast—is the use of intellectuals as party leaders and not just as political ornaments useful mainly to dangle before a middle-class world.

The prominence of intellectuals within the Italian party can be traced back to the clandestine period of the 1920s when the small PCI, in hiding from the Fascists, fought for survival. In that period it was neither subject to the strict discipline of Moscow nor in a position to quibble about the social backgrounds of leaders. Intellectuals continue to feel comfortable as members of the PCI, for the party has traditionally taken theory seriously. However, when theoretical positions are developed that are perceived by the top leadership as undermining basic party policy, the PCI has not hesitated to discipline, and at times expel, wayward intellectuals. In recent years the expulsion of the *Dialogo* group is the best case in point. Several important PCI leaders have intellectual interests; the most prominent among them, of course, is Secretary Berlinguer, who not only has an intellectual background but springs from Sardinian aristocratic stock.

The class background of this key party leader and several prominent members of his central committee brings us to another plank in the PCI strategy to seek wide societal presence: the decision to welcome and indeed seek support among the middle classes. To court the so-called *ceti medi produttivi* (the productive middle class) requires a very broad definition of potential friends and a very narrow conception of societal opponents. At times, indeed, it appears that the PCI would exclude only a handful of "monopoly capitalists" and their closest allies from the category of potential recruits. Togliatti, the key PCI leader in the pre-Berlinguer era, told his party that the PCI wished to guarantee "the freedom of small and medium property to develop and grow without being crushed by avid, egoistic groups of plutocrats, that is, by monopoly capitalism."[5] The PCI's courting of social-class diversity was fueled in part by its backward glance toward a strong Church and the appeals of Fascism, and in part by its desire to attract the growing numbers of relatively prosperous voters that were multiplying amidst the European "economic miracle" of the 1950s and early 1960s.

Decisions to seek supporters among sectors in the population not traditionally associated with Communist parties helped the PCI build an extremely impressive organizational network. Indeed the determination to build a mass party, made soon after World War II, may have helped to stimulate the class alliance strategy. At any event, today the party has 1.7 million members, an impressive roster.

This organizational depth, built mainly around the party section, which has replaced the cell as the most fundamental organizational unit, has enabled the PCI to foster the network of groups necessary to build and maintain a subculture comparable to that of its Catholic opponents. In areas of special strength such as the central Italian regions of Emilia, Tuscany, and Umbria, the party maintains a dense system of associations that appeal to many groups in the population: women, young people, veterans, sportsmen, peasants, book discussants—each group has its own club. And while the attractions of media, automobiles, and big-city diversions in general drain off some devotion to politically oriented events featured in their subcultural bastions, the PCI-dominated communities of central Italy still foster a loyalty to the PCI that borders on being a regional cultural value, passed on through the generations, in many segments of the population, not just among the working classes.

Strong organizational resources have helped the party demonstrate that its alliance strategy works in subnational governments. That is to say, emphasis upon collecting wide-ranging support has contributed to the establishment of Communist administrations, first at the community level in the so-called Red Belt cities of the central Italian provinces mentioned above, and, when they were initiated, in regional governments. Most recently PCI supporters have come to dominate the administration of most of the large northern cities, and they have even moved into the municipal offices in Naples.

While dramatic expansion of the Communist share of municipal power is a new phenomenon, PCI control of some localities, Bologna being a famous case in point, is of long standing. And so is Communist participation in various institutions of parliamentary life, especially its vital committee work. In the Parliament, the PCI has been content to cooperate quietly with other groups, including the Christian Democrats, in achieving mutual objectives without fanfare, even though in more public areas their sometime Catholic partners usually deny any cooperative efforts.

Rather similar acceptance of indirect benefits seems to characterize some PCI behavior in regions where the Communists have long been weak and their respectability in the community most marginal. In areas like northeastern Italy, the party seems ready, at least for a while, to encourage the success of the more progressive elements of the dominant Christian Democrats, even though in the short run tacit support of such politicians may bring no new supporters to the PCI itself. Yet varieties of tacit, nonpublic cooperation with opponents in areas as varied as the national legislature and small communal councils help gain the PCI a measure of legitimacy and acceptance among formerly hostile opponents.[6]

Courting a socially diverse membership even among the party elite, building a very strong mass-party structure on the basis of those supporters, and gradually accumulating control of municipalities whose numbers and importance have vastly expanded in recent years, together with a willingness to accept indirect gains in a variety of government forums, seem to be bringing to fruition at the mass level the carefully planned and patiently nurtured *compromesso storico*.

COMPLICATIONS IN THE PCI STRATEGY

Yet, paradoxically, it may be that in some ways the measures adopted to enhance the possibilities of achieving a measure of national power will make exercising that power relatively difficult. That is to say, the strategies pursued for most of the post-World War II years by the PCI may be best suited to defensive efforts to prevent opponents from undermining PCI support and to achieving limited goals, each important to one of its many constituent groups. The overall diversity of policy commitments can hamper efforts to stimulate fundamental social and political change. Let me illustrate this possible dilemma with reference to middle-class supporters and the needs of local administrators.

In the early postwar years, the PCI, under the leadership of Palmiro Togliatti, himself invoking the theoretical guidance of Gramsci, sought to extend its mantle to nonworkers in the then limited industrial society. Natural targets were small farmers of various sorts, especially sharecroppers, ex-sharecroppers, renters, and in some cases small independent holders, as well as the large numbers of small shopkeepers and even owners of small manufacturing plants. The limited nature of the operations engaged in by

these occupational groups needs to be noticed. The PCI was vigorously supporting small productive units.

As Italy increasingly participated in the general European
economic boom and became integrated rather successfully in the
Common Market, the Italian economy was increasingly characterized by a large public sector and concentrated productivity in
large firms, a growing service group, and a shrinking agricultural
population. A party that had attracted small holders found it hard
to shift positions so as to take progressive positions in line with
dynamic economic change. At times some subunit of the party
found itself fighting against a supermarket or even a cooperative
that offered a wide range of merchandise at rather low prices because such enterprises threatened a number of small store owners
who had long been supporters of the PCI.

A closely related problem, because it also involved deep reluctance to endanger established electoral support, involves the
growing group of municipal officials, including many mayors and
town councilors, who are PCI members. These officials are apt to
be relatively preoccupied with local affairs and have foremost in
their minds community-level goals and the protection of safe electoral margins to enable them to attain those goals. Inherent in
such activity is a tendency to deemphasize political doctrine and a
similar tendency to emphasize the use of varieties of political patronage. The priorities of local administrations and the custodians
of successful party organizational units may make a PCI leadership out of national office more congenial than a group of PCI
leaders striving to bring about basic changes in Italian society.

It remains to be seen whether the gathering of electoral support from a variety of social-class groups with sometimes contradictory policy preferences and the efficient, honest administration
of communities that range in size from hamlets to great cities can
be coordinated with bold national leadership in a coalition government with the Christian Democrats. Some commentators, notably State Department officials including the ex-American Secretary of State, have warned of the dire consequences of Communist
participation in an Italian cabinet. Certainly the nature of the Italian commitment to the Atlantic Alliance might alter in quality, no
matter how sincere the PCI statements of intention to keep Italy
in NATO.[7]

But such apprehensions should not be exaggerated. In the
first place American pressures, Church insistence, and perhaps
PCI reluctance to inspire right-wing attempts at military solutions
will keep PCI members out of sensitive cabinet posts such as

Defense, Interior, and Foreign Affairs. Secondly, and perhaps more significantly for those interested in the domestic impact of possible direct PCI participation in the government, the legacy of the very groundwork that allowed the *compromesso storico* to succeed at the level of the mass electorate may act to restrain and inhibit the range of Communist options.

In many ways the historic compromise suggests itself as a preferred alternative to abortive efforts by left-wing governments to exercise power in previously hostile democratic environments supported by bare majorities. For years many observers believed the *compromesso storico* could not, at the electoral level, bring sufficient strength to ensure a share of government power. Such observers expected, if anything, an accommodation among elites. It may well prove to be the case that skepticism about success at the mass level was misplaced. The *compromesso storico* may yield a share of national decision-making power and may not stimulate right-wing or military *coups*. However, the leftist parties that may come to participate in the forums of national power through steady, gradual accumulation of alliances and supports have special limiting parameters of their own to contend with.

Having made these points, it remains to be said that avoidance of a strategy aimed at the construction of a narrow left-wing coalition makes it likely that the PCI has also avoided the social schisms and military solutions surrounding the efforts of Salvador Allende to change Chilean society. Even with the important constraints on its freedom enumerated above, the PCI is now in a good position to insist on a renewal of an Italian national elite that has been remarkably stable for thirty years and to press for long delayed, significant, if perhaps not revolutionary societal changes.

NOTES

1. Berlinguer has published several articles on the "Chilean lesson" in the PCI journal *Rinascita*. Many of Berlinguer's recent positions are reported in the widely available article by Alvin Shuster, "Communism Italian Style," *New York Times Magazine*, May 9, 1976, p. 13.

2. See for example Quinton Hoare and Geoffrey Smith (eds.), *Selections from the Prison Notebooks of Antonio Gramsci* (New York: International, 1971), and the discussion of Gramsci's perception of the Italian right in Sidney Tarrow, "Adaptation and Change," in Donald L. M. Blackmer and Sidney Tarrow (eds.), *Communism in Italy and France* (Princeton: Princeton University Press, 1975), pp. 584–585. Tarrow's concluding chapter in this volume is an excellent synthetic guide to recent studies of the two

major West European Communist parties. The volume edited by Blackmer and Tarrow brings together most of the recent empirical work on the PCI and PCF.

3. The studies of the two communities is reported in Alan J. Stern, "Political Legitimacy in Local Politics," in Blackmer and Tarrow (eds.), pp. 221–258. For a discussion of the dynamics of political legitimacy, see Jean Blondel, *Comparative Government* (New York: Praeger, 1969), p. 63.

4. Stephen Hellman accents the importance of the Fascist experience in "The PCI's Alliance Strategy and the Case of the Middle Classes," in Blackmer and Tarrow (eds.), p. 375.

5. Palmiro Togliatti, "La Politica di Unità Nazionale dei Comunisti." This speech as well as Togliatti's famous "Ceto Medio e Emilia Rossa" is reprinted in *Critica Marxista* 2(July-October, 1964). Hellman's discussion, *op. cit.*, of the whole question is enlightening.

6. Parliamentary behavior is very helpfully analyzed in Franco Cazzola, "Consenso e Opposizione nel Parlamento Italiano: Il Ruolo del PCI dalla I alla IV Legialatura," *Rivista Italiana di Scienza Politica* 2(April, 1972), pp. 71–96. For local examples, see Stern, *op. cit.*

7. A sensible and stimulating brief discussion of the foreign policy impact of possible PCI collaboration in government is presented in Peter Lange, "What Is to Be Done—About Italian Communism," *Foreign Policy* 21(Winter, 1975–1976), pp. 224–240.

Impressions
of an Authoritarian Model

GLAUCIO DILLON SOARES

This essay offers a brief analysis of the Brazilian military regime, which many have called the successful dictatorship. Indeed, in recent years it has achieved a degree of popular support as well as a high growth rate in GNP.

To analyze any military dictatorship, of course, it is necessary to consider first what preceded it. It is one thing when the military overthrows a civilian government characterized by considerable anarchy, high inflation, low economic growth, and a discredited political system. It is another when the military replaces a government in which there is faith, a high growth rate, considerable social justice, and little if any corruption.

There is sufficient empirical data to show that in Brazil everything political was discredited in the eyes of the public. A survey undertaken by the United States Information Service (USIS) between January and March, 1964, in the state of Guanabara showed the preoccupation with political corruption. Of those interviewed, 62 per cent said that what Brazil needed most was an honest government, without corruption. Response to another question reflected the weakness of the party system. Few reported that they felt the existing political party system to be satisfactory: 38.7 per cent preferred a one-party system, another 26.6 per cent a two-party system. The question did not recognize the possibility that part of the population might prefer no party, a response which in other polls received significant support. In either case, one third or less of those surveyed defended the existing party system.

Another survey, in this case of candidates for a degree in an important engineering school, showed the low opinion students held of politicans. Three fourths of the students (77 per cent) dis-

450

agreed with the statement that political corruption had decreased in Brazil in recent years. There is no doubt that by 1964 the public attitude toward politics and political parties was one of complete lack of confidence.

Other investigations show the ineffectiveness of the legislature before 1964. Less than 20 per cent of all bills submitted were discussed, and still fewer became laws.[1] Congress was characterized by tremendous debate over nothing substantial. In general, the most relevant bills had been under consideration for seven or more years. As a result, when they were finally approved, often their *raison d'être* had already disappeared. By no standard could the Congress be considered efficient.[2]

Another problem was the high and growing inflation rate. It was 23.8 per cent in 1960; 41.9 per cent in 1961; 55.8 per cent in 1962; 80.2 per cent in 1963; and 86.6 per cent in 1964. High inflation continued even after drastic controls were introduced by the government.[3] Inflation in Brazil was not a technical invention of the economists. It was a reality felt and resented by the population. The same USIS study found in Guanabara that 55 per cent of the population interviewed saw the rise in the cost of living as the principal problem facing the government.

From 1962 on the economic growth rate dropped radically, a trend that ran counter to the trend toward more or less continuous growth ever since the Second World War. Except in 1953 and 1956, the Brazilian postwar economy had grown at a very rapid rate. Growth was particularly rapid between 1957 and 1961: 8.1 per cent; 7.7 per cent; 5.6 per cent; 9.7 per cent; and 10.3 per cent.[4] These high growth rates generated optimism, and the opposition prudently shifted its attack to other themes. Thus, the Brazilian population, accustomed for decades to sustained growth, was surprised by the economic stagnation that began with the creation of the parliamentary government in 1962.

As a result, conditions in 1964 favored a change toward authoritarian rule. Someone has already mentioned that if forced to choose between anarchy and dictatorship, the people always prefer dictatorship. I believe this was the case in Brazil. Yet it was exactly the opposite of what had been hoped for. Goulart reassumed presidential powers after a plebiscite in which five votes were cast in favor to every one against (82 per cent, or 9,457,488 votes in favor, 2,073,582 votes against). This overwhelming majority was far greater than that he had obtained in the vice-presidential elections of 1960 (when he received only 4.5 million votes). In other words, the results of the plebiscite were a *rejection of the institutional anarchy* that had been created in Brazil under the parlimentary regime. The latter had been an attempt to wrest presidential powers from Goulart. The position of President was maintained, but its powers were transferred to the Parliament, a Parliament totally incapable of governing the country. In two and one-half years there was a parade of Prime Ministers.[5] The plebiscite thus indicated the depth of feeling of the opposition supporting Goulart, who was able to gather 800,000 people in the streets of Rio and 500,000 in Sao Paulo—according to modest estimates. Yet the hope that Goulart could control inflation, regenerate rapid economic growth, and control anarchy rapidly disappeared. It is in these circumstances that the *coup* of 1964 emerged. It was based on the total discrediting of the political system in the eyes of the population, particularly the middle sectors.

There are also more structural causes of the *coup*. José Nun has emphasized the importance of military *coups* supported by the middle class.[6] In 1945, when democracy was reintroduced into the Brazilian political process following the dictatorship of Getulio Vargas, the Brazilian Workers party (*Partido Trabalhista Brasileiro*) obtained twenty-two deputies. In the elections of 1962 it received 116. Thus it grew from a relatively insignificant party into the second largest in Brazil.[7] Moreover, various parties on the left also increased in size. In 1962 the left, labor, and populist parties together received more than 40 per cent of the total vote. This phenomenon is explained by the growing level of electoral participation. At first only the middle classes and a small group of workers were incorporated into the electoral process. Once the entire middle class participated, however, other groups were progressively added. The great expansion of electoral participation from 1945 to 1962 was not due to vegetative growth in the same population but to the addition of *new* social sectors which had previously been excluded. The addition of these sectors meant a political shift from right to left. In 1962 the PTB for the first time in the history of Brazil was able to defeat the *Union Democratica Nacional* (UDN), the party of the moralistic and conservative middle class. The growing strength of the PTB threatened the domination of the conservatives, whose position had not been endangered since 1899.[8] Thus the military *coup* also responded to pressures from the middle class, symbolized by the great movement of masses marching through the streets, a movement similar to the March of the Empty Pots against the *Unidad Popular* government in Chile, but on the scale of a country with 100 million inhabitants—that is, with 800,000 persons in the streets.[9]

The period following 1964 has often erroneously been treated as a homogeneous unit. It was not. The same sector was not always in control, and we can and should distinguish different periods. Stepan has published an interesting study of the military group that assumed power in 1964. It was a generational group based on shared experiences that created a number of binding ties. All its members had participated in the Italian campaign of the Brazilian Expeditionary Forces in World War II, all but one had taken advanced training courses in the United States, and all had a history of participating in prior political and military conspiracies.[10] The great intellectual architect of the *coup* was General Golbery do Couto e Silva, a man who had been active in various military plots, both successful and frustrated.[11]

This faction known as the "Sorbonne Group" had a reasonably liberal-democratic program, *always insofar as the possibility of an extreme left electoral victory did not exist.* In its political model, the alternatives were two: conservatives and laborites. Once in power, the regime created two new parties—eliminating those that already existed. The two parties were created by decree, as if partisan loyalties to them could be created at the same time. By a stroke of the pen the Labor party, the PSD (*Partido Social Democratico*—which had nothing to do with socialism and much less with democracy; it was a party of the right, conservative and rural), and the thirteen parties that had existed until 1964 ceased to exist. What is interesting is that the legal, institutional apparatus that was imposed, that did not correspond to political reality, bit by bit acquired significance and value—a fact which surprised many, including myself.

The method of domination was first to reduce the powers of Congress. This was achieved by Institutional Act #2, which denied Congress the power of initiating legislation and restricted it to a function of supervising, of criticizing the Executive. This was done through so-called subpoenas for information, by which a minister might be called to testify before the legislature. This activity grew phenomenally—in 1967 there were 3,598 subpoenas for information. In 1970, following Institutional Act #5 and a year-long congressional recess, the number of subpoenas dropped to six. Institutional Acts #2 and #5 were powerful instruments, denying Congress its fundamental function of legislating and keeping it from erecting obstacles to the plans of the Executive. Thus, in 1971, the Congress approved all bills originating from the Executive—sixty-seven in all—and rejected all but 9 per cent of its own bills. It virtually committed legislative suicide. If we note from whom the legislative initiative came in Congress, we find that almost everything was proposed by the opposition. The few bills that the Congress did approve were all projects originating in the Executive but presented by the leadership of the *Alianza Renovadora Nacional* (ARENA), the official party. These were approved as a matter of course.[12]

Until Institutional Act #5 certain liberties continued to survive in Brazil. The press still continued to function, students organized demonstrations, and deputies denounced and argued. After Institutional Act #5, however, and above all with the military triumvirate following Costa e Silva, a new and more repressive period began. Brazilians clearly lost what was left of their citizenship. (It is said that never did so few do so much damage to so many in so short a time—the triumvirate was in power only a few months, but it promulgated most of the restrictive legislation.) The triumvirate was followed by Garrastazu Medici, who in his first two years consolidated the regime and eliminated the few sources of armed resistance.

Medici acquired considerable public legitimacy, founded above all on the myth of a great national program. Economic growth, which was heavily stressed in government publicity, was the major basis of his legitimacy. How do we know? If we analyze presidential speeches, we find that Castello Branco at first spoke with frequency of a return to democracy. By mid-1965 such references had disappeared, and he spoke instead of security, and then of development followed by security. The theme of development occupies more than half of the space in presidential speeches, an emphasis that persists through the end of the Medici government and continues to the present.[13] The themes of security and national integration, and other themes, alternate and have a clearly secondary importance. Indeed, the emphasis on democracy only reappears with the Geisel government. Geisel, for the first time in ten years, picks up anew the theme of democratization and introduces also the idea of income redistribution.

There is no doubt that after a certain moment the major preoccupation of the military government has been economic growth. It has oriented all its efforts in this direction. Nor can we deny that it has had considerable success. Thus polls conducted in 1971 and 1972 show a high level of popular support for the government. But how can these surveys be valid, given that the results of the November, 1974, elections were adverse to the government? It is a difficult question, but I believe it can be answered. To the extent that the surveys are valuable, they show a great preoccupation with and acceptance of the project of a *Great Brazil*. Everyone is ready to make considerable personal sacrifice so that the country can grow, so that it can become a world power of first magnitude. There is also a great preoccupation with order and peace (once again a rejection of anarchy). This is the origin of the government's legitimacy in the eyes of wide sectors of the population.

In 1974 the opposition did not attempt to attack these strengths, as it had on earlier occasions. Instead, it emphasized that "growth is not helping you." Various surveys at the time begin to capture the fact that the parties, created as empty organs, as superimposed political structures, had obtained some social significance. The followers of both the *Movimiento Democratico Brasileiro* (MDB) and the ARENA accept that the latter is the party of the rich and the former that of the poor.[14] The opposition had found a class basis upon which to mount an effective opposition to the government. It would have been absurd to deny that the growth rate was high. One could discuss just how high it was—a little bit more or a little less; one could even affirm that the gross national product, as it was measured, was meaningless. But to deny the existence of growth was to deny what people were seeing materially in the street. What took place was an attack on the problem of distribution, affirming that the growth benfited not everyone but only a few. This attack, coupled with the secondary emphasis on individual freedom, gave the MDB a spectacular electoral victory.

It was fascinating to see how an academic topic, discussion of which was initially prohibited, gradually became a theme that could be considered and then a topic of political debate. Many of us knew the concentration of wealth was high, but no one published the fact—no one dared. The first step had to come from outside, and it came through an advisor from the World Bank, Al Fishlow, who wrote a study that had practical impact on Robert McNamara, the president of the institution. In his study Fishlow showed that concentration of income, whether by class, sector, or region, was a fact in Brazil.[15] Once published and mentioned by McNamara in a speech, it was impossible to avoid the topic, which soon became the subject of political controversy. This was the great electoral issue of the MDB. Five years earlier it could not have been mentioned, but a certain liberty, a certain openness in politics, permitted it to be touched upon directly in the campaign and in the press.

We have information on what the Brazilian people were thinking at the time. Their opinion did not count for much, but it is interesting to note that the people had no clear idea of what they wanted. In one survey, the majority—78 per cent—did not want a military government (which is different from an authoritarian one), nor did they believe the military should intervene in politics. But 71 per cent continued to say the politicians are corrupt. And no less than 82 per cent preferred "a government that is not very capable but honest to one that is capable but corrupt."[16] That is, the image of politics as "dirty" persisted. In addition, as a result of the repeated humiliations suffered by Brazilians at the hands of the military, a second negative view of politicians was added. In Brazil, subservience is a requisite for political survival. This has created an even more negative image of politicians, who are seen as not only corrupt but also servile and without honor. Thus the population wants redistribution and it wants nationalization, but it does not have its own political program. If the people do not want politicians and they do not want the military, then who can direct the country? It is a very unstructured situation, but one that is rather normal for a country that has suffered oppression for twelve years.

There is also a lack of leadership. When oppression lasts for many years, old leaders disappear. The age pyramid in Brazil has a wide base. There are many young and few adults. In twelve years an immense number who have never had any effective political participation have become old enough to vote. They were only seven, eight, or nine years old when there was last representative democracy in Brazil. They do not remember the political figures of that time: Kubitschek, Quadros, Carlos Lacerda. . . . There is a vacuum of names. If the government in fact seeks political evolution in Brazil, this is a serious problem. Partisan ties continue as before, but the leaders have disappeared.

There are a number of additional points we could note. First, I sensed in a recent visit to Brazil that political discussion has become somewhat more open. For the first time in years the people speak their minds. The first thing my taxi driver did was criticize members of the military, saying they did not stand in line, they earned too much, and I do not remember what else. The people speak up. In academic circles people converse with one another. They lead classes. They do not feel fear—above all at the advanced and postgraduate levels. Two years ago fear was present, five years ago terror. Censorship of the mass media is much more relaxed. Prior censorship is limited to three newspapers, *Opiniao, O Pasquim,* and the diocesan newspaper of Sao Paulo. This is because the Church, at this moment, is the only organized opposition to the regime.

Second, it is quite clear that the concept of the state we inherited from German general theory of the state is not adequate. The state is not the unitary, homogenous, and synchronized body we studied in the university. In concrete terms, the Geisel term, which forms part of the sector that followed Castello Branco, does not hold complete power at a military level. Perhaps it holds greater power, but it does not want to risk a confrontation. Likewise, torture continues, even though it is much less frequent than before. Still, it continues. Who tortures? In general paramilitary organs, usually at a very local level, are responsible. We know that Sao Paulo and Recife are much more hard line than, for example, Rio Grande do Sul. The commander of the first army, Reynaldo Almeida, communicates with the relatives of detainees. He informs them officially that there are regular processes within the structure of military justice that, if one accepts the parameters, are legal. At least it is a legal process, with the possibility of defense. This is a tremendous advance from the earlier situation. Before, people simply disappeared. Sometimes they reappeared six months, two years, or three years later; sometimes they never reappeared. In Congress there is an extremely active opposition. One need only read the speeches of the members—Marcos Freire, Lysaneas Miciel, and others—to note this relaxation.

Yet, this limited relaxation is not irreversible. Although our attention is drawn by the participation that now exists, we must also inquire as to what members of the military are thinking. The answer to this question we do not know, and we have no information. Yet it does not seem farfetched to me for there to be a process of "civilianizing" in the government. I think there are various reasons. Relative military expenditures have increased considerably during the last ten years. Not only have salaries risen, but so have appropriations for military expenditures. Many officers are active now in both private enterprise and public administration. For example, in the Education Ministry under Jarbas Passarinho there were thirty-three officers of a rank of colonel or higher in important administrative posts. There are numerous advantages in occupying such positions: prestige, power, salary, a car, and so forth. Are they going to give all this up? Almost all large Brazilian private enterprises have a general or one or more high-ranking officers among their directors. General Golbery himself is (or was) the president of Dow Chemical in Brazil. Companies have reacted realistically to the fact that the military as an institution controls power. Private enterprise has sought to co-opt officers to serve its own ends. Is the military voluntarily going to give this up?

My interviews with several deputies, a few business executives, and even fewer military officers suggested the following: the distribution of opinions within the Congress and in the higher ranks of the armed forces is normal. That is, in each there is a certain middle position that gathers more support, and extreme positions that gather less. Nevertheless, the two distributions do not have the same middle values. There are two opposing bell-shaped curves—one on one side, the other on the other—but in no way are the central points of these the same. In the Federal Senate there is perhaps one individual who favors an extreme right position, while in the army there are a good many who do. In the Chamber of Deputies those who are in most virulent opposition, the *"autenticos,"* oppose any program of national conciliation by steps that would arrive at something we might call "normalization." In contrast, such a program seems acceptable to the Geisel government. Yet what might be the minimal demands—the nonnegotiables—of the right? I think that for the military there are two points on which there can be no compromise. The first is an institutionalization of national security legislation. A constitutional reform would have to be introduced leaving the military real power—which they already have—as well as legal power for taking charge of national security. Second, they will not accept discussion of the budget by politicians. They are afraid that if civilians return to power, a spirit of revenge, however limited, may result in a decrease in the military budget. For the civilians, the nonnegotiables appear to be an immediate cessation of torture (which would include punishment of infractors), reestablishment of a state of law, return to Congress of its normal functions (particularly supervision of the Executive, but also certain legislative functions), and direct elections. These nonnegotiables do not seem incompatible, and I believe an agreement at the center of the two distributions is possible.[17]

Other lessons: Some institutions lose functions. Others, though created completely in air, create their own functions. Not only do they create functions, but they acquire a certain reality. The case of the MDB is an ideal example. Though created by decree, it is today an opposition party with a real class base. Socioeconomic reality is given, and the parties must reflect the socioeconomic parameters more or less faithfully. Contrary to the theory that the worse it is, the better, small cumulative advantages are worth pursuing. It is important to support the process of redemocratization. I believe all of us who have suffered the vicissitudes of politics know how important is the existence of *habeas corpus*. In the 1950s many unthinking extremists laughed at democratic institutions, at civil rights, the rights of man. After the 1964 *coup* they realized just how important these rights and institutions are. Certain individual guarantees, direct elections in certain cases—the crumbs of liberty that one can obtain and guarantee—should not be ridiculed. I believe this lesson serves us all. These are some of the similarities between the Brazilian experiences, which I do not pretend in any way to report exhaustively, and the Chilean.

NOTES

1. See Sergio H. H. De Abraches and Glaucio Ary Dillon Soares, "As Funcões do Legislativo," *Revista de Administração Pública* 7(January-March, 1973), pp. 73–98; Spanish version in the *Revista Lationamericana de Ciencia Política* 3(August, 1972), pp. 256–280. See also the thesis of Clovis Brigagao, *Poder e Legislativo no Brasil* (Rio de Janeiro: IUPERJ, Master's Thesis, 1971).

2. Various works by politicians also emphasize the inefficiency of the legislature, as well as other problems affecting its functioning. See in particular José Bonifacio de Andrada, "A Reforma do Poder Legislativo," *Revista Brasilera de Estudios Politicos* 20(January, 1966), pp. 21–38. Oswaldo Trigueiro, "A Crise Legislativa e o Regime Presidencialista," *Revista Brasileira de Estudios Politicos* 7(November, 1959), pp. 45–74; and Alfonso Arinos de Mello Branco, *Evoluçao de Crise Brasileira* (Saõ Paulo: Cia Editôra Nacional, 1965).

3. Data from *Conjuntura Económica* 28 (May, 1974). The data refer to the increase in the cost of living.

4. *Ibid.*

5. Tancredo Neves was the first Prime Minister. When he resigned, Goulart nominated San Tiago Dantas, who was rejected by the Congress (174 votes against to 110 for). The following Prime Minister resigned after less than forty-eight hours. Approval was finally obtained for Brochado da Rocha, who resigned in September, 1961. The new Prime Minister, Hermes Lima, was not confirmed by the Congress until November. When the plebiscite was held at last on January 6, 1963, the parliamentary regime had been totally discredited.

6. See José Nun, "A Latin American Phenomenon: The Middle-Class Military Coup," in James Petras and Maurice Zeitlin (eds.), *Latin America: Reform or Revolution?* (Greenwich, Conn.: Fawcett Publications, 1968), pp. 145–185.

7. See my description of the evolution of political parties during this period: Glaucio Ary Dillon Soares, *Sociedade e Politica no Brasil* (Saõ Paulo: Difusão Européia, 1973), chap. IV.

8. *Ibid.*

9. Estimates vary considerably. High guesses put the number at 1.5 million in Sao Paulo and 800,000 in Rio; low estimates suggest a half million in Sao Paulo and 300,000 in Rio.

10. See Alfred Stepan, *The Military in Politics: Changing Patterns in Brazil* (Princeton, N.J.: Princeton University Press, 1971).

11. General Golbery do Costa e Silva is, without doubt, one of the most important strategists of the Brazilian armed forces. He has been preoccupied, above all, with questions of geopolitics, a theme which has absorbed his interest in three books, *Planejamento Estratégico* (Rio de Janeiro: Biblioteca do Exercito, 1955); *Aspectos Geopolíticos do Brasil* (Rio de Janeiro: José Olympio, 1957); and *Geopolítica do Brasil* (Rio de Janeiro: José Olympio, 1967). The last is a collection of articles and speeches. In one sense, the doctrine of national security and internal war was elaborated by General Golbery long before such topics interested the North American military.

12. Abranches and Soares, *op. cit.*, pp. 94–96.

13. Cándido Mendes presents an interesting analysis of presidential speeches: "O Discurso Político Domo Indicador nos Sistemas de Elite de Poder na America Latina," in Cándido Mendes (ed.), *Crise e Mudança Social* (Rio de Janeiro: Livraria Eldorado, 1974), pp. 147–195. Between 1965 and 1970 development is the theme mentioned with greatest frequency in presidential speeches.

14. This was shown in a survey made in Belo Horizonte by a group of political science students led by Fabio Wanderley Reis.

15. The study, "Brazilian Size Income Distribution," has been published in the *American Economic Review* 62(May, 1971), part II. A similar essay, also by Fishlow, is "Reflections on Post-1964 Brazilian Economic Policy," in Alfred Stepan (ed.), *Authoritarian Brazil* (New Haven: Yale University Press, 1973).

16. See Vera Maria Candido Pereira, *Authoritarismo e Preconceito: Un Estudo Exploratorio* (Rio de Janeiro: IUPERJ, Master's Thesis, 1972), pp. 78–79.

17. For a more detailed analysis of this problem, see Helio Jaguaribe, *Brasil: Crise e Alternativas* (Rio de Janeiro: Zahar, 1974).

Observations on the Nature of Authoritarian Regimes

JOSE NUN

THE CHANGES IN DEPENDENCY RELATIONS

I begin with Radomiro Tomić's affirmation that capitalism in Chile had exhausted itself. I would rather say that a certain kind of capitalism had been exhausted and with it a certain kind of political system. Precisely because in many ways the latter had achieved in Chile a far higher level of development than in other Latin American countries, its collapse has been more catastrophic and, for many, more shocking. However—as has already been suggested—the crisis was not unleased by the *Unidad Popular*. The Allende government was at once both an expression of that crisis and a bold effort to find a solution to it from the left. (In this duality I believe we can find the origin of many of its contradictions.) Today what we are observing is less a solution from the right than a brutal transition to such a solution—a solution that, though precarious, may yet be found. Tortures, concentration camps, unemployment, and mass misery can only be seen as indications of the end of capitalism if we forget to what extent capitalism is a system of exploitation whose principal end is personal enrichment, a system that has even found it proper to make use of slavery where it has been able to do so profitably. Moreover, both in the Chilean crisis and its present *denouement*, I believe we can perceive similarities with what had occurred earlier in Brazil and Uruguay and what is presently occurring in Argentina. There are even certain shared characteristics with recent history in Peru and Mexico. These similarities, in real-life situations that in other ways seem so dissimilar, reflect the two great, interrelated processes that have been slowly gaining force ever since the 1950s.

461

On the other hand, there is the reconstruction or transformation of the imperialist chain of domination—a chain in which the various Latin American countries occupy specific positions. On the other, there is the notable intensification of the struggle for mass justice throughout the continent.

The well-known transformations in the nature of dependency relations that have occurred in the last quarter century have undoubtedly affected different countries in the area unequally. However, almost everywhere these changes have involved from the first: (1) an increasing presence of large international capital—today ever more interested in controlling new internal markets; (2) an ever more powerful trend toward centralization and concentration of capital; and (3) a considerable expansion of the public sector. These three changes have been accompanied by deepening disequilibria between and within sectors and a deterioration (or at best a partial, unstable, and very limited improvement) in the relative position of the majority of the population. The intensification of the struggle for popular justice has been tightly linked to all of these transformations. In each concrete context, of course, it has assumed varied forms and intensity, ranging from "peronist resistance" in Argentina, to the workers' strikes of Santiago, Sao Paulo, and Montevideo, to the peasant movement of the Peruvian Andes.

The worldwide capitalist system is today passing to a new stage in the relationship between the imperialist metropolis and peripheral formations such as those found in the majority of Latin American nations. It is here that we find the decisive difference. In the central nations, hegemonic monopoly capital under the control of the so-called multinational corporations was consolidated after the war. In the process, there was produced an economic boom which was reflected in increasing employment and rising real salaries for a considerable portion of the labor force. In the short and medium term, this contributed both to cushioning the social impact of the important transformations that were occurring and to fragmenting the masses or at least making their demands less explosive. Simultaneously, the economic boom provided resources for an increasingly interventionist state—a state which was also increasingly deficit financed. The resources were used to ameliorate the most negative effects of the new forms of domination. Thus, regardless of the ever more visible limitations of such a strategy, it was in general possible to transform the process of production without deeply affecting the processes of ideological and political socialization.

In the periphery, the situation was different for two reasons: first, the beginning point was different, and, second, the periphery continued to enjoy a subordinate position. Because of the latter, conditions simply did not exist for an extended economic boom like the European, Japanese, or, even less, the North American. Even capitalist "miracles," when they are dependent, tend to be short-lived and restricted to reach. The Latin American proponents of "developmentalism" sought by whatever means available to maintain their basic alliances with more traditional groups—at least to the extent possible. In the past the apogee of the import substitution era had permitted these alliances to be preserved. Think in terms of Kubitschek, Frondizi, Alessandri, Prado, López Mateos. . . . Resort to foreign capital seemed the "modernizing" solution *par excellence*, particularly for those who placed their highest hopes in a rapid increase in the rhythm of accumulation and, consequently, rapid growth in "Our Lord," the Gross National Product. A better distribution of income or greater system legitimacy would follow in due time as a matter of course—if the jump could be made without the masses arising on their own. It was the hour of planning and technocracy but not of collective will. Thus, though governments might change, the technocrats—backed by an efficient international bureaucracy—continued to be the same, in spite of the growing discontent of the population.

THE CRISIS OF THE CHILEAN LIBERAL STATE

I have noted these processes because I do not think sufficient attention has yet been given to the complex nature of the transformation to this new stage. Certainly, we understand the broad characteristics of many of the principal economic trends. Our understanding of the key problem of the state, however, is much less clear. By "the state" we mean not just an institutional system but also the crystallization of a specific relationship among social forces. The state is the specific entity that links political and civil society. The changes that the state is undergoing require our careful analysis, yet we can take only limited advantage of the concepts and hypotheses drawn from the evolution of the central countries.

Is it really possible, for example, to compare the Chilean political system that took form during the last twenty years to the European liberal democracies? (This has often been done.) The basic premise of the "classic" bourgeois liberal state is a strict separation between private and public domains. More concretely, the liberal state does not intervene in either the process of economic accumulation or the ideological process of civil society. But if this is to be so, there must be two necessary preconditions. There must simultaneously be, first, a widespread diffusion of the capitalist mode of production and, second, a considerable degree of integration between the economic and ideological levels, i.e., a high degree of correspondence between the processes of production and those of socialization in capitalist social relations. Only if this is so can the state be limited to the basic function of a watchman over an order that can be presented ideologically as arising prior to that state. Both the bourgeois defenses of capitalism and the criticisms of Marx and Gramsci use the liberal state as a point of reference. For this reason they must be used in the Latin American case with great care.

In general terms, the bourgeois liberal state never existed in Latin America, in spite of the letter of our constitutions. Specifically, the creation of peripheric capitalism—at least at first—was based on a restricted and distorted diffusion of the capitalist means of production and socialization. In Chile the enclave economy that gave early prominence to the public sector, combined with the oligarchic control of land, laid the basis for a very unequal capitalist development. Under such conditions a typical bourgeois state simply could not operate. What appeared superficially as a liberal state in fact rested on the political exclusion of wide sectors of the population. In other words, in Chile civil society could be portrayed as the domain of private interests existing prior to the state only by those who sought to avoid perceiving that what gave shape to the Chilean state was its narrow political nature. One example is sufficient: When at the end of the 1930s there was an attempt to promote the formation of rural labor unions, the *latifundistas*—represented by the National Agricultural Society—screamed bloody murder. In effect, they reminded the government of the limits of the system, the strict margins within which the mechanisms preserving civil society could operate. Result: the government immediately intervened and halted the process. I need not remind you that it was the government of the Popular Front.

Beginning in the 1950s, this "atypical" Chilean bourgeois-liberal state began to enter a crisis. In the context of a stagnant economy, as mass pressures forced expanding political participation, the institutional scaffolding began to creak. It is no coincidence that following Ibañez's "broom," Alessandri began to attack the very system of political parties. Simultaneously the changes occurring in the structure of accumulation forced new and more rigorous methods of social control.

I consider this point of greatest importance. It is this that gives rise to the dialectic in the processes to which I referred in the beginning. If democratization of the system was a certain risk to the interests of the enclaves and the bourgeois oligarchy, it was no less so to the interests of new monopoly capital producing for the internal market—a monopoly capital that was being incorporated into the prevailing structure of domination. In one sense, the risk for this new capital—represented above all by subsidiaries of the multinationals—was even greater. The copper companies, for example, could enforce their control not only over the sources of international financing but also, and in particular, over external markets. In contrast, "internal market" capital lacked a similarly powerful sanction. It depended much more on the economic policy decisions of the national government and the maintenance of a specific pattern of income distribution. As a result, any opening in the system that might lead to a question of existing priorities threatened its ability to exert political pressure. Yet this was in fact what had to occur. This is not to deny that in Chile, as elsewhere, such capital seems more modern than the earlier type, nor that it has been interested in certain reformist measures of the kind advocated by the Alliance for Progress. What I want to emphasize is the relative narrowness of the area in which this "internal" capital has to maneuver, i.e., that of a democracy "for the democrats," a democracy that has little in common with any genuine expression of a mass will. Yet there was a mass will that was groping for a way to express itself. It is quite significant that in 1963, two years after proclaiming the Alliance for Progress, the United States for the first time offered the Latin American armies financing for the "anti-subversive" battle. In 1964 Thomas Mann, Under Secretary of State for Latin American Affairs, did not hesitate to admit that what was sought was not so much to defend representative democracy south of the Rio Grande as to maintain dependable allies. At the close of the decade Nelson Rockefeller, a "modern" Republican, toured Latin America evoking the phantom of communism and singing the praises of military regimes and brutal police.

I think that Luis Maira made a very pertinent comment. During the Eduardo Frei administration, when the penetration of foreign capital became increasingly rapid, the economic strategy of Raúl Saez was accompanied both by a growing escalation of repression and by efforts such as Roger Vekemans' to divide the masses, to fragment organization of the workers in the city and countryside. This was done by organizing the so-called marginals corporatively, from above. By "marginals" I mean those excluded Chileans who were blamed for their own misery and whose potential force was so feared. Note that Popular Promotion was so much an effort to redefine politically the nature of civil society that it was proposed as a supra-ministerial agency, subject only to the authority of the President.

Authoritarian and anti-mass tendencies form part of the very logic that the transformation of this movement to a new stage of capitalism requires. It is because the *Unidad Popular* triumph interrupted this process that the Allende government was forced to work within the framework of a bourgeois legality in which—as was shown by events—the Chilean bourgeoisie no longer believed. In other words, the liberal state had ceased to be the most adequate means for them to dominate. In this, as in the noteworthy achievements of the *Unidad Popular* and the important advances in the people's struggle, can be found the principal reasons for the virulence of the 1973 *coup*. It is true that the "pentagonized" faction led by Pinochet represents the old financial oligarchy more closely than the "internal-market" industrialized sectors. The latter are one of the possible bases of support for Eduardo Frei. However, the link between the two, which forms their profound unity, is this need for repression to which I have alluded. The present regime has carried it to a paroxism.

This is why I called attention to the possible similarities between the Chilean case and those of other Latin American countries. It would be absurd, of course, to overlook the importance of the many differences. However, I think it is no coincidence that the new phase in accumulation has been closely followed by attempts at a drastic redefinition of the political system in Brazil, Argentina, and Uruguay. (Mexico seems a counter-example because the system has shown a greater ability to adapt. Note, nevertheless, the failure of the "opening" proposed by President Luis Echeverría, a policy that threatened to destabilize the system and that prominent spokesmen for monopoly capital quickly labelled "allendist.")

We find ourselves in the midst of a process of movement toward a new kind of state, a process that makes the already precarious border that has existed in our countries between civil society and state structures more tenuous every day. Think of the Brazilian government "inventing" its official party and opposition, or of General Onganía in Argentina decreeing the "freezing" both of "political time" and "social time" while he sought to articulate a kind of vertical communitarianism. Or think of the Peruvian Revolution. Its undeniable achievements have occurred within the framework (and the limitation) of a constant preoccupation with channeling mass demands into predetermined channels of participation that, coincidentally, block any possible unity.

It is true that I am discussing tendencies and do not want to imply uniformity or any sense of fatalism about their success. Above all, one must keep in mind that I am alluding to a *double* process: not only a redefinition of dependency but also a sharpening of contradictions and social conflicts. The latter seriously affect the course of that redefinition and affect its results, but at the same time they are conditioned by those results. For example, the Brazilian *coup* of 1964 occurred during a phase when the mass movement was on the offensive. Therefore, its initial effort was to smash its class adversary, and the key to its program was terror. Almost four years had to pass before the new model of domination began to take form. In contrast, the Argentine *coup* of 1966 and the Peruvian of 1968 occurred at moments when the struggle between classes was relatively quiet. Thus they represented offensive efforts by certain dominant factions that sought to implement immediately a more or less articulated program. The nature of these programs and their successes varied, but they reflect the uniqueness of each specific situation, the kinds of alliances and commitments that were possible, the efficacy of the measures adopted, and so forth.

If I have insisted on speaking of a moment of transition, of a restructuring of social relations, of a crisis in the mechanisms of socialization, it is because I believe there is a degree of flexibility in the directions actions may take. Alternative options are possible, both for the dominant classes or factions of classes and for the classes or factions that are dominated. Yet the options of the former are far fewer than those of the latter, because they are limited simply to different tactics for negotiating dependency. Moreover, it is becoming clear that all tactics of the dominant classes have as a common denominator strong state intervention directed at eliminating any autonomous expression of the will of the people.

ROLE OF THE MILITARY WITHIN A CHANGING STATE

In my judgment, one must situate the renewed frequency of military *coups* within this complex context. To paraphrase Horkheimer rather freely, he who does not want to speak of peripheric capitalism should also refrain from commenting on the *coups* or political instability of our countries.

Ricardo Lagos has referred to an article I wrote on this topic ten years ago. I note the date intentionally, for the essay coincided almost exactly with the intensification of the processes to which I have been referring. As a result, I was not really at that time in a position to be clearly aware of them.* It is worth making a brief observation. My analysis began with an assumption of a very specific kind of unity between civil society and the structure of the state in Latin America. Within that unity I sought to understand the potentials and limits of the evolution of each, emphasizing the pressures the former exercised over the latter. In this fashion, in contrast to the liberal or developmental interpretations then in vogue, I sought to show among other things the extent to which the military had acted to protect the interests of the middle classes, channeling or supporting their demands and fears.

For reasons already explained, I believe that some substantial aspects of the situation have changed. When I wrote that essay, the social origin of officers was one of the most significant factors conditioning their political behavior. This is no longer the case. Today behavior seems to depend more on the strategic position of the military within the structure of a state undergoing profound transformation. It is worth repeating that this transformation in the state has a degree of indeterminacy, though it occurs within and not outside the imperialist chain. Today one finds a primacy of force that articulates programs running from an illusory return to the past to a more or less integrated effort to rechannel mass participation. In every case, however, what lies behind the invocations of Western and Christian civilization is a profound redefinition of civil society—a redefinition directed by the state. It is for this reason that we must seek new explanations for military intervention.

To those who despair of ever finding a simple and universal formula for explaining these phenomena, I remind them that to understand one single *coup d'état* Marx found it necessary to write *Eighteenth Brumaire*.

* "A Latin American Phenomenon: The Middle Class Military *Coup*," in *Trends in Social Science Research in Latin America* (Berkeley: Institute of International Studies, University of California, 1965), pp. 55–91.

Conference Participants

*CLODOMIRO ALMEYDA Professor, University of Chile. Minister of Foreign Relations, 1970–1973. Presently, Professor, Universidad Nacional Autónoma de México.

*DAVID BAYTELMAN Agronomist. Professor of Agrarian Economics, University of Chile. Vice-President, Agrarian Reform Corporation, 1970–1973. Presently in Paris.

SERGIO BITAR Civil Engineer. Postgraduate studies in economics at Harvard University. Minister of Mining, 1973. Presently at the Institute for International Development, Harvard University.

*PÍO GARCÍA Economist and sociologist. Director, Center of Socioeconomic Studies, University of Chile. Cabinet Head, Ministry of Economics. Coordinator, CORFO, 1970–1973. Presently, Professor, Center of Latin American Studies, Universidad Nacional Autónoma de México.

RICHARD R. FAGEN Professor of Political Science at the Institute of Political Studies, Stanford University. Advisor, Ford Foundation, Santiago, Chile, and Professor, Latin American Faculty of Social Sciences (FLACSO–UNESCO), Santiago, Chile, 1971–1973. Author of books and articles about Cuba, Chile, and forces of change in Latin America.

FEDERICO G. GIL Director, Institute of Latin American Studies, and Kenan Professor of Political Science, University of North Carolina at Chapel Hill. Author of *The Political System of Chile*.

*Unable to attend the conference.

RICARDO LAGOS E.   Economist. Professor, University of Chile, 1963–1973. Director, Institute of Economics. Provost, University of Chile, 1969–1971. Secretary General of FLACSO, 1972–1974. Presently with the U.N. Development Program. Author of *La Concentración del Poder Económico: Su Teoría, Realidad Chilena.*

HENRY A. LANDSBERGER   Professor, Department of Sociology, University of North Carolina at Chapel Hill. Professor, University of Chile, 1961–1965. Publications about working-class and peasant movements in Chile and Latin America in general.

JUAN J. LINZ   Professor, Department of Sociology and Political Science, Yale University. Author of books and articles about the sociostructural bases of different political systems, with special reference to Europe.

LUIS MAIRA   Lawyer, University of Chile. Deputy, National Congress, 1965–1973. Staff writer for *Chile Hoy.* Presently, Research Associate, Center for Research and Teaching in Economics (CIDE), Mexico.

JOSÉ NUN   Political Scientist. Researcher, Latin American Institute of Economic and Social Planning (ILPES), 1967–1969. Visiting Professor, UCLA and Berkeley. Presently, Professor, University of Toronto. Author of "The Middle-Class Military Coup" and other articles.

PHILIPPE SCHMITTER   Professor, Department of Political Science, University of Chicago. His books and articles deal with the political development of Brazil and the role of the armed forces in Latin America.

PAUL SIGMUND   Professor, Department of Political Science, Princeton University. Books and articles about the political systems of Latin America, with special reference to Chile. Author of *The Overthrow of Allende and the Politics of Chile, 1964–1976.*

JULIO SILVA SOLAR   Lawyer. Deputy, National Congress, 1969–1973. Permanent staff writer for the newspaper *Ultima Hora.* Author of various books, including *The Development of the New Society in Latin America* (with Jacques Chonchol). Presently in Rome.

GLAUCIO A. DILLON SOARES   Sociologist. Professor, Getulio Vargas Foundation at the University of Brazil since 1970. Director,

Latin American School of Sociology of FLACSO, 1965–1968. Presently, Visiting Professor, University of Florida. Author of numerous books and articles on Latin American social problems.

ALAN STERN   Professor, Department of Political Science, University of North Carolina at Chapel Hill. Publications in the field of comparative analysis of industrialized societies with special reference to the Italian political system.

JOHN STRASMA   Professor, Department of Economics, University of Wisconsin at Madison. Professor, University of Chile, 1959–1973. Advisor in agrarian reform and the taxation system in Chile and Peru. Author of articles and monographs on these subjects.

JORGE TAPIA VALDÉS   Lawyer, University of Chile. Professor of Theory of Law and of Constitutional Law. Minister of Justice in 1972 and Minister of Education in 1973. Author of *Técnica Legislativa*. Presently in the Netherlands.

JORGE TAPIA VIDELA   Professor, University of Chile and Catholic University, 1963–1974. Author of books and articles on social security and the Chilean political system. Presently, Professor, Wayne State University.

RADOMIRO TOMIĆ   Lawyer. Senator in 1950–1953 and in 1961–1965. Ambassador to the United States, 1965–1968. Presidential candidate of the Christian Democratic party, 1970. Professor, Catholic University of Chile, 1970–1973. Research Associate, Woodrow Wilson International Center for Scholars, Washington, D.C., 1975. Presently in Geneva.

ARTURO VALENZUELA   Professor, Department of Political Science, Duke University. Author of, among other works, *Chile: Politics and Society* (with J. Samuel Valenzuela) and *The Breakdown of Democratic Regimes: Chile*.

HERNÁN VERA   Sociologist. Professor, University of Florida. Participated in the formulation of agrarian policies during the Christian Democratic period of government in Chile, 1964–1968.

HUGO ZEMELMAN   Sociologist. Professor, University of Chile, until 1973. Researcher in ICIRA and FLACSO. Author of various books and articles. Presently, Research Associate, Center for Sociological Research, El Colegio de México.

Index